D1578761

Sustainable Marketing

Sustainable Marketing

Diane Martin
University of Portland

John Schouten
University of Portland

Prentice Hall

Boston   Columbus   Indianapolis   New York   San Francisco   Upper Saddle River
Amsterdam   Cape Town   Dubai   London   Madrid   Milan   Munich   Paris   Montreal   Toronto
Delhi   Mexico City   São Paulo   Sydney   Hong Kong   Seoul   Singapore   Taipei   Tokyo

Editorial Director: Sally Yagan
Editor in Chief: Eric Svendsen
Executive Editor: Melissa Sabella
Editorial Project Manager: Kierra Bloom
Editorial Assistant: Elisabeth Scarpa
Director of Marketing: Patrice Lumumba Jones
Marketing Manager: Anne Fahlgren
Marketing Assistant: Melinda Jensen
Project Manager: Debbie Ryan
Production Project Manager: Clara Bartunek
Art Director: Jayne Conte
Cover Designer: Bruce Kenselaar

Manager, Cover Visual Research & Permissions:
Karen Sanatar
Cover Art: Fotolia
Media Editor: Denise Vaughn
Media Project Manager: Lisa Rinaldi
Full-Service Project Management: Chitra
Ganesan / PreMediaGlobal
Composition: PreMediaGlobal
Printer/Binder: Edwards Brothers
Cover Printer: Lehigh Phoenix / Hagerstown
Text Font: Times

Photo Credits: Pages 7, 112, istockphoto; pages 17, 74, 127, 156, 179, 187, 206, 207, 227, Alamy; pages 18, 73, 106, 136, 189, 191, Shutterstock; page 62, Courtesy of The California Cars Initiative (CalCars); page 98, Courtesy of Office Depot; page 125, Courtesy of Seventh Generation; page 126, Courtesy of gDiapers; page 130, Courtesy of K2 Sports; page 132, Courtesy of NOAA; page 220, Thinkstock.

Library of Congress Cataloging-in-Publication Data
Martin, Diane
  Sustainable marketing / Diane Martin, John Schouten.
    p. cm.
  Includes bibliographical references and index.
  ISBN-13: 978-0-13-611707-0 (alk. paper)
  ISBN-10: 0-13-611707-4 (alk. paper)
  1. Green marketing. 2. Green marketing—Case studies. I. Schouten, John. II. Title.
  HF5413.M37 2012
  658.8'02—dc22

                                                    2010042390

10 9 8 7 6 5 4 3 2 1
Prentice Hall
is an imprint of

This book is not for sale or distribution in the U.S.A. or Canada

www.pearsonhighered.com

ISBN 10: 0-13-611707-4
ISBN 13: 978-0-13-611707-0

Dedication

This book is dedicated to the visionaries who came before us, to the colleagues who work beside us, and to you, the future leaders and managers who will usher in a more sustainable society.

TABLE OF CONTENTS

Preface   xiii

Chapter 1 An Introduction to Sustainable Marketing   1
Introduction: Interesting Times   1
Coming to Terms with Sustainability   2
  Three Dimensions of Sustainability   3
Declining Supply and Increasing Demand   4
  ▶ MINI CASE STUDY: The Collins Companies   5
A Brief History of Unsustainable Marketing   6
Environmental Awakening   7
  Pioneers and Visionaries   8
  Government Efforts   8
  Engaging the Citizenry   9
  Reaching the Business World   9
The Evolution of a New Paradigm: Sustainable Marketing   10
  A Definition of Sustainable Marketing   10
  Virtual Field Trip: Searching for Sustainability on the Web   11
  The Collaboration Advantage   11
  Critical Thinking Activity: Debate the Issues   11
    Chapter Summary   12

Chapter 2 Sustainable Marketing Strategy   14
Introduction: Marketing Strategy in 20/20 Hindsight   14
Competitive Advantage and the Business Case for Sustainability   15
  Staying Ahead of Environmental Regulation   15
  Lower Costs   16
  Innovation   16
  A Better Workforce   16
  Differentiation   16
  ▶ MINI CASE STUDY: Humdinger Wind Energy, LLC   17
  Virtual Field Trip: Competitive Advantage   18
Frameworks for Sustainable Marketing   18
  Beginning with Brundtland   18
  The Triple Bottom Line   19
  Natural Capitalism   19
  The Natural Step Framework   21
Creating and Implementing a Sustainable Marketing Strategy   23
  Building a Team   23
  Creating the Strategy   24
  Critical Thinking Activity: Can an Oil Company Become Sustainable?   25
    Chapter Summary   25

Chapter 3 Ethical Dimensions of Sustainable Marketing   28
Introduction: The Problem with Mother's Milk   28
The Responsibilities of Business in Society   29

Economic Consequences of Ethical Decisions   29

Corporate Social Responsibility   30

Virtual Field Trip: Find the CSR Statements of Some Well-Known Firms   30

The Fundamentals of Responsible Business   31

Creating Value   31

Finding Balance   32

Being Accountable   32

Sustainability: The New Ethics   33

Barriers to Success   33

TNSF, Ethics, and Responsible Business   34

▶ MINI CASE STUDY: Scandic Hotels   35

What Is the Responsibility of the Individual Consumer?   35

Critical Thinking Activity: The Natural Step Framework   38

Chapter Summary   39

Chapter 4   The Marketing Environment and Processes   42

Introduction: An Unusual Coalition   42

Sustainability and the Social-Cultural Environment   43

Educational Influences   43

Marketing and Media Influences   44

The Economic Environment   46

The Competitor Environment   47

The Technology Environment   47

The Political-Legal Environment   49

Muncipalities   49

Virtual Field Trip: Take a Web-Based Field Trip to Your Hometown and See What Evidence You Can Find of Sustainability   50

States   50

Federal: Government Regulatory Agencies and Legislation   50

▶ MINI CASE STUDY: Urban Growth Boundaries   51

The Natural Environment   51

Critical Thinking Activity: What Are the Implications of a Global System (the Earth) Being Managed by Multiple Regional Managers (Nations) with Competing and Conflicting Interests?   53

Chapter Summary   53

Chapter 5   Consumer Behavior and Sustainable Marketing   57

Introduction: The Cheeseburger Footprint   57

Sustainable Consumption   58

▶ MINI CASE STUDY: Carrotmob   59

Consumer Engagement in Marketing Processes   59

Consumer Motivation and Sustainable Consumption   60

Subsistence or Survival   61

Safety   61

Belonging   61

Esteem   62

Self-Actualization   62

Consumer Decision Processes and Sustainable Consumption   63

Need Recognition   63

Information Search   63

Virtual Field Trip: Digging Deep in the Information Mine   64

Evaluation of Alternatives   65

Purchase Decision Process   65

Post-Purchase Behaviors   66

Sustainability and Consumer Involvement   67

The Role of Culture in Sustainable Consumption   67

Critical Thinking Activity: Living Sustainably   68

Chapter Summary   68

Chapter 6   **Measurement and Research for Sustainable Marketing   71**

Introduction: Good and Evil are Equal in the Eyes of the GDP   71

The Importance of Measurement   72

▶ MINI CASE STUDY: IBM's Real Estate and Site Operations (RESO) Group   73

Virtual Field Trip: Patagonia's Footprint Chronicles   74

Principles for Measurement in Sustainable Marketing   74

Principle #1: Begin with a Whole-System Perspective of Success   75

Principle #2: Measure All the Relevant Dimensions of Success   75

Principle #3: Use Good Metrics   75

Principle #4: Develop Benchmarks and Performance Indicators   76

Uncovering Information   76

Secondary Research   76

Virtual Field Trip: Digging Deep in the Information Gold Mine   77

Primary Research   77

Uses and Types of Sustainability Metrics   77

CERES and the Global Reporting Initiative   77

ISO 14000 and EMAS   79

Sustainability Audits   80

Company Metrics and Scorecards   80

Monitoring the Green Economy   82

Life-Cycle Assessment   82

Metrics for Everyone   82

Critical Thinking Activity: Calculate Your Own Carbon Footprint   85

Chapter Summary   85

Chapter 7   **Market Segmentation, Targeting, and Positioning for Sustainability   89**

Introduction: LEGOmaniacs   89

The Emerging Green Market   90

Segmenting the Green Market   91

LOHAS and the Cultural Creatives   95

Alternative Consumption Segments   97

Virtual Field Trip: Dee Williams's Dream House   97

Positioning for Sustainability   97

Virtual Field Trip: Walk, Run or Fload a Mile in My Shoes   98

Taking the Green Position in the Business-to-Business Sector   100

▶ MINI CASE STUDY: Rocky Mountain Recycling   101

Critical Thinking Activity: Talkin' 'bout My Generation (Apologies to the Who)   102

Chapter Summary   102

Chapter 8   Global Problems, Global Opportunities   105

Introduction: Transoceanic Toxins   105

Global Environmental Challenges   106

World Water   106

Bottled Water   107

Water Privatization   108

The Global Greenhouse   109

Global Economic Challenges   110

Global Workforce   111

Sustainable Marketing and Levels of Development   112

Developed Nations and Sustainable Marketing   112

Developing Nations and Sustainable Marketing   113

Emerging Nations and Sustainable Marketing   113

▶ MINI CASE STUDY: A Sustainable Rural Village   114

Global Government and Regulatory Challenges   114

Virtual Field Trip: NAFTA   115

Global Consumers and Sustainable Marketing   116

Sustainability in Global Business-to-Business Markets   117

Critical Thinking Activity: One Man: Global Effort   118

Chapter Summary   118

Chapter 9   Sustainable Products and Services   122

Introduction: How Do You Like My Medicine?   122

Product Stewardship   123

Service-Dominant Logic   123

Product Sustainability Using The Natural Step Framework   124

System Conditions One and Two   124

System Condition Three   128

System Condition Four   128

Developing Sustainable New Products   129

Consumer Products   129

▶ MINI CASE STUDY: Interface   131

Giant Opportunities: Designing Products for Business and Government   131

Sustainable Services   132

Sustainable Business-to-Business (B2B) Services   133

Sustainable Consumer Services   134

Virtual Field Trip: Or Maybe Not So Virtual   135

Critical Thinking Activity: A Balance Sheet for Human Capital   136

Chapter Summary   136

Chapter 10   Sustainable Branding and Packaging   139

Introduction: Behind Great Brands   139

Sustainable Branding   140

Principles of Sustainable Branding   141

▶ MINI CASE STUDY: Stonyfield Farms   143

Ten Keys to Sustainable Branding   143

The Internal Brand   144

Virtual Field Trip: Examining Brand Sustainability   144

Sustainable Packaging 145

Packaging and the Triple Bottom Line 146

Remove, Reduce, and Recycle 146

Sustainable Labeling 148

Third-Party Certifications: Telling the Sustainability Story 148

Truth in Labeling 150

Critical Thinking Activity: How Much Information Is Too Much Information When It Comes to Product Labeling? 150

Chapter Summary 150

Chapter 11 Marketing Channels: Sustainability in the Value Chain 153

Introduction: Sell Your Trash 153

Marketing Channels: From Value Chains to Sustainable Value Circles 154

Linear Flows and Waste 155

Cradle to Cradle 156

Virtual Field Trip: Waste = Food 157

Reversing Flows of Materials, Money, and Ideas 157

Secondary Markets 158

▶ MINI CASE STUDY: The ReBuilding Center 159

Marketing Opportunities 159

Overlapping Value Circles: Cooperation across Industries 160

Building Sustainable Channel Relationships: Communication and Collaboration 160

Transparency and Chain of Custody 161

▶ MINI CASE STUDY: Bon Appétit Management Company 162

Building Sustainable Channel Capacity 162

Developing Sustainable Channel Operations 163

Greener Facilities and Warehousing 163

Greener Transportation 165

Shorter Channels 165

Sustainability in Retailing 166

Influencing Suppliers 166

Educating Consumers 166

Taking Back Recyclables 167

Critical Thinking Activity: Identify a Favorite Possession 167

Chapter Summary 167

Chapter 12 Sustainable Pricing 170

Introduction: The Value of a Healthy Planet 170

Sustainable Pricing: Recovering the Real Product Cost 171

Externalized Costs 172

Life-Cycle Costing 173

Virtual Field Trip: The Price of Food 173

Barriers to Sustainable Pricing 174

Competitive Barriers 174

Political Barriers 174

Cultural Barriers 175

Beyond Costs: Sustainable Pricing Strategies   177
    Discounts and Promotions in Sustainable Pricing   178
        ▶ MINI CASE STUDY: Traverse City Light & Power   179
    Prestige Pricing   179
Complementary Currencies and Exchange Schemes   180
    Critical Thinking Activity: Different Pricing Strategies   181
        Chapter Summary   181

Chapter 13 **Sustainable Marketing Communication   184**
Introduction: Beyond Petroleum or Backpedaling?   184
The Nature of Sustainable Marketing Communication   185
The Keys to Sustainable Marketing Communication   186
    Integration   186
    Leverage   186
    Brand Community   187
    Communities of Purpose   188
    Accountability and Transparency   189
    Credibility   190
    Consumer Education   192
    Value Congruence   192
    Virtual Field Trip: The Fun Factor   193
    Back to Basics: AIDA   193
Barriers to Sustainable Marketing Communication   194
    Losing Sight of the Basics   194
    Clouding the Brand Story   194
    Misreading the Target Audience   194
The Cardinal Sins of Sustainable Marketing Communication:
Greenwashing, Astroturfing, and Other Green Lies   195
    Greenwashing   195
        ▶ MINI CASE STUDY: Johnson & Johnson   196
    Astroturfing   196
    Government Actions   197
    Critical Thinking Activity: Developing an SMC Strategy   198
        Chapter Summary   198

Chapter 14 **Sustainability in the Promotion Mix—Methods, Media,
and Customer Relationships   201**
Introduction: Toyota's Unfortunate Secrets   201
Advertising   202
    Advertising Appeals   203
    Storytelling   204
    The Power of Pictures   205
    Virtual Field Trip: Explore the Visual   205
    Advertising Agencies: Partners in Sustainable Marketing
    Communication   205
Public Relations and Publicity   206
    Sharing from the Top   208
        ▶ MINI CASE STUDY: Positive Publicity from an Unlikely Source   208
    Tapping into Celebrity   209

Sustainability, Risk, and Investor Relations   209

Voluntary Reporting   210

Sales Promotions   210

Personal Selling and Trade Shows   212

Customer Relationship Management and Direct Marketing   213

Customer Relationship Management   213

Direct Marketing   214

Critical Thinking Activity: TNSF and the Nuts and Bolts of SMC   214

Chapter Summary   215

Chapter 15   **Digital Media and Sustainable Marketing   218**

Introduction: High Stakes Skirmish in Social Media   218

Digital Communication and Sustainable Marketing   219

Principle #1—Rapid Innovation and Change Are the Norm   220

Principle #2—Consumers Increasingly Prefer Digital Media   221

Principle #3—Digital Products Dematerialize Consumption   224

Principle #4—Digital Communication Aids Process Sustainability   224

Principle #5—Digital Communities Drive Sustainability   225

Current Uses of Digital Media in Sustainable Marketing Communication   226

Who Communicates to Whom?   226

Virtual Field Trip: Starbucks Crowdsourcing   228

How and Why Do They Communicate?   229

▶ MINI CASE STUDY: HP Blog Central   229

What Are They Communicating?   231

Digital Danger Zones and Antisocial Media   231

Critical Thinking Activity: Dell and the Blogs   232

Chapter Summary   232

Glossary   234

Index   240

PREFACE

WELCOME TO THE NEW WORLD OF SUSTAINABLE MARKETING

The defining challenge facing humanity in the twenty-first century is to learn how to live sustainably, meaning to live well, while at the same time preserving the natural systems that make it possible for all people, including future generations, to enjoy a similarly high quality of life.

Marketing has a vital and unique role to play in creating a more sustainable society. It is through marketing systems that most of humanity's material needs and many of our psychological needs are met. As the engine that drives the global economy, marketing has an enormous footprint on both the environment and society. As the interface between business and society, marketing also has great potential as a force for shaping cultural change. *Sustainable Marketing* is about understanding and managing marketing's pivotal role in the future of business and society.

The main premise of this book is that marketing, as a contributor to a sustainable society, has two imperatives. The first is to *market sustainably*, meaning that all marketing functions must be done in a fashion that preserves or increases environmental and human well-being while making reasonable profits. The second imperative is to *market sustainability*, which means to use the powers of influence and market infrastructure to help bring about a global culture of sustainability.

Sustainable Marketing is written for students who have already completed a principles-level course in marketing. This book preserves and reinforces basic marketing concepts while integrating principles of environmental and social sustainability. Rather than an afterthought or add-on topic, sustainability is treated as a fundamental objective of all marketing activity.

In *Sustainable Marketing*, you will learn:

1. What constitutes environmental and social sustainability
2. What is meant by sustainable marketing
3. Why sustainable marketing is vitally important, both to society and to a successful business strategy
4. How sustainability can drive a successful marketing strategy from the mission statement and marketing objectives down through segmentation, targeting, and positioning
5. How sustainability can inform and improve marketing practices as an integral part of a competitive marketing plan

Sustainable Marketing draws on state-of-the-art thinking about sustainability. This book incorporates important concepts such as the Triple Bottom Line, Natural Capitalism, cradle-to-cradle design, and The Natural Step Framework into a holistic approach to sustainability in marketing practice. In addition, it is grounded in the practices of leading companies around the world. Leadership and innovation in sustainable marketing come from a wide range of companies, large and small. This book draws from the best ideas of those companies, providing rich examples of marketing practice in the quest for a more sustainable world.

Perhaps most important, *Sustainable Marketing* provides you with the tools you need to optimize every marketing decision with respect to profits, the natural environment, and human well-being. This is more than a book about marketing. It is a guidebook to a meaningful career in a world that is rapidly embracing the reality of sustainability as the basis for business success.

An Approach to Learning

We believe learning should be fun as well as rewarding. We are also aware that many textbooks seem unnecessarily dense and dry. With that in mind, we have written *Sustainable Marketing* with the intention of telling a compelling and highly readable story. The subject of sustainability in marketing is complex, and *Sustainable Marketing* does not shy away from that complexity. Instead, it provides a framework for understanding and dealing with it in a relatively simple, step-by-step fashion.

Each chapter opens with a set of remarkable facts about sustainability that we hope will pique your interest. Following the introduction, you will find a list of the chapter's key learning objectives. We have made every attempt to present the concepts in a way that is clear, straightforward, and understandable. To help increase your understanding, we have included several features in each chapter that we hope will provoke thought, discussion, and additional exploration:

1. "Think about It" questions provide food for thought and fodder for engaging discussions about issues that may have more than one side to them.
2. "Virtual Field Trips" provide links to further exploration of important topics via the Internet.
3. "Mini Case Studies" and abundant examples draw links to contemporary marketing application and decision making.
4. "Critical Thinking Activities" set the stage for stimulating debates about potentially thorny problems of marketing and sustainability.

The Organization of the Book

The first three chapters of *Sustainable Marketing* are foundational. They establish the need for sustainable marketing; they explain the concepts of sustainability and sustainable marketing; they outline the underlying intellectual traditions; and they relate sustainable marketing to other initiatives such as business ethics and corporate social responsibility. Perhaps most importantly, they present a framework for strategic and tactical decision making that is used and reinforced throughout the text.

Chapters 4 and 5 deal with external marketing environments and consumer behavior with respect to sustainability. Chapter 6 focuses on marketing information and metrics as they relate to sustainable marketing. Chapter 7 examines segmentation, targeting, and positioning for sustainability, and Chapter 8 discusses the implications of operating in a global context. Chapters 9 through 15 cover the marketing mix, exploring the meaning of sustainability and its importance in decisions regarding products and services, branding, pricing, marketing communication, and channels of distribution.

Because You are the Future

We wrote this book for you. We hope you will enjoy reading it, and that you will take away from it a clear understanding of marketing as a force for shaping a more sustainable society. As a future marketing leader, you will have opportunities not only to forge a meaningful and rewarding career, but also to have a hand in making the world a better place for every living creature.

THANKS TO REVIEWERS AND CONTRIBUTORS

Writing this book was a labor of love and a journey of discovery. In the process, two people above all others gave generously of their time, ideas, support, and creative energy. Chas Martin and Jenny Mish, you are gentle but thorough critics, and true and inspiring friends. Thank you.

Many experts and visionaries also gave freely of their time, stories, and experiences. To Ray Anderson, Susan Chambers, Tyler Elm, Regina Hauser, Paul Hawken, Karl-Henrik Robért, Andy Rubin, Susan Sokol Blosser, Robert Swan, Adam Werbach, Marsha Willard, and Ian Yolles we extend our admiration and gratitude.

We also want to thank the people at Pearson Prentice Hall who helped us turn an idea into a reality: Dennis Fernandes, the world's most magnanimous former book rep; Sally Yagan and Melissa Sabella, who first believed in this project; and Kierra Bloom and Anne Fahlgren, who helped us bring it to market.

Many of our colleagues and fellow scholars also encouraged, challenged, and inspired us to write this groundbreaking text. We are particularly grateful to Doug Albertson, Robin Anderson, Eric Arnould, Bill Barnes, Elena Bernard, Claudia Bridges, Nicole DeHoratius, Howard Feldman, Greg Hill, Christina Jarvis, William Kilbourne, Steven Kolmes, Tracy Marafiote, Jim McAlexander, Jill Mosteller, Melea Press, Mellie Pullman, Fredrica Rudell, Heidi Senior, John F. Sherry Jr., Laura Steffen, Debra Stephens, Wendy Wilhelm, and Carolyn Woo.

Several students at the University of Portland helped us along the way: Harli Lozier, Daniele Moreni, and Scott Swearingen, in particular, saved us hours of work. In addition, several classes of undergraduate and graduate business students served as the first audiences for many of the concepts and exercises included in this book.

Finally, several reviewers helped us to refine and focus this book. Once again we thank Jenny Mish of the University of Notre Dame. Reviewers who remained anonymous throughout the writing process, but who contributed greatly to the final results included:

Megan Ball, Marymount University

Ken Fairweather, LeTourneau College

Cathy Ferris McPherson, Mary Baldwin College

George Kelley, Eerie Community College, City Campus

Susan McCabe, Kellogg Community College

Michael McCall, Ithaca College

Richard Sharman, Lone Star College

Deb Utter, Boston University

Carol Vollmer Pope, Alverno College

To all others: If we somehow left you out, please let us know. We'll toast you with a glass of wine from one of Oregon's most sustainable wineries.

ABOUT THE AUTHORS

A lifelong environmentalist, **Diane M. Martin** currently works as an associate professor of marketing at the University of Portland, where she has spent the last several years studying sustainability in marketing organizations. Her research appears in the *Journal of Business Ethics*; *Consumption, Markets & Culture*; *Journal of Qualitative Marketing Research*; and *Journal of Applied Communication Research* among others. Prior to her academic career, Dr. Martin was owner and CEO of Oregon Attractions Marketing, a consulting firm specializing in tourism marketing. During that time, she served as the president of the Columbia River Gorge Visitors Association, which was instrumental in the creation of the United States' first National Scenic Area. She is a senior consultant with Stebbins Consulting Group, a senior associate of Ethos Market Research and is a senior fellow in the American Leadership Forum.

John W. Schouten is also an associate professor at the University of Portland as well as cofounder and chief creative officer of Ethos Market Research, a firm specializing in applied ethnographic research. Dr. Schouten's academic research, which pioneered the exploration of consumer communities and subcultures, appears in *Journal of Marketing*; *Journal of Consumer Research*; *Journal of the Academy of Marketing Science*; and *Consumption, Markets & Culture* among others. He has devoted his recent study and teaching to the pursuit of sustainability in marketing. Dr. Schouten is also a poet and novelist. His poetry appears in numerous scholarly and literary journals. His first novel, *Notes from the Lightning God*, was published in 2009 by BeWrite Books, United Kingdom.

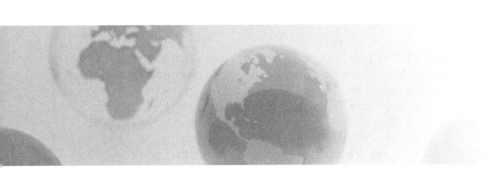

An Introduction to Sustainable Marketing

INTRODUCTION: INTERESTING TIMES

A so-called Chinese curse says, "May you live in interesting times." If by "interesting" the curse means perilous, troubled, or outright frightening, then these are certainly some of the most interesting times the human race has ever faced. Consider the following quotes:

> Water from melting ice sheets and glaciers is gushing into the world's oceans much faster than previously thought possible, sending scientists scrambling to explain why. The unexpected deluge is raising global sea levels, which scientists say could eventually submerge island nations, flood cities, and expose millions of coastal residents to destructive storm surges.[1]
>
> For the first time in human history, human use and pollution of fresh water have reached a level where water scarcity will potentially limit food production, ecosystem function, and urban supply in the decades to come.[2]
>
> If fishing around the world continues at its present pace, more and more species will vanish, marine ecosystems will unravel and there will be "global collapse" of all species currently fished, possibly as soon as midcentury.[3]
>
> The potential consequences of [climate change] … include food and water shortages, population shifts and economic losses. These in turn may increase a range of risks to human security, including the risk of deadly conflict.[4]

THINK ABOUT IT

Assume for a moment that the above scenarios are the findings of proper forecasting methods based on reliable scientific data. Does that mean such sobering circumstances are inevitable? What are the limitations of forecasting? What actions, if any, might bring about different results than those predicted? On what scale would those actions need to be taken?

Scientists agree that by practicing business as usual, humankind is careening toward unparalleled crises, which could even include global economic collapse, widespread disease, starvation, and violence.[5] The roots of the crisis lie in economic development that is unsustainable. Put simply, humans are using up or destroying the Earth's vital resources much faster than those resources that can be replenished.

The problems of unsustainable growth are environmental, social, and economic. They are real; they are accelerating; they are global; and they won't go away on their own. But all is not doom and gloom. Scientists also agree that the worst-case scenarios of climate change and environmental degradation can be avoided.[6] In a commencement address at University of Portland, the author and entrepreneur Paul Hawken had this to say about the relative places of pessimism and optimism:

> If you look at the science about what is happening on earth and aren't pessimistic, you don't understand the data. But if you meet the people who are working to restore this earth and the lives of the poor, if you aren't optimistic, you haven't got a pulse.[7]

Marketing and the stimulation of consumer demand have often been criticized as a major part of the problem of unsustainable economic growth.[8] However, this book takes the position that marketing offers a set of tools that can be used for either good or ill. In that spirit, this book presents marketing as part of the solution to the problems of unsustainable development. This is a book about the principles and practices of **sustainable marketing**, which will be defined later in this chapter and explained more fully throughout the book. Each chapter will build on concepts of marketing you've already learned, and each will examine the meaning of those concepts with respect to principles of **sustainability**.

CHAPTER OBJECTIVES

In this chapter, you will learn:

- The meaning of sustainability
- The root of the current crisis of unsustainable growth
- The problem of declining supply and increasing demand
- The history of unsustainable marketing and environmental awakening
- The evolution of a new paradigm: sustainable marketing

COMING TO TERMS WITH SUSTAINABILITY

Many people and organizations have offered definitions of sustainability. Chapter 2 discusses some of them in depth. Simply put, however, sustainability is the ability of a system to maintain or renew itself perpetually. All of the Earth's natural systems function this way. Take, for example, the cycle of photosynthesis and respiration. Plants take energy from the sun, carbon dioxide from the atmosphere, and minerals from the soil, and they produce vegetation and oxygen. Animals eat vegetation (and other animals) and breathe oxygen, and they produce carbon dioxide and mineral wastes, which in turn become food for plants. Everything in the cycle is renewable, and the cycle is, therefore, sustainable.

Humankind, with the ability to create and use technology, has found ways to convert the Earth's resources into new kinds of materials, machines, and sources of power. The technologies that define modern life rely on substances from the **lithosphere**, or the Earth's crust, such as petroleum, coal, and metal ores. The problem is these materials are not renewable; as they are used up, they become harder and harder to find. What's more, when sufficient concentrations of these substances from deep in the Earth's crust, and the compounds formed from them, accumulate in the **biosphere**, where every living thing lives, they eventually create big problems.

Since at least the time of the industrial revolution, every generation has left the human race in better shape technologically than they found it. Medicines are more advanced and more effective (of course, so are weapons), food production is more efficient, transportation is faster and

Home.

more reliable, entertainment is more varied and sophisticated, and communication has brought the people of the world closer together than ever before. At the same time, however, every generation has left the Earth in worse condition than they found it; that is, with fewer precious resources and with more toxins in the environment. It turns out that at some point technology for natural resources isn't such a good trade-off. The Earth is humanity's life-support system. If we interrupt the Earth's ability to renew itself, we are effectively shutting off the supplies of clean air, fresh water, and food for future generations.

Sustainability comes naturally to the Earth, but not so naturally to humankind. **Human sustainability**, as we define it, is the opportunity for all people to maintain fulfilling, productive lives while preserving or replenishing the natural and economic systems that make their well-being possible. From here forward, the term *sustainability* will refer specifically to human sustainability.

THINK ABOUT IT

Think of a product you recently bought for yourself. Do you know how it was made, or where the materials originated? Do you know which, if any, were toxic? Do you know what waste was created? What will become of it when you are through with it? How might the product be made more sustainable? Would that add to its value for you? Whom else would it benefit?

The concept of sustainability represents an ideal for the human condition, and for human endeavors such as business or development, it makes perfect sense. However, the distance between current practices and truly sustainable practices is enormous. The first step in creating solutions is to have a clear understanding of the problems to be solved. There are three critical dimensions of sustainability, and the world's current crises must be understood and addressed at all three levels.

Three Dimensions of Sustainability

This book discusses three dimensions of sustainability—environmental, social, and economic—that are entwined and interdependent. Human well-being requires economic activity, and economic activity depends on natural systems. Consider the following finding of the United Nations' World Commission on Environment and Development:

Environmental stress has often been seen as the result of the growing demand on scarce resources and the pollution generated by the rising living standards of the relatively affluent. But poverty itself pollutes the environment, creating environmental stress in a different way. Those who are poor and hungry will often destroy their immediate environment in order to survive: They will cut down forests; their livestock will overgraze grasslands; they will overuse marginal land; and in growing numbers they will crowd into congested cities. The cumulative effect of these changes is so far-reaching as to make poverty itself a major global scourge.[9]

In 1971, biologist Barry Commoner articulated four laws of ecology, the first being that "everything is connected to everything else."[10] Social problems exacerbate environmental problems, and environmental problems intensify social ones. Environmental degradation leads directly to humanitarian problems such as malnutrition and disease. In the case of water, it can even lead to territorial conflicts.[11] Given the absolute necessity of natural systems to human survival, all human activity should be conducted with the aim of **environmental sustainability**, defined here as the ongoing preservation of essential ecosystems and their functions.[12]

Economic sustainability is also a must for human welfare. It can be defined as the ongoing ability of an economic system to provide for all human needs. The global economy is, without a doubt, the system with the greatest impact on both society and the natural environment. The world's human population depends on economic systems for virtually all our material needs. When the economy suffers, people suffer. And the reverse is also true. The economy depends on human productivity. People who are hungry, homeless, or ill have less opportunity to contribute economically to their communities than people who are healthy and prosperous.

Social sustainability refers to the ongoing ability of communities to provide for the well-being of their members. Healthy, thriving communities provide for the overall health and welfare of their members. In order to lead fulfilling and productive lives, people need access to goods such as food, medicines, and clothing, and to services such as housing, transportation, health care, education, and recreation. In addition, people need opportunities to participate in and contribute to community processes.

The mini case study on page 5 examines how one American company, Collins Pine, has worked to develop all three of the dimensions of sustainability.

The bitter division between timber companies and environmentalists has been hard fought for many decades. Why do you think Collins has continued to thrive while moving toward greater environmental sustainability? What sets Collins apart from the forest management of other timber companies? How does this approach increase its productivity? What evidence can you find of social sustainability practices?

DECLINING SUPPLY AND INCREASING DEMAND

Two major forces contribute to the current crisis of unsustainable economic activity (see Figure 1-1):

1. A continuous decline in natural resources and ecosystem services, and
2. A continuous increase in the demand for those resources and services.

Natural resources, such as wood, water, soils, and minerals, are the material building blocks of human economy. Many natural resources, such as coal and petroleum, are finite and nonrenewable, meaning that they become scarcer as they are used. Scarcity ultimately leads to higher prices and less reliable supplies. Other natural resources, such as soils and forests, are subject to degradation and diminishing productivity. **Ecosystem services** are the collective activities of natural systems that renew resources and sustain life. Healthy ecosystems perform vital services such as the production of oxygen, purification of water, enrichment of soils, and decomposition of waste. They provide food and habitat for fish and wildlife. Ecosystems that are stressed, contaminated, or overburdened are, however, less able to provide the services on which humanity relies.

In order for human activity to be sustainable, we cannot continuously exceed the Earth's capacity to provide the resources and services we need. Currently, however, we do. The amount of the Earth's resources required to support a population depends on two factors: the size of the population and its level of consumption, which together determine a population's **ecological footprint**,[13] or the amount of Earth's resources required to support a particular lifestyle. Right now, the world's population requires the equivalent of more than one complete planet Earth to live as it does[14] (see Figure 1-2).

Mini Case Study

The Collins Companies

The Collins Companies, formerly called Collins Pine, has always operated with a mentality of sustainability. When most timber companies viewed forests as little more than woodlots, Collins viewed them as living systems to be cared for and nurtured. From Collins's perspective, the productive engine of a forest isn't the trees; it's the soil. With that in mind, the company has always managed its forests for biodiversity and total-system health. The company's wood harvests never exceed or compromise the forest's generative capacity. The operation is, in a word, sustainable.

Despite its history of relatively sustainable operation, Collins recognizes the need and the opportunity to be even more sustainable. In 1997, the firm set out on what it calls JTS, its Journey to Sustainability. With teams from across the company, and using a strategic framework called The Natural Step (which is described in Chapter 2), Collins targeted three main areas for environmental gains—energy, waste, and water.

Sustaining the Environment

Investments in energy conservation and reuse include heat exchangers that use excess heat from curing ovens to heat the building and a new high-output electric motor that replaces six older motors and saves over $100,000 per year in electricity costs. The energy team continues to innovate and improve, finding new ways to reduce power consumption and to recapture and use wasted heat.

Reducing and utilizing material wastes have turned costs into both savings and revenue. For example, the waste team found a way to incorporate wasted sander dust into a particleboard product rather than burning it in a boiler, thereby improving the product and reducing carbon emissions. Wood chips previously sent to a landfill found a paying customer in an energy recovery business. Tanker-sized bulk purchasing of glue for the particleboard plant saved on fuel for transportation and reduced the amounts of unusable glue residue.

The team assigned to water use found ways to conserve tens of thousands of gallons of fresh water a day with investments in air-conditioning and plumbing systems. Heated wastewater that had flowed into the Klamath River now flows through wetlands. This cools and filters the water before it goes into the river.

Collins follows the Forest Stewardship Council certification rules for ecological processes and uses a set of eco-indicators to track its environmental progress in all its target areas.[15]

Sustaining Communities

The Collins Companies and many of its competitors in the timber industry make meaningful donations to their local communities. For Collins, one of those communities is Chester. Chester, California, is a timber town, and in an era when timber towns are turning into ghost towns, Chester continues to be a vibrant community. Many residents are second- or third-generation wood-products workers, and they owe their continued livelihoods to the sustainable practices of Collins, which has been doing business in Chester since 1943. Collins employs nearly 200 people in the area. Taxes paid by the company and its workers support schools and public services. But Collins does more for the community than just pay taxes. For example, the company sponsors Little League, Girl Scouts, Boy Scouts, and other children's groups. Collins has ceded land for civic projects such as school expansions, a cemetery, and a senior living center. Scholarship funds from Collins award graduates of Chester High School from $1,800 to $2,400 per year, depending on their course loads, if they maintain at least a 3.0 grade point average. Over 1,000 Chester graduates have received scholarships since the program began in 1944.[16]

Sustaining Profits

The first year of Collin's JTS achieved monetary savings of approximately $1 million. By 2003, the savings amounted to $1,373,818 per year or a cumulative figure of over $3 million. Costs for capital purchases, salary, seminars, and travel were estimated to be about $50,000 or about six percent of the [overall financial] benefits.[17]

In summary, a healthy economy depends on ecosystem services from the natural environment, but environmentally unsustainable economic activity undermines the abilities of ecosystems to function properly. A healthy economy relies on productive workers and prosperous consumers, but socially unsustainable practices harm both productivity and prosperity. There can be no economic sustainability without healthy environmental and social systems.

The situation gets worse as populations grow and their appetites for higher standards of living increase. The world population in 2009 was estimated at nearly 7 billion.[18] By the year 2040, it is expected to pass 9 billion.[19] According to the Global Footprint Network, "China's ecological footprint has quadrupled in the last four decades, with the country now demanding more from the planet than any nation except the United States. If China were to follow the consumption patterns of the United States, it would demand the available biocapacity of the entire planet."[20]

FIGURE 1-1 The current crisis of unsustainable growth—A continuous decline in resources and ecosystem services and a continuous increase in demand.

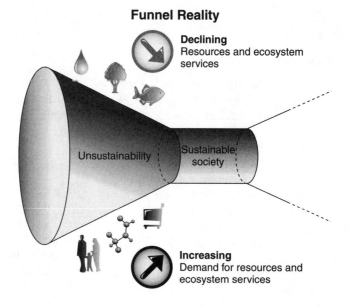

FIGURE 1-2 Projected increases in the global eco-footprint.

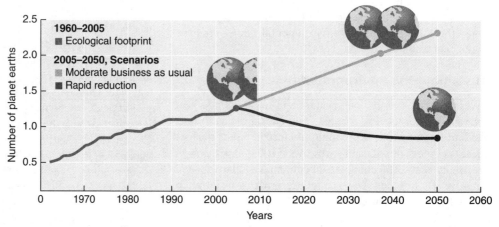

How, then, is it possible for nearly 7 billion people to survive on the Earth today? First, not everyone has enough. Food, shelter, fuel, arable soil, clean water, and clean air are in desperately short supply in many parts of the world. Second, at current levels of consumption, humanity is living on borrowed resources. When we use more of the Earth's capacity than it can replace, we are essentially borrowing from future generations. So far, we are in no position to pay them back. You may well ask: How did we get to this point of squandering Earth's natural and human capital?

A BRIEF HISTORY OF UNSUSTAINABLE MARKETING

Modern marketing is the grandchild of the industrial revolution. Since the beginning of the era of mass production, the practices and the philosophies of marketing have evolved considerably. Initially, businesses focused on what they could produce, with little or no concern for customer preferences, and consumer demand was sufficient to drive sales. The philosophy was, "If we can build it, we can sell it." In the next generation, firms competed with each other through aggressive advertising and sales tactics. The reigning philosophy became caveat emptor, or "let the buyer beware." In marketing's third generation, the needs and wants of consumers took center stage, and the marketing concept became the guiding philosophy.

The marketing concept dictates that a business focus on satisfying the needs and desires of consumers, and in doing so, the business will also achieve its goals. The marketing concept became the guiding philosophy of the discipline. The satisfaction of customer desires was the ultimate justification for any marketing activity. The idea of societal marketing has extended the marketing concept to include concern for social responsibility, which means that, while fulfilling consumer needs, firms need to do so in ways that are not damaging to society.[21] Some would

The natural environment cannot absorb all industrial waste.

argue that this model leaves the determination of what is best for society up to businesses.[22] The definition of marketing currently sanctioned by the American Marketing Association is, "The activity, set of institutions, and processes for creating, communicating, delivering, and exchanging offerings that have value for customers, clients, partners, and society at large."[23]

One legacy of marketing's birth in the industrial revolution is that it operates on a set of underlying assumptions that no longer work. Patterns of thinking established during the industrial revolution have turned out to be faulty. During the 1800s, as first Britain and then the rest of the Western world began a coal-powered shift to mechanization and mass production, natural resources were so abundant that they seemed virtually unlimited. The environment's capacity to absorb waste seemed equally inexhaustible, and consumer demand for new products appeared to be insatiable. Labor, on the other hand, was relatively scarce. The obvious job of business, then, was to convert natural resources into goods as fast and efficiently as possible, thereby creating enormous wealth for the owners of factories and the captains of industry.

It turns out that the above assumptions—unlimited resources, scarce labor, and the harmless assimilation of waste—are precisely backward in today's world. The Earth's natural resources are not limitless; in many cases, they are in short supply. Waste never truly goes away, and it is seldom harmless. And, thanks to globalization, automation, and massive population growth, labor is now so abundant that much of the world's population is unemployed, underemployed,[24] or inhumanely exploited.[25]

As a result of faulty assumptions, the traditional paradigm of business, in general, and marketing, in particular, is no longer in sync with the reality of the natural and human systems that provide the foundation for life.[26] The old paradigm is broken. We need a new one—one that is sustainable.

ENVIRONMENTAL AWAKENING

It's not as if we couldn't see the new paradigm coming. In one form or another, people have been advocating for sustainability for a long time. Naturally, their voices haven't always penetrated the business world. Innovative ideas that question long-held beliefs and upset power structures typically face tremendous opposition. However, the proof of necessary change is eventually upheld by the impartiality of history. For instance, slavery was once an unquestioned economic necessity, but soon after abolishing the practice in 1833, Britain's economy accelerated.[27] The case of human advocacy for the natural world has had a similar history.

Pioneers and Visionaries

The first efforts to protect public land for national parks began in the United States in 1832 when President Andrew Jackson set aside the lands of Hot Springs, Arkansas, for the U.S. government. President Abraham Lincoln preserved the Yosemite Valley and Mariposa Grove of Giant Sequoias in California, which later became Yosemite National Park. President Theodore Roosevelt was instrumental in establishing the world's first national park with the creation of Yellowstone National Park in 1872.[28] Naturalist John Muir spearheaded further efforts to protect natural lands, and in 1892, he founded the Sierra Club.[29] Seventy years later, ecologist Rachel Carson wrote *Silent Spring*[30] wherein she challenged the use of industrial chemicals as being dangerous to humans and the natural world. Her work was roundly criticized as alarmist by the chemical industry and by some government officials, but her arguments led to congressional testimony in 1963 and to greater interest in policies to protect human health and the environment.[31]

Influential individuals from all walks of life have followed these pioneers. Economist E. F. Schumacher, author of *Small Is Beautiful*,[32] questioned the desirability of Western economics in 1973. National efforts for sustainability have been led by such people as Friends of the Earth leader and early Green Party activist Jonathon Porritt,[33] NASA scientist James Hansen, television naturalist David Attenborough, U.S. politicians Al Gore and Arnold Schwarzenegger,[34] New Zealand Prime Minister Helen Clark, and Swedish minister for the environment, Lena Sommestad.[35] Entertainers like Leonardo DiCaprio and Natalie Portman attract the spotlight to issues related to sustainability. Biologists and researchers Anne H. Ehrlich and Karen Eckert and activists Julia Butterfly Hill and Van Jones[36] are examples of people who currently push social and environmental agendas, much like the British Quakers did in their efforts to abolish slavery nearly 200 years ago.

Government Efforts

While scientists and activists drew attention to the needs of nature, governments began seeing economic benefits in consumer recycling. In the early 1900s, citizens in Chicago and Cleveland were encouraged to find "Waste as Wealth" by sorting and reselling their cans. During the height of U.S. involvement in World War I (1916–1918), the citizenry recycled old rags, wastepaper, foil, books, and newspapers for the war effort. These efforts were later repeated for a wider variety of items during World War II. When the all-aluminum can was introduced in 1964, industry began to realize the value of using used aluminum for making beverage containers and began its own efforts to encourage recycling.

THINK ABOUT IT

What would the United States look like today if there had been no environmental protections during the last 50 years? Alternatively, what if for the last 50 years the U.S. government had required businesses to be environmentally sustainable and socially responsible?

Recognizing trash as a growing issue of national importance, Congress passed the Solid Waste Disposal Act in 1965. The state of Oregon was the first to require consumers to pay a deposit on bottles and cans by passing the nation's first "bottle bill" in 1972. The first polyethylene terephthalate (PET) plastic bottle was patented by chemist Nathaniel Wyeth in 1973, and in 1977, plastic recycling began. The federal government once again took an interest in legislating solid waste and mandated close monitoring of landfills with the Federal Resource Conservation and Recovery Act in 1976. In 1987, media images of the *Mobro 4000,* a barge carrying garbage from New York up and down the east coast for six months looking for a place to dump its load, brought new interest to recycling as an alternative to adding to solid waste.[37] In 1990, Congress focused on the source of the problem and passed the Pollution Prevention Act, which states "that pollution should be prevented or reduced at its source whenever feasible."[38]

Engaging the Citizenry

While governments were beginning the task of regulating on behalf of the environment, groups of citizens were also organizing on their own. Among the first to bring the environment into the national spotlight was Senator Gaylord Nelson of Wisconsin, the founder of Earth Day. With an activist's enthusiasm, Nelson organized a "huge grassroots protest over what was happening to our environment," and invited everyone in the nation to participate.[39]

Earth Day was an instant success, drawing 20 million participants the first year. The spirit of Earth Day reached well beyond one day. In 1970, April 22 fell on a Wednesday. One of the authors of this text was a young student who felt that students could do something for the first Earth Day even though the principal did not cancel classes. Along with 11 classmates, this student organized an event for the following Saturday, when the participants rode their bikes for 11 miles, picking up trash along the roadside.

By the twentieth anniversary of Earth Day, best-selling books such as *50 Simple Things You Can Do To Save the Earth*[40] and *The Green Consumer*[41] had helped make the environment a top concern for millions of people around the globe. Although these books offered only simple and easy changes for individual action, their popularity demonstrated the growing interest in environmental sustainability among the population.

Numerous nongovernmental organizations (NGOs) have also been successful in engaging citizens with a variety of environmental concerns through direct volunteerism, financial donations, and political activism. NGOs have tended to leverage citizen involvement to put pressure on businesses to change their practices and on governments to change their policies. Among the most successful and long lived of these are the Sierra Club, the National Wildlife Federation, the World Wildlife Fund, the Nature Conservancy, Friends of the Earth, and the Natural Resources Defense Council (see Table 1-1).

Reaching the Business World

Citizen groups and governments embraced environmental issues earlier than businesses did, but the business world has also come around to an appreciation of the value of sustainability. From about 1970 to the mid-1980s, businesses showed a general unwillingness to incorporate environmental concerns into their strategies or operations.[42] Government-mandated environmental protections were localized in various plants and factories rather than being integrated into company-wide programs, measurement systems were not developed, and environmental issues were not seen to have a place in business strategy.

By the mid-1980s, many industries began embracing environmental issues, but without innovating. Government regulations and societal efforts to affect public policies combined to move companies toward more sustainable practices. Pollution controls, monitoring systems, and solid waste programs became more common.[43] However, the lack of real innovation meant that pollution controls entailed added costs, perpetuating the mindset that the environment is the enemy of profits and jobs.

The environmental movement has continued to gain traction as more and more economies have become disrupted by resource shortages, natural disasters, and problems of public health,

TABLE 1-1 Nongovernmental Organizations

Organization	Date of Inception	Global Membership	Mission
Sierra Club	1892	1.3 million	To explore, enjoy, and protect the planet
The National Wildlife Federation	1937	4 million	To inspire Americans to protect wildlife for our future generations
The Nature Conservancy	1951	1 million	To protect ecologically important lands and waters for nature and people
The World Wildlife Fund	1964	5 million	To promote conservation of nature
Friends of the Earth	1969	80,000	To create awareness about climate change, forests, fair trade, proper use of taxes, and the banning of genetically modified organisms
The Natural Resources Defense Council	1970	1.2 million	To protect wildlife and wild places and to ensure a healthy environment for all life on earth

all of which can be traced to unsustainable economic practices. In the last few years, real concern for the environment has also penetrated corporate boardrooms, where even the most ardent devotees of the profit motive have begun to see the advantages of moving toward sustainability.

Corporations are major instruments of economic production and the world's biggest users of natural resources. The outputs of greenhouse gases, solid wastes, air pollution, water pollution, and soil pollution are all results of the economic engine of the free market. Environmental economists have begun to realize that these outputs and the resulting damage to ecosystems and to human health have an economic cost that must be included in the value to shareholders.[44] At the beginning of the twenty-first century, business leaders have begun to understand that environmental and social sustainability can contribute positively to their profits and their competitive positions in the marketplace.

THE EVOLUTION OF A NEW PARADIGM: SUSTAINABLE MARKETING

While public interest in the environment grew, governments legislated and environmental groups campaigned for changes in humanity's relationship with the natural world. Some business leaders and business scholars were also realizing the importance of sustainable practices.[45] **Green products**, generally meaning products that are less damaging to the environment or human health than traditional equivalents, began to emerge.[46] For example, in 1970, Tom's of Maine began to produce environmentally friendly products, beginning with phosphate-free laundry detergent. Over the years, the company developed a line of all-natural personal care products such as toothpaste, deodorant, soap, and mouthwash. Tom's of Maine was bought by Colgate-Palmolive in 2006.

Marketing and management thought leaders began to incorporate the limitations of the natural world into their theories.[47] Rather than considering the environment, society, and profits as separate, competing interests, innovative business thinkers developed holistic propositions, such as the triple bottom line, to simultaneously increase the economic, environmental, and social value of a business.[48] Paul Hawken's 1993 book, *The Ecology of Commerce: A Declaration of Sustainability*,[49] became highly influential among a few pioneering business leaders. Now, at the beginning of the second decade of the millennium, a consciousness of sustainability has made major inroads into mainstream business strategies and practice. Some observers believe that society's awareness of the need for sustainability has finally reached a tipping point.[50]

A Definition of Sustainable Marketing

Marketing, along with virtually every other business function, is undergoing a major shift toward environmental and social sustainability.[51] The role of marketing is particularly important in that it is the primary interface between any business and its customers. It is the marketing function that identifies customer needs and values and communicates them to the rest of the organization. Marketing influences every aspect of providing value to customers, including the design, development, and distribution of products and services. In its external communication functions, marketing also has the ability to influence the way people think, feel, and behave.

Because marketing essentially begins and ends with the customer, it follows that any marketing system must deliver value to its customers. At the same time, marketing institutions must be able to meet their own economic and financial goals. Sustainable marketing is no different in this respect. However, to be sustainable, marketing must also attend actively to its impact on the natural environment and on human well-being. In that spirit, we advance a definition of sustainable marketing:

> *Sustainable marketing* is the process of creating, communicating, and delivering value to customers in such a way that both natural and human capital are preserved or enhanced throughout.

This very concise definition requires some further explanation. First, it isn't intended to replace the definition of marketing advanced by the American Marketing Association,[52] which also includes references to institutions, exchange processes, and a list of stakeholders beyond the customer. This definition merely makes more explicit the need for sustainability throughout the marketing process.

Second, this definition does not conflict with the principles in the marketing concept. Sustainable marketing must still deliver a competitive advantage to an organization through superior performance in meeting the needs of target customers.

Third, the definition makes reference to both natural and human capital, terms we have not yet defined. **Natural capital** consists of all the resources nature provides, including both materials and ecosystem services. **Human capital** consists of all the resources that people provide, including labor, talent, and creativity. Note the differences in terminology between *natural capital* and *natural resources*, and between *human capital* and *human resources*. Both capital and resources are valuable, but our orientation to them is different. Resources are something to be used. Capital is something in which to invest.

As a final clarification, we suggest that sustainable marketing has two key objectives with respect to environmental and social sustainability. First, sustainable marketing means marketing in a sustainable manner. This aspect of an organization's marketing is directed inward such that all the marketing processes are environmentally and socially benign. Second, sustainable marketing means marketing sustainability—as a concept, a cultural value, and a set of practices. In other words, sustainable marketing's outward function is to help bring about a society in which striving for sustainability is the norm.

VIRTUAL FIELD TRIP

Searching for Sustainability on the Web

Pick a product or service category with which you are relatively unfamiliar. Search for it along with the term "sustainable" on the Web.

- Which brands or models are most highly recommended?
- What kinds of critiques, cautions, or dissatisfactions do you encounter?
- Do you believe what you are reading? Why or why not?

The Collaboration Advantage

Sustainable marketing is not and cannot be business as usual. For organizations struggling to become sustainable, the biggest challenge also turns out to be one of the biggest benefits: collaboration. Becoming sustainable requires new ways of creating value. This requires new thinking and new business relationships.

Although experts in their core competencies, many managers may not be well versed in the philosophies, communication strategies, and systems-level thinking that true sustainability requires. Some organizations develop internal sustainability teams that work alongside engineers, buyers, and product developers. For instance, in the 1980s, Nike created the Nike Environmental Action Team (NEAT) to integrate sustainable practices into the company's products and processes. Other firms look for outside assistance. Many have turned to the very environmental NGOs that may have once been their nemeses. General Motors partners with the Nature Conservancy, Coca-Cola works with the World Wildlife Fund, Wal-Mart works with Conservation International and the National Resources Defense Council, and Clorox works with the Sierra Club.[53] Some NGO members remain wary of the intentions of their corporate partners,[54] but close, collaborative relationships between businesses and NGOs offer advantages to both sides.[55] The environmental and social NGOs have expertise that businesses lack in the areas of sustainability. Businesses give the NGOs new avenues of participation that allow them to be more effective with their messages and activities.

CRITICAL THINKING ACTIVITY

Debate the Issues

Some people argue that *sustainability* is just the business buzzword of the day and that if they ignore it, it will go away. Others see sustainability as the new "must do" that business must embrace, or die. Argue the merits of both sides.

This chapter has presented a brief history of sustainability, ending with a definition of sustainable marketing. Chapter 2 delves into the economic and strategic rationales for sustainability in marketing, and Chapter 3 explores the ethical implications.

Chapter Summary

The world faces extraordinary and unprecedented challenges relating to both the environment and society. Rapidly increasing demand is colliding with declining resources. Vital ecosystems are under stress. Millions of people lack the most basic resources to sustain life. The problems lie in social and economic systems that are unsustainable. Awareness of the need for environmental and social sustainability has grown among citizens, governments and, finally, mainstream businesses. Recently, that awareness appears to have reached a tipping point, triggering impulses for widespread change in business priorities and practices. Marketing has a vital dual role in making businesses and society more sustainable. The concept of sustainable marketing is explained and defined.

Review of Chapter Objectives

- The meaning of sustainability
- The root of the current crisis of unsustainable growth
- The problem of declining supply and increasing demand
- The history of unsustainable marketing and environmental awakening
- The evolution of a new paradigm: sustainable marketing

Key Concepts

Sustainable Marketing 2	Human Sustainability 3	Social Sustainability 4	Green Products 10
Sustainability 2	Environmental	Natural Resources 4	Natural Capital 11
Lithosphere 2	Sustainability 4	Ecosystem Services 4	Human Capital 11
Biosphere 2	Economic Sustainability 4	Ecological Footprint 5	

Endnotes

1. Roach, John (2006), *National Geographic News*, March 23, http://news.nationalgeographic.com/news/2006/03/0323_060323_global_warming.html, accessed May 10, 2009.
2. Jury, William A. and Henry J. Vaux, Jr. (2007), "The Emerging Global Water Crisis: Managing Scarcity and Conflict among Water Users," *Advances in Agronomy Volume 95*, ed. Donald L. Sparks, New York: Elsevier Science & Technology.
3. Dean, Cornelia (2006), "Study Sees 'Global Collapse' of Fish Species," *New York Times*, November 3; see also Worm, Boris et al. (2006), "Impacts of Biodiversity Loss on Ocean Ecosystem Services," *Science*, 314 (5800) November 3: 787–790.
4. International Crisis Group, "Climate Change and Conflict," http://www.crisisgroup.org/home/index.cfm?id=4932, accessed May 20, 2009.
5. The Intergovernmental Panel on Climate Change 2007 report, http://www.ipcc.ch/, accessed May 20, 2009.
6. The Intergovernmental Panel on Climate Change 2007 report, http://www.ipcc.ch/, accessed May 20, 2009.
7. "Commencement: Healing or Stealing," http://www.up.edu/commencement/default.aspx?cid=9456, accessed December 28, 2009.
8. Kleanthous, Anthony and Jules Peck (2004), "Let Them Eat Cake: Satisfying the New Consumer Appetite for Responsible Brands," World Wildlife Fund, http://assets.wwf.org.br/downloads/let_them_eat_cake_full.pdf, accessed May 20, 2009.
9. United Nations General Assembly, Chapter 1: A Threatened Future, Report of the World Commission on Environment and Development: Our Common Future, Document A/42/427, 1987, http://www.un-documents.net/ocf-01.htm#I, accessed May 20, 2009.
10. Commoner, Barry (1971), *The Closing Circle*, New York: Bantam Books.
11. Giordano, Meredith A. and Aaron T. Wolf (2003), "Sharing Waters: Post-Rio International Water Management," *Natural Resources Forum*, 27:163–171.
12. Hawken, Paul (2007), *Blessed Unrest*, New York: Penguin Group (p. 13).
13. Moffatt, Ian (2000), "Ecological Footprints and Sustainable Development," *Ecological Economics*, 32: 359–362.
14. Global Footprint Network, http://www.footprintnetwork.org/en/index.php/GFN/page/world_footprint/, accessed May 20, 2009.
15. Castle, Duke and Jeanne Roy (1997, 2006), "The Collins Companies, Portland, Oregon, USA, The Natural Step Network," http://www.naturalstep.org/en/usa/collins-companies-portland-oregon-usa, accessed January 31, 2010.
16. Collins Almanor Forest, http://www.collinswood.com/CertifiedForests/AlmanorProfile.html, accessed July 27, 2009.
17. Castle, Duke and Jeanne Roy (1997, 2006), "The Collins Companies, Portland, Oregon, USA, The Natural Step Network," http://www.naturalstep.org/en/usa/collins-companies-portland-oregon-usa, accessed January 31, 2010.
18. U.S. Census Bureau, International Programs, World POPClock Project, http://www.census.gov/ipc/www/popclockworld.html, accessed May 20, 2009.
19. U.S. Census Bureau, World Population Information, http://www.census.gov/ipc/www/idb/worldpopinfo.html, accessed May 20, 2009.
20. Global Footprint Network, http://www.footprintnetwork.org/en/index.php/GFN/page/national_assessments/, accessed May 20, 2009.

21. Prothero, Andrea (1990), "Green Consumerism and the Societal Marketing Concept: Marketing Strategies for the 1990s," *Journal of Marketing Management*, 6 (2): 87–103

22. Crane, Andrew and John Desmond (2002), "Societal Marketing and Morality," *European Journal of Marketing*, 36 (5/6): 548–569.

23. American Marketing Association, http://www.marketingpower.com/AboutAMA/Pages/DefinitionofMarketing.aspx, accessed May 20, 2009.

24. Köhler, Gernot (2008), "The Global Stratification of Unemployment and Underemployment," Argentine Center for International Studies, working paper, http://www.caei.com.ar/es/programas/teoria/t12.pdf, accessed May 20, 2009.

25. Bussel, Robert (2003), "Taking on 'Big Chicken': The Delmarva Poultry Justice Alliance," *Labor Studies Journal*, 28 (2): 1–24.

26. Brown, Lester R. (2001), *Eco-Economy: Building an Economy for the Earth*, New York: W.W. Norton.

27. Kennedy, Robert F. Jr., (2008), Foreword to *The Green Collar Economy: How One Solution Can Fix Our Two Biggest Problems*, by Van Jones, New York: HarperCollins Publishers.

28. Yellowstone Net, Yellowstone National Park History, http://www.yellowstone.net/history.htm, accessed May 20, 2009.

29. Fox, Stephen R. (1985), *The American Conservation Movement: John Muir and His Legacy*, University of Wisconsin Press: 107–108.

30. Carson, Rachel (1962), *Silent Spring*, Boston, MA: Houghton Mifflin.

31. Lear, Linda (1997), *Rachel Carson: Witness for Nature*, New York: Henry Holt and Company.

32. Schumacher, E.F. (1973), *Small Is Beautiful: Economics as if People Mattered*, London, UK: Blond & Briggs.

33. Adam, David (2006), "Earthshakers: The Top 100 Green Campaigners of All Time," *Guardian*, November 28, http://www.guardian.co.uk/environment/2006/nov/28/climatechange.climatechangeenvironment, accessed May 9, 2009.

34. Environmental Graffiti, http://www.environmentalgraffiti.com/ecology/5-most-influential-environmental-leaders-in-the-world/141, accessed May 9, 2009.

35. United Nations Environment Programme, http://www.unep.org/women_env/w_details.asp?w_id=138, accessed May 9, 2009.

36. Jones, Van (2008), *The Green Collar Economy: How One Solution Can Fix Our Two Biggest Problems*, New York: HarperCollins Publishers.

37. History of Recycling, www.p2pays.org/ref/26/25070.pdf, accessed November 24, 2008.

38. United States Environmental Protection Agency, Pollution Prevention (P2), http://www.epa.gov/p2/pubs/p2policy/act1990.htm, accessed May 9, 2009.

39. Envirolink, http://earthday.envirolink.org/history.html, accessed May 5, 2009.

40. Javna, John (1990), *50 Simple Things You Can Do to Save the Earth*. Ashland, OR: Earthworks Group.

41. Makower, Joel, John Elkington, and Julia Hailes (1990), *The Green Consumer*, Oakland, CA: Tilden Press.

42. Walley, Noah and Bradley Whitehead (1994), "It's Not Easy Being Green," *Harvard Business Review*, May/Jun: 46–51.

43. Fischer, Kurt and Johan Schot, eds. (1993), *Environmental Strategies for Industry: International Perspectives on Research Needs and Policy Implications*, Washington, D.C.: Island Press.

44. Pearce, David (2002), "An Intellectual History of Environmental Economics," *Annual Review of Energy and the Environment*, 27:57–81.

45. Fuller, Donald, A. (1999), *Sustainable Marketing: Managerial-Ecological Issues*, Thousand Oaks, CA: Sage.

46. Ottman, Jacquelyn, A. (1993), *Green Marketing: Challenges and Opportunities for the New Marketing Age*, Lincolnwood, IL: NTC Business Press; also see Waski, John F. (1996), *Green Marketing and Management: A Global Perspective*, Cambridge, MA: Blackwell Publishers, Inc.

47. Hart, Stuart L. (1995), "A Natural-Resource-Based View of the Firm," *Academy of Management Review*, 20 (4): 986.

48. Savitz, Andrew W. and Karl Weber (2006), T*he Triple Bottom Line: How Today's Best-Run Companies Are Achieving Economic, Social, and Environmental Success—And How You Can Too*, New York: John Wiley.

49. Scott London, Book Review, http://www.scottlondon.com/reviews/hawken.html, accessed May 20, 2009; BNet, News Publications, http://findarticles.com/p/articles/mi_m1510/is_n81/ai_14656480/, accessed May 20, 2009; also see http://www.wdi.umich.edu/ResearchInitiatives/BottomPyramid/Resources/BooksReports/accessed May 20, 2009.

50. Verde Nieto, Diana (2008), "White Paper: The Long Journey to Sustainability Begins with a Single Step," *Awareness into Action: The Sustainable Enterprise*, http://www.awarenessintoaction.com/whitepapers/clownfish-marketing-sustainability-in-business.html, accessed July 25, 2009.
Friend, Gil (2006), "Sustainability: At the Tipping Point?" World Changing, March 5, http://www.worldchanging.com/archives/004172.html, accessed July 25, 2009.

51. Hart, Stuart, L. (1995), "A Natural-Resource-Based View of the Firm," *Academy of Management Review*, 20 (4): 986.

52. About AMA, http://www.marketingpower.com/AboutAMA/Pages/DefinitionofMarketing.aspx, accessed December 29, 2009.

53. Sustainability Partners, http://www.sustainabilitypartners.com/html/ourclientsnikereport.html, accessed May 20, 2009.

54. Marafiote, Tracy and Diane M. Martin (2007), "Meeting the In-Laws: How Unanticipated Heterodoxy Complicates the Marriage of Business and Environmental Organization Sustainability Alliances," Paper presented at the Sustainability in the Supply Chain International Conference, November 2, in Portland, Oregon.

55. Organic Consumers Association, http://www.organicconsumers.org/articles/article_11150.cfm, accessed May 20, 2009.

Sustainable Marketing Strategy

INTRODUCTION: MARKETING STRATEGY IN 20/20 HINDSIGHT

In June 2006, General Motors was still the world's largest automobile manufacturer, but Toyota was gaining ground on it. Rumors about a possible Chapter 11 bankruptcy at GM were floating around at the time. In an interview with *Motor Trend* magazine, then-CEO Rick Wagoner denied the bankruptcy rumors and tried to bolster public confidence in the company. Asked point blank, what was his worst decision, Wagoner answered, "Axing the EV1 electric-car program and not putting the right resources into hybrids. It didn't affect profitability, but it did affect image."[1]

THINK ABOUT IT

Did Wagoner get it right? Was it a mistake to terminate GM's electric car program? Should GM have invested more in the research and development of hybrids? What market conditions influenced GM to take the strategic direction it did? Wagoner claims the decisions affected GM's image but not its profitability. In hindsight, was that correct? Why or why not? How might GM look different today if it had made electric cars and hybrids a key part of its marketing strategy?

When executives, managers, and entrepreneurs chart the courses of their companies into uncertain futures, they develop marketing strategies based on their best estimates of what those futures will look like. They take into account their companies' strengths and weaknesses, and they attempt to predict likely changes in customer preferences, economic conditions, geopolitical situations, regulatory environments and, of course, competitors' actions.

Certain things now seem relatively certain about the future. Finite natural resources will become scarcer and more expensive, and their supplies will remain volatile. Populations will continue to grow, and people in developing and emerging nations will continue to demand higher standards of living. Environmental regulations will get stricter, not laxer. And, as always, the competition will never rest.

This chapter deals with the necessity and the methods of creating marketing strategies that can succeed in our changing world. If we can agree that business must become sustainable, then it follows that we need **sustainable marketing strategies**.

A sustainable marketing strategy is the statement of an organization's marketing goals and a plan for achieving them while preserving or enhancing both natural and human capital.

CHAPTER OBJECTIVES

In this chapter, you will learn:

- How to make the business case for sustainability
- Useful frameworks for understanding sustainable marketing
- How to create and implement a sustainable marketing strategy using The Natural Step Framework
- The sustainable strategy process

COMPETITIVE ADVANTAGE AND THE BUSINESS CASE FOR SUSTAINABILITY

The ultimate goal of any marketing strategy is to give a business an edge in a competitive market.[2] The success of a strategy is measured in economic terms such as sales revenues, market share, profits, and stock prices. The economic pulse of a business is monitored closely, and its indicators are the basis of management compensation, hiring and firing, and other important decisions. However, when managers pay too much attention to short-term profits, they tend to overlook, ignore, or devalue longer-term problems that may be detrimental to the company.

If short-term economic success were the only goal for business, there would be very little interest in sustainability. Clearly, this is not the case. Business publications and the popular press, political and nongovernmental groups, and citizen organizations have been increasingly concerned about sustainability.[3] There are many reasons for the concern. Some are moral and ethical. More and more, however, the reason for interest in sustainability is also economic. There are many economic reasons for businesses to pursue environmental and social sustainability in their marketing strategies. In the end, the reasons all come down to long-term **competitive advantage**, and together they make the business case for sustainability.

Staying Ahead of Environmental Regulation

One reason to become more sustainable is to stay ahead of inevitable **environmental regulation.** Environmental regulations are the laws designed to protect the natural environment against undue harm by individuals or organizations.[4] For example, the Clean Water Act (1972) and Air Quality Act (1967) were designed to regulate industrial pollution. Business groups fought the statutes, citing the costs of compliance and resulting threats to their economic success. There is no doubt that complying with environmental laws can be expensive. But environmental regulations and standards can trigger innovation that results in competitive advantage.[5] For example, the 1992 Energy Policy Act limited the amount of water showerheads could deliver to 2.5 gallons per minute.[6] One company, Teledyne, met this new regulation with ease and capitalized on the market strength of its brand, Shower Massage.[7]

While it's true that new laws apply to all players in an industry, not all players are affected equally. Automobile industry manufacturers have generally resisted increased federal and state fuel economy standards. A few though, like Honda and Toyota, were more aggressive in pursuing fuel-efficient technologies in anticipation of changing laws. When gas prices nearly doubled during 2008, Honda and Toyota, with their line-ups of hybrids and new compact models, enjoyed a competitive advantage over companies like GM that were still focusing their production on more fuel-thirsty SUVs.[8] The U.S. House of Representatives recently passed a historic bill to cap emissions of greenhouse gases. "By 2020, emissions must be reduced 17% over 2005 levels. By 2050, emissions must be reduced 80% or more."[9] If the U.S. Senate also passes the bill, this Congress will succeed in passing the nation's first comprehensive climate change legislation. Industries that have started down the path toward sustainable strategies will be in prime positions to take advantage of, or to meet, these new regulations.

Lower Costs

Another major source of competitive edge is having **cost advantages** over your rivals. The company that operates at lower costs has a greater margin for profits. Companies are rapidly learning that sustainability saves money. In the short term, conserving energy and reducing waste can reduce costs significantly. For example:

> Kohlberg, Kravis & Roberts (KKR) recently announced a pilot program with the Environmental Defense Fund that yielded an initial $16 million in savings in three of its portfolio companies. By reducing truck fuel usage (at US Foodservice), cutting paper consumption (at Primedia), and using more recycled feedstocks (at Sealy), the companies were able to generate significant savings in their operations. One of the promising things about the KKR effort is that the firm plans to apply its results across its diverse portfolio companies.[10]

In many cases, companies can actually convert waste into revenue streams, turning costs into earnings. For example, when Wal-Mart changed from wooden shipping pallets to cardboard ones, they saved money on the disposal of wooden pallets and made money by recycling the cardboard. They also saved money through reduced worker injuries (wood pallets are heavier and harder to move), and reduced building maintenance (nails in wood pallets are damaging to floors).

The above examples deal with short-term, repeated costs. In the longer term, sustainability gives an even greater cost advantage. In the future, fossil fuels and other finite resources will only become scarcer and more expensive. In severe cases, certain resources could become completely unavailable, whether by depletion or by government restriction. Businesses that are more sustainable, that is, that are less dependent on diminishing resources, are more likely to survive and to thrive.

Innovation

Yet another important source of competitive advantage is **innovation**, or the development of new products, services, and processes, that can keep a business running ahead of its competitors. Continuous innovation is the foundation of competitive advantage.[11]

It turns out that innovation blossoms when people are forced to find creative solutions to constraining problems.[12] After the 1992 Earth Summit in Rio de Janeiro, where international business leaders met to craft a vision of sustainable business development, many skeptics doubted the abilities of companies to become sustainable and remain competitive.[13] Yet others pointed out that becoming more sustainable was a catalyst for innovation, wealth creation, and new market opportunities.[14]

In one example of creative problem solving, Unarco Industries, a supplier of shopping carts to Wal-Mart, recently developed new methods for refurbishing old shopping carts to like-new condition. This innovation saved Wal-Mart over $8 million in one year on about a quarter million carts that would otherwise have been destined for landfills; at the same time, it made Unarco more competitive in the fight for Wal-Mart's business.[15] For another example of the power of innovation, consider the case of Humdinger Wind Energy, LLC on page 17.

A Better Workforce

A company's people can also be a source of competitive advantage. The ability to attract and retain talented workers is enhanced for businesses that are actively working to become sustainable. Not only do such businesses foster creativity and innovation, but they also tend to create healthier, more stimulating, and more productive work environments.[16] In one poll, "75% of graduating MBA students said that a company should consider its impact on society in such areas as the environment, equal opportunity, family relationships, and community involvement. A full 50% said that they would take a cut in salary to work for a socially responsible company."[17]

Differentiation

A company's market position is defined in the minds of its customer market. A strong **market position,** based on meaningful differentiation, is also a source of competitive advantage. Increasingly, sustainability is a critical component of a successful business's market position.[18]

Mini Case Study

Humdinger Wind Energy, LLC

Windbelt™ technology was originally conceived in 2004, during a trip to Petite Anse, Haiti. This fishing village near the coast was not connected to an electrical grid, and the only lighting available was diesel-powered or kerosene-based. Shawn Frayne, a member of a team from MIT and Petite Anse working in the area, recognized that instead of kerosene lamps, white LEDs powered by a very inexpensive wind generator might be able to better light homes and schools in the area. However, when Shawn tried to design this affordable, turbine-based wind generator, he hit a brick wall: turbine technology is too inefficient at these scales to be a viable option.

It was these difficult constraints of cost and local manufacture that led to a new invention, the world's first nonturbine wind generator, the Windbelt™ generator. Since then, the Windbelt™ technology has undergone several transformations. The small tabletop proof-of-concept of the world's first membrane-based, nonturbine generator has been transformed into the microBelt, the Windcell, and most recently the Windcell Panel. Taking wind power into places and applications previously inconceivable, the Windbelt aims to be one of the key tools of energy harvesting in the twenty-first century.[19] Investigate this innovation further at http://www.humdingerwind.com.

How did the problem (diesel-powered or kerosene-based lighting) lead to innovation (invention of the Windbelt)? How did Shawn Frayne's work improve the social sustainability of Petite Anse? What changes would you expect to the economic sustainability of the community due to this innovation?

If a business develops a consistent reputation for quality, and for caring for people and the environment, then customers will reward it with their loyalty. An authentic market position of sustainability can produce a payoff in terms of increased revenue from loyal customers and expanded markets among new customer segments.[20]

THINK ABOUT IT

IKEA's market position is, "Your partner in better living. We do our part, you do yours. Together we save money."[21] IKEA operates in 39 countries and the typical IKEA store features about 10,000 items. While other home store giants were faltering, IKEA gained ground. "Ikea has gained market share in the United States from home furnishings rivals like Levitz Furniture, which liquidated, and Linens 'N Things, which filed for bankruptcy protection in early May (2009)."[22] IKEA was one of the first large companies to develop and monitor company-wide sustainability efforts. Starting with a yearlong trial period in June 1990, IKEA has prioritized sustainability into all its operations.[23] What sets IKEA apart from its competitors? What role, if any, do you think IKEA's internal emphasis on sustainability has in helping the company maintain a competitive market position?

IKEA—Growth with an emphasis on sustainability.

VIRTUAL FIELD TRIP
Competitive Advantage

Pick a company that you believe enjoys a competitive advantage in its market. Search the company's website for examples of sustainable marketing activities.
- What kind of competitive advantage is evident?
- Look at a competitor's website. What opportunities exist for improving competitive advantage? How can this company use sustainability to create greater competitive advantage?

In summary, becoming sustainable provides businesses with a source of competitive advantage through anticipating regulatory changes, reducing costs, stabilizing supplies of limited resources, driving product and process innovation, attracting and retaining talented workers, and establishing a strong and authentic market position. Given that competitive advantage is the primary goal of marketing strategy, it makes sense that marketing should include sustainability goals and move companies closer to sustainable models of business.

FRAMEWORKS FOR SUSTAINABLE MARKETING

As global awareness of the need for sustainability has grown, so have attempts to understand and apply sustainability principles. The result has been different conceptual frameworks that have become increasingly applicable to marketing strategy and practice.

Beginning with Brundtland

In 1983, the United Nations called for the first World Commission on Environment and Development (headed by Norwegian Prime Minister Gro Brundtland and commonly known as the Brundtland Commission). After four years of work, the commission concluded that governments and industry need to show more environmental and social responsibility. The commission coined the term **sustainable development** and defined it as "development that meets the needs of the present without compromising the ability of future generations to meet their own needs."[24]

The commission called for governments and industries to deal with economic and ecological problems simultaneously through **ecologically sustainable development (ESD)**.[25] ESD addresses sustainable economies, ecosystem management, worldwide food security, and population impacts on ecosystems. The Brundtland Commission is commonly credited with the first widely used definition, philosophy, and compelling vision of sustainability. And though the usefulness of sustainable development has been widely debated and criticized, it certainly set the stage for other visionaries to develop strategy and comprehensive frameworks for sustainability

The United Nations Headquarters in New York City.

in business. Two of the most influential frameworks that emerged as foundations on which to build marketing strategy are the Triple Bottom Line and Natural Capitalism.

The Triple Bottom Line

Businesses that do well are colloquially described as being "in the black," the accounting term for being profitable. The "black" shows up in the bottom line of the financial statement, which shows if the business has profit or a loss. Managers learn early on that although sales may be increasing and customers may be happy, if the costs are also increasing and the competition is gaining, the bottom-line story may not have a happy ending.

Business practices that simultaneously benefit the business, society, and the environment achieve a win-win-win situation and help a firm to become more sustainable. Entrepreneur John Elkington developed the triple-win idea and coined the term **Triple Bottom Line (TBL)**, meaning the net economic, environmental, and social impacts of an organization.[26] The TBL framework encourages managers to find opportunities to build competitive advantage through three dimensions of sustainability: economic, environmental, and social. This is achieved in part by reaching out to **stakeholders**, meaning people and groups that have legitimate interests in a business and its conduct but are not necessarily its shareholders.

Each component of the TBL includes several specific, measurable points of reference that may be useful in the pursuit of competitive advantage. Economic measures include sales, profits, return on investment (ROI), taxes paid, monetary flows, and jobs created. Environmental measures include air and water quality, energy usage, and waste produced. Social measures include labor practices, health and injuries, community impacts, human rights, and product safety.[27]

While a TBL orientation increases a business's environmental and social responsibility, the framework is not without its critics. Some suggest that the approach is insufficient and may even be a smoke screen for businesses to hide behind.[28]

Other critics argue that the TBL perspective ignores a fourth pillar of sustainability, namely culture. One important aspect of culture, emphasized by UNESCO (the United Nations Educational, Scientific and Cultural Organization), is diversity. According to UNESCO's "Universal Declaration on Cultural Diversity," "As a source of exchange, innovation and creativity, cultural diversity is as necessary for humankind as biodiversity is for nature."[29] Sustainability consultant Adam Werbach describes this cultural pillar as, "actions through which communities manifest their identity and cultivate traditions from generation to generation."[30] As mentioned in Chapter 1, shaping cultural values is one of the main imperatives of sustainable marketing.

Natural Capitalism

Capital is the stuff of business. Without it, not much gets done. Businesses that are the most adept at creating and managing capital often enjoy a competitive advantage. But what happens when capital is limited or decreasing? If they use up all their capital, businesses won't survive. There are four kinds of capital: financial, manufactured, natural, and human. Businesses are acutely aware of the value of **financial capital** (cash and investments) and **manufactured capital** (infrastructure and technology), but they traditionally have not fully valued natural capital

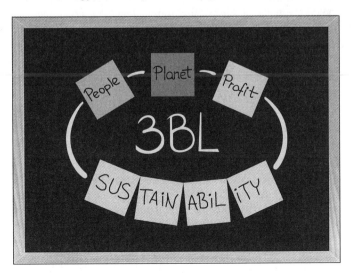

The Triple Bottom Line.

(natural resources and ecosystem services) or human capital (labor, talent, intelligence, and creativity). Instead, businesses too often treat both nature and people as expendable resources.

This old way of thinking is not sustainable. Natural Capitalism[31] is an approach to business that fully values all sources of capital, but places special emphasis on building both natural and human capital. By failing to take into account the degradation of the natural world, business-as-usual practices have greatly decreased global levels of natural capital, which has enormous economic value and no known substitutes.[32]

Meanwhile, while natural capital has been decreasing at alarming rates, human capital is ever increasing. Rapidly growing global populations and the growing availability of health care, information, and education are producing large and capable workforces, the likes of which didn't exist during the industrial revolution. Now that people are abundant and natural resources are scarce, businesses must adapt and innovate accordingly.[33]

Natural Capitalism stresses four interlinked principles: radical resource productivity, biomimicry, service economies, and reinvestment.[34] **Radical resource productivity** refers to making the most of limited and irreplaceable resources, leading to slower depletion of natural resources, the reduction of pollution, and increased worldwide employment. An example of radical resource productivity in a product distribution center might include dramatic energy conservation, conversion to renewable power sources, and a program for capturing all wastes for reuse, recycling, or composting.

Biomimicry refers to the **redesign of industrial processes** according to biological models. In nature, nothing is wasted. The waste from one organism is food for another. "Waste equals food" forms the central principle of **cradle-to-cradle design**,[35] in which all industrial waste and consumer waste are recovered and returned to productive uses. For example, General Mills used to pay to have oat hulls, a by-product of making Cheerios, hauled away. Now the hulls are used as fuel, and General Mills makes money on the sales of what was once a wasteful expense, both increasing its profits and reducing its dependence on fossil fuels.[36]

THINK ABOUT IT

Using recycled materials (such as paper, aluminum, and polyester) is better for the environment than using virgin materials (such as trees, bauxite ore, and petroleum). In many cases, the recycled materials are also cheaper to use. For example, "*Plastics News*, a trade magazine, lists the recent price of PET virgin bottle resin pellets between 83 and 85 cents a pound, compared to only 58 to 66 cents a pound for PET recycled pellets."[37] And the cost advantage only increases as virgin materials become scarcer. What are some of the advantages to a business of using recycled polyester (PET) to replace virgin polyester manufactured from petroleum? What kinds of systems could be put in place to recapture polyester (including beverage bottles and textiles) for recycling? What business opportunities might this suggest?

Service economies emphasize meeting consumer needs with services and viewing goods as means of service delivery. Video rental is a good example. A DVD you might rent for your entertainment is rented again and again by other movie watchers. The movie studio doesn't have to manufacture one DVD for each person who desires to see a film. The trend toward streaming video over the Internet is yet another step closer to a service economy. Pay-per-use models have been extended to product/services as diverse as carpeting, computing, air-conditioning, and lighting.[38] Substituting services for product ownership is consistent with the principles of dematerialization and service-dominant logic, which will be described in detail in Chapter 9.

THINK ABOUT IT

What other kinds of products could be rented or shared? What kinds of cost savings would that mean for customers? In addition to the purchase price of an item, what other expenses could be spared? What are the likely disadvantages to customers of rent/share arrangements? What kinds of profitable business opportunities could be developed through creatively addressing those disadvantages?

Bioswales cool and clean runoff before they flow to the river, and they provide natural riverbank habitat for wildlife.

Reinvestment, or the use of dividends, interest, or profits from an investment to buy additional productive capital, is a foundation of good business practice. This is as true for natural capital and human capital as it is for the financial and manufactured varieties. Reinvestment in natural and human capital often can be financed by cost savings or efficiencies gained through more efficient use of resources. For example, one of the vehicle distribution centers of Toyota Logistics Services, which moves thousands of new cars a week through the Port of Portland, Oregon, used construction savings from redesigned facilities along the Willamette River to reinvest in the local ecosystem. Among many improvements to enhance sustainability, the company added bio-swales between its acres of parking lots and the river. The bio-swales cool and clean runoff before it flows to the river, and they provide natural riverbank habitat for wildlife.[39]

Neither Natural Capitalism nor the TBL claims to be a how-to manual for becoming sustainable, but they outline the general direction for a major shift in the direction business needs to move in a world of diminishing natural capital and a growing global population of increasingly demanding consumers.

The Natural Step Framework

For something closer to a how-to manual, we look to a strategic framework called The Natural Step, developed by the Swedish oncologist Karl-Henrik Robèrt in conjunction with ecologists, chemists, physicists, and medical doctors from around the world. **The Natural Step Framework** (TNSF) is founded on "a set of guiding sustainability principles based on the laws of thermodynamics and natural cycles."[40]

TNSF identifies four essential characteristics, or system conditions, of a sustainable society. Together, these four **system conditions** constitute a working definition of sustainability that, unlike previous definitions, provides concrete guidelines for planning sustainable processes and policies. A truly sustainable society, business, or other organization is one that:

1. causes no systematic increases in environmental concentrations of substances from the Earth's crust,
2. causes no systematic increases in environmental concentrations of synthetic substances,
3. causes no systematic increases in ecosystem degradation, and
4. creates no systematic barriers to people meeting their own needs.[41]

To understand the system conditions, it's helpful to first understand what a naturally sustainable system looks like, and then how that system can be made unsustainable.

FIGURE 2-1 **Naturally Sustainable Cycles.**

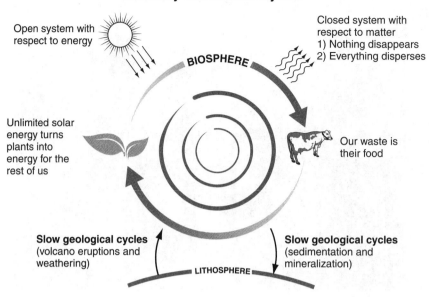

Naturally Sustainable Cycles

Open system with respect to energy

Closed system with respect to matter
1) Nothing disappears
2) Everything disperses

BIOSPHERE

Unlimited solar energy turns plants into energy for the rest of us

Our waste is their food

Slow geological cycles (volcano eruptions and weathering)

Slow geological cycles (sedimentation and mineralization)

LITHOSPHERE

FIGURE 2-2 **Human Influences on the Sustainable Cycles.**

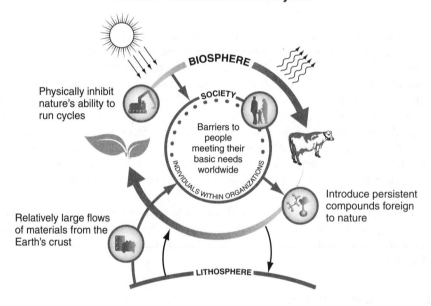

Human Influences on the Cycles

BIOSPHERE

SOCIETY

Physically inhibit nature's ability to run cycles

Barriers to people meeting their basic needs worldwide

INDIVIDUALS WITHIN ORGANIZATIONS

Introduce persistent compounds foreign to nature

Relatively large flows of materials from the Earth's crust

LITHOSPHERE

Figure 2-1 depicts a balanced and sustainable biosphere, which is a perfectly sustainable system. In contrast, Figure 2-2 depicts the four ways that human activity interferes with the biosphere's ability to function properly: first, by extracting substances (e.g., coal, petroleum, and heavy metals) from the lithosphere, or the Earth's crust, faster than the Earth can recapture and reabsorb them; second, by introducing man-made substances (e.g., pesticides and other toxic chemicals) to the biosphere that the Earth can't break down or neutralize; third, by hindering the Earth's ability to provide essential ecosystem services (e.g., through mass deforestation and overfishing); and fourth, by undermining people's ability to meet their own needs (e.g., through abuse of economic or political power) and thereby forcing them to sacrifice their environment, their health, or their well-being for the survival of their families.

Note that the four system conditions do not call for the complete elimination of plastics or metals or the harvesting of trees. We need those materials for our economy to function. Instead, TNSF calls for the management of such substances so that they don't end up in the air, water, or soil where nature can't adequately reabsorb and reintegrate them. One way to manage toxic or harmful substances is through cradle-to-cradle design and manufacturing, which confines those substances to closed-loop manufacturing cycles and keeps them from polluting the environment.

The system conditions also hold that ecosystems need to be preserved or, if possible, restored so that they can continue to perform their life-giving services. And finally, TNSF holds that all people must have the means to provide for the well-being of their families and communities without resorting to environmental destruction.

The four system conditions constitute a vision of success for an organization working on becoming sustainable. Developing a sustainable marketing strategy begins with a process called **backcasting** in which managers evaluate their organizations' current positions with respect to their vision of a sustainable future. They then work from this desired end state and identify possible steps to create this future. For example, a team of managers may determine that the company has significant opportunities to eliminate toxic chemicals in its products, to save fossil fuels in product distribution, and to reduce waste to landfills from its retail locations.

Once the teams have identified opportunities for action, the next step is to evaluate and prioritize these opportunities. TNSF provides three criteria to optimize progress on all fronts: environmental, social, and financial. All actions and investments should:

1. move the firm in the right direction toward sustainability, assuring that gains in one area aren't offset by losses elsewhere,
2. provide the flexibility to take advantage of future opportunities, and
3. yield an acceptable ROI.

The combination of backcasting and strategic action allows managers to optimize progress toward sustainability, **strategic flexibility**, and profitability. For triple-bottom-line sustainability, this process is strategically superior to maximizing ROI on a project-by-project basis.[42] It focuses creative energy on solving environmental and social problems in ways that also make the company more competitive in both the short and long run. In the early stages of a transition to sustainability, companies should focus on **quick wins,** the kinds of actions that create cost savings and efficiencies in the short term. Examples of quick wins would include packaging reductions that save materials costs, reduce waste to landfills, and create major savings on shipping, fuel, and storage. Savings from quick wins can then be reinvested into systems and innovations that will have even greater impact on sustainability, profits, and competitive advantage.

More and more U.S. companies are beginning to embrace TNSF in their efforts to become sustainable, and there are ample precedents for success in The Natural Step's home country of Sweden. Author Donald Fuller noted that, by 1999, 29 corporations and 49 municipalities in that country had used TNSF principles in their strategic planning.[43]

CREATING AND IMPLEMENTING A SUSTAINABLE MARKETING STRATEGY

This section reinforces what you know about the process of forming a marketing strategy and provides guidelines for making sure the end result is sustainable. Sustainable marketing strategy needs to flow from a company's vision based on system-level thinking and a mission that reflects ambitious goals for both marketing and sustainability. Because creating a sustainable strategy often involves expertise outside of current marketing job descriptions, we look first at some organizational tactics that can make the process easier and more successful.

Building a Team

A popular adage says, "Culture eats strategy for breakfast." Even the most brilliant strategy can be made worthless by an organization that doesn't comprehend it, doesn't believe in it, or simply doesn't find it as important as other aspects of a job or career. The first step in creating a sustainable strategy, then, is to involve the right people and prepare them to participate fully in the exercise.

Because sustainability requires systems-level thinking, it's important to create strategy with cross-functional teams. **Cross-functional teams** ideally consist of people from top to bottom across a broad spectrum of a company's operations, which may include information management, people management, manufacturing, accounting, finance and, of course, sales and marketing. Such teams contribute different perspectives of a business's strengths, limitations, and opportunities, and they will often identify "out of the box" solutions to problems outside their expertise. They also help to achieve a whole-system perspective so that sustainability gains in one area don't have negative consequences elsewhere.

A good example of a cross-functional team is QUEST (Quality Utilizing Employee Suggestions and Teamwork), a waste-reduction management group within Interface Inc., the floor-covering giant. Beginning with training in The Natural Step Framework, QUEST teams meet regularly to address a host of sustainability challenges.[44] Their efforts have resulted in massive reductions in waste to landfills, water, and air; they have yielded millions of dollars in savings; and they have converted hundreds of millions of dollars in revenue to sustainable business. To learn more about QUEST and Interface, check out CEO Ray Anderson's book, *Mid-Course Correction*.[45]

Once a team is assembled (or ideally beforehand), participants need to be tuned in to a common definition of success. In other words, everyone needs to understand the company's mission in terms of both business goals and sustainability goals (Imagine a road trip where each driver has a different understanding of the destination!). The four TNSF system conditions provide an excellent understanding of sustainability goals that apply to any organization. Training is an important and often overlooked aspect of strategic planning. Nike, in its efforts to become sustainable, has provided sustainability training for hundreds of employees throughout the company.[46] Similarly, Electrolux has provided its EcoKnow training for over 100,000 employees in over 60 countries.[47] Interface has created "One World Learning (OWL), a company within our company" to advance sustainability training.[48]

A company's employees can be counted on to know their own places with respect to the core business, but they may lack expertise in other areas, such as public policy, ecology, or the supply chain. Again, because good strategy requires systems-level approaches, it's often useful to create **strategic alliances** with people from outside the company for planning purposes. Industry people, such as suppliers and distributors, and nonindustry people, such as thought leaders from NGOs, government, and academia, can bring valuable perspectives, knowledge, skills, and ideas to the process. For example, Wal-Mart uses Sustainable Value Networks (SVNs), comprising "leaders from our company, supplier companies, academia, government, and non-governmental organizations" to integrate sustainable solutions into 13 business areas including buildings, transportation and logistics, packaging, and products ranging from seafood to clothing and from jewelry to electronics. One SVN focuses specifically on the supply chain in China.[49]

Creating the Strategy

Once the strategy team is in place and everyone has agreed to the basic objectives for marketing and sustainability, then the more familiar process of planning can begin. As you probably know, the fundamental steps of creating a marketing strategy include some version of the following:

1. Identify marketing opportunities
2. Select a target market and market position
3. Plan and implement a marketing mix, including a
   a. product strategy,
   b. pricing strategy,
   c. communication strategy, and
   d. distribution strategy
4. Monitor, adapt and repeat as necessary

The first step, to identify **marketing opportunities**, should make ample use of the back-casting and brainstorming aspects of the TNSF, helping the cross-functional team to explore a wide range of innovative possibilities. Marketing opportunities include any possible actions for creating or increasing value for customers, the firm, and stakeholders; and they can be found anywhere in an organization's marketing functions and processes. For example, a marketer of smart phones may identify an opportunity to incorporate GPS navigation into a phone, creating more value for users, giving the firm a competitive edge, and reducing the need for separate navigation devices. Each potential opportunity should then be screened using the three TNSF prioritization criteria (right direction, strategic flexibility, and acceptable ROI) in order to identify the most promising alternatives.

Once an opportunity is identified and screened, the next step is to select a **target market,** typically a market segment with which the company has some competitive advantage or special expertise, and determine an appropriate market position. The selected target market may not be interested primarily in sustainable practices. That's not important at this point. What does matter is that the marketing offering is as sustainable as possible in addition to meeting whatever specific needs the target customer has. Nike, for example, famously targets athletes, worldwide, with little mention of sustainability as a customer value,[50] even though sustainability now lies at the heart of the company's vision and practices.[51] Wal-Mart, on the other hand, has adapted its "Always Low Prices" market position to accommodate its expanded business goals. The current market position, "Save Money, Live Better" captures both its pricing strategy and its commitment to sustainability.

With the target customers in mind, it's time to create a **marketing mix** that does an excellent job of meeting their needs while also advancing the company's sustainability goals. For strategic planning purposes, it's important to scrutinize each element of product, place, price, and promotion in terms of the system conditions for sustainability. In each case, answer the four questions: (1) Does this action systematically increase environmental carbon or other substances from the Earth's crust? For example, does this outdoor clothing line require petroleum-derived fabrics? Or are there recycled alternatives? (2) Does the action systematically increase concentrations of man-made substances? For example, is the supply chain for this food product committed to the use of synthetic pesticides and herbicides? Or are there organic alternatives? (3) Does the action contribute to the increased degradation of ecosystems? For example, does this seafood product contribute to overfishing? Or is there a sustainably fished or farmed option? (4) Does this action contribute to barriers against people meeting their own needs anywhere in the value chain? For example, are the workers in the suppliers' factories paid living wages and protected from hazardous substances or conditions? If not, how can the situation be remedied? Finally, there is a fifth question that must be asked: Do these proposed actions have negative consequences elsewhere in the value chain with respect to the four system conditions?

If the answers to these questions are satisfactory, then the marketing mix passes the first of the prioritization criteria; that is, it moves the company closer to sustainability. The next step is to make sure that the proposed marketing mix leaves the business with the flexibility to make additional positive changes in the future. In other words, for each element of the mix, ask the following questions: Does this action lock the business in to solutions that may become less than optimal as technologies and markets change? Or does it add to the capacity to grow sustainably in the future? For example, a lighting company that overinvests in compact fluorescent technology may find itself at a competitive disadvantage if new lighting breakthroughs make fluorescents obsolete from both a cost and a sustainability standpoint.

If the projected financial return on any marketing action is sufficiently positive, then the strategy should be fully sustainable. Consistent with the principles of Natural Capitalism, TBL and TNSF, the key to successful marketing strategy is not to maximize short-term profits at all costs. Rather, it is to optimize solutions that make money in the short term while building natural, human, and financial capital for long-term, sustainable business.

The final step in strategic planning is to build in systems for measuring, monitoring, and improving the marketing strategy and processes. Marketers understand how to monitor performance outcomes such as sales, market share, and profits. Many tools also exist for charting progress toward sustainability goals. They include international standards such as ISO 14001 and increasingly popular measures such as carbon footprints, ecological footprints, and life-cycle assessments, all of which will be discussed in greater detail in Chapter 6.

CRITICAL THINKING ACTIVITY

Can an Oil Company Become Sustainable?

Can an oil company become sustainable? What about a mining company? Assume for a moment that the chairman of the board of a multinational oil or mining company decided that it was going to become sustainable. What would be an appropriate corporate vision statement? What would be appropriate but ambitious sustainability goals? What elements of marketing strategy would enhance the company's competitive advantage?

Chapter Summary

In this chapter, we have learned that sustainability is critical to an organization's long-term competitive advantage. We discussed several frameworks for sustainability, including ESD, the TBL, Natural Capitalism, and The Natural Step. Finally, we examined the process of creating a sustainable marketing strategy using TNSF.

Review of Chapter Objectives

- How to make the business case for sustainability
- Useful frameworks for sustainable marketing

- How to create and implement a sustainable marketing strategy using The Natural Step Framework
- The sustainable strategy process

Key Concepts

Sustainable Marketing Strategies   14
Competitive Advantage   15
Environmental Regulation   15
Cost Advantages   16
Innovation   16
Market Position   16
Sustainable Development   18

Ecologically Sustainable Development (ESD)   18
Triple Bottom Line (TBL)   19
Stakeholders   19
Financial Capital   19
Manufactured Capital   19
Natural Capitalism   20
Radical Resource Productivity   20

Biomimicry   20
Redesign of Industrial Processes   20
Cradle-to-Cradle Design   20
Service Economies   20
Reinvestment   21
The Natural Step Framework (TNSF)   21
System Conditions   21
Backcasting   23

Strategic Flexibility   23
Quick Wins   23
Cross-Functional Teams   23
Strategic Alliances   24
Marketing Opportunities   24
Target Market   24
Marketing Mix   25

Endnotes

1. Interview with Rick Wagoner (2006), *Motor Trend*, June: 94.
2. Porter, Michael, E. (1985), *Competitive Advantage: Creating and Sustaining Superior Performance*, New York: The Free Press.
3. Willard, Bob (2007), presentation at the 10th Anniversary of the Natural Step, Nike World Headquarters, October 10, in Portland, Oregon.
4. Environmental Law, Legal Information Institute, Cornell University Law School, http://topics.law.cornell.edu/wex/Environmental_law, accessed July 23, 2009.
5. Porter, Michael E. and Claas van der Linde (1995), "Green and Competitive: Ending the Stalemate," *Harvard Business Review*, Sep/Oct: 120–134.
6. Flex Your Power, http://www.fypower.org/res/tools/products_results.html?id=100160, accessed July 25, 2009.
7. Ottman, Jacquelyn A. (1998), *Green Marketing: Opportunity for Innovation*, New York: J. Ottman Consulting Inc.
8. Collier, Robert (2006), A Step Ahead of the Curve: Success of Its Hybrid Cars Fuels Toyota's Rise in Industry, *San Francisco Chronicle*, April 24, http://www.sfgate.com/cgi-bin/article.cgi?f=/c/a/2006/04/24/TOYOTA.TMP, accessed May 12, 2009.
9. Business Week (2009), House Passes Cap and Trade Bill, June, 26, http://www.businessweek.com/blogs/money_politics/archives/2009/06/house_passes_ca.html, accessed July 26, 2009.
10. My Green Element (2009), Sustainability + Private Equity = Cost Savings, March 6, http://www.mygreenelement.com/?p=496, accessed May 12, 2009.
11. Lengnick-Hall, Cynthia A. (1992), Innovation and Competitive Advantage: What We Know and What We Need to Learn, *Journal of Management*, 18 (2): 399–429.
12. Mayer, Marissa Ann (2006), Creativity Loves Constraints, *Business Week*, February 13, http://www.businessweek.com/magazine/content/06_07/b3971144.htm, accessed May 10, 2009.
13. Walley, Noah and Bradley Whitehead (1994), It's Not Easy Being Green, *Harvard Business Review*, May/Jun: 46–51.

14. Clarke, Richard A., Robert N. Stavins, J. Ladd Greeno, Joan L. Bavaria, Frances Cairncross, Daniel C. Esty, Bruce Smart, Johan Piet, Richard P. Wells, Rob Gray, Kurt Fischer, and Johan Schot (1994), "The Challenge of Going Green," *Harvard Business Review*, Jul/Aug: 37–48.
15. Martin, Diane M. and John W. Schouten (2009), "Engineering a Mainstream Market for Sustainability: Insights from Wal-Mart's Perfect Storm," in *Explorations in Consumer Culture Theory*, ed. John F. Sherry, Jr., and Eileen Fisher, 150–167, London, UK: Routledge.
16. Willard, Bob (2002), *The Sustainability Advantage*, British Columbia, Canada: New Society Publishers.
17. Dorsey, David (2007), "The New Spirit of Work," *Fast Company*, December 18, http://www.fastcompany.com/magazine/16/barrett.html?page=0%2C0, accessed May 18, 2009.
18. Brady, Arlo (2005), *The Sustainability Effect: Rethinking Corporate Reputation in the 21st Century*, London, UK: Palgrave/Macmillan.
19. Our Company: About, Humdinger Wind Energy, http://www.humdingerwind.com/#/oc_about/, accessed July 27, 2009.
20. Willard, Bob (2002), *The Sustainability Advantage*, British Columbia, Canada: New Society Publishers.
21. Press Room, Student Information, IKEA, http://www.ikea.com/ms/en_GB/about_ikea_new/press_room/student/index.html, accessed July 26, 2009.
22. IKEA Sticks to Growth Strategy Despite Housing Market Woes, *Tampa Bay Online*, http://www2.tbo.com/content/2008/jun/20/bz-ikea-sticks-to-growth-strategy-despite-housing-/, accessed July 25, 2009.
23. Nattrass, Brian and Altomare, Mary (1999), *The Natural Step for Business: Wealth, Ecology, and the Evolutionary Corporation*, Gabriola Island, British Columbia, Canada: New Society Publishers.
24. Center for a World in Balance, http://www.worldinbalance.net/agreements/1987-brundtland.html, accessed May 18, 2009.

25. Shrivastava, Paul (1995), "The Role of Corporations in Achieving Ecological Sustainability," *Academy of Management Review*, October: 936–960.
26. Elkington, John (1994), "Towards the Sustainable Corporation: Win-Win-Win Business Strategies for Sustainable Development," *California Management Review*, 36: 90–100.
27. Savitz, Andrew W. and Karl Weber (2006), *The Triple Bottom Line: How Today's Best-Run Companies Are Achieving Economic, Social and Environmental Success—And How You Can Too*, New York: John Wiley (xiii).
28. Norman, Wayne and Chris MacDonald (2004), "Getting to the Bottom of the Triple Bottom Line," *Business Ethics Quarterly*, April: 243–262.
29. UNESCO (2001), "The Universal Declaration on Cultural Diversity," http://www.un-documents.net/udcd.htm, accessed December 30, 2009.
30. Werbach, Adam (2009), *Strategy for Sustainability: A Business Manifesto*, Boston, MA: Harvard Business Press (p. 10).
31. Hawken, Paul, Amory Lovins, and L. Hunter Lovins (1999), *Natural Capitalism: Creating the Next Industrial Revolution*, Boston, MA: Little Brown.
32. Natural Capitalism, http://www.natcap.org/sitepages/pid5.php, accessed May 18, 2009.
33. SlideShare, "The Basics of Natural Capitalism," http://www.slideshare.net/RichCEI/The-Basics-of-Natural-Capitalism-994510?src=related_normal&rel=741036, accessed May 19, 2009.
34. Hawken, Paul, Amory Lovins, and L. Hunter Lovins (1999), *Natural Capitalism: Creating the Next Industrial Revolution*, Boston, MA: Little Brown.
35. McDonough, William and Michael Braungart (2002), *Cradle to Cradle: Remaking the Way We Make Things*, New York: North Point Press.
36. SlideShare, "The Basics Of Natural Capitalism," http://www.slideshare.net/RichCEI/The-Basics-of-Natural-Capitalism-994510?src=related_normal&rel=741036, accessed May 19, 2009.
37. Intagliata, Christopher (2008), "Does It Cost More to Recycle a Plastic Bottle than to Make a New One?" *Scienceline*, http://www.scienceline.org/2008/05/05/ask-intagliata-plastic/, accessed January 3, 2010.
38. SlideShare, "Natural Capitalism by Assif Strategies," http://www.slideshare.net/sitblog/natural-capitalism-by-assif-strategies-presentation, accessed May 19, 2009.
39. The authors have toured the TLS facility several times and examined numerous documents regarding its environmental efforts. To view a PowerPoint presentation, see http://www.aapa-ports.org/files/SeminarPresentations/06_HNE_Corbin.pdf.
40. The Natural Step, "Our Story," http://www.naturalstep.org/en/our-story, accessed May 19, 2009.
41. The Natural Step, "The System Conditions," http://www.thenaturalstep.org/the-system-conditions, accessed May 19, 2009.
42. Robèrt, Karl-Henrik (2002), *The Natural Step Story: Seeding a Quiet Revolution*, Gabriola Island, BC: New Society Publishers.
43. Fuller, Donald, A. (1999), *Sustainable Marketing: Managerial-Ecological Issues*, Thousand Oaks, CA: Sage.
44. The Natural Step, A Natural Step Network Case Study: "Interface, Atlanta, Georgia, USA," http://www.thenaturalstep.org/en/usa/interface-atlanta-georgia-usa, accessed May 20, 2009.
45. Anderson, Ray C. (1998), *Mid-Course Correction*, White River Junction, VT: Chelsea Green.
46. The Natural Step, A Natural Step Network Case Study: "Nike," http://www.thenaturalstep.org/sites/all/files/Nike%20Case%20Study_Jan2009.pdf, accessed May 20, 2009.
47. The Natural Step, A Natural Step Network Case Study: "Electrolux," http://www.thenaturalstep.org/en/usa/electrolux, accessed May 20, 2009.
48. Anderson, Ray C. (1998), *Mid-Course Correction*, White River Junction, VT: Chelsea Green.
49. Wal-Mart, Inc., "Sustainable Value Networks," http://walmartstores.com/Sustainability/7672.aspx, accessed May 20, 2009.
50. Nike, "Company Overview," http://www.nikebiz.com/company_overview/, accessed May 20, 2009.
51. Nike, "Responsibility," http://www.nikebiz.com/responsibility/, accessed May 20, 2009.

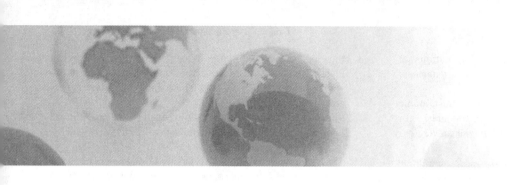

Ethical Dimensions of Sustainable Marketing

INTRODUCTION: THE PROBLEM WITH MOTHER'S MILK

Most people agree that societies should strive to protect babies and young children, their most vulnerable citizens. Most also agree that mother's milk is the most pure and wholesome food for newborns. So consider this: "Researchers discovered an average of 91 industrial chemicals, with a total of 167 chemicals, in the breast milk of nine women in six (American) states."[1] A *New York Times Magazine* article provides a partial list of the toxins found in mother's milk. It includes DDT, PCBs, dioxin, trichloroethylene, perchlorate, mercury, lead, benzene, and arsenic. The sources of these poisons are all around us, all the time, in such common products as "paint thinners, dry-cleaning fluids, wood preservatives, toilet deodorizers, cosmetic additives, gasoline byproducts, rocket fuel, termite poisons, fungicides and flame retardants."[2]

THINK ABOUT IT

What responsibility does a business have to keep industrial chemicals out of the environment? Should businesses be required to know the downstream effects of their products and processes? Should businesses openly communicate those effects to the public? To what extent should businesses be allowed to systematically contribute to environmental harm and risks to human health and well-being?

The role of marketing in society inspires much interest and discussion. Marketing decisions may have consequences for stakeholders other than just customers and stockholders. Questions about the responsibilities of businesses and their managers include issues of legality, morality, and philosophy, and, as we saw in the case of mother's milk, they may even touch the natural and social sciences as well.

Ethical questions may seem complex and confusing, and at times even unanswerable. Nevertheless, they deserve special attention. Ethical concerns in marketing must be understood in both social and environmental contexts, which, as we learned in Chapters 1 and 2, are deeply interrelated.

THINK ABOUT IT

What is the responsibility of marketing toward the environment? What is marketing's responsibility to society, including its most vulnerable populations? Consider the following questions: Can marketing actions be considered ethical if they are fundamentally unsustainable? Is it ethical to steal resources and opportunities from future generations in order to increase profits today? And as a consumer, is it ethical to buy and use a product manufactured with slave labor? With child labor? Where should marketers draw the line between lower prices to customers and dangerous conditions for workers?

This chapter attempts to untangle marketing ethics and make the topic more approachable by examining it through the lens of environmental and social sustainability.

CHAPTER OBJECTIVES

In this chapter, you will learn more about:

- The relationship between business and society
- Underlying principles of responsible business: Value, balance, and accountability
- Sustainability as a science-based framework for ethics
- The relationship between individual consumption and ethics

THE RESPONSIBILITIES OF BUSINESS IN SOCIETY

The influential economist Milton Friedman famously said that the one and only social responsibility of business is to increase its profits "so long as it stays within the rules of the game, which is to say, engages in open and free competition without deception or fraud."[3] This view, although extreme and often refuted,[4] frames one side (unrestrained free-market capitalism) of an ongoing argument about the proper roles of business in society.

In fact, social and environmental concerns are becoming more prevalent in discussions of business ethics and social responsibility. A list of "major global trends and issues at the beginning of the twenty-first century"[5] includes:

- population growth,
- poverty and inequality,
- water supply sanitation,
- changes to global biogeochemical cycles,
- climate change,
- environmental degradation,
- habitat destruction, and
- loss of biodiversity.

The movement in business toward triple-bottom-line thinking[6] reinforces the societal demand for businesses to assume broader responsibilities and clearer accountability for their impacts on the environment and the human condition.

Economic Consequences of Ethical Decisions

Indifference to environmental and social concerns has landed many financially successful companies in hot water with government agencies, citizen groups, and consumers. The economic consequences to such companies can be substantial. One source of economic risk comes from fines and government-mandated reparations.

For example, in a 2007 Clean Air Act settlement, American Electric Power (AEP) "agreed to spend as much as $4.6 billion to reduce emissions of sulfur dioxide and nitrogen oxides"[7] emitted from their coal-burning power plants. In this case, "doing the right thing" environmentally and socially didn't come naturally to AEP; it only came about after a costly battle with government regulators.

Consider two other costly battles over environmental and social responsibility, both involving Shell. In 1995, Shell UK planned to sink an obsolete oil storage facility called the Brent Spar in British-controlled waters of the North Sea. The structure was known to contain oil sludge, radioactive scale, and heavy metals, which would leak out into the water. The alternative disposal method, considered preferable to environmentalists, was to dismantle the facility on land, recover its contents, and recycle its components. The process had been proven feasible, and the cost was estimated at £41 million. Shell maintained that sinking the rig was preferable in terms of both environmental and worker safety, and it was by far the cheapest option at an estimated cost of between £17–20 million. The UK government supported Shell's position. Greenpeace brought pressure through protests and boycotts that mobilized consumers and governments across Europe, especially in Germany. Citing losses to both revenues and reputation, Shell relented and had the Brent Spar dismantled in a Norwegian port. The ultimate cost to Shell, including lost sales (but not damaged reputation), was estimated at between £60–100 million.[8]

At about the same time, Shell Petroleum Development Company was coming under fire for its dealings with the Ogoni people of the Nigerian Delta. After decades of suffering with the consequences of massive environmental destruction from oil spills and fires, including the loss of fish, fresh water and farmlands, and health problems, such as asthma, lung cancer, and other diseases, due to drilling on their lands, the Ogoni began to protest.[9] Meanwhile, Shell's interests were protected brutally by the Nigerian Government,[10] which received huge payments from the company. The international press and NGOs took up cause of the Ogoni, and public opinion once again fell hard on Shell, which departed from the Nigerian Delta in 1993. More recently, Shell settled a court case with the Ogoni, agreeing to a payment of $15.5 million.[11] In a similar case, Chevron, which acquired Texaco in 2001, also inherited a lawsuit filed in Ecuador over pollution in the Amazon Basin. At stake for the company is as much as $27 billion, or seven times the cost of the Exxon Valdez spill in Alaska.[12]

Corporate Social Responsibility

Many companies use **corporate social responsibility (CSR)** statements and policies to address issues of social and environmental ethics. CSR generally refers to corporate policies for self-regulation, intended to integrate triple-bottom-line concerns into the business plan. CSR often begins as a risk-reduction strategy. Companies rely on CSR programs as defenses against problems such as consumer boycotts, public relations disasters, and increased government regulation. Proponents of CSR claim that it provides tangible business benefits, such as employee retention, corporate image, and brand image.[13] CSR initiatives can even influence customers to support corporate-sponsored charities.[14] Opponents of CSR on the economic right (such as Milton Friedman) view CSR as an impediment to market forces. On the economic left, opponents of CSR find fault with its strictly voluntary basis and its potential as window dressing or a smoke screen for conducting business as usual.

VIRTUAL FIELD TRIP
Find the CSR Statements of Some Well-Known Firms

Find the CSR statements of some well-known firms. Look for both U.S. and foreign companies. What do you think about the CSR statements? Are they meaningful? How do the CSR statements compare with the corporate mission statements? Do the CSR statements seem to provide real guidance for marketing decisions? Can you find any evidence of system-wide efforts to measure and improve actual sustainability performance?

The case of Shell once again proves instructional. After its financial and public relations disasters resulting from the Brent Spar and Ogoni affairs, Shell became a strong public advocate for CSR, earning a top-ten spot in *Fortune's* rankings of the world's "most accountable big companies."[15] As in Shell's case, however, taking a strong public position on corporate responsibility also invites extra scrutiny from groups on the lookout for hypocrisy and dishonesty in public

relations. For example, in response to Shell's favorable *Fortune* ranking, the watchdog organization Royal Dutch Shell plc reports that the rankings reflected a firm's apparent commitment to social and environmental goals rather than its actual environmental and social performance, and concludes that, "Many companies are spending more money hiring consultants and brand masters to make their firm look like they care about measuring their environmental and social performance than mitigating their actual impact."[16]

Acting responsibly with respect to society and the environment yields significant benefits in terms of legal risks, company reputation, and even sales revenues. However, publicly proclaiming CSR values and then failing to perform may be especially damaging on the same dimensions.

According to ethics scholar Joseph DesJardins, CSR efforts are hampered by two fundamentally flawed assumptions of traditional economics.[17] First is the assumption that problems of poverty and environmental degradation can best be solved with economic growth. But economic growth often favors an affluent minority and fails to improve the lives of a nation's poor. Moreover, economic growth is more likely to create environmental problems than to solve them unless it is done sustainably. The second assumption is that businesses can operate independently of environmental concerns. As you learned in Chapters 1 and 2, any separation between business, society, and the environment is artificial and detrimental.

Perhaps the greatest weakness of even well-intended CSR programs is that they focus company efforts too narrowly. Without a comprehensive view of global society and ecosystems, fixing problems in one area can ignore or even create bigger problems elsewhere.

THE FUNDAMENTALS OF RESPONSIBLE BUSINESS

A recent analysis of various approaches to ethical business conduct, including CSR, reveals three principles that lie at the heart of all of them: Value, balance, and accountability.[18]

Creating Value

Value stresses the creation of long-term value for both the business and society.[19] The ideal value proposition would occur when a firm achieves its profit goals while also helping to restore ecosystems and decrease global poverty. In triple-bottom-line terms,[20] this would equate to profits in all three columns. In terms of natural capitalism,[21] it would amount to simultaneously building financial, natural, and human capital. Creating value in one area (e.g., stock value) at the expense of another (e.g., risks to public health) is unacceptable from virtually every perspective on socially responsible business.

Problems arise in trying to assess or measure social and environmental value. For example, is economic development, measured as rising GDP, an indication of a nation's social betterment? What if income disparities within a country actually result in deepening poverty? Or what if the development comes at the expense of environmental catastrophe, or lost markets for local farm production? In the case of Shell and the Ogoni, the company's oil extraction added billions of dollars to Nigeria's GDP, but it came at the cost of massive environmental and humanitarian disasters.

The value proposition for sustainability also plays out in the forest products industry. According to a 2005 report titled "The Global Impact of SmartWood Certification," over 15 million acres of U.S. forests were certified by the Forest Stewardship Council (FSC) for environmentally and socially sustainable management. This had led to measurable environmental improvements including the protection of sensitive ecosystems and wildlife habitat. In human terms, the report cited improvements in worker safety, training, communication, and conflict resolution with stakeholders. Finally, it also reaffirmed the long-term economic viability of FSC-certified forestry operations through advantages such as improved understanding of profitability and efficiency, greater accountability, transparency and compliance with laws, and better management planning, monitoring, and chain-of-custody practices. The global market for FSC-certified wood in 2005 was worth over $5 billion, with certified wood and paper products carried by major retailers including Home Depot, IKEA, FedEx Kinko's, and many others.[22]

Finding Balance

Balance refers to a business's ability to accommodate conflicting stakeholder interests or moral standards.[23] Truly balancing economic, social, and environmental responsibilities may require going beyond assessing individual stakeholder interests and identifying where different responsibilities overlap and possibly reinforce each other.[24] Perfect balance would take away the cause for complaint from any of a firm's stakeholders, including shareholders, suppliers, employees, customers, and society at large. Sometimes, reconciliation of different stakeholder values is extremely difficult, if not impossible. For example, it may be difficult for a coal company to balance societal interests, such as greenhouse gas reduction and ecosystem preservation, with the interests of shareholders, who demand growth and profits, and with the interests of miners, who rely on jobs to support their families and communities.

Recognizing the legitimacy of various stakeholders can force businesses to prioritize the importance of different groups. A company may well decide that investors' interests are equally important to customers' interests, but more important than the interests of workers, communities, or environmental advocates. As we shall see in the following British Petroleum example, such thinking can lead to trade-offs that ultimately backfire in big ways.

The question of balance also brings up other important issues, such as the scope and definition of the stakeholder. For example, ethicist Peter Singer argues that the realities of economic globalization and a shared global atmosphere mean that every citizen of every nation is a legitimate stakeholder in virtually every business's environmental and social conduct.[25] Similarly, even the most basic definition of sustainability implies that future generations also deserve stakeholder status in every business decision.

Being Accountable

Accountability means taking responsibility for actions and consequences and acting in a transparent manner.[26] **Transparent**, in this context, means open and visible to outside observers. A fully accountable business would operate openly, truthfully, and without hypocrisy. According to the principle of accountability, a business that creates harm to the environment or to people, and then seeks to cover up or minimize that harm, acts in bad faith and should be made to change or desist in its operations and perhaps to make reparations.

THINK ABOUT IT

British Petroleum's former chairman, John Browne, made history in 1997 by pledging to cut the company's greenhouse gas emissions by 10 percent by 2010, and again in 2002 when he announced that the goal had been attained eight years early while saving money in the process.[27] However, an investigation following a fatal 2005 Texas refinery explosion found that BP had been inattentive to issues of worker safety, even in the face of warnings.[28] In 2006, BP was hit with another scandal when its inadequate maintenance of the Alaska Pipeline led to a massive oil spill in the frozen tundra.[29] Browne retired suddenly and amid controversy in 2007.[30]

1. How does BP fare in the *value* equation? Does the fact that BP saved money while reducing greenhouse gas emissions indicate a win-win-win for company profits, the

environment, and society? How might that value be offset by other operations of the oil company, such as the massive oil spill in Alaska or the deaths of 15 refinery workers in Texas?

2. Does BP need to refigure the *balance* equation? Which stakeholders, if any, deserve greater or less consideration by the company?

3. Does BP maintain adequate *accountability*? Might greater transparency in its operations and communications have helped it avoid environmental and safety crises? How might greater accountability have affected its overall *value* and *balance* equations?

According to the logic of value + balance + accountability, a business acts ethically or responsibly to the extent that it generates triple-bottom-line profits, while balancing the interests of all its stakeholders in a fashion that is open to public scrutiny.

SUSTAINABILITY: THE NEW ETHICS

The ideal situation for any business organization is to be able to achieve reasonable profitability goals while at the same time building natural and human capital. As we have previously established, a business that could achieve consistent gains in terms of people, profits, and the planet would reap benefits in risk management, public relations, employee talent and retention, innovation, and the development of new markets.[31] Many businesses understand the arguments in favor of ethics, CSR, and sustainability. What they too often lack is a comprehensive means of achieving those goals.

Barriers to Success

Common practices of CSR and business ethics face many impediments to success. Let's look at two of the most persistent barriers. First, businesses have trouble dealing with different moral systems or **conflicting ideologies** among their stakeholders. Two common and potentially conflicting ideological systems are **deontology**, which prioritizes moral duty and the adherence to rules, and **teleology**, which focuses on the consequences of action. For example, from a deontological point of view, operating a polluting factory in a foreign country might be acceptable if it complies with that country's laws and accepted practices. From a teleological standpoint, the legality of polluting is beside the point; what matters is the outcome. Another common conflict pits **libertarian** viewpoints, which prioritize individual rights, against **communitarian** perspectives, which emphasize individual sacrifice for the common good. For example, a libertarian might assert the right of an individual (or a corporation) to pollute or degrade its own private property, whereas a communitarian would condemn the action as harmful to broader societal interests.

Conflicting ideologies ultimately boil down to different beliefs or values, which is precisely what makes them ethically problematic. But what if businesses could base their decisions on principles that were not based on beliefs or values but, instead, on scientific facts that were universally accepted by people, regardless of their religious, moral, political, or economic beliefs? A **science-based decision framework** built on incontrovertible facts, instead of moral relativities, could potentially transcend ideological differences and put an end to such conflicts.

The second major barrier to successful CSR is **reductionism**, or the tendency to focus on individual components of a system rather than on the system as a whole. Selective or nonsystemic approaches to doing good can lead to undesirable trade-offs and unintended harm. For example, hydroelectric power generation emits far less atmospheric carbon than coal- or gas-powered plants; however, the dams required for their operation can create serious problems for fish, ecosystems and cultures that depend on free-flowing rivers. Compact fluorescent light bulbs (CFLs) are widely promoted as more sustainable than traditional incandescent bulbs because they use a fraction of the energy and therefore help reduce greenhouse gases; however, CFLs also contain mercury, which is toxic in the environment. Biofuels, such as ethanol and biodiesel, appear to be sustainable from a greenhouse gas perspective; however, many biofuel crops are farmed in highly unsustainable ways, and they compete with food crops for water and soil nutrients.

A business's attempts to do good are less meaningful when they carry unintended negative consequences, or if they are offset by harmful practices elsewhere. But what if businesses could base their decisions on a **whole-system approach** in which every action was considered in the context of global ecosystems and society? What if businesses could better safeguard themselves against unforeseen negative consequences? A decision framework with a comprehensive systems approach could effectively anticipate and control ecological and social downsides.

TNSF, Ethics, and Responsible Business

The Natural Step Framework (TNSF), introduced in Chapter 2, is just such a science-based, systems-oriented framework for strategic decision making. TNSF recognizes that the natural cycles that sustain life, such as photosynthesis and water cycles, are completely self-perpetuating as long as they aren't undermined by disruptive human activities. The first three environment-related system conditions are derived from basic principles of physical science.[32] The following facts are irrefutable. First, substances (such as coal or mercury) extracted by humans from the Earth's crust accumulate in the biosphere (air, water, and soil) because the Earth can only replace them in geologic time. Second, synthetic substances (such as pesticides and chemical waste) accumulate in the biosphere because natural systems are unable to adequately nullify or break them down. Third, physically degrading the Earth's ecosystems (such as forests, oceans, and watersheds) reduces nature's ability to perform essential eco-systems services (such as cleaning the air and water).[33]

The fourth system condition, the social one, recognizes that humans, when struggling to meet their basic needs, will understandably ignore the needs of nature rather than see their families suffer or perish. Therefore, a sustainable society must make sure that all people have access to what they need for their well-being. TNSF's understanding of human needs draws from the work of Manfred Max-Neef, who identifies nine fundamental conditions that are essential for human well-being:[34]

1. subsistence (e.g., food, shelter, and work)
2. protection (e.g., civil security and access to health care)
3. affection (e.g., friendships, family, and companionship)
4. understanding (e.g., access to information and education)
5. participation (e.g., community and rights to assemble)
6. leisure (e.g., fun, games, and relaxation)
7. creation (e.g., invention, problem solving, and self-expression)
8. identity (e.g., a sense of self and a valued place in the world)
9. freedom (e.g., access to choice regarding one's activities)

These needs are universal and consistent across all cultures. The only difference is in how and with what resources different people attempt to meet them. Max-Neef also holds that the needs are not substitutable, meaning that a lack of any of them is felt as a kind of poverty. An organization or a society striving to be sustainable must find ways to meet the full spectrum of human needs without violating the other system conditions.

THINK ABOUT IT

Consider the nine human needs listed above. Is there any area where you feel you are lacking something personally? If so, what kinds of goods, services, or experiences could correct this? In your community, is any of the nine needs difficult to fulfill for some segment of the population? What kinds of marketing opportunities might that need create?

TNSF, used as a practical and strategic guide to sustainability, is a valuable tool for making an organization more socially and environmentally responsible. Let's hold TNSF up to the ethics template of value, balance, and accountability.

First, TNSF helps a company to create value in every aspect of the triple bottom line. It focuses on profitability, or return on investment, in every strategic decision. At the same time, every decision moves a firm closer to environmental and social sustainability as embodied in the four system conditions. In addition, TNSF's whole-system perspective helps avoid unintended consequences or undesirable trade-offs elsewhere in the firm's operations.

Second, with respect to balancing stakeholder interests and viewpoints, TNSF's basis in fundamental science promotes decisions that are free of conflicting viewpoints, morals, or

Mini Case Study

Scandic Hotels

In the early 1990s, the Scandinavian hotel chain, Scandic, was in bad financial straits. The need to become profitable led it, in 1994, to hire a new CEO, Roland Nilsson, to shake things up. Nilsson saw the connection between profitability and sustainability. Needing to cut costs, Scandic turned first to waste reduction and innovation, and it engaged The Natural Step for assistance. The Natural Step then involved workers from throughout the organization in the change process. Workers received training in TNSF, and then they began actively suggesting ways to improve both the environmental and the social sustainability of the company. The best 1,500 suggestions were used as targets for innovation. The company developed new systems for cleaning, dishwashing, and laundering, which allowed it to switch to more environmentally safe detergents and cleaning products and to dramatically decrease water usage. The company took measures to reduce its energy usage, and eventually, it shifted all its electricity to renewable sources. It shifted its fleet of vehicles from gas and diesel to hybrid or alternative-fuel vehicles. All new construction and remodeling was done according to the most advanced green building techniques. Food service throughout the hotel chain began sourcing ingredients from the most sustainable sources available. In addition to ongoing training in sustainability, service, and diversity, employees also received support for health and fitness improvement and for service to their communities. As for profitability, the turnaround was fast and enduring. In the first three years, Scandic's sales rose more than 25 percent, and its operating margin increased from 3.5 percent to 5.2 percent. Scandic was once again profitable.[35] Now explore more deeply and interactively what Scandic has done since the mid-1990s to continuously improve sustainability.

How did Scandic approach the problem of financially unsustainable operations? What evidence do you see of increased financial value? What about value to the environment? And to people and communities? Can you find examples of Scandic balancing different stakeholder interests? And what has it done to increase its transparency and accountability?

ideologies. Even among stakeholders with widely varied values and ideologies, it's possible, using TNSF, to begin every decision or deliberation with complete agreement about core issues regarding profits, people, and the planet.

Third, TNSF's use of cross-functional teams and strategic alliances (see Chapter 2) promotes accountability and transparency as well as innovative thinking. It's difficult for a business to hide its practices behind a cloak of secrecy when environmental and social organizations are invited to strategy party.

WHAT IS THE RESPONSIBILITY OF THE INDIVIDUAL CONSUMER?

Businesses strive to be competitive by matching their competencies to the needs of consumers. For this reason, understanding customer needs is among the top concerns in major corporations' CSR messages.[36] If marketing decisions are driven by consumer wants and needs, then it is worth asking: What are the responsibilities of the individual consumer in the efforts to create a more sustainable society?

The ethics of individual consumers have traditionally been treated as private and personal, based on moral or religious values.[37] People who embrace the needs for environmental sustainability or social justice have developed many different tactics or approaches for expressing and addressing those needs. Some have championed anti-consumption agendas, efforts to avoid purchasing goods and services while increasing their own sense of personal empowerment.[38] Others have organized various kinds of nonprofit groups with environmental[39] or social goals.[40] Still others work through religious organizations.[41] And still others resign themselves to inaction, believing that any individual effort to create positive change is futile.

Once we realize that all people are consumers, and that all consumers are connected to society and the environment, it will be clear that the principles of value, balance, and accountability also pertain to individuals. As consumers, our stakeholders are each other, the businesses and organizations we interact with, the environment that supports us, and the generations to come.

Returning briefly to the principles of value, balance, and accountability, which we applied to business sustainability, may also help us to better understand individual responsibility and sustainable consumption. First, consider the value proposition. What kinds of value do people strive to create in their individual lives? The answers lie in the nine human needs articulated by Max-Neef.[42] Building wealth is a common consumer goal, but wealth alone can't substitute for any of the other needs.

THINK ABOUT IT

What is happiness? What is well-being? Write out the list of nine needs or fundamental conditions that are essential for human well-being according to Max-Neef. Next, for each need, write down the percentage of how completely you feel that need is met for you (for example, you may feel that your subsistence need is met 100 percent, but that your leisure need is met only about 50 percent). Now, for each need that is met at less than 100 percent, think about what's missing.

Marketing relies, in part, on advertising that shows people fulfilling their dreams and desires through the purchase and use of products and services. Can you identify any ways that your own consumption falls short in contributing to your overall happiness or well-being? Can you think of one way that you could consume more sustainably and, at the same time, increase your own well-being?

Living sustainably doesn't necessarily require sacrificing our current needs and caring only for the future. TNSF can work as well for individuals as it does for organizations, and that means adding value to one's life from day one. An individual that followed The Natural Step principles would begin by visualizing individual success in both sustainability and personal well-being. It would mean clarifying one's own values and answering the question: What will make me happy? Every key consumption decision would be held to the same criteria as in an organization, as follows:

1. Does this purchase move me closer to a sustainable way of living? In other words, does it reduce my negative impact, or increase my positive impact, with respect to the four system conditions? Are there any negative consequences of the purchase that outweigh the gains?
2. Does this purchase leave me with the flexibility to continue making positive impacts as my conditions change? In other words, can I keep from overcommitting resources (such as health, time, or money) that I may need or prefer to use elsewhere?
3. Does this purchase provide me with adequate gains, in terms of overall well-being, right now? Does it enrich my life in any meaningful way?

It may seem excessive, or even a little silly, for an individual to make these kinds of deliberations about every purchase. That, also, is unnecessary. If followed deliberately for any length of time, TNSF becomes a frame of mind, a way of sizing up any major decision.

Sustainable consumption also is not necessarily or simply about consuming less. It's about consuming differently, imaginatively, wisely, and thoughtfully. In moving toward sustainability, both marketers and consumers can refocus on desired benefits and experiences rather than on the ownership of material goods.[43] We may find that different models of consumption, such as renting, leasing, and sharing, can satisfy many of our needs as well as product ownership.[44] A benefits-and-experiences focus may allow consumers to achieve significant reductions in tied-up financial resources and in the costs of product maintenance, home-storage space, insurance, depreciation, and obsolescence. One example of resources (money and land) tied up for the sake of owning products that may not deliver justifiable returns of well-being comes from the self-storage industry. "According to the Self Storage Association, one out of every 10 households in the US rents a unit, and, with more than seven square feet for every man, woman and child, every American could stand—all at the same time—under the total canopy of self-storage roofing."[45] Some of the cost savings and land resources from this kind of consumption could likely be diverted to other uses, arguably improving standards of living and enhancing overall well-being. From a value perspective, then, sustainable consumption is about building a fulfilling personal life while also contributing to the overall quality of the environment and of life in our families, in our communities, and in the world at large.

Personal sustainability certainly has the potential to add value to individual lives. Now, consider the balance proposition. What does it mean to balance stakeholder interests in the context of our personal consumption? First, conflicting interests can occur in our own internal battles. A balanced approach to individual consumption would result in decisions that do not create harm in one essential area (such as affection or leisure) for the sake of advancing another area (such as subsistence or its extreme version, amassing wealth). A balanced approach to consuming also takes into consideration the

ZipCar and other car sharing services provide automobile transportation without the need for ownership.

needs of others. For example, urban dwellers may find that automobile ownership entails too many environmental and social costs (e.g., pollution, parking expense, crowding, and conflict) and violates too many system conditions to be sustainable. A more balanced approach to urban transport might include walking, biking, public transportation, and the occasional use of a Zipcar[46] or a U-Haul truck. In Switzerland, a company called Mobility Car Sharing serves as much as 20 percent of all Swiss transportation needs,[47] including service in towns with populations as small as 20,000.[48] Mobility Car Sharing is similar to Zipcar, but has more options for rentals, from Ford Fiestas to sportscars.[49]

THINK ABOUT IT

Can you think of a leisure activity you enjoy that violates one of the system conditions? Now, can you think of ways that you might achieve the same enjoyment more sustainably? How might the activities of backcasting and brainstorming help you find more sustainable solutions? Can you imagine how innovative solutions might open up new market opportunities?

Finally, consider accountability. Business accountability means taking responsibility for actions and consequences and acting in a manner that is both trustworthy and transparent. What does it mean for individual consumers to be accountable? And to whom must we account for our choices and behaviors? As members of communities and of civil society we are accountable to each other. With our own actions, we help to set the standards by which all behavior is measured in our respective communities.

Earlier in the chapter we established that, for businesses, traveling the road to sustainability is a pretty good assurance of continued social and environmental responsibility, especially if that road follows a comprehensive framework like The Natural Step. The same is true for individuals.

Savage Chickens   by Doug Savage

Author Terry Gips has established a "personal action checklist" based on the four system conditions of TNSF to help individuals live more sustainably.[50] The list of actions is far from complete, and not every action is relevant to every consumer. Nevertheless, it gives a sense of the kinds of actions that matter at an individual level.

CRITICAL THINKING ACTIVITY

The Natural Step Framework

Answer the questions on the personal action checklist (see Table 3-1 If you're currently taking the action described, check the box "now." If you are committed to taking up the action, check the box "commit."

TABLE 3-1   Four Conditions for Sustainability

Four Conditions for Sustainability	Now	Commit	Three months
1. What we take from the Earth's crust—metals/minerals and fossil fuel			
Conserve energy by turning off lights and computers; when not in use, unplug chargers			
Use compact fluorescent light bulbs (then recycle) and efficient Energy Star appliances			
In winter, decrease heating (68° if home, 58° if not or at night), insulate, have energy audit			
In summer, use fan, reduce cooling (72° if home, 85° if not), and use trees for shading			
Reduce hot water use with showers, baths, laundry, dishwasher, and frontloading washer			
Use natural landscaping, use human or electric-powered lawn mower, and avoid leaf blowers			
Use alternative energy (solar, wind, and geothermal) and purchase green energy			
Bike, walk, use public transit, telecommute, carpool, or use clean/energy-efficient vehicle			
Eco-drive: properly inflate tires, drive at speed limit, avoid sudden stops/starts, and tune car			
Recycle cans, fluorescents, cell phones, and computers			
Use rechargeable batteries (recycle at end of their life) and nonmercury thermometers			
Avoid heavy metals (use nonuranium fire alarms and avoid leather tanned with chromium)			
Avoid mined fertilizers (potassium and phosphorous) and use natural ones			
Other			
2. What we make—hazardous chemicals, pesticides, and plastics			
Use nontoxic, nonchlorine cleaning products, avoid dry cleaning, and use "green cleaners"			
Use natural personal care products and avoid anti-bacterial soaps			

Reduce plastics with reusable bags, plates, cups, cutlery, and water bottles			
Recycle plastic bottles and containers and purchase bio-based, reusable, compostable ones			
Replace hazardous pesticides with natural pest control in home, yard, garden, and work			
Grow your own organic food or buy certified organic food, preferably local			
Buy clothes made from organic cotton and hemp; wear reused clothes			
Other			
3. What we do to the Earth—species, trees, water, and other Eco-systems			
Reduce paper use with two-sided copying, cloth napkins, and handkerchiefs			
Use 100% post-consumer recycled copy paper, stationery, towels, and tissue and toilet paper			
Get off junk mail lists, pay online, and ask for email-only bills if available			
Reuse wood and use non–old growth, certified, sustainably harvested wood products			
Compost waste food and yard and garden material			
Reduce water use with efficient shower heads, faucets, and toilets and by using gray water			
Protect and enhance wildlife habitat, minimize paving and runoff, and use green roof			
Address sprawl, reduce work commute, and encourage sustainable building development			
Avoid sea food from endangered species and factory fish and shrimp farms			
Eat lower on the food chain (plant-based foods) and more organic produce and grains			
Other			
4. How we meet human needs—health and well-being, social justice, and community			
Smile, treat everyone with respect, and practice random acts of kindness			
Practice a healthy lifestyle: diet, exercise, meditation, yoga, massage, art, Sabbath, and sleep			
Develop a sense of community and participate in community activities and organizations			
Work to create a just society; donate time, money, and resources to help the disadvantaged			
When traveling, practice eco-tourism and better understand different cultures			
Assure that investments and pension funds are in socially responsible businesses			
Buy fair trade products and products from artisans and shop at co-ops and local sustainable businesses			
Other			

Check the list in three months; are you still taking action? Why or why not? Have you influenced anyone else to take action? Consider the consequence of your action and think about what would it be like to live in a community where everyone held themselves accountable for the four systems conditions.

Chapter Summary

In a capitalist society, we depend on goods and services to meet many of our most basic needs, from subsistence and safety to the pursuits of leisure and creativity. Businesses compete for our attention and our money, and as members of society, we demand that they do so fairly and morally. This chapter explores the responsibilities of businesses toward nature and society. Underlying all major systems of business ethics and social responsibility are three main principles: Value, balance, and accountability. Value must be assessed at a triple-bottom-line level. Balancing stakeholder interests is critical for developing collaboration and synergy in the pursuit of complex goals. Accountability motivates an organization, its leaders, its employees, and its suppliers to act honestly and without hypocrisy, building trust with customers and other stakeholders. Barriers to the successful practice of these principles include the lack of a whole-system perspective, which leads to unforeseen consequences and undesirable trade-offs, and conflicting stakeholder interests and ideologies, which can lead to antagonism among parties that would be better off working together. TNSF, with a whole-system perspective grounded in universally accepted scientific facts, potentially gets past the barriers in a way that unifies strategy and ethics. TNSF serves individual consumers as well as organizations as a path to sustainability.

Review of Chapter Objectives

- The relationship between business and society
- Underlying principles of CSR and business ethics: Value, balance and accountability
- Sustainability as a science-based framework for ethics
- The relationship between individual consumption and ethics

Key Concepts

Corporate Social
  Responsibility
  (CSR)   30
Value   31
Balance   32

Accountability   32
Transparent   32
Conflicting
  Ideologies   33

Deontology   33
Teleology   33
Libertarian   33
Communitarian   33

Science-Based Decision
  Framework   33
Reductionism   33
Whole-System Approach   33

Endnotes

1. DesJardins, Joseph R. (2007), *Business, Ethics, and the Environment: Imagining a Sustainable Future*, New Jersey: Pearson Education.
2. Williams, Florence (2005), "Toxic Breast Milk?" *New York Times Magazine,* January 9.
3. Friedman, Milton (1970), "The Social Responsibility of Business Is to Increase Its Profits," *New York Times Magazine,* September 13.
4. Liechty, Daniel (1985), "On the Social Responsibilities of Business: Contra Milton Friedman," *Management Decision*, 23 (4): 54–62.
5. Harris, Graham (2007), *Seeking Sustainability in an Age of Complexity*, London, UK: Cambridge University Press (p. 3).
6. Savitz, Andrew W. and Karl Weber (2006), *The Triple Bottom Line: How Today's Best-Run Companies Are Achieving Economic, Social, and Environmental Success—And How You Can Too*, xiii, New York: John Wiley.
7. Mufson, Steven (2007), "Utility to Pay Large Sum in Clean Air Settlement," *Washington Post*, October 9, p. D1, http://www.washingtonpost.com/wp-dyn/content/article/2007/10/08/AR2007100801689.html, accessed August 3, 2009.
8. The Brent Spar, Greenpeace, http://www.greenpeace.org/international/about/history/the-brent-spar; "Brent Spar Gets Chop," *BBC News*, http://news.bbc.co.uk/2/hi/europe/221508.stm; "Brent Spar's Long Saga," *BBC News*, http://news.bbc.co.uk/2/hi/science/nature/218527.stm; "Brent Spar," Wikipedia, http://en.wikipedia.org/wiki/Brent_Spar; accessed January 3, 2010; Hollender, Jeffrey and Stephen Fenichell (2004), *What Matters Most: How a Small Group of Pioneers Is Teaching Social Responsibility to Big Business, and Why Big Business Is Listening*, New York: Basic Books.
9. "The Curse of Oil in Ogoniland," http://www.umich.edu/~snre492/cases_03-04/Ogoni/Ogoni_case_study.htm, accessed January 3, 2010.
10. Boele, Richard, Heike Fabig, and David Wheeler (2001), "Shell, Nigeria and the Ogoni." A study in unsustainable development: I. "The Story of Shell, Nigeria and the Ogoni people—Environment, Economy, Relationships: Conflict and Prospects for Resolution," *Sustainable Development*, 9 (2): 74–86.
11. Vidal, John (2009), "Shell Settlement with Ogoni People Stops Short of Full Justice: Payout of $15.5m Could Backfire Now That Precedent of a Nigerian Community Suing a Oil Company Has Been Set," *Guardian*, June 10, http://www.guardian.co.uk/environment/cif-green/2009/jun/09/saro-wiwa-shell, accessed January 3, 2010.
12. Forero, Juan (2009), "In Ecuador, High Stakes in Case against Chevron," *Washington Post*, April 28,http://www.washingtonpost.com/wp-dyn/content/article/2009/04/27/AR2009042703717.html, accessed January 4, 2010.
13. Sen, Sankar and C. B. Bhattacharya (2001), "Does Doing Good Always Lead to Doing Better? Consumer Reactions to Corporate Social Responsibility," *Journal of Marketing Research,* May: 225–243.
14. Lichtenstein, Donald R., Minette E. Drumwright, and Bridgette M. Braig (2004), "The Effect of Corporate Social Responsibility on Customer Donations to Corporate-Supported Nonprofits," *Journal of Marketing,* 68 (October): 16–32.
15. Ten Most 'Accountable' Big Companies, *Fortune*, CNN Money, http://money.cnn.com/galleries/2008/fortune/0811/gallery.accountability.fortune/10.html, accessed January 4, 2010.
16. Donovan, John (2008), "Stop the CSR Spin, Royal Dutch Shell plc," December 16, http://royaldutchshellplc.com/2008/12/16/stop-the-csr-spin/, accessed January 4, 2010.
17. DesJardins, Joseph R. (2007), *Business, Ethics, and the Environment: Imagining a Sustainable Future,* New Jersey: Pearson Education (p. 3).
18. Schwartz, Mark S. and Archie B. Carroll (2008), "Integrating and Unifying Competing and Complementary Frameworks: The Search for a Common Core in the Business and Society Field," *Business & Society*, 47 (June): 148–186.
19. Schwartz, Mark S. and Archie B. Carroll (2008), "Integrating and Unifying Competing and Complementary Frameworks: The Search for a Common Core in the Business and Society Field," *Business & Society*, 47 (June), (p. 168).
20. Savitz, Andrew W. and Weber, Karl (2006), *The Triple Bottom Line: How Today's Best-Run Companies Are Achieving Economic, Social And Environmental Success—And How You Can Too,* New York: John Wiley.
21. Hawken, Paul, Amory Lovins and L. Hunter Lovins (1999), *Natural Capitalism: Creating the Next Industrial Revolution*, Boston, MA: Little Brown (p. 10).
22. GreenBiz.com (2005), New Study Shows Benefits of Sustainable Forestry Certification, July 22, http://www.enn.com/ecosystems/article/9445, accessed August 14, 2009.
23. Schwartz, Mark S. and Archie B. Carroll (2008), "Integrating and Unifying Competing and Complementary Frameworks: The Search for a Common Core in the Business and Society Field," *Business & Society*, 47 (June): 148–186.
24. Enderle, Georges and Lee A. Tavis (1998), "A Balanced Concept of the Firm and the Measurement of its Long-Term Planning and Performance," *Journal of Business Ethics,* 17 (August): 1129–1144.
25. Singer, Peter (2002), *One World: The Ethics of Globalization,* New Haven, CT: Yale University Press.
26. Schwartz, Mark S. and Archie B. Carroll (2008), "Integrating and Unifying Competing and Complementary Frameworks: The Search for a Common Core in the Business and Society Field," *Business & Society*, 47 (June): 148–186.

27. M2 Presswire (2002), "BP Beats Greenhouse Gas Target by Eight Years and Aims to Stabilise Net Future Emissions," March 12, http://www.highbeam.com/doc/1G1-83705088.html, accessed June 25, 2009.

28. Schwartz, Nelson D. (2006), "BP Was Warned," *Fortune,* October 2, http://money.cnn.com/2006/10/02/magazines/fortune/BP_leak_short.fortune/index.htm?postversion=2006100210, accessed June 25, 2009.

29. *Associated Press* (2006), "Alaska Pipeline Spill Amount Debated," March 6, http://www.msnbc.msn.com/id/11696601/, accessed June 25, 2009.

30. Schwartz, Nelson, D. (2007), "The Final Days of BP's John Browne," *Fortune* (January 16), http://money.cnn.com/2007/01/16/news/companies/browne_downfall.fortune/?postversion=2007011617, accessed June 25, 2009.

31. "Business Link: The Business Benefits of Corporate Social Responsibility," http://www.businesslink.gov.uk/bdotg/action/detail?type=RESOURCES&itemId=1075408491, accessed June 25, 2009.

32. "TNS-Basic Science," Forum for the Future, http://www.forumforthefuture.org/node/371, accessed August 14, 2009.

33. The Natural Step, http://www.naturalstep.org/, accessed June 30, 2009.

34. Max-Neef, Manfred A. (with contributions from Antonio Elizalde and Martin Hopenhayn) (1991), *Human Scale Development: Conception, Application and Further Reflections,* New York: Apex Press.

35. The Natural Step, "Scandic Hotels," http://www.naturalstep.org/en/usa/scandic-hotels, accessed August 14, 2009; Scandic, http://www.scandic-campaign.com/betterworld/index.asp?languageid=en, accessed January 10, 2010.

36. Snider, Jamie, Ron Paul Hill, and Diane M. Martin (2003), "Corporate Social Responsibility in the 21st Century: A View from the World's Most Successful Firms," *Journal of Business Ethics,* 2: 175–187.

37. Singer, Peter (2000), *Writings on an Ethical Life,* London, UK: Harper Collins.

38. Denzin, Norman K. (2001), "The Seventh Moment: Qualitative Inquiry and the Practices of a More Radical Consumer Research,"*Journal of Consumer Research*, 28 (September): 324–330; also see Michael S.W. Lee, Karen V. Fernandez, and Michael R. Hyman (2009), "Anti-Consumption: An Overview and Research Agenda," *Journal of Business Research,* 62 (February): 45–147.

39. Conservation International, http://www.conservation.org/Pages/default.aspx and Friends of the Earth, http://www.foe.org/.

40. Doctors without Borders, http://doctorswithoutborders.org/.

41. Catholic Charities, http://www.catholiccharitiesusa.org/NetCommunity/Page.aspx?pid=1174.

42. Max-Neef, Manfred A. (with contributions from Antonio Elizalde and Martin Hopenhayn) (1991), *Human Scale Development: Conception, Application and Further Reflections,* New York: Apex Press.

43. "New American Dream," http://www.newdream.org/, accessed December 26, 2009.

44. Ray, Paul, H. and Sherry R. Anderson (2000), *Cultural Creatives: How 50 Million People Are Changing the World,* New York: Harmony Books.

45. Overconsumption Stats, http://www.scribd.com/doc/23319445/Over-consumption-Stats, accessed on December 26, 2009.

46. ZipCar, http://www.zipcar.com/webpdx/?crcat=ppc&crsource=gsnpdx&crkw=zipcar&engine=google&keyword=zipcar, accessed June 25, 2009.

47. Belz, Frank-Martin and Ken Peattie (2009), *Sustainability Marketing: A Global Perspective,* Chichester, UK: Wiley.

48. Car Sharing in Small Cities, MOMO, http://www.uitp.org/knowledge/pdf/factsheet9esmallcities.pdf, accessed January 11, 2010.

49. Car Sharing in Small Cities, MOMO, http://www.uitp.org/knowledge/pdf/factsheet9esmallcities.pdf, accessed January 11, 2010.

50. Copyright November 13, 2006, Terry Gips, tgips@sustainabilityassociates.com, 612-374-4765, Alliance for Sustainability, www.afors.org, 612-331-1099, may be reproduced with full credit.

The Marketing Environment and Processes

INTRODUCTION: AN UNUSUAL COALITION

Q. What do the following companies and environmental organizations have in common?

AES, Alcoa, Alstom, Boston Scientific, BP America, Caterpillar, Chrysler, ConocoPhillips, Dow Chemical, Duke Energy, DuPont, Environmental Defense Fund, Ford, General Electric, General Motors, Johnson & Johnson, Natural Resources Defense Council, The Nature Conservancy, NRG Energy, PepsiCo, Pew Center on Global Climate Change, PG&E, Rio Tinto, Shell, Siemens, and World Resources Institute.

A. They are all members of the United States Climate Action Partnership (USCAP), a coalition of major companies and environmental organizations dedicated to influencing the U.S. government to enact legislation to require dramatic reductions in greenhouse gas (GHG) emissions. USCAP's report, titled "A Blueprint for Legislative Action," is "a detailed framework for legislation to address climate change . . . a direct response to federal policymakers who recognize, as we do, that well-crafted legislation can spur innovation in new technologies, help create jobs and provide a foundation for a vibrant, low-carbon economy."[1]

THINK ABOUT IT

Why would major industrial and energy companies join with environmental groups to press the federal government for stricter GHG emission standards? Isn't stricter regulation counter to the interests of oil companies and huge energy consumers? Why might a strict federal standard for GHGs be preferable to widely differing state standards?

As you have already learned, businesses formulate their marketing strategies in consideration of several external environments, including prevailing social and cultural trends, economic trends, competition, technological developments, government regulations and, of course, the natural environment or biosphere. In their attempts to maintain some kind of competitive advantage, businesses attempt either to predict what's going to happen in these various realms or, even better, to directly influence events in their own favor.

In the previous example, the USCAP actively tries to influence legislators to strengthen federal environmental laws in part because it believes such action "would encourage innovation, enhance America's energy security, foster economic growth, improve our balance of trade and provide critically needed U.S. leadership on this vital global challenge."[2] Interestingly, some of the same companies that now form USCAP formerly belonged to the Global Climate Coalition, a lobbying group that until 1997 worked against legislation to curb GHG emissions.[3]

This chapter considers marketing's external environments as they affect and are affected by strategies for sustainable marketing. And because each of the external environments is part of the same larger system, we must also consider how they affect each other.

CHAPTER OBJECTIVES

In this chapter, you will learn about influences of major business environments on sustainable marketing:

- The social-cultural environment
- The economic environment
- The competitor environment
- The technology environment
- The political-legal environment
- The natural environment

SUSTAINABILITY AND THE SOCIAL-CULTURAL ENVIRONMENT

No organization exists in a social vacuum. Businesses survive by serving markets, and the markets they serve are greatly influenced by the **social-cultural environment**, that is, by society's values and belief systems. The influences can occur at the level of **macroculture**, which encompasses the value systems and ways of life of an entire society, or **microculture**, which relates to the defining characteristics of distinct subgroups within society.

Macroculture reflects the character and priorities of a nation or a civilization. As such, when macroculture-level changes occur, they have huge impacts on business. Evidence indicates that the growing awareness of the need for environmental and social sustainability is such a macrocultural shift. The values and life patterns of a society are influenced by a number of major institutions. One of those is education.

Educational Influences

Sustainability is coming to education in a big way. At the global level, the United Nations has declared the years 2005–2014 to be the Decade for Education for Sustainable Development. The educational efforts, headed by UNESCO (the United Nations Educational, Scientific and Cultural Organization), are intended to "integrate the principles, values, and practices of sustainable development into all aspects of education and learning, in order to address the social, economic, cultural and environmental problems we face in the 21st century."[4]

Sustainability education is coming to business schools. At the graduate level, market forces are driving the change. One study finds that "88% of MBA students want to see their future employers actively address sustainability issues. More than three-quarters (77%) believe that being responsible leads to corporate profits."[5] Sustainability education in business is also available through self-guided professional development forums.[6]

In general, higher education in the United States is advancing toward sustainability goals through leadership at the highest levels. As of its 2008 report, the American College & University Presidents' Climate Commitment (ACUPCC) had the support and participation of more than 600 universities and colleges.[7] A 2009 ACUPCC report describes what many universities are doing to build sustainability education into basic undergraduate and graduate curricula.[8] Other organizations, such as the Association for the Advancement of Sustainability in Higher Education,[9] support sustainability education with resources such as information, training programs, awards, newsletters, conferences, and assessment systems.

We are also seeing increased attention to sustainability in elementary and secondary education.[10] The *Sustainability Education Handbook: A Resource Guide for K-12 Teachers*[11] is one resource intended to help teachers integrate sustainability principles and exercises into their curricula. Another example is the Cloud Institute for Sustainability Education, which states, "We believe that K-12 education can substantially influence beliefs, attitudes, values and behaviors related to sustainability. This is the most fertile ground for helping to shape a society committed to sustainable development."[12]

THINK ABOUT IT

Can you think of something you learned in grade school that has shaped the way you see the world? How might the widespread teaching of sustainability principles help shape our society? And how might society in turn affect the way marketing is done?

Education tends to shape values, such as sustainability, formally and deliberately. The business sector, especially as manifested in marketing and the media, is also driving a macroculture shift toward sustainability.

Marketing and Media Influences

You already know that social and cultural trends affect marketing practice. The reverse is also true. Marketing practices have direct influence over society's values, beliefs, and behaviors through mechanisms such as advertising and product design.[13] There is a reinforcing cycle between society and marketing. Marketing organizations pick up on social changes, and then they design products, services, and messages to capitalize on these changes. Marketing activities, in turn, strengthen those very changes.

Increasing awareness of the need for sustainability is such a change in the social-cultural realm. Businesses' efforts to embrace sustainability are, in part, a response to the growth in societal concern.[14] A wide variety of popular and business magazines have featured sustainability issues in their cover stories. Popular movies have also spread the message of sustainability. Perhaps most influential film is the 2006 Academy Award winning documentary *An Inconvenient Truth*, written in part by former vice president, Al Gore. Other films shaping societal views of sustainability include actor Leonardo DiCaprio's *The 11th Hour*.[15]

The sheer numbers of sustainability-related claims in advertising make it clear that marketers believe the cultural trend is real and powerful. Green or sustainability claims in advertising are now sufficiently popular that the Federal Trade Commission (FTC) publishes consumer protection notices to help people know how to interpret them. Advertising agencies specializing in sustainability have been springing up. The GreenBiz directory lists over a hundred marketing communication firms specializing in sustainability.[16] These firms commonly reject work if they feel clients are seeking to misrepresent their commitment and progress toward sustainability. Some, such as Saatchi & Saatchi S, combine basic sustainability consulting with communication services in order to help clients create more sustainable marketing strategies.

Few people would deny that sports and sports marketing influence culture, not only in the United States, but all over the world. There is evidence that the world of sport is making concerted and public efforts to operate more sustainably. Greg Menken, vice president and director of sustainability at Beckerman Public Relations, pointed out the following:

- The 2010 Vancouver Winter Olympics were the first to make sustainability part of their mission statement, and they claim to be the most environmentally sustainable games in history;
- The planning committee for the 2012 London Olympics has stated that it will be the most sustainable games ever;
- The NFL's Philadelphia Eagles have made a point of becoming "green" in more than the color of their uniforms;
- Tennis's US Open has officially greened up with programs for renewable energy, materials procurement, waste diversion, and public awareness;

- Several major sporting events are actively influencing their corporate sponsors to become more sustainable; and finally,
- "According to a poll of sports executives released by the *Sports Business Journal*, eco-efforts are being driven by business decisions and the desire by brands to be seen as green leaders. The poll showed that 87% of sports teams are incorporating green because it is an important issue or for its PR value. When asked where sports properties can make the biggest green impact, the second-highest response (29%) was by leveraging the brand to increase awareness of green initiatives."[17]

To the extent that businesses strive honestly to achieve sustainability and involve stakeholders, such as customers and suppliers, in their efforts, they can help create more societal demand for sustainable products and services.[18] The implications for sustainable marketing are simple and clear. First, like all business activities, marketing must be done in more sustainable ways. Second, marketing institutions should focus energy on bringing about macroculture-level change in society's awareness and values regarding sustainability.

Marketing is also in a position to influence change at the microculture level. Within any society there exist groups and subgroups of people, which may define themselves by any number of characteristics, including ethnicity, religion, hobbies, passions, occupations, educational affiliations, political goals, and so on.[19] The list of reasons people have to affiliate with each other is virtually endless, and the groups they form tend to have overlapping boundaries.[20] Any marketing institution influences a whole web of different communities or social networks through its supply chain, workers, customers, and other stakeholders. For example, workers at a local supermarket are also likely to its customers. Likewise, many of those workers' friends, families, and neighbors will also be customers. These customers may belong to various other religious, civic, or recreational groups through which they interact, share stories, and compare experiences. Moreover, those groups may be local and interact primarily face-to-face, or they may exist largely in the nongeographical space of the Internet.

Microculture groups or communities organize through communicative processes,[21] create meaning, and coordinate action with a sense of common goals and purpose.[22] In other words, they get together to make things happen. One way microcultural groups are relevant to sustainable marketing is that they often form market segments (which we discuss in Chapter 7) for sustainable products and services (which we discuss in Chapter 9).

Other than market segments, other microculture groups that influence marketing include citizen watchdog groups and **nongovernmental organizations** (NGOs). Much like their predecessors in the environmental movements of the last two centuries, citizen watchdog groups and NGOs often function as voluntary overseers, following corporate and even government activities for signs of legal and ethical violations.

One active and well-organized watchdog group is Wal-Mart Watch, which began in 2005 with a nationwide public campaign "to challenge the world's largest retailer, Wal-Mart, to become a better employer, neighbor, and corporate citizen" and to "challenge Wal-Mart to embrace its moral responsibility as the nation's biggest and most important corporation."[23] To what extent the group is a grassroots citizens' organization isn't clear. According to the *Washington Post*, Wal-Mart Watch received its initial funding from the Service Employees International Union.[24] Wal-Mart Watch has partnered with a number of environmental NGOs (ENGOs) (e.g., Sierra Club), community groups (e.g., Sprawl Busters, New Rules Project), labor groups (e.g., Service Employees International, Jobs with Justice), and religious organizations (e.g., Clergy and Laity United for Economic Justice) to pressure the nation's largest retailer to enact positive change. The effects of watchdog organizations on Wal-Mart, through public opinion, ultimately forced the company to begin engaging critics actively.[25] Former CEO Lee Scott openly admits that his first inclination to consider Wal-Mart's environmental impacts grew from public pressures and the question of where future attacks were likely to come from.

At the regional, state, and community levels, **citizen groups** have brought local media attention to societal ills. These are community- and Internet-based groups of people who seek to influence public policy and business practices. For example, New York State's Citizens' Environmental Coalition pressures corporations to clean up toxic sites and promote better environmental practices.[26] The Alliance for Sustainability in Minneapolis works to build awareness and influence behaviors around sustainability through community efforts including neighborhood workshops and conferences, sustainability awards, and training in The Natural Step Framework.[27]

The Internet provides interested individuals and groups easy access to media reports of corporate ethical misdeeds and infractions. Websites such as Treehugger.com act as media consolidators. Their writers scour the Web for sustainability stories and then provide context, editorial comments, and links to the original story. Their goal is to mainstream sustainability and provide readers with green news, solutions, and product information.[28]

THINK ABOUT IT

How do community- and Internet-based citizen groups influence marketing practices? What methods do they use? The relations between businesses and social and environmental groups have often been adversarial. Can you think of ways that businesses could benefit from more cooperative relations with advocacy groups?

Some of the most forward thinking businesses pursue sustainability by partnering with "green" organizations or ENGOs. These strategic alliances provide environmental sustainability expertise for business and access and influence for ENGOs. Development of these alliances should include care that businesses are truly moving toward sustainability, not just using ENGOs for window dressing.[29]

THE ECONOMIC ENVIRONMENT

As this book is being written, the United States and the world are in the midst of the deepest recession since World War II.[30] Economies rise and fall, expand and contract; and with them, consumers' spending patterns also fluctuate. The *Economist* predicts that this downturn will have lasting impact on how people shop and what they buy. Among the changes predicted is that, "Interest in things such as green products and healthy foods will continue to grow in a post-crisis world, but customers will be less willing to pay a premium for them, and will demand more value for money when they do."[31] Currently, the segments most inclined to pay a premium for more sustainable products are also among the least affluent and youngest. "Miller Zell, a retail and strategy design firm, finds that lower income shoppers are driving the sustainable product marketplace, not the higher income, lifestyle consumers many think of as supporting sustainability."[32] Attitudes toward sustainability may have more to do with youth than with affluence. Environmental and social changes predicted for 20, 30, or even 50 years in the future tend to seem more personally relevant to someone who expects to be alive through those times.

Although it's tempting to assume that sustainability efforts would suffer when money is tight, it turns out that the opposite may be true. During the current recession, overall building is down, but green building is up.[33] Andrew Burr of the CoStar Group reports that green building appears to be resistant to economic downturns. Citing a McGraw Hill *2009 Green Outlook* study, he states, "The value of green construction increased five-fold from $10 billion in 2005 to as much as $49 billion this year, and could triple by 2013 to nearly $150 billion."[34]

Sustainability initiatives can help grow jobs and revitalize economies. One study reports that every dollar invested in renewable energy and energy efficiency creates three to five times more jobs than a dollar invested in the fossil fuels sector.[35] Similar logic appeared in President Obama's "American Recovery and Reinvestment Plan," which called for doubling the production of alternative energy in the United States over the first three years of his presidency.[36] The lesson for marketing seems clear. The business case for sustainability holds true even, or especially, in struggling economic conditions.

Changes in **the economic environment** can have profound effects on major industries. Consider the automotive sector. When the United States experienced record-high gasoline prices surpassing $4/gallon in the summer of 2008, Americans changed their driving habits and began to look for fuel efficiency in their new cars. In spring of 2008, the U.S. Department of Transportation called the 4.3 percent decline the "first year-on-year decline since the 1979 oil shock, and the sharpest decline ever."[37] At the same time, the popular automotive website, cars.com, noted that the Toyota Prius had become the most searched for model, surpassing even the popular Honda Accord and Toyota Camry.[38] Industries that can predict and prepare for major economic changes (e.g., increasing energy prices) are in better positions to take advantage of them.

THE COMPETITOR ENVIRONMENT

The competitor environment consists of the actions of firms vying for the same consumers. Sustainability efforts and a firm's ability to compete interact in different ways. As we learned in Chapter 2, being sustainable can be a powerful source of competitive advantage. Alternatively, acting slowly on sustainability may create competitive disadvantages.[39]

In the short run, large investments in sustainability may create a competitive disadvantage by tying up capital. In such cases, companies in a given industry may look to the government to level the competitive playing field. In the opening story of this chapter, we described how certain companies and NGOs were on the forefront of calling for tougher legislation of GHG emission standards. A closer look at the list of members of the USCAP reveals direct competitors (e.g., ConocoPhillips and Shell) among the members. It may seem strange for direct competitors to work together, but it turns out that some sustainability efforts are too large or too expensive for a single company to tackle.[40]

There are circumstances where **competitor collaboration** creates mutual advantages. First, companies may strike agreements on standards in areas where they prefer not to compete, such as labor conditions in foreign plants or environmental practices throughout the supply chain. The Electronic Industry Citizenship Coalition (EICC) is an example of industry-wide collaboration, which "promotes an industry code of conduct for global electronics supply chains to improve working and environmental conditions."[41] EICC provides such benefits as a carbon reporting system for electronics companies, supplier training programs, and facilities audits.

Second, industry rivals may band together to create, change, or stimulate entire markets. For example, the Green Power Market Development Group,[42] with a membership that includes Dow, Johnson & Johnson, and Dupont, is working to build the entire renewable energy market by purchasing renewable energy at prices that are significantly higher than prices for coal-generated power.

Third, when market leaders take action, competitors soon follow.[43] Companies such as Wal-Mart have changed the directions of entire industries through unilateral decisions regarding suppliers. In October 2008, Wal-Mart held a Sustainability Summit in Beijing for "1,000 top officials from its leading global suppliers, the Chinese government and NGOs,"[44] in which Wal-Mart executives, including then CEO Lee Scott, presented new, tougher standards for social and environmental practices.[45] When manufacturers change their products or practices to accommodate Wal-Mart, the changes are felt throughout the retail sector.

THE TECHNOLOGY ENVIRONMENT

Firms also compete in **the technology environment** with new and existing technologies that influence products and marketing systems. Where sustainability is concerned, technology can be a double-edged sword. For example, the efficiencies created by new fishing technologies in the 1960s greatly improved fishing yields, but they also contributed to the collapse of once-abundant North Atlantic cod fisheries.[46] During the 1990s, North American commercial fish populations of cod, haddock, and flounder fell by 95 percent (see Figure 4-1). "The value of the British catch alone declined $300 million from 1994–2002. The U.N.'s Food and Agriculture Organization estimated that sustainably managed fisheries would yield $16 billion in higher revenues."[47]

Biotechnology and genetically modified foods and organisms have the potential to yield great benefits for the environment and society, but they also create new risks.[48] The fact remains that much of the hope for a more sustainable society depends on the development of new technologies.

Innovation is an important source of competitive advantage. In Chapter 2, you learned that commitments to sustainability can drive innovation in products and processes. One area of great importance, renewable energy, is driving innovation in such areas as lighting, battery development, and smart power grids. General Electric has invested more than $150 million in sodium battery technology for use in hybrid vehicles and as backup power for cell phone towers and data centers. The company expects sodium batteries to generate $500 million in sales by 2015.[49]

In 2007, Congress enacted new efficiency standards that appeared destined to make traditional incandescent bulbs obsolete. Scheduled to take effect in 2012, the standards have instead led to rapid innovation in an industry that many people thought was doomed to extinction. In 2009, according to a *New York Times* article, "One company is already marketing

FIGURE 4-1 Decline in North Atlantic Cod

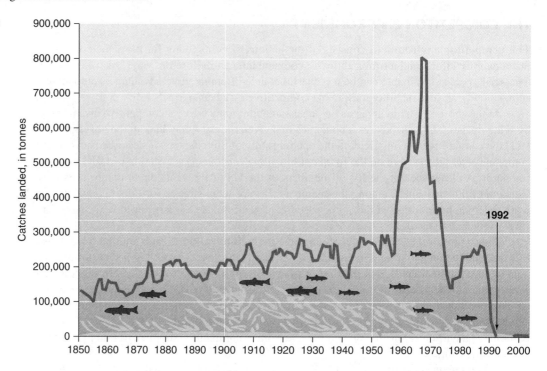

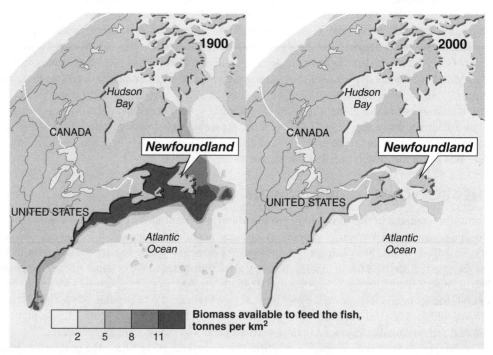

limited quantities of incandescent bulbs that meet the 2012 standard, and researchers are promising a wave of innovative products in the next few years."[50] The article goes on to conclude that government policy can be an effective stimulus for innovation in the area of more sustainable products.

THINK ABOUT IT

What conditions accelerate technological advancement? Are the effects of government regulation generally perceived to be negative or positive for business? In what ways is regulation potentially harmful to innovation? In what ways is it helpful?

THE POLITICAL-LEGAL ENVIRONMENT

The relationship between the social environment and the political environment underscores the interdependence of all environments on markets and marketing strategy. "Government not only reacts to the demands of its citizens, it also shapes and directs the attitudes, beliefs and values of those citizens."[51]

Municipalities

Portland, Oregon, is considered to be the one of the most sustainable U.S. cities[52] (see Figure 4-2). The local government includes a bureau of sustainability and planning, which "develops and implements policies and programs that provide environmental, economic and social benefits to residents, businesses and government . . . ."[53] These efforts are evident in the way local government works to attract and support more sustainable business. Portland supports grants for biofuel development and uses these fuels in city trucks.[54] Rainwater that used to run down city streets is now diverted to rain gardens, bioswales (landscape elements designed to remove silt and pollution from surface runoff water),[55] and vegetated curb extensions.[56] The city was among the first in the United States to adopt LEED (Leadership in Energy and Environmental Design) building ratings.[57] Portland architectural firms, such as SERA Architects, are known and respected by their peers for their emphasis on green building. IDC Architects has created green designs around the world, including a Nike factory in Ho Chi Minh City and the technology city, Dubai Silicon Oasis, scheduled to be completed in 2020.[58]

Other major U.S. cities are also taking steps toward environmental sustainability. San Francisco is serious about waste. The San Francisco Board of Supervisors mandated a goal of 75 percent waste diversion for the entire city by 2010, and instituted a 3-cart recycling program to make recycling easier, reduce waste, and control litter.[59] Although many cities provide curbside recycling, this program provides a bin for food scraps as well as yard trimmings, increasing composting and decreasing food waste in the landfills.[60] Seattle along with other major U.S. cities has committed to the greenhouse emission reduction levels developed in the Kyoto Protocol, a 141-nation effort to cut worldwide emissions that was not adopted at the federal level.[61] Chicago bears the moniker of the "Green Roofs City" thanks to the 4.5 million square feet of vegetation on downtown building roofs. The vegetation sequesters carbon and provides a cooling effect.[62] Chicago is also the first major U.S. city to offer a voluntary pilot program for trading of greenhouse gas, the Chicago Climate Exchange. This program is a cap-and-trade system for members who make voluntary and legally binding commitments to meet annual carbon emission reduction targets.[63] Other major U.S. cities, including Boston, Baltimore, New York, Austin, Minneapolis, Oakland, Philadelphia, and Milwaukee, have developed a variety of programs and initiatives.[64]

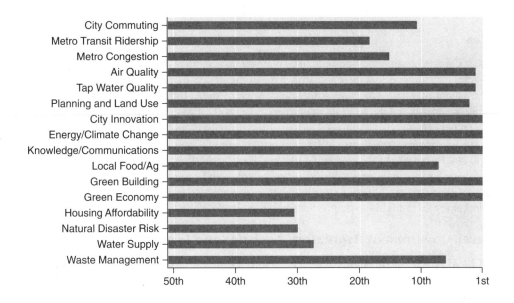

FIGURE 4-2 Portland, Oregon's ranking among U.S. Sustainable Cities

services

ARCHITECTURE
INTERIORS
URBAN DESIGN + PLANNING
SPECIALTY CONSULTING
green building
cultural resource evaluation
seismic design
strategic visioning
team oregon

SERA approaches sustainable design and planning as a basic responsibility. A 'whole building' design process that applies sound strategies of construction and planning will yield long-term economic benefits, healthier communities and environmentally sound solutions.

SERA is a national leader in sustainable design, with extensive depth and experience in LEED and other green building strategies. Our experience in adaptive re-use and building "recycling" led to our early involvement in sustainable design. Today, we provide guidance and expertise in a wide range of environmental issues that extend well beyond green building. SERA's in-house Sustainability Resources Group (SuRG) provides an array of sustainable design services including: LEED consulting, early energy analysis and programming, daylighting design and modeling, efficient lighting design, water efficiency and re-use analysis and calculations, building envelope analysis, and a variety of digital performance analyses.

In addition to our broad experience with LEED projects, SERA is involved with several projects that go beyond LEED in pursuit of the Living Building Challenge (LBC). We are very involved in the advocacy and policy realm of green building, and have participated in the development of numerous green building policies.

For more information about SERA Green Building, please contact Clark Brockman.

Portland, Oregon firm SERA Architects specializes in green buildings

VIRTUAL FIELD TRIP

Take a Web-Based Field Trip to Your Hometown and See What Evidence You Can Find of Sustainability

Dorothy may not have said it first, but she said it best: "There's no place like home." Take a Web-based field trip to your hometown and see what evidence you can find of sustainability. What government programs are in place? Is curbside recycling available? Is public transportation easy to use, safe, and reliable? Are there public green spaces within city limits? How is the air quality? The water quality? Is the city government planning for green industries? Are citizens aware of and actively supporting environmental issues and programs?

Move to Action

Identify the most urgent needs of your hometown and write a letter to the mayor. Send a copy to the local newspaper. Watch what happens.

States

In 2003, Oregon became the first state to implement an executive order for statewide sustainability planning.[65] Oregon had been the first state in the nation to create strict industrial emission standards and plans for emission reduction.[66] Several states followed with stricter automotive emission standards and the federal government may soon follow.[67] California's Governor Arnold Schwarzenegger famously embraced sustainability initiatives and in 2007 rolled out a statewide program for cleaner cars, energy efficiency, smart growth, renewable energy, power plant upgrades, and forestry.[68] In the case of California, because of the state's buying power, state regulations have had national repercussions, forcing entire industries to change their practices. For example, a ban by the California state legislature on bromated flame retardants effectively killed the market for these highly toxic products nationwide.[69]

Federal: Government Regulatory Agencies and Legislation

In an ideal world, businesses would always create healthy, sustainable products and promote them with honest and clear advertising. Consumers would buy them regularly and in quantities that returned a nice profit for the businesses. In this ideal world, the FTC would

Mini Case Study
Urban Growth Boundaries

Many cities and metropolitan areas have adopted urban growth boundaries (UGBs), borders designed to separate land for urban development apart from protected agricultural and forest lands. Within the UGB, land is developed for residential and commercial uses, with an emphasis on high density and efficiency of infrastructure. Outside the UGB, rural tracts are preserved to ensure vital agriculture and wild areas. Administered by a tri-county regional government called Metro, Portland, Oregon, has had a gradually expanding UGB since 1980. According to Metro:

> The urban growth boundary is one of the tools used to protect farms and forests from urban sprawl and to promote the efficient use of land, public facilities and services inside the boundary. Other benefits of the boundary are as follows:

- Motivation to develop and redevelop land and buildings in the urban core, helping keep core "downtowns" in business.

- Assurance for businesses and local governments about where to place infrastructure (such as roads and sewers), needed for future development.
- Efficiency for businesses and local governments in terms of how that infrastructure is built. Instead of building roads further and further out as happens in urban "sprawl," money can be spent to make existing roads, transit service and other services more efficient.

UGBs have their critics. Conduct an Internet search on UGBs. See what arguments people are making for and against them. What are their various vested interests? What marketing opportunities might arise from increased urban density and planning? What would sustainable cities look like? What kinds of marketing opportunities could be created or preserved by protecting agricultural lands and natural spaces close to urban areas?

---

have nothing to do, nothing to regulate, and no laws or statues needing enforcement. FTC jurisdiction includes both consumer protection and competition through law enforcement.[70] The U.S. Consumer Product Safety Commission works "to protect the public from unreasonable risks of serious injury or death from thousands of types of consumer products under the agency's jurisdiction" including toys, power tools, and household cleaners.[71] The 17,000-person U.S. Environmental Protection Agency (EPA) enforces environmental regulations and relies on the expertise of engineers, scientists, and other specialists.[72] The environmental work of the U.S. Congress is a continuing story of slow movement toward climate change responsibility. Vagaries in the political winds have played a major role in efforts to pass federal statutes. For example, the first comprehensive U.S. federal legislation toward climate change has taken many years,[73] and is still in doubt. At the heart of this legislation is the goal of reducing industrial carbon dioxide (CO_2) emission. Other ideas for federal legislation coupled with business opportunities to address this problem include the following:

- Replacement of employment-based taxes with pollution-based taxes
- Modernization of the electrical grid
- Reduction of investment risk in clean energy
- Federal legislation for a loophole-proof cap and trade system
- Requirement of long-time polluters to follow current regulations
- Increased funding for home weatherization
- Research, development, and deployment of alternative fuels and green technology
- Separate energy consumption from utility profits[74] (see Figure 4-3).

THE NATURAL ENVIRONMENT

Traditionally, the natural environment has been treated as one of business's external environments. This is wrongheaded thinking based on the economic fallacy that nature is part of the economy.[75] We now know that the natural environment, or the Earth, constitutes the one, grand system upon which all other systems depend (see Figure 4-4). Without functioning ecosystems, social and economic systems break down.

FIGURE 4-3 Target Global Warming: Here's How

The Earth is a closed system inside which all other business environments operate and interconnect as subordinate systems. It is no longer justifiable for any nation or any people to act with disregard to the consequences of their actions for the Earth's vital ecosystems.

Perhaps the most pressing issue today with respect to the natural environment is the mounting scientific evidence of human-caused global warming and its enormous potential consequences (see Figure 4-5). In 1988, the United Nations created the Intergovernmental Panel on Climate Change, and in 1990, the panel's first report noted that Earth had warmed by 0.5°C in the past century. The panel's third report noted the increase had been 0.6°C. By the time the panel issued it's fourth report in 2007, warming in the past century had caused a 0.74°C increase in global average temperature.[76] The panel's next report is due in

FIGURE 4-4 Sustainable Marketing Management in the Natural Environment

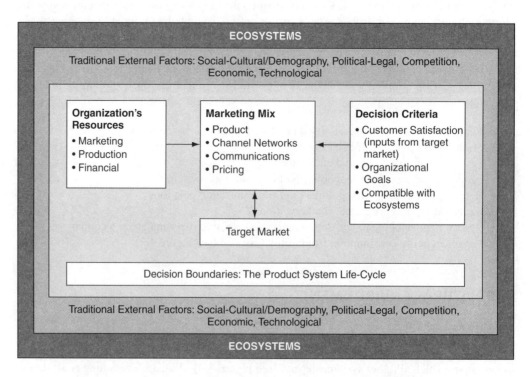

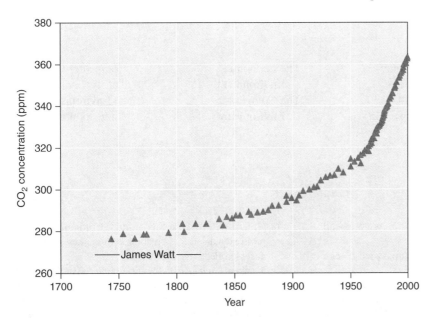

FIGURE 4-5 Since the invention of the steam engine by James Watt, there has been a continual rise of CO_2. This graph is based on carbon dioxide measurements from ice cores of Siple, Antarctica, and from Mauna Loa, Hawaii (Keeling Curve).

2014. Meanwhile, progress toward action on climate change is rocky. In a recent summit of the G8 plus 5, political leaders from the largest industrialized and emerging nations agreed to the need for arresting global warming, but were unable to agree on specific short-term goals, actions, or benchmarks.[77] U.S. leaders have been reluctant to commit to greehouse gas goals without participation from emerging giants like China and India. Disagreements about the need for developed nations to assist developing countries with money and technology have also impeded progress.

CRITICAL THINKING ACTIVITY

What are the Implications of a Global System (the Earth) Being Managed by Multiple Regional Managers (Nations) with Competing and Conflicting Interests?

What are the implications of a global system (the Earth) being managed by multiple regional managers (nations) with competing and conflicting interests? How does the global situation reflect the problem of multiple stakeholders with conflicting interests as discussed in Chapter 3? Is there any wisdom to be found in The Natural Step Framework that could help world leaders come to agreements on climate change?

Chapter Summary

As organizations formulate their marketing strategies, they attempt to understand, anticipate, adapt to, and influence numerous factors in their external environments. These include social-cultural trends and influences, economic conditions, competition, technology, and regulatory conditions. These forces both influence and are influenced by marketing activities. The task for sustainable marketing is twofold. First, marketing must be conducted in a manner that is sustainable. Second, businesses need to participate in the creation of a sustainable society by marketing sustainability as a desirable mainstream value.

Review of Chapter Objectives

- The social-cultural environment
- The economic environment
- The competitor environment
- The technology environment
- The political-legal environment
- The natural environment

Key Concepts

Social-Cultural
   Environment 43
Macroculture 43
Microculture 43

Nongovernmental
   Organizations
   (NGOs) 45
Citizen Groups 45

The Economic
   Environment 46
The Competitor
   Environment 47

Competitor Collaboration 47
The Technology
   Environment 47
Biotechnology 47

Endnotes

1. United States Climate Action Partnership, http://www.us-cap. org/index.asp, accessed July 6, 2009.
2. United States Climate Action Partnership, http://www.us-cap. org/index.asp, accessed July 6, 2009.
3. Global Climate Coalition, http://web.archive.org/web/200601 27223742/ http://www.globalclimate.org/, accessed July 5, 2009.
4. United Nations Educational, Scientific and Cultural Organization, "Education: Education for Sustainable Development," http:// www.unesco.org/en/esd/, accessed February 15, 2010.
5. Net Impact, Publications and Research, http://www.netimpact. org/displaycommon.cfm?an=1&subarticlenbr=80#research accessed July 9, 2009.
6. Net Impact, Making Your Impact Work, http://netimpact.org/associations/4342/files/MakingYourImpactatWork.pdf, accessed July 9, 2009. Also see Sustainability: Step by Natural Step™ and Sustainability 101, http://www.thenaturalstep.org/en/elearning.
7. American College & University Presidents' Climate Commitment, 2008 Annual Report, Climate Leadership for America, http://www. secondnature.org/documents/ACUPCC_AR2008.pdf, accessed July 9, 2009.
8. American College & University Presidents' Climate Commitment, 2008 Annual Report, Climate Leadership for America. Also see http://www.secondnature.org/documents/ EducationforClimateNeutralitySustainability_2009.05.07_ finalWEB.pdf, accessed July 9, 2009.
9. Association for the Advancement of Sustainability in Higher Education, AASHE Features, http://www.aashe.org/, accessed July 9, 2009.
10. Keith A. Wheeler and John M. Byrne (2003), "K-12 Sustainability Education: Its Status and Where Higher Education Should Intervene," *Planning for Higher Education*, 31 (3, March–May): 23–29.
11. Urban Options, Sustainablity Education Handbook, http:// www.michiganenergyoptions.org/education/sustainable-education-handbook, accessed July 9, 2009.
12. Sustainability Education, "Our Mission," http://www.sustainabilityed.org/who/our_mission/index.html, accessed July 9, 2009.
13. Grant D. McCracken (1986), "Culture and Consumption: A Theoretical Account of the Structure and Movement of the Cultural Meaning of Consumer Goods," *Journal of Consumer Research*, 13 (1, June): 71–84.
14. Esty, Daniel C. and Andrew S. Winston (2006), *Green to Gold: How Smart Companies Use Environmental Strategy to Innovate, Create Value, and Build Competitive Advantage*. New Haven, CT: Yale University Press.
15. Resources for Better Living, "Movies and Films about Sustainability and Environmental Issues," http://www. resourcesforlife.com/docs/item626, accessed July 9, 2009.
16. GreenBiz, "Marketing and Communications," http:// professional-services.greenbiz.com/marketing-communications/, accessed February 16, 2010.
17. Menken, Greg (2010), "Sporting Enterprises Race To Be Green," http://www.mediapost.com/publications/?fa=Articles.showArticle& art_aid=122646#comments, accessed February 17, 2010.
18. John Grant (2007), *The Green Marketing Manifesto*, West Sussex, UK: Wiley.
19. Schouten, John W. and James H. McAlexander (1995), "Subcultures of Consumption: An Ethnography of the New Bikers," *Journal of Consumer Research*, 22 (June): 43–61.
20. McAlexander, James H., John W. Schouten, and Harold J. Koenig (2002), "Building Brand Community," *Journal of Marketing*, 66 (January): 38–54.
21. Martin, Diane M. and John W. Schouten (2007), "Hyper-organizations: Communication and the Organizing Grammars of the Marketplace," Proceedings of the Asia Pacific Association for Consumer Research Conference in Sydney, Australia: 201–207.
22. Muñiz, Albert M., Jr. and Thomas C. O'Guinn (2001), "Brand Community," *Journal of Consumer Research*, 27 (March): 412–432.
23. Wal-Mart Watch, "About Us," http://walmartwatch.com/pages/ about/, accessed February 18, 2010.
24. Joyce, Amy and Matthew Mosk (2006), "Unions Hope Wal-Mart Bill Has Momentum," *Washington Post*, January 14, http:// www.washingtonpost.com/wp-dyn/content/article/2006/01/13/ AR2006011301861_pf.html, accessed February 18, 2010.
25. Zimmerman, Ann (2005), "Wal-Mart Boss's Unlikely Role: Corporate Defender-in-Chief," *Wall Street Journal*, July 26, http://www.mindfully.org/Industry/2005/Wal-Mart-Lee-Scott26 jul05.htm, accessed February 18, 2010.
26. Citizen's Environmental Coalition, "About Us," http://www. cectoxic.org/about1.html, accessed July 9, 2009.
27. Alliance for Sustainability, http://www.afs.nonprofitoffice. com/, accessed July 9, 2009.
28. TreeHugger, "About Us," http://www.treehugger.com/about/? dcitc=th_nav_top_about#1, accessed July 9, 2009.
29. Tracy Marafiote and Diane M. Martin (2007 November), "Meeting the In-Laws: How Unanticipated Heterodoxy Complicates the Marriage of Business and Environmental Organization Sustainability Alliances," Presentation at the Sustainability in the Supply Chain International Conference, Portland, Oregon.
30. Economic Cycle Research Institute, Professional Report Excerpt, http://www.businesscycle.com/, accessed July 9, 2009.
31. "From Buy, Buy to Bye-Bye," *Economist*, April 2, 2009, http://www.economist.com/displaystory.cfm?story_id=13415207, July 9, 2009.

32. *Sustainable Business Weekly* (2009), "Low Income Consumers Drive Sustainable Purchasing," Sustainable Life Media, July 22, http://sustainablelifemedia.com/content/story/strategy/low_income_consumers_drive_sustainable_purchasing, accessed Aug. 14, 2009.

33. Paul Howard, "Can Sustainability Survive the Recession?" *Contract Journal*, February 16, 2009, http://www.contractjournal.com/Articles/2009/02/16/64928/can-sustainability-survive-the-recession.html, on July 9, 2009.

34. Burr, Andrew C. (2008), "Studies Suggest More Gains for Green Building in 2009," December 5, http://www.costar.com/news/Article.aspx?id=F8DB0499285CA048F2AF712287D92BAB, accessed February 8, 2010.

35. Daniel M. Kammen, Kamal Kapadia, and Matthias Fripp (2004), "Putting Renewables to Work: How Many Jobs Can the Clean Energy Industry Generate?" A study by the Renewable and Appropriate Energy Laboratory, accessed at http://californiaedgecampaign.org/download/KammenPres.pdf, on July 9, 2009.

36. Sheppard, Kate (2009), "The First Step toward Recovery: Obama Lays Out His Economic Stimulus Plan," *Grist*, http://www.grist.org/article/The-first-step-toward-recovery/, accessed July 9, 2009.

37. "U.S.: A Record-Setting Change in Driving Habits," Straftor Global Intelligence, May 23, 2008, http://www.stratfor.com/analysis/u_s_record_setting_change_driving_habits, accessed February 8, 2010.

38. Car.com, June 11, 2008, http://www.cars.com/go/about/us.jsp?section=P&content=rel&date=20080611, accessed February 8, 2010.

39. Fuller, Donald, A. (1999), *Sustainable Marketing: Managerial-Ecological Issues,* Thousand Oaks, CA: Sage (p. 39).

40. Winston, Andrew (2007), "Collaborating with Rivals: Industry Partnerships," *Eco-Advantage Strategies*, December 3, http://www.sustainablelifemedia.com/files/webform/documents/ecoadvantagestrategies12032007.htm, accessed July 10, 2009.

41. Electronic Industry Citizen Coalition, http://www.eicc.info/, accessed July 9, 2009.

42. Green Power, Market Development Group, http://www.thegreenpowergroup.org/, accessed July 9, 2009.

43. Willard, Bob (2002), *The Sustainability Advantage: Seven Business Case Benefits of a Triple Bottom Line.* Gabriola Island, BC, Canada: New Society Publishers (p. 101).

44. GreenBiz, News, "Wal-Mart Ramps Up Standards for Suppliers in China, Around the Globe," http://www.greenbiz.com/news/2008/10/23/wal-mart-suppliers, accessed July 9, 2009.

45. Wal-Mart, China Sustainability Summit: Fact Sheet, http://walmartstores.com/download/3274.pdf, accessed July 9, 2009.

46. "Codfishes: Atlantic Cod and Its Fishery," http://science.jrank.org/pages/1563/Codfishes.html, accessed July 9, 2009.

47. Esty, Daniel C. and Andrew S. Winston (2006), *Green to Gold: How Smart Companies Use Environmental Strategy to Innovate, Create Value, and Build Competitive Advantage*, New Haven, CT: Yale University Press (p. 57).

48. Human Genome Project, Information, "Genetically Modified Foods and Organisms," http://www.ornl.gov/sci/techresources/Human_Genome/elsi/gmfood.shtml, accessed July 9, 2009.

49. "GE Invests Heavily in Sodium Battery Technology" (2009), *Environmental Leader,* May, 12, http://www.environmentalleader.com/2009/05/12/ge-invests-heavily-in-sodium-battery-technology/, accessed July 12, 2009.

50. Vestal, Leora Broydo (2009), "Incandescent Bulbs Return to the Cutting Edge," *New York Times*, July 5, http://www.nytimes.com/2009/07/06/business/energy-environment/06bulbs.html?emc=eta1, accessed July 6, 2009.

51. DesJardins, Joseph R. (2007), *Business, Ethics and the Environment: Imagining a Sustainable Future,* Upper Saddle River, NJ: Pearson Prentice Hall (p. 6).

52. Sustain Lane, "The 2008 U.S. City Rankings," http://www.sustainlane.com/us-city-rankings/, accessed July 12, 2009.

53. City of Portland, Bureau of Planning and Sustainability, http://www.portlandonline.com/bps/index.cfm, accessed July 12, 2009.

54. Dworkin, Andy, "Outlook 2008: Green Living ," *Oregonian*, April 20, 2008, p. W33.

55. Wikipedia, Bioswale, http://en.wikipedia.org/wiki/Bioswale, accessed July 12, 2009.

56. *Oregonian*, May 21, 2009. Joe Fitzgibbon, Living p. 4–5.

57. Hill, Gail Kinsey, "Outlook 2008: Green Living ," *Oregonian*, April 20, 2008, p. W30.

58. Reed, Richard, *Oregonian*, December 14, 2006, Business C-1. Also see http://www.idcarchitects.com/portfolio/green-buildings/nike.asp.

59. Recology San Francisco, Residential Services, http://www.sfrecycling.com/residential/index.php?t=r, accessed July 12, 2009.

60. Recology San Francisco, Residential Services, http://www.sfrecycling.com/residential/index.php?t=r, accessed July 12, 2009.

61. Anne Underwood, *Newsweek*, April 16, 2007 (p. 68).

62. Sustain Lane, "The 2008 U.S. City Rankings, Chicago," http://www.sustainlane.com/us-city-rankings/chicago, accessed July 12, 2009.

63. Chicago Climate Exchange, http://www.chicagoclimateexchange.com/, accessed July 12, 2009.

64. Sustain Lane, "The 2008 U.S. City Rankings," http://www.sustainlane.com/us-city-rankings/, accessed July 12, 2009.

65. State of Oregon, Office of the Governor, Executive Order Number EO-03-03, "A Sustainable Oregon for the 21st Century," http://www.oregon.gov/Gov/pdf/ExecutiveOrder03-03.pdf, accessed July 12, 2009.

66. Energy Facility Siting Standards, http://www.oregon.gov/ENERGY/SITING/standards.shtml#Carbon_Dioxide_Emissions, accessed July 12, 2009.

67. Broder and Baker, *New York Times,* "Obama's Order Is Likely to Tighten Auto Standards," January 25, 2009, http://www.nytimes.com/2009/01/26/us/politics/26calif.html, accessed July 12, 2009.

68. Karen Breslau, *Newsweek*, April 16, 2007 p. 50–59.

69. Daub, Tracy (2005), California—Rogue State or National Leader in Environmental Regulation? An Analysis of California's Ban of Bromated Flame Retardants," *Southern California Interdisciplinary Law Journal*, 14 (2, Spring), 345–370, http://www-bcf.usc.edu/~idjlaw/PDF/14-2/14-2%20Daub.pdf, accessed August 5, 2009.

70. Federal Trade Commission, "About the FTC," http://www.ftc.gov/ftc/about.shtml, accessed August 5, 2009.

71. U.S. Consumer Product Safety Commission, http://www.cpsc.gov/about/about.html, accessed August 5, 2009.

72. U.S. Environmental Protection Agency, "About EPA," http://www.epa.gov/epahome/aboutepa.htm, accessed August 5, 2009.

73. Richard Cowan, "House Democrats Reach Deal on Climate Change Bill," *Reuters,* January 23, 2009, http://www.reuters.com/article/environmentNews/idUSN23156520090623?feedType=RSS&feedName=environmentNews, accessed August 5, 2009.

74. Hoey, Peter, "Target Global Warming, Here's How" *Sierra,* May/June 2007, p. 52.

75. Brown, Lester R. (2001), *Eco-Economy: Building an Economy for the Earth*, Earth Policy Institute.

76. Climate Change 2007: Synthesis Report, Intergovernmental Panel on Climate Change, http://www.ipcc.ch/ipccreports/ar4-syr.htm, accessed August 5, 2009.

77. Jonathan Weisman (2009, July 9), "G-8 Climate-Change Agreement Falls Short," *Wall Street Journal*, http://online.wsj.com/article/SB124704550659510745.html?mod=rss_com_mostcommentart, accessed July 12, 2009.

Consumer Behavior and Sustainable Marketing

INTRODUCTION: THE CHEESEBURGER FOOTPRINT

We may not often think about the atmospheric impact of food production, but it is substantial. According to a lifecycle analysis performed by Jamais Cascio (using data from a food industry study by Stockholm University and the Swiss Federal Institute of Technology), the production and marketing of a single cheeseburger creates the equivalent of approximately 6.75 pounds of atmospheric carbon dioxide[1] (see Figure 5-1). The actual number varies according to a number of factors, such as whether the electricity involved is generated by coal or natural gas. Cascio points out that in the United States, the amount of greenhouse gas impact from all cheeseburger consumption in one year is roughly equal to the total emissions of all SUVs on the road during that same year.

THINK ABOUT IT

Our diets, like every other aspect of our consumption, vary widely in terms of how sustainable they are. Here is some food for thought. What kind of diet is most sustainable? In addition to the economic costs, what are some of the environmental and social costs of eating a burger? What, if anything, could be done to make hamburgers more sustainable?

At this point, you should already have a basic understanding of consumer behavior and why understanding it is vital to marketing efforts. To recap, **consumer behavior** consists of the activities and experiences of people engaged in buying, using, and disposing of goods and services. Consumers' behaviors are motivated by a variety of needs and wants, which may be biological, social, or psychological, and influenced by both internal and external forces. This chapter explores the concept of sustainable consumption and how it fits into efforts to make marketing sustainable.

FIGURE 5-1 The carbon footprint of a cheeseburger. The ecological impact of eating a burger doesn't stop with atmospheric carbon. Every 1/3-pound burger also requires the use of over 630 gallons (2400 liters) of fresh water. And these footprint measures don't even factor in stream degradation, soil erosion, and the damage to fish from pesticide and fertilizer runoff.

Carbon Facts

Product Size 1 Cheeseburger (130g)

Amount Per Serving

Kilograms CO_2 Equivalent 3.08

Kilograms CO_2 .243   Kilograms CH_4 .123

Total C: Energy Sources	**243g**
Transportation	
Fossil Fuel (Diesel)	120g
Fossil Fuel (Gasoline)	48g
Electricity Production	
Fossil Fuel (Natural Gas)	75g
Fossil Fuel (Coal)	0g
Other	

Total C: Non-Energy Sources	2840gCO_2E
Enteric Fermentation	81.0g (1854gCO_2E)
Manure	25.8g (656gCO_2E)
Other	5.2g (120gCO_2E)

Carbon/Product Ratio	23.7

Localism Rating	C+
Sustainable Production Rating	D+

Overall Carbon Code: Orange

CHAPTER OBJECTIVES

Upon completion of this chapter, you should have a better understanding of:

- The nature of sustainable consumption
- Consumer engagement in marketing processes
- Consumer motivation and sustainable consumption
- Consumer decision processes and sustainable consumption
- Sustainability and consumer involvement
- The role of culture in sustainable consumption

SUSTAINABLE CONSUMPTION

Simply put, **sustainable consumption** is that which meets people's needs without compromising the ability of other people to meet their needs, either now or in the future. Using The Natural Step Framework, sustainable consumption is that which meets the four conditions of a sustainable system. In other words, individuals or households would not systematically contribute to environmental increases in synthetic substances or substances extracted from the Earth's crust. Their consumption would not contribute to increasing environmental degradation, and it would in no way hinder the ability of other people to consume adequately and sustainably.

THINK ABOUT IT

Consider your own household ecology:

- What activities of acquiring, using, and disposing of products violate the four system conditions? What's in your trash? In what ways do you contribute to atmospheric carbon? What's your water usage?

- What kinds of changes in behavior would move your household toward more sustainable consumption?
- What kinds of barriers limit or prohibit your household consumption from becoming sustainable?

Consumption occurs not only in and by households. It also occurs in business and in government. The same principles that guide sustainable consumption at home also apply to the workplace. Regardless of where it occurs, consumption can always be made more sustainable.

A key role of sustainable marketing is to remove as fully as possible the barriers to sustainable consumption. In traditional thinking, successful marketing culminates in a sale, ideally to a customer who will develop some level of loyalty or long-term relationship to the marketer. Successful sustainable marketing would culminate in the sale of a product that is sustainable (i.e., that doesn't violate the system conditions for a sustainable society) to a customer in such a way that the customer has the knowledge, motivation, and resources to use and dispose of the product in a sustainable manner. Ideally, the customer and the marketer would develop a relationship that creates value for the marketer, the customer, society, and the environment.

Consumers of sustainable marketing become active collaborators in caring for the planet and creating positive social change. Through their spending choices, consumers ultimately help determine the success or failure of any marketing effort. American consumers spend trillions of dollars each year.[2] As our social world more fully grasps the importance of becoming sustainable, consumers increasingly will reward companies that work honestly toward more sustainable efforts and outcomes.[3] One consumer organization, called Carrotmob, has taken proactive spending choices to a new level of activism.

Mini Case Study

Carrotmob

According to its website, Carrotmob is "a method of activism that leverages consumer power to make the most socially-responsible business practices also the most profitable choices. Businesses compete with one another to see who can do the most good, and then a big mob of consumers buys products in order to reward whichever business made the strongest commitment to improve the world. It's the opposite of a boycott."[4] Carrotmob organizes "**buycotts**," all over the world as "a way for anyone to make a real difference with the environment by buying ordinary things in a targeted way."[5] Carrotmob negotiates with a business to use a substantial portion of revenues from a specific time window to invest in sustainability projects, and then it organizes hundreds of consumers to support the business with their purchases during that time frame. It also seeks to focus on particular behavior change. For instance, its first campaign focused on climate change, but it plans to focus on other social issues as well. It also plans on a future that includes reaching global companies along with small businesses on a local level.[6] Would it surprise you to learn that Carrotmob is organized as a for-profit organization? What are some of the challenges facing Carrotmob? How does Carrotmob membership affect individual consumers? How does it reduce barriers to sustainable consumption? What are the benefits for participating retailers?

CONSUMER ENGAGEMENT IN MARKETING PROCESSES

Sustainable marketing engages consumers meaningfully in marketing processes. Consumers are more than just sales targets. In many important ways, they are also **co-marketers** or even, at times, adversaries of businesses and their marketing programs.[7] They actively influence other consumers through word of mouth and through word of mouse. The latter, which is the prime medium of viral marketing,[8] results from Internet-mediated communication such as forums, blogs, customer review sites, and social media (for more on social media and viral marketing, see Chapter 15).

Word-of-mouth marketing occurs when people share their stories, opinions, or experiences about a product in a way that motivates others to also consider or try the product as a result. According to the Word of Mouth Marketing Association, this type of marketing works best when satisfied customers have access to open and transparent communication with companies. Companies can enhance the likelihood of word of mouth by:

- educating people about their products and services,
- identifying other people likely to share their customers' opinions,

- making it easier for their customers to share information,
- studying and understanding the context of information sharing, and
- engaging in dialogue with supporters, detractors, and neutrals.[9]

One of the most powerful contexts for word-of-mouth marketing is within and at the edges of **brand communities**, which consist of relationships among customers and between customers and companies, along with their products and brands.[10] People who feel strong connections with a brand tend to understand and share the brand's story with others. Marketers can strengthen the relationships in a brand community by providing opportunities for customers to gather and share positive, brand-relevant experiences.[11] Word-of-mouth marketing, or storytelling, is especially sustainable, or self-sustaining, in that it becomes woven into the cultural narratives, myths, or larger stories by which consumers make sense of their own lives and behaviors.

Consumers can also function as **co-producers** in the marketing process, adding their labor or expertise to make the product or service available for its intended use. For example, purchasers of furniture from IKEA assume certain tasks of manufacturing. IKEA ships its furniture products disassembled in flat and extremely compact boxes, making it possible to maximize the amount of product it can ship and, thereby, reducing each item's costs and emissions from shipping. Consumers assemble the products in their homes, which gives many people a sense of satisfaction and allows them to purchase the products more cheaply than if someone else had provided the labor for assembly.

Do-it-yourselfers purchase materials to remodel homes or create arts and crafts, even at times for resale or profit, as well as for personal enjoyment. In a slightly different role of co-production, callers to the popular National Public Radio program, *Car Talk*, actively participate in the production of entertainment.[12] At automatic grocery store checkouts, consumers take on traditional roles of retailers by scanning and bagging their own purchases. At ATMs, they function as bank tellers with the assistance of a machine.

Finally, in sustainable marketing, consumers actually take on roles as members of the marketing supply chain. Through activities such as recycling, consumers can collect and supply many of the resources that are important for manufacturing. Postconsumer paper, metals, glass, and certain plastics already have commercial value. In a world with increasing demand for finite resources, the need for marketers to include consumers in the supply chain becomes ever more critical. For example, many retailers now reclaim and aggregate recyclables such as plastic shopping bags, which in turn are used in decking and home composters.

Marketers can make it easier for customers to participate in the supply chain by designing products to be easily deconstructed into component parts that can then be reused or recycled. For example, Herman Miller, a Michigan-based office furniture company, designs its products to encourage customers to return them for recycling at end of life. In 2009, Herman Miller reached the point where over half of its sales come from products that qualify as cradle to cradle. The company's goal was to reach 50 percent by 2010. It has now revised its 2010 goal to 60 percent of sales. According to a 2009 report from GreenerDesign, "Around 1991, the company sent about 40 million pounds of material to landfills and recycled 3 million pounds of material. Last year it recycled 26 million pounds of material and trashed 3 million pounds of waste, mostly ash, residual paint powder and wood."[13]

Similarly, BMW has led the automotive world in design for disassembly: "The foundations for the environmentally friendly recycling of vehicles are already laid during the development and production phases of each BMW vehicle. By consistently applying the Design for Recycling concept, BMW ensures that its vehicles can be efficiently recycled."[14] Consumers might not participate directly in the recycling of their luxury sedan, but the attribute is one that sets this luxury car company apart.

Understanding consumer behavior has always been fundamental to successful marketing. It becomes even more essential for successful sustainable marketing, which directly involves consumers in increasing numbers of important roles. This chapter next examines the sustainability implications of some of the basic principles underlying consumers' motivations, influences, and behaviors.

CONSUMER MOTIVATION AND SUSTAINABLE CONSUMPTION

At various times in our lives, different motivations may take precedence in guiding our consumption. A **motivation** is a desired end state, or the activation of consumer behavior for the purpose of achieving some desired end state. Motivation takes many forms and comes from many places and situations. For instance, a new mother may find that her role as provider and caregiver for a newborn infant has a great influence on her decision to purchase organic produce, meats, and dairy products. Knowing this, the Organic Agriculture and Products Education Institute recently launched a national marketing campaign, "Organic. It's worth it." According to Organic Trade Association director, Laura Batcha, "Helping mothers make the connection between the personal health of their families and the health of the environment is key to this education and marketing initiative"[15]

As consumers, we purchase goods and services in order to satisfy needs and desires. What we really are buying are benefits and solutions. The humanistic psychologist Abraham Maslow developed a theory of needs that suggests that people are motivated to fulfill basic needs before moving on to other, higher-order needs. **Maslow's hierarchy of needs** includes basic survival and safety, belonging and esteem, and, ultimately, self-actualization or the desire to express one's full potential and unique talents.[16] As you learned in Chapter 3, The Natural Step Framework recognizes a broader set of human needs, but Maslow's model will do nicely to illustrate the implications of motivation for sustainable consumption.

FIGURE 5-2 LEED certified buildings appeal to an expanded set of safety needs.

Subsistence or Survival

Consumers are beginning to recognize a broader set of physiological needs. Not only do we recognize the need for food and clean water, but we also recognize the need to sustain the social and environmental systems that provide them. We are becoming more aware and less tolerant of toxins in our food and water supplies, leading to increasing demand for organic food and textile production. Brands that may appeal to an expanded set of physiological needs include Earthbound Farm, Organic Valley, and others that display the USDA's (United States Department of Agriculture) organic certification. Organic Valley's marketing message makes the case for organic foods as healthier for consumers, "We think it's a simple truth. The Earth's most delicious, most healthful foods are made when farmers work in harmony with nature. That's how this farmer-owned co-op produces organic milk, organic cheese, organic butter, organic eggs, organic juice, organic soy beverages, organic produce, and organic meats."[17]

Safety

Safety requires secure shelter and transportation. However, in the long term, shelter and transport that contribute heavily to greenhouse gases may actually counter our safety. An increasing awareness of the reality and consequences of global climate change can influence how we understand and assess our safety needs. Businesses may signify their commitment to an expanded set of safety needs by displaying brands such as LEED (Leadership in Energy and Environmental Design) and Forest Stewardship Council certifications. According to the U.S. Green Building Council, a LEED-certified home, "uses less energy, water and natural resources; creates less waste; and is healthier and more comfortable for the occupants (see Figure 5-2). Benefits of a LEED home include lower energy and water bills; reduced greenhouse gas emissions; and less exposure to mold, mildew and other indoor toxins. The net cost of owning a LEED home is comparable to that of owning a conventional home."[18]

Belonging

The human need for social recognition and being part of a social group or system is fundamental to human well-being. Each of us can identify groups to which we feel like we belong. For example, the friendships you've nurtured since high school may provide a sense of belongingness to a social group. It may be that the forces of globalization are expanding our sense of community. As we recognize our shared humanity with people around the globe and future generations, our desire for environmentally and socially sustainable products and practices is bound to increase. Brands that appeal to our expanded belonging needs include Fairtrade-certified products and Conflict-Free Diamonds. FLO International, a Fairtrade certification agency, makes the humanitarian case for Fairtrade coffee: "World market prices for coffee, rice and other commodities are highly volatile and often below the costs of production. A stable price, that covers at least production and living costs, is an essential requirement for farmers to escape from poverty and provide themselves and their families with a decent standard of living"[19] (see Figure 5-3).

FIGURE 5-3 Fairtrade products appeal to consumers with a sense of belonging to a global society.

PHOTO 5-1 Unusual and expensive purchases often appeal to a desire for status or esteem.

Esteem

People need to feel valued, to feel like we matter, like we make a difference somewhere. In many circles, esteem is equated with status displayed as the conspicuous consumption of resources. However, to the extent that society begins to view consumer wastefulness as anti-social, the more compelling signs of status may be linked to our contributions to people and to the planet. In many affluent circles, hybrid vehicles have already become status symbols. In 2008, the company OurPower.org converted Toyota Prius hybrids to plug-in technology, lifting the vehicle to even greater heights of efficiency, allowing them to achieve better than 100 miles per gallon (see Photo 5-1). The conversion's $10,000 price tag made little economic sense, but it conferred significant status on the Silicon Valley CEOs who had signed on for the service.[20] Significant numbers of Hollywood celebrities have already replaced gas-guzzlers with hybrids as the new status symbol.[21] And major corporations are drawing eco-prestige from activities such as placing their company brands on sponsored wind farms.[22]

Self-Actualization

The highest-level need, self-actualization, has always been understood in nonmaterial terms. It is more about the qualities of a human being, rather than the quantities or quality of what the human consumes. Self-actualization occurs when we bring our efforts, accomplishments, and personal growth in line with our deepest values. Services that promote self-actualization include eco-tourism and service trips, such as Sierra Club Outings and volunteer vacations from Globe Aware (see Figure 5-4). Globe Aware offers weeklong volunteer-vacation opportunities, or "volun-tourism," in Peru, Costa Rica, Thailand, Cuba, Nepal, Brazil, Cambodia, Laos, Vietnam, Jamaica, Romania, Ghana, Mexico, and China, and compares the experiences to a "mini Peace Corps."[23]

Numerous studies show that, beyond a certain point, increased wealth and consumption have no positive effect on human well-being.[24] In fact, the core values of consumer culture (e.g., materialism and individualism) may actually undermine individuals' health and well-being and society's overall sustainability.[25] Within the Association for Consumer Research, a

FIGURE 5-4 Services like volunteer vacations appeal to consumers that seek non-material growth or self-actualization.

movement called Transformative Consumer Research examines the fundamentals of consumer well-being. This group of scholars "seeks to encourage, support, and publicize research that benefits consumer welfare and quality of life for all beings affected by consumption across the world."[26]

CONSUMER DECISION PROCESSES AND SUSTAINABLE CONSUMPTION

By now you should also be familiar with the various decision processes that order and guide purchasing and consumption. The **consumer decision process** is the string of mental processes involved in purchasing, using, and disposing of a product. It includes need recognition, information search, evaluation of alternatives, purchase decisions, and post-purchase behaviors. Consumers may take these steps out of order or skip some steps entirely, depending on their levels of involvement with the product or decision. The basic decision process is the same whether or not a person is attempting to consume sustainably. However, some differences are noteworthy in the realm of sustainable consumption, probably because of the relative newness of the concept and practices.

Need Recognition

Need recognition is the onset of awareness of a need or a goal. Usually considered an individual phenomenon, need recognition can also occur at a mass or cultural level. Recall the dramatic spike in oil prices in the summer of 2008. Suddenly millions of Americans recognized the need for alternatives to gas-guzzling vehicles, resulting in a sharp downturn in the sales of large SUVs. The release and popularity of Al Gore's movie, *An Inconvenient Truth*, and its subsequent Academy Award sparked need recognition in millions more for solutions to global climate change.

Need recognition can at times be a humbling and powerful experience. Ray Anderson, founder and chairman of Interface, the world's largest manufacturer of modular carpet, described his own experience as a "spear in the chest"[27] while he was reading *The Ecology of Commerce* by Paul Hawken. Anderson's awakening was so powerful that it moved him to completely rethink and redesign Interface with the goal of manufacturing and marketing flooring products sustainably and profitably, with zero negative impact on the planet.[28]

Information Search

The desire to consume sustainably introduces new dimensions to the process of information search. **Information search** is the active pursuit of information regarding any aspect of a potential purchase. Most people probably enter the world of sustainable consumption with less prior knowledge than they are used to having. Internal searches of memory yield less, and learning is more elementary. External searches often require finding and screening new information sources. In-store messages and packaging are especially useful, as is the dynamic environment of the World Wide Web.

Increasing numbers of consumers turn to the Internet first for virtually any external information search. Whether they seek nothing more than a phone number for a local store, or engage in all-out product and price comparisons, the Internet provides abundant information quickly and conveniently. Many seek no farther than the popular search engine, Google. Others use online versions of the Yellow and White Pages. For more extensive information searches, they may rely heavily on product review sites (e.g., Epinions) or referral services (e.g., Angie's List), which provide consumer feedback and ratings regarding product performance and service quality. Still others use customized feedback from retail sites like Amazon to find book and music recommendations tailored to their interests. Ethically driven or activist consumers may turn to special directories, such as Co-op America's online National Green Pages,[29] which screens all its business listings for practices that are socially and environmentally sustainable.

As useful as it is, the Internet can also complicate the information search by spreading misinformation about sustainability. Conclusions that may be insufficiently tested, misinterpreted by news media, or even patently false can spread rapidly and persistently, especially if they support vested interests. For example, consider the relative prevalence of denials of global warming, even though they run directly counter to the vast accumulation of scientific data and analysis.[30]

Co-op America/ Services like the National Green Pages assist consumers in the search for information about more sustainable products.

VIRTUAL FIELD TRIP
Digging Deep in the Information Mine

As a consumer, finding the facts about sustainability sometimes requires a bit of effort. Take a plunge into cyberspace and see what people are saying about global warming. Who is saying what? What sources of information do they cite?

For another example of dubious information, consider the controversy about the sustainability of hybrid cars. In 2005, the market research firm CNW released a report that contained analysis of several vehicles' lifetime energy costs.[31] Probably the most attention-grabbing and hotly contested conclusion was that a hybrid Toyota Prius used more energy than a Hummer in its total manufacture, use, and disposal. The report was picked up and accelerated by news media and soon after was rebutted vigorously by environmental groups.[32]

Another challenge to information search is the practice known as *greenwashing*, which refers to an organization's use of vague or misleading environmental claims in order to present a false image of ecological friendliness. Combating such misinformation are watchdog organizations, such as the Greenwashing Index, and the increasing use of third-party certification providers, such as the Marine Stewardship Council, which conduct objective evaluations of companies' environmental and labor practices.

Finally, in the growing market for sustainable goods and services, both the technology that creates the goods and services and consumers' understanding of these goods and services are constantly changing. What consumers conclude to be true at one point in time may later be proven false. Think about the old supermarket cashier question, "Paper or plastic?" The ideal answer is, of course, neither. It turns out that both paper and plastic bags are harmful to the environment, albeit in different ways,[33] making reusable cloth bags the more sustainable option. As technology and available information continue to change, consumers must constantly reevaluate what we think we know.

Evaluation of Alternatives

Consumers use available information to make choices among products and services that can meet their needs. The **evaluation of alternatives** involves mentally weighing the potential costs and benefits associated with one or more products being considered for purchase. A product's sustainability is only one of many attributes we are likely to consider. Others include price, features, performance, style, and prestige; and consumers differ regarding the importance we place on each attribute. For example, in choosing a household cleaner, a consumer who prioritizes sustainability may choose a product from Seventh Generation,[34] whereas someone who focuses on brands known for cleaning power may opt for Clorox Green Works products.[35]

THINK ABOUT IT

Like many other products, cosmetics are going every shade of green. Some cosmetic companies that are dedicated to sustainability, such as Nvey Eco,[36] stress organic certification and natural sourcing throughout the supply chain, and their marketing communication often emphasizes the list of toxic substances that their products *do not* contain. Other companies, like Pür Minerals,[37] focus on one or two key natural ingredients that differentiate their products. Other popular brands are marketed with messages that imply (sometimes misleadingly) natural or organic content while stressing beauty or sensory benefits. What kind of process of evaluating alternatives would lead a consumer interested in sustainability to choose one brand of cosmetics over another?

Some firms voluntarily provide consumers information about their products' sustainability. For example, the clothing company Patagonia provides a behind-the-scenes look at sourcing and manufacturing processes through its "Footprint Chronicles."[38] Wal-Mart has taken a huge step in cutting through supplier companies' competing sustainability claims. The retail giant has announced that it is developing an index that will provide comparative environmental information on every product it sells, making it easier for shoppers to evaluate alternatives on the basis of their sustainability.[39] We'll take a closer look at sustainability indices and scorecards in Chapter 6.

Purchase Decision Process

The **purchase decision process** involves more than deciding whether and what to buy. It also involves all the other decisions necessary to complete the transaction. Those decisions may include things like method of payment, method of delivery, and whether or not to use a shopping bag. The purchase stage becomes more complex as retailers seek to become more sustainable. For example, some bricks-and-mortar retailers and grocery stores also offer home delivery options. Oregon's New Seasons Market provides an online shopping and delivery program that uses biodiesel-powered delivery vans, fueled in part by the cooking oil from the stores' delis. New Seasons Market claims it can, "prevent up to 240 trips to the grocery store per day and potentially save over 80 metric tons of carbon dioxide per year."[40]

Attempting to reduce the use of single-use shopping bags, many stores now sell reusable bags, and many, like Kroger's Fred Meyer, Safeway, and WinCo, even pay consumers to use them (see Photo 5-2).

Increasing numbers of retailers now donate a percentage of sales to humanitarian or environmental projects, and in some cases, customers are asked to choose their preferences from a

PHOTO 5-2 The purchase process includes more than just paying. What kind of bags would you prefer?

list of charities. For example, Nau, a sportswear company, donates 2 percent of every sale to one of five charities that shoppers select at the point of purchase.[41] New Seasons Market donates 10 percent of after-tax profits to community organizations and remits 20 percent to its employees.[42]

Post-Purchase Behaviors

As consumers' awareness, knowledge, and attitudes become more tuned toward sustainability, we consume and dispose of products and energy more mindfully. **Post-purchase behaviors** include both **product usage behaviors** and **disposition or disposal behaviors**. More sustainable product usage may include behaviors such as turning down thermostats or combining automobile trips for greater efficiency. More sustainable disposition or disposal behaviors

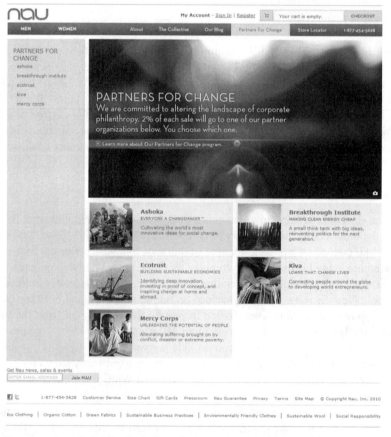

Every purchase from Nau includes a decision about charitable giving.

include composting vegetable waste and thinking twice before consigning anything to a trash bag destined for the landfill. In product disposal behaviors, consumers have opportunities to reduce waste and direct valuable resources back into the supply chain through recycling.

SUSTAINABILITY AND CONSUMER INVOLVEMENT

The study of consumer behavior commonly differentiates between high-involvement purchases, which require **extensive problem solving**, and low-involvement purchases that lend themselves to **limited problem solving** or **routine purchasing**. As opposed to routine or habitual purchasing, extensive problem solving involves an extended or intensified information search and evaluation of alternatives, generally to reduce the perceived risk associated with a purchase. Because concepts, practices, and technologies associated with sustainability are relatively unfamiliar to many consumers, purchase decisions that have traditionally been routine or habitual can suddenly become demanding, high-involvement situations. For example, take the purchase of electricity for a household. With limited choices of suppliers, consumers typically sign up for electric service without much information search or evaluation of alternatives, and then they pay their bills every month as a matter of routine. Many consumers now consider the option of investing in residential solar power.

As utilities' prices continue to rise alongside public levels of environmental awareness and concern over greenhouse gases, more people have begun to consider options for using photovoltaic (solar or PV) energy to power their homes. Using PV cells, usually installed on rooftops or freestanding installations on the ground, consumers can generate their own electricity from the sun, defray their electric bills, and even sell surplus power back to the utilities company. Many states even offer tax incentives for doing so. Still, the required investment is significant, and payback periods may be long. Even as a purely economic decision, installing a PV system is a high-involvement process requiring extensive information search. And it is not a purely economic decision. For many consumers, the decision is a matter of principle. Some of the decisions a consumer must make include the following:

- Is a PV system the best way for me to get renewable power? What about commercially available green power, which supports investment in developing renewable energy?
- Is my home location suitable for solar power generation? How big would the system need to be?
- What are the options for installation? Where would it work best? Where would it look best?
- How much would it cost to install? What kind of financing is available? How long would it take to pay for itself?
- Who sells and installs PV systems? How should I evaluate different suppliers?
- What do I need to know about permits? Insurance? Connection agreements with the electric company?[43]

THINK ABOUT IT

What other examples can you think of where previously low-involvement purchases suddenly require extensive problem solving (EPS)? Is the shift to EPS a barrier to sustainable consumption? If so, how might marketing help reduce the barriers?

THE ROLE OF CULTURE IN SUSTAINABLE CONSUMPTION

Many forces shape people's consumer behaviors and buying processes. They include societal influences, interpersonal influences, individual factors, such as self-concept and personality, and even situational factors at any given time. The overarching influence, affecting all the others, is culture.

Culture, the learned system of behaviors and beliefs that guide and structure life in society, can be separated into both material and nonmaterial components. **Material culture** refers to human-made objects (such as buildings, roads, tools, and toys) and natural objects that have been given special purpose for human use (such as wilderness areas or soil in a garden). Nonmaterial aspects of culture include mental constructs such as knowledge, beliefs, and values. Material and nonmaterial aspects of culture are highly interrelated. People create, interpret, and interact with material objects according to their knowledge, beliefs, and values. The importance of automobile ownership in American culture is a case in point. In 2006, the Pew Research Center reported that 91 percent of Americans viewed automobile ownership as a necessity.[44] This fundamental belief is linked to American material culture, characterized by extensive freeway systems, sprawling suburbs, drive-ins, drive-throughs, and a general media fascination with cars.[45] In 2009, the number of Americans who considered car ownership as a necessity had dropped to 88 percent,[46] and Americans were driving less, despite lower gas prices.[47] Current trends eroding the American culture of automobile ownership include urban revitalization,[48] the increasing use of public transportation,[49] the growing popularity of bicycle commuting,[50] and the increasing availability of car-sharing services like Zipcar.[51]

Although certain social groups, or subcultures, attempt to live sustainably, such as through voluntary simplicity,[52] at this point in history, environmentally and socially sustainable practices are not central to most cultures, either materially or nonmaterially. It can be argued that consumption will not be sustainable until we can bring about a mainstream culture of sustainability, in which most people understand, value, and demand ecologically sound and humane practices in a physical world that is altered to make such practices easy and commonplace.

CRITICAL THINKING ACTIVITY

Living Sustainably

Imagine a society in which sustainable living is the behavioral norm.

- What kinds of values would be privileged?
- What kinds of physical systems would need to be in place? How would homes, work, and transportation be different?
- In what ways would life be better?
- What would members of society have to give up to make sustainable living possible?
- What institutions could accelerate change toward a culture of sustainability? How could they do it?

As you have already learned, many other kinds of forces influence consumer behavior. However, even the most personal and internal of them, such as individual self-concept, are formed against the basic blueprint of culture. Culture provides the norms, values, and social expectations against which we assess our own behaviors, and culture provides the material building blocks with which we learn and ultimately define ourselves.

Chapter Summary

The marketing concept holds that the success of a business relies on its ability to meet its customers' needs, and to do it better than competing businesses. The principle of sustainable marketing adds the necessity of meeting current customer needs without compromising the ability to also meet the needs for future generations. The duty falls to marketing professionals to understand consumer needs and desires, and to create sustainable means to fulfill them. This chapter has introduced the fundamentals of human needs and consumer behavior as they relate to sustainability. It explained the basic process of consumer decision making, and it outlined many of the internal and external forces that influence that process.

Review of Chapter Objectives

- The nature of sustainable consumption
- Consumer engagement in marketing processes
- Consumer motivation and sustainable consumption

- Consumer decision processes and sustainable consumption
- Sustainability and consumer involvement
- The role of culture in sustainable consumption

Key Concepts

Consumer Behavior   57
Sustainable Consumption   58
Buycotts   59
Co-marketers   59
Brand Communities   60
Co-producers   60
Motivation   60

Maslow's Hierarchy of
    Needs   61
Consumer Decision
    Process   63
Need Recognition   63
Information Search   63
Evaluation of Alternatives   65

Purchase Decision
    Process   65
Post-Purchase Behaviors   66
Product Usage Behaviors   66
Disposition or Disposal
    Behaviors   66

Extensive Problem
    Solving   67
Limited Problem Solving   67
Routine Purchasing   67
Culture   67
Material Culture   67

Endnotes

1. Cascio, Jamais (2006), "The Cheeseburger Footprint," http://openthefuture.com/cheeseburger_CF.html, accessed July 16, 2009.
2. The World Factbook, July 2007, https://www.cia.gov/library/publications/the-world-factbook/index.html, accessed July 16, 2009.
3. Willard, Bob (2002), *The Sustainability Advantage*, Gabiola Island, BC, Canada: New Society Publishers.
4. Carrot Mob, http://carrotmob.org/, accessed September 15, 2009.
5. Carrot Mob Charleston Blog, http://carrotmobcharleston.blogspot.com/, accessed September 15, 2009.
6. Personal correspondence with CarrotMob representative Brent Schulkin, October 8, 2009.
7. Gummesson, Evert (2005), "From One-to-One to Many-to-Many Marketing in the Network Society," Paper presented at the annual meeting for the Academy of Marketing and AMA Conference, DIT, July 5–7, in Dublin, Ireland.
8. Scott, David Meerman (2008), "The New Rules of Viral Marketing: How Word-of-Mouse Spreads Your Ideas for Free," free e-book available at:http://www.davidmeermanscott.com/documents/Viral_Marketing.pdf, accessed July 16, 2009.
9. Word of Mouth Marketing Association, http://womma.org/wom101/, accessed February 24, 2010.
10. McAlexander, James H., John W. Schouten, and Harold J. Koenig (2002), "Building Brand Community," *Journal of Marketing*, Vol. 66 (January): 38–54.
11. Schouten, John W., James H. McAlexander, and Harold F. Koenig (2007), "Transcendent Customer Experience and Brand Community," *Journal of the Academy of Marketing Science*, 35 (3-Fall): 357–368.
12. Martin, Diane M. and John W. Schouten (2007), "Hyperorganizations: Communication and the Organizing Grammars of the Marketplace," Proceedings of the Asia Pacific Association for Consumer Research Conference in Sydney, Australia, pp. 201–207.
13. GreenerDesign (2009), "Herman Miller Earns Design for Recycling Award," May 12, http://www.greenerdesign.com/news/2009/05/12/herman-miller-earns-design-recycling-award, accessed September 15, 2009.
14. BMW, "BMW Recycling," http://www.bmw.co.uk/bmwuk/about/corp/recycling/, accessed September 15, 2009.
15. Organic Trade Association, 2009 Press releases, http://www.organicnewsroom.com/2009/02/organic_its_worth_it.html, accessed September 15, 2009.
16. Maslow, Abraham, H. (1943), "A Theory of Human Motivation," *Psychological Review*, 50 (4): 370–396.

17. Organic Valley Family of Farms, http://www.organicvalley.coop/, accessed July 16, 2009.
18. U.S. Green Building Council, http://www.usgbc.org/, accessed July 16, 2009.
19. Fairtrade Labeling Organizations International, http://www.fairtrade.net/impact, accessed July 16, 2009.
20. Kanellos, Michael (2008), "Latest Silicon Valley Status Symbol: The Plug-In Hybrid," *CNET: Green Tech*, February 11, http://news.cnet.com/8301-11128_3-9869592-54.html, accessed July 16, 2009.
21. d'Estries, Michael (2007), "How Did All of Hollywood End Up with A Prius?" *Ecorazzi*, May 23, http://www.ecorazzi.com/2007/05/23/how-did-all-of-hollywood-end-up-with-a-prius/, accessed July 16, 2009.
22. SustainableBusiness.com (2008), "Sustainability as a Status Symbol," May 5, http://www.sustainablebusiness.com/index.cfm/go/news.feature/id/1556, accessed July 16, 2009.
23. Globe Aware Adventures in Service, http://www.globeaware.org/, accessed July 19, 2009.
24. Easterbrook, Gregg (2003), *The Progress Paradox: How Life Gets Better While People Feel Worse*, New York: Random House.
25. Eckersley, Richard (2005), "Is Modern Western Culture a Health Hazard?" *International Journal of Epidemiology*, 35: 252–258.
26. Association for Consumer Research, http://www.acrwebsite.org/fop/index.asp?itemID=325, accessed July 24, 2009.
27. Dean, Cornelia, (2007), "Executive on a Mission: Saving the Planet," *New York Times*, May 22, http://www.nytimes.com/2007/05/22/science/earth/22ander.html, accessed July 21, 2009.
28. Anderson, Ray (1998), *Mid-Course Correction: Toward a Sustainable Enterprise: The Interface Model*, Atlanta, GA: Peregrinzilla Press.
29. National Green Pages, http://www.coopamerica.org/pubs/greenpages/, accessed July 19, 2009.
30. Joseph Romm, Joseph (2008), "The Cold Truth about Climate Change," *Salon,* February 27, http://www.salon.com/news/feature/2008/02/27/global_warming_deniers/index.html, accessed July 21, 2009.
31. "Dust to Dust: The Energy Cost of New Vehicles from Concept to Disposal," http://cnwmr.com/nss-folder/automotiveenergy/DUST%20PDF%20VERSION.pdf, accessed July 21, 2009.
32. Gleick, Peter H. (2007), "Hummer versus Prius: Dust to Dust Report Misleads the Media and Public with Bad Science," Pacific • Institute, May, http://www.pacinst.org/topics/integrity_

of_science/case_studies/hummer_vs_prius.pdf, accessed July 21, 2009.

33. "Reusable Bags," http://www.reusablebags.com/facts.php?id=7, accessed July 21, 2009.

34. Seventh Generation, http://www.seventhgeneration.com/, accessed July 24, 2009.

35. Clorox, http://www.clorox.com/products/overview.php?prod_id=gw, accessed July 24, 2009.

36. Nvey eco, http://www.econveybeauty.com/, accessed October 11, 2010.

37. Pürminerals, http://www.purminerals.com/, accessed October 11, 2010.

38. Patagonia, http://www.patagonia.com/web/us/footprint/index.jsp, accessed July 21, 2009.

39. Judkis, Maura (2009), "Wal-Mart Announces Sustainability Index," *U.S. News & World Report*, July 16, http://www.usnews.com/blogs/fresh-greens/2009/07/16/wal-mart-announces-sustainability-index.html, accessed July 21, 2009.

40. New Seasons Market, http://www.newseasonsmarket.com//-images/media/pdf/report2009.pdf, accessed July 25, 2009.

41. Nau, http://www.nau.com/partners-for-change/, accessed July 22, 2009.

42. New Seasons Market, http://www.newseasonsmarket.com//-images/media/pdf/report2009.pdf, accessed July 25, 2009.

43. National Renewable Energy Laboratory, http://www.nrel.gov/solar/, accessed July 24, 2009.

44. Pew Research Center, Publications, "Luxury or Necessity," http://pewresearch.org/pubs/323/luxury-or-necessity, accessed September 15, 2009.

45. Foster, Mark S. (2003), *A Nation on Wheels: The Automobile Culture in America Since 1945*, Belmont, CA: Wadsworth.

46. The Infastructurist, The Data, New Poll, http://www.infrastructurist.com/2009/05/19/new-poll-americans-cant-imagine-life-without-cars-even-while-using-them-less/, accessed September 15, 2009.

47. CNNMoney.com (2009), "Not Road Tripping: Americans Drive Fewer Miles—Again," February 19, http://money.cnn.com/2009/02/19/autos/miles_driven.reut/index.htm, accessed September 15, 2009.

48. Dugan, Matthew M. (2005), "Trends in Downtown Revitalization," *Virginia Review*, June/July, http://www.timmons.com/news-and-events/TrendsinDowntownRevitalization.asp, accessed September 15, 2009.

49. Tanneer, Manav (2008), "U.S. Cities Scrambling to Meet Rising Mass Transit Demands," CNN.com, July 16, http://www.cnn.com/2008/US/07/16/mass.transit/index.html, accessed September 15, 2009.

50. Chan, Sewell (2008), "Commuter Cycling Is Soaring, City Says," *New York Times*, October 30, http://cityroom.blogs.nytimes.com/2008/10/30/commuter-cycling-is-soaring-city-says/, accessed September 15, 2009.

51. Zipcar, http://www.zipcar.com/, accessed September 15, 2009.

52. The Simple Living Network, http://www.simpleliving.net/main/, accessed July 24, 2009.

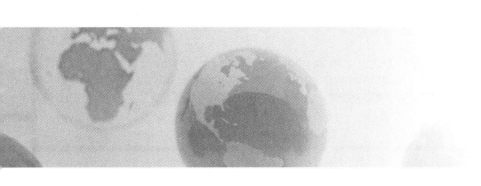

Measurement and Research for Sustainable Marketing

INTRODUCTION: GOOD AND EVIL ARE EQUAL IN THE EYES OF THE GDP

There is a saying that "we measure what we value, and we value what we measure." In a speech at the University of Kansas on March 18, 1968, Robert F. Kennedy had this to say about the standard measure of economic development in America and throughout the world:

> Our gross national product counts air pollution and cigarette advertising, and ambulances to clear our highways of carnage. It counts special locks for our doors and the jails for those who break them. It counts the destruction of our redwoods and the loss of our natural wonder in chaotic sprawl. It counts napalm, and the cost of a nuclear warhead, and armored cars for police who fight riots in our streets.
>
> Yet the gross national product does not allow for the health of our children, the quality of their education, or the joy of their play. It does not include the beauty of our poetry or the strength of our marriages, the intelligence of our public debate or the integrity of our public officials. It measures neither our wit nor our courage; neither our wisdom nor our learning; neither our compassion nor our devotion to our country. It measures everything, in short, except that which makes life worthwhile.

Robert Kennedy made an interesting point. Gross national product (GNP) and its more common cousin, gross domestic product (GDP), make no distinction for the quality of a society's economic activity, regardless of whether it leads to constructive or destructive ends. These measures also fail to recognize valuable productive activities, such as parenting, that can't be measured easily in economic terms. What, then, is the ultimate result of a nation attempting to maximize GNP?

Probably few of us value war above peace, misery above happiness, or violence above beauty. Yet in many cases, our measurement and management systems tend to reduce them all to economic measures and, therefore, to equate or even invert their value in practice. In response to this problem of measurement, the European Union recently announced that it "will introduce an index in 2010 to track life qualities such as a clean environment, social cohesion and wellbeing to complement the gross domestic product (GDP) indicator in shaping policy."[1] The country of Bhutan has developed a measure of gross national happiness (GNH) to replace GDP as its measure of successful development. The GNH theoretically puts a positive value on anything that promotes human well-being and a negative value on anything that impedes it.[2] A similar measure, the genuine progress indicator (GPI), attempts to distinguish between good growth, which benefits society, and growth that creates more harm than good for society.[3]

THINK ABOUT IT

Businesses get very skilled at managing the things they can measure and track. We have elaborate, sophisticated systems to track financial costs and earnings. It might also be argued that we need equally sophisticated systems to track indicators of human well-being and the health of ecosystems.[4] What kinds of things would we measure if we were trying to maximize the well-being of workers and customers? What items would appear on a balance sheet of gains and losses of natural capital?

A superior ability to gather, process, and interpret information is a major source of competitive advantage in the marketplace.[5] This is equally true for information relating to sustainability, which, as we have learned, is also an important source of competitive advantage. In the process of creating and executing a sustainable marketing strategy, **research** and **measurement**, or **metrics**, are useful at every step of the way. They help managers to quantify market opportunities, select target markets, and develop effective marketing programs. Once a business has decided on a course of action, metrics are essential for monitoring performance, for increasing both efficiency and effectiveness, and for identifying new marketing opportunities. This chapter examines the roles of measurement and research in making marketing more sustainable.

CHAPTER OBJECTIVES

In this chapter, you will learn about:

- The importance of measurement
- Principles for measurement in sustainable marketing
- Uncovering information
- Uses and types of sustainability metrics

There is another saying: "What we measure, we can manage." For this reason measurement, or the use of metrics, is an area of rapidly growing importance to sustainable marketing.

THE IMPORTANCE OF MEASUREMENT

Measurement is crucial to marketing activities such as setting prices, managing costs, increasing distribution efficiencies, and choosing advertising media. Marketing measurement, analysis, and decision making also are fundamental to responding to changes in the various business environments, such as competition, technology, and the economy. The same is true for the natural and social environments. To make real improvements in sustainability requires the ability to measure and track key aspects of performance in the areas of natural and human capital.

No company or organization is fully sustainable. Sustainability is at best a goal and a journey, albeit a critically important one. Making meaningful progress toward sustainability requires a clear understanding of **baseline performance**, or a starting point from which to measure and track improvements, and accurate methods of monitoring and recording performance. For example, in 2003, Alcoa found that its efforts to measure and manage energy efficiency had reduced its emissions 26 percent below 1990 levels and resulted in energy savings of over $16 million per year[6] (see Photo 6-1).

As it has become more apparent that competitive advantage and profits are linked to both natural and human capital, companies have increasingly begun to incorporate social and

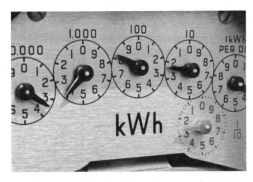

PHOTO 6-1 Making improvements in sustainability requires accurate measurement.

environmental indicators into their measurement and management systems.[7] For example, Sony Ericsson, among its many programs for improving sustainability, has put systems in place to measure and manage the energy requirements and carbon footprints of its factories, offices, and business travel. The company also engages in research to test for possible health-related effects of product usage, such as exposure to electromagnetic fields and the absorption of radiation from cell phones.[8]

Businesses traditionally use economic or financial measures to form a basis for evaluating and managing performance. This may also carry over into measurement for sustainability. Regarding the reliance of the economy on the natural environment, one economist notes that, "Environmental issues are fundamentally economic ones."[9] This does not mean, however, that all environmental and social performance can be reduced to economic terms. Many companies, in industries ranging from textiles to consumer electronics, attempt to require manufacturing suppliers to adhere to codes of conduct regarding worker health, safety, and human rights. Codes, which typically are enforced through mechanisms such as external audits and self-administered questionnaires, include requirements governing things like work hours, housing conditions, and the provision of protective clothing. Because compliance with codes of conduct in foreign factories can be difficult to measure and enforce, some companies, including Sony Ericsson, are also increasing their efforts in the areas of training and support.

Mini Case Study

IBM's Real Estate and Site Operations (RESO) Group

Large marketing firms often entail complex systems within systems. Managing complex systems may require complex measurements. For example, IBM's Real Estate and Site Operations (RESO) group manages energy use and conservation programs across all of the company's operations. RESO engineers were already good at energy conservation when they were asked to reduce consumption by a further 3.5 percent over baseline 2007 levels. Finding that they lacked adequate data on energy consumption throughout the system, they installed additional electric meters and connected all the meters at 20 large facilities into a central information system. Measurements formerly limited to monthly bills were now available at 15-minute intervals.

By analyzing real-time data, RESO engineers were able to identify more than 100 energy conservation projects resulting in a total savings of 16,500 megawatt hours of electricity and $1.35 million in savings.[10]

For IBM, certain sustainability gains were possible because real-time measurement was better at revealing energy waste than measurements at longer intervals. In terms of greenhouse gas (GHG) emissions, how meaningful is a two-to-five percent reduction in electricity use? What could IBM do to make far deeper reductions in its GHG impact? Is it possible for IBM to achieve zero emission in its operations? How would you recommend that IBM invest its $1.35 million savings?

It turns out that the same principle applies to individual consumer behavior as well. For example, the instrumentation in a Toyota Prius hybrid provides drivers with instant feedback on drivetrain operation and fuel consumption (see Photo 6-2). This leads drivers to modify their driving behaviors to achieve significantly higher fuel efficiency. As an added benefit, it also introduces a game-like quality to driving that enhances the overall experience.[11]

PHOTO 6-2 For some drivers, the energy monitor display on a Prius dash turns fuel conservation into a game.

THINK ABOUT IT

How can individual drivers more drastically reduce the GHG emissions of their cars? Is the goal of zero emissions possible in either case? What would zero-emission manufacturing look like? Zero-emission driving?

For companies attempting to become sustainable, it is crucial not only to measure human and environmental impacts, but also to report them.[12] Accurate **internal reporting** of sustainability performance helps managers improve products and marketing operations. Transparent **external reporting** helps outside stakeholders to evaluate risks and make more informed purchasing and investment decisions.

VIRTUAL FIELD TRIP
Patagonia's Footprint Chronicles

Not all external reporting focuses on numbers and statistics. Visit the Patagonia website's Footprint Chronicles at (http://www.patagonia.com/web/us/footprint/index.jsp?slc=en_US&sct=US) and explore the sustainability stories of the products featured there. What do you think Patagonia intends to achieve by providing this information? What is the effect of listing both "the good" and "the bad" aspects of each product? What can you learn about such topics as materials sourcing, recycled fibers, and factory conditions? What can you learn about each product's environmental footprint? Is the information useful? How does the Footprint Chronicles influence your attitude toward the Patagonia brand?

As important as measurement is to managing and reporting marketing performance, including in the area of sustainability improvements, it is equally important that the measurement be done well. As we shall learn, measuring the wrong things, or measuring only some of the right things, can potentially be more damaging than not measuring at all.

PRINCIPLES FOR MEASUREMENT IN SUSTAINABLE MARKETING

Good measurement facilitates good management. By the same logic, managing marketing processes to make them more sustainable requires measurement that conforms to the principles of sustainability. For those principles, we refer back to The Natural Step Framework (TNSF), which we introduced in Chapter 2. As you may recall, TNSF emphasizes the importance of maintaining a whole-system perspective so that improvements in one area don't bring about unintended harm in another. Backcasting from principles involves establishing clear goals, determining baseline performance, and developing strategies that enhance sustainability and deliver suitable financial performance. The proper use of metrics is critical to developing and evaluating strategies for sustainable marketing. Let's examine some of the key principles of sustainability and see how they relate to marketing measurement.

Principle #1: Begin with a Whole-System Perspective of Success

Measurement that fails to account for all the effects of change in a system can be problematic. Managers tend to follow the maxim, "If it ain't broke, don't fix it." Once systems are in place for measuring and managing performance, those systems tend to be allowed to operate unimpeded as long as they keep producing measurable improvements. Problems arise, however, if the systems produce unwanted side effects that escape measurement. Imagine, for example, that you are managing the performance of a racecar, and that you have an excellent system for measuring and improving the engine's output. Due to your efforts, the car likely will get faster and faster. However, the increased speed may accelerate the wear and tear on a critical steering mechanism. Now imagine that you've failed to measure that wear and tear. The increased speed of the car is useless, maybe even dangerous and detrimental, if the steering fails in the middle of a race. In this racecar analogy, we can probably agree that the real goal isn't simply having the fastest car; it's winning races. In addition to a well-maintained and tuned car, winning races also requires a skilled driver in peak condition, and a skilled pit crew to minimize the time required for refueling and tire changes during the race. Correct management of the system, that is, the racing team, will include identifying, measuring, and monitoring all of these necessary components.

There are two requirements for bringing a whole-system perspective to the job of measurement: (1) identifying the correct systems and (2) understanding how the systems work. In the case of sustainable marketing, the main system of concern is the biosphere, including all the natural ecosystems and human systems that are affected by the marketing processes. An important subsystem to consider is the value chain for the company's products, including suppliers and customers, all of whom affect the company's ability to market more sustainably. Understanding how the systems work requires the use of cross-functional teams, including people who are familiar with all aspects of the organization as well as people who understand stakeholder interests with respect to the natural environment and human well-being.

Principle #2: Measure All the Relevant Dimensions of Success

This principle flows directly from the previous one. Once a cross-functional team has achieved a system perspective, it must be able to identify all the relevant dimensions of success in sustainable marketing. This begins with an understanding of the four system conditions for sustainability. With the goal of eliminating all violations of the system conditions, the team should identify every aspect of the company and its operations that have some affect on either natural or human capital.

In the process of backcasting from principles (as explained in Chapter 2), an organization will identify actions that can make it more sustainable. The outcomes of those actions need to be measured. This applies not only to the positive outcomes. Any possible negative consequences will also need to be measured. For example, a company may focus on reducing energy use and air pollution, and in doing so, it may achieve impressive reductions and incur significant cost savings. However, if the pollution-reduction mechanisms produce flows of toxins into a local river, then the trade-offs may be unacceptable. Making that call requires the kind of information that comes from measurement. Meaningful gains in sustainable marketing require measuring all the right stuff, not just the stuff that's easy to measure and easy to report to stakeholders.

Principle #3: Use Good Metrics

The principles of quality measurement are widely understood. First, any good metric or scale must be reliable, meaning that it will consistently return the same results when measuring the same phenomenon. Second, a good measurement also must provide a valid or meaningful representation of the phenomenon being measured and not of some other related concept or phenomenon. The principles of reliability and validity are covered in detail in the study of market research.

Another aspect of good measurement is its sensitivity to meaningful variations in the phenomenon being studied. For example, a scale that records a simple "yes" or "no" response to a question regarding stakeholder involvement in a marketing strategy probably can't provide useful information about the level or quality of stakeholder involvement. A good general rule in measurement is to use **higher-order scales**, that is, metrics that provide more rather than less information about the differences in a phenomenon.

Principle #4: Develop Benchmarks and Performance Indicators

Measuring improvement in sustainability not only requires knowing what your ultimate goals are, it also requires you to know where you're starting and what constitutes real progress. For this purpose, we establish **benchmarks**, which are standards to which we can compare our performance. Common benchmarks for an organization's carbon emissions include the levels measured at some earlier point in time. For example, General Electric reports that in 2008 it had, "reduced greenhouse gas emissions by 13% compared to 2004 levels."[13] Typically, benchmarks are chosen based on the earliest available data about the phenomenon being measured.

Sometimes, it's more important to know immediately that something is happening than it is to measure accurately what is happening. Think of the smoke detector in a home or office. Its function isn't to measure the amount of smoke in the air. It only needs to alert occupants that there is a potential problem. **Performance indicators** are like smoke detectors. They are summary measurements meant to give a quick and general assessment of a situation and, in some cases, to trigger some kind of immediate response. The proverbial canary in the coal mine is a performance indicator. Your GPA is an indicator. So is your credit score. Common indicators of environmental and social sustainability might include:

- customer complaints;
- public protests;
- bills for power, water, or waste disposal;
- worker health claims or complaints;
- alarms for radiation or chemical presences;
- orders for paper and other work supplies; and
- amounts and types of business travel.

UNCOVERING INFORMATION

In gathering information, both its cost and its quality are important factors. Secondary research is the most cost effective, having already been gathered for some other purpose, but it may not be timely or directly applicable to an organization's needs. Primary research can be tailored to meet an organization's needs and has the added advantage of being proprietary, that is, owned and controlled by the organization and unavailable to competitors except as an organization chooses to reveal it. On the other hand, primary research is far more expensive because it must be specially conducted or commissioned with all costs borne by the organization. Let's look at both secondary and primary sources of information as they relate to research in marketing and sustainability.

Secondary Research

Secondary sources of sustainability information offer content from a wide variety of people and organizations. Content ranges from **substantive information**, such as the size, structure, and segmentation of markets, to **methodological information**, such as strategic frameworks, measurement processes, and individual metrics.

Potential secondary sources of sustainability information include academic publications, trade publications, governmental and nongovernmental organizations, and commercial research firms. Academic publications, such as journal articles, are peer reviewed and highly trustworthy but may not be a good fit with a particular industry's needs. Trade publications and organizations provide excellent data and information pertaining to specific industries, usually with something of a pro-industry bias. Both academic and trade publications can be accessed via the Internet, using search engines, such as Google and Google Scholar, and research databases, such as ProQuest and Academic Search Premier.[14] Government agencies, such as the U.S. Environmental Protection Agency,[15] are excellent sources of trustworthy information, especially regarding laws, regulations, and aggregate industry data. NGOs, such as the World Business Council for Sustainable Development,[16] also provide abundant sustainability information, and they tend to have strong presences on the World Wide Web. Finally, research firms and consultancies, such as the Hartman Group[17] and RiskMetrics Group,[18] offer specialized research reports at a price.

VIRTUAL FIELD TRIP

Digging Deep in the Information Gold Mine

Take a plunge into cyberspace and discover some of the available secondary sources for information about measurement in sustainable marketing. Combine the search terms "sustainability" and "metrics," with the name of any industry, such as "tourism," "jewelry," or "packaging." Now search the same combination of terms on Google Web, Google Scholar, and a research database, such as ABI/Inform. How do the results differ?

Without a doubt, the single-most important tool for secondary research is the Internet. However, great caution should be exercised before accepting the truthfulness, completeness, or timeliness of information gleaned from the World Wide Web. Sources such as blogs and news stories can be accurate and very useful or highly biased, poorly researched, and taken out of context. Always trace information back to its original source wherever possible. Then examine the source's credibility and the methods and context in which the information was first discovered and used. Finally, compare the information with that of other credible sources.

Primary Research

When secondary research is inadequate for its needs, an organization may need to conduct primary research. You should already be somewhat familiar with the most common marketing research methods. Monitoring performance and processes usually is accomplished with internal data and a firm's information systems. Researchers use surveys for a wide range of studies, such as market segmentation and determining market potential. Product design research may couple customer surveys with analytical methods such as conjoint analysis.[19] Firms use focus groups to test products and positioning concepts. Other qualitative methods, such as in-depth interviews and observation, allow deeper understanding of customer behaviors and experiences.

Much of the primary research in the area of sustainable marketing focuses on the attitudes and behaviors of consumers. In January 2009, the Hartman Group released a major study of this type titled, "Sustainability: The Rise of Consumer Responsibility." To profile American consumers, the Hartman Group used a combination of both quantitative survey methods and in-depth qualitative methods. Quantitative findings were drawn from an online survey conducted with a nationally representative sample of over 1,800 U.S. consumers. For its qualitative data, the Hartman Group conducted more than 100 hours of ethnographic interviews in consumers' homes and in retail settings.[20]

Individual companies conduct sustainability-related research in order to improve products and develop new ones. For example, research by Procter & Gamble revealed that the single largest carbon impact of laundry detergent came during consumer product usage and was associated with heating water. This finding led to the development of Tide Coldwater.[21]

USES AND TYPES OF SUSTAINABILITY METRICS

In order for sustainability metrics to be really useful, they must be standardized, which requires agreement across organizations and governments as to what should be measured, how it should be measured, and how it should be reported. Government regulation and public demand have spurred much of the growth in sustainability standards and metrics. Some standards are a direct result of regulations, such as the Clean Air Act. Others come about through the efforts of nongovernmental organizations. Let's take a closer look at a few of the most widely used sustainability standards and measures.

CERES and the Global Reporting Initiative

In 1989, the Coalition for Environmentally Responsible Economies (CERES), a nonprofit network of investors and NGOs, created a 10-point code of corporate environmental conduct and invited businesses to adopt it as a form of environmental mission or ethic. The CERES principles, which have been adopted by more than 50 companies, including several of the Fortune 500, are:

Protection of the Biosphere

We will reduce and make continual progress toward eliminating the release of any substance that may cause environmental damage to the air, water, or the earth or its inhabitants. We will safeguard all habitats affected by our operations and will protect open spaces and wilderness, while preserving biodiversity.

Sustainable Use of Natural Resources

We will make sustainable use of renewable natural resources, such as water, soils and forests. We will conserve non-renewable natural resources through efficient use and careful planning.

Reduction and Disposal of Wastes

We will reduce and where possible eliminate waste through source reduction and recycling. All waste will be handled and disposed of through safe and responsible methods.

Energy Conservation

We will conserve energy and improve the energy efficiency of our internal operations and of the goods and services we sell. We will make every effort to use environmentally safe and sustainable energy sources.

Risk Reduction

We will strive to minimize the environmental, health and safety risks to our employees and the communities in which we operate through safe technologies, facilities and operating procedures, and by being prepared for emergencies.

Safe Products and Services

We will reduce and where possible eliminate the use, manufacture or sale of products and services that cause environmental damage or health or safety hazards. We will inform our customers of the environmental impacts of our products or services and try to correct unsafe use.

Environmental Restoration

We will promptly and responsibly correct conditions we have caused that endanger health, safety or the environment. To the extent feasible, we will redress injuries we have caused to persons or damage we have caused to the environment and will restore the environment.

Informing the Public

We will inform in a timely manner everyone who may be affected by conditions caused by our company that might endanger health, safety or the environment. We will regularly seek advice and counsel through dialogue with persons in communities near our facilities. We will not take any action against employees for reporting dangerous incidents or conditions to management or to appropriate authorities.

Management Commitment

We will implement these Principles and sustain a process that ensures that the Board of Directors and Chief Executive Officer are fully informed about pertinent environmental issues and are fully responsible for environmental policy. In selecting our Board of Directors, we will consider demonstrated environmental commitment as a factor.

Audits and Reports

We will conduct an annual self-evaluation of our progress in implementing these Principles. We will support the timely creation of generally accepted environmental audit procedures. We will annually complete the Ceres Report, which will be made available to the public."[22]

CERES extended its influence and partnered with the United Nations Environmental Programme (UNEP) in 1997 to create the Global Reporting Initiative (GRI). The GRI pioneered the development of what has become "the world's most widely used sustainability reporting framework."[23] A hallmark of the GRI is its commitment to continuous improvement and the development of guidelines over time. GRI regularly revises its guidelines "through a consensus-seeking process with participants drawn globally from business, civil society, labor, and professional institutions."[24]

GRI guidelines focus on both what to report and how to report. Its guidelines currently include 87 performance metrics, covering the full range of triple-bottom-line concerns, and are free to any organization that wishes to use them.[25] For example, one department of the federal government that is moving toward sustainability and measuring its progress is the U.S. Army (see Figure 6-1). "The Army's 2007 Sustainability Report marks the first time a U.S. government agency reports its sustainability measure using the framework and indicators established under the Global Reporting Initiative."[26] The Army released this report to "inform and engage the Army's primary shareholders on their progress to embody the principles of sustainability."[27]

ISO 14000 and EMAS

Whereas the GRI covers both environmental and social interests as found in most corporate social responsibility initiatives, its standards, including ISO 14000 and the European Union's Eco-Management and Audit Scheme (EMAS), focus primarily on environmental standards.[28] Based in Switzerland, the International Organization for Standardization (ISO) is a network of national standards institutes of 161 countries. ISO membership includes business, industry, engineering, and NGO experts. ISO's declared goal is to meet the needs of both business and society[29] by attempting to harmonize several independent standards, such as the criteria for eco-labeling of consumer products.[30] (Uses and benefits of eco-labeling standards will be addressed in Chapter 9.) ISO 14000 standards adoption is useful for firms hoping to improve their environmental responsibility. Some scholars suggest it may also be a marketing opportunity, helping to positively influence purchase decisions of "green consumers" who want environmental-friendly products.[31]

FIGURE 6-1 The U.S. Army is serious about measuring its progress toward sustainability.

Army FY07 Sustainability Highlights

Released the first Army-wide Annual Sustainability Report—first of any major U.S. Federal Agency using the GRI sustainability reporting framework

Sixteen Army installations with comprehensive Installation Sustainability Plans in place

78% (301) of FY07 Army Military Construction projects designed to at least U.S. Green Building Council's LEED® new construction certification standards

FY04–FY07 Environmental Performance Trends

✤ 100% (161) installations with an Environmental Management System (EMS) in place with 31% in conformance to ISO14001

✤ 8.4% reduction in facility energy use intensity (KBtu/gross square foot/per year, since FY03)

✤ 35% increase in Hazardous Waste (HW) generation as reported for CY03 to CY06 and an 8% increase in pounds HW generated per $1000 net Army cost of operations

✤ 11% increase in absolute Toxic Release Inventory (TRI) releases as reported for CY03 to CY06, but a 13% decrease in pounds TRI released per $1000 net Army cost of operations

FY04–FY07 Soldier and Community Well-being Performance Trends

✤ 3% and 18% increases in total Army retention and recruitment, respectively

✤ Held steady military accident fatalities rate per 1000 service members

✤ 62% decrease in Army civilian lost time injuries and fatalities rate per 1000 civilians

A similar standard developed for Europeans (EMAS) is a voluntary initiative for European Union members. EMAS's main purpose is to provide "a management tool for companies and other organizations to evaluate, report, and improve their environmental performance."[32] In 2009, in an attempt to strengthen the influence of EMAS standards, the European Parliament went so far as to suggest that European government agencies should: "Consider how registration under EMAS may be taken into account in the development of legislation or used as a tool in the enforcement of legislation. They should also, in order to raise the appeal of EMAS for organisations, take account of EMAS in their procurement policies and, where appropriate, refer to EMAS or equivalent environmental management systems as contract performance conditions for works and service."[33]

Sustainability Audits

Standards for measuring environmental responsibility are constantly changing.[34] Firms looking to build credibility and win public confidence often turn to certified, independent third parties for comprehensive **sustainability audits**.[35] For example, AccountAbility assesses sustainability reports based on three principles:

- Materiality: Does the sustainability report provide an account covering all the areas of performance that stakeholders need to judge the organization's sustainability performance?
- Completeness: Is the information complete and accurate enough to assess and understand the organization's performance in all these areas?
- Responsiveness: Has the organization responded coherently and consistently to stakeholders' concerns and interests?[36]

Company Metrics and Scorecards

Often an organization's sustainability measurement objectives can't be fully met by existing standards and metrics. When this is the case, companies may develop their own internal metrics. For example, SC Johnson subjects all products to its internal Greenlist process, which gives every ingredient a score based on environmental attributes including toxicity and biodegradability. "SC Johnson has evaluated over 3,000 raw materials—far more than the federal government has regulated under its toxic laws."[37] SC Johnson's Greenlist metrics are used primarily for the internal management of product sustainability improvements.

Nike has developed its Considered Design Index for internal sustainable-product development purposes (see Figure 6-2). The index assigns scores or metrics to preproduction product designs based on solvent use, waste, materials, innovation, and garment treatments.[38] According to a 2008 report, "The overall Considered Design Index is now being integrated into accountability systems to be evaluated alongside cost and performance in the design process."[39] Author Adam Werback reports that, "Nike has committed to having 100 percent of its footwear meet baseline Considered standards by 2011. This equates to real numbers. That's a 20 percent increase in environmentally preferred materials. A 17 percent reduction in waste. And maintaining their reduction of volatile organic compounds—VOCs—at 95 percent."[40]

Other companies may develop standards to guide internal processes such as procurement and to influence suppliers to develop more sustainable products. For example, in November 2006, Wal-Mart revealed a "packaging **scorecard**" aimed at saving money and reducing the environmental impact of packaging throughout its global supply chain. The scorecard is a measurement tool comprising multiple indicators created by a "Packaging Sustainable Value Network," which includes Wal-Mart managers, suppliers, and leaders in the global packaging industry. Based on Wal-Mart's "7 R's of Packaging" (remove, reduce, reuse, recycle, renew, revenue, and read), the network established criteria for the packaging scorecard that included GHG (CO_2) production, product-to-package ratios, cube utilization (compactness), transportation, amounts of recycled content, materials recovery value, use of renewable energy, and levels of innovation.[41]

The scorecards criteria were designed to allow suppliers to compare their packaging-sustainability performance with that of peers and competitors. Suppliers receive overall scores relative to other suppliers, as well as scores in each category. For support in using the scorecard, Wal-Mart offered suppliers online demonstrations, such as a Packaging Supplier Virtual Trade Show. Use of the scorecard began with a one-year trial and learning period, after which it became mandatory for all suppliers.[42]

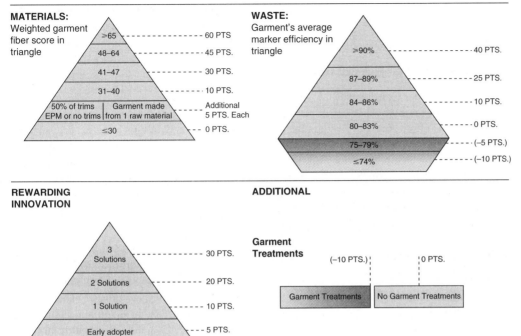

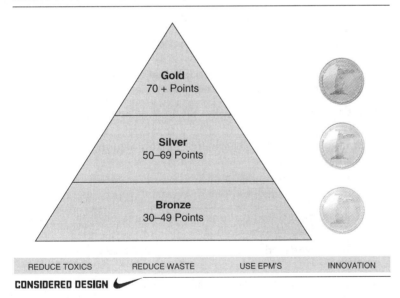

FIGURE 6-2 Nike, an industry leader in sustainable practices, is developing sustainability scorecards to track it own progress and to monitor suppliers.

THINK ABOUT IT

Who Wins with the Scorecard?

What are the advantages to Wal-Mart of instituting a packaging scorecard among its suppliers? What are the possible advantages to customers? Are there advantages for the suppliers themselves? Are there disadvantages? How important was it that Wal-Mart engaged other stakeholders (the Packaging Sustainable Value Network) in the scorecard development process?

Wal-Mart is expanding its scorecard concept from packaging to core products. With the help of a consortium jointly administered by Arizona State University and the University of

Arkansas, the company is developing product-sustainability scorecards intended to cover a wide spectrum of the goods it sells. As part of its comprehensive effort toward overall organizational sustainability, the company is asking its 60,000 suppliers to measure the environmental impact of their products using the sustainability scorecards.[43]

Monitoring the Green Economy

The U.S. Consumer Confidence Index is a measure of American consumers' confidence in the economy. It is used by businesses in planning things like inventories and production, especially of expensive durable goods. A similar measure, called the Green Confidence Index, has been devised to take the pulse of consumers' confidence in the green economy. According to GreenBiz.com, which helped develop the metric, "The Green Confidence Index builds on the rich tradition of index scores, tracking changes in marketplace perceptions, and highlighting shifts in market confidence as bellwethers of future intentions. It's the first to focus specifically on environmental beliefs and behaviors and is the only such study conducted monthly to provide an ongoing, real-time gauge of the evolving green economy."[44]

Life-Cycle Assessment

Companies need to account for the environmental impact of products-in-use as well as the ease of composting, reuse, or recyclability once the consumer disposes of the product.[45] The comprehensive analysis of a product's impact throughout all aspects of design, manufacture, use, and final disposition is called a **life-cycle assessment** (LCA).[46] LCA is a common feature of many companies' sustainability programs.[47] LCA analyzes raw material acquisition; materials manufacture; production; use, reuse and maintenance; and waste management.[48]

THINK ABOUT IT

Paper or Plastic?

Which is a better choice at the grocery store, a paper bag or a plastic one? LCA helps to answer that question. Here's a simplified version of the LCA:

> *The paper bag:* Trees → Logs Trucks → Pulp and Paper Mills → Truck → Store → Landfill
>
> *The plastic bag:* Oil → Ship → Refinery → Manufacturing → Warehouse → Truck → Store → Landfill.

Important considerations for the LCA:

- Paper is much heavier than plastic, so transportation is more important.
- Plastic takes a sequestered carbon (fossil fuels) and puts it into another carbon sequestration location (the landfill).
- Paper takes sequestered carbon (the forest) and converts it into methane (in the landfill).

The result: Unrecycled paper bags are 2 to 10 times more polluting in terms of GHGs than plastic bags, but neither is sustainable. The best solution: A reusable cloth or plastic grocery bag. Use it once a week, save 33kgs CO_2 per year over paper bags, and help keep tons of plastic out of landfills.[49]

The illustration (see Figure 6-3) deals strictly with the life cycle of a bag in terms of atmospheric carbon, meaning that its analysis is restricted to only one aspect of the first system condition as put forth by The Natural Step Framework (see Chapter 2). A more thorough LCA would take into account a product's impact on all four of the system conditions.

Metrics for Everyone

Measurements also exist to help consumers manage their own environmental impacts. **Carbon footprint calculators** help individuals, households, and organizations estimate how many tons of carbon dioxide and other GHGs they create each year.[50] In one year, the average American

(a)

**Life Cycle Thinking at Home:
Paper vs. Plastic Grocery Bags**

FIGURE 6-3 (a) LCA Paper Vs. Plastic Grocery Bags, (b) LCA Plastic Bag, (c) Paper VS Plastic Comparison, (d) Reusable Plastic Bag

CH_4 emission

(b) **Plastic Bags**

No emissions

(c) **Paper vs. Plastic**

- Paper is much heavier than plastic, so transport is more important

- Plastic takes sequestered carbon (fossil fuels) and puts it into another carbon sequestration location (the landfill)

- Paper takes sequestered carbon (the forest) and converts it into methane (in the landfill)

- Result: Paper grocery bags are 2 to 10 times more polluting than plastic bags

FIGURE 6-3 *(Continued)*

(d)

**Best Solution
Reused Plastic Grocery Bags**

■ Use it once a week, save 33 kgs CO_2 per year over paper bags

household could save 1,000 pounds of carbon dioxide by recycling glass, plastic, and paper; 800 pounds by taking the bus to work instead of driving; 720 pounds by line-drying half its laundry loads instead of using the dryer; 700 pounds by maintaining its refrigerator door seal and keeping its coils clean; and 55 pounds for each replacement of a 75-watt incandescent light bulb with a 20-watt compact fluorescent[51] (see Figure 6-4).

THINK ABOUT IT

According to an article in the Christian Science Monitor, "American meat eaters are responsible for 1.5 more tons of carbon dioxide per person than vegetarians every year. . . . Livestock are a major emitter of greenhouse gases that cause climate change. . . . It's not just the well-known and frequently joked-about flatulence and manure of grass-chewing cattle that's the problem, according to a recent report by the Food and Agriculture Organization of the United Nations (FAO). Land-use changes, especially deforestation to expand pastures and to create arable land for feed crops, are a big part. So is the use of energy to produce fertilizers, to run the slaughterhouses and meat-processing plants, and to pump water.... Livestock are responsible for 18 percent of greenhouse-gas emissions as measured in carbon dioxide equivalent. . . . This includes 9 percent of all CO_2 emissions, 37 percent of methane, and 65 percent of nitrous oxide. Altogether, that's more than the emissions caused by transportation."[52]

If all the people in the world consumed meat like Americans, what would be the effect on the atmosphere? Does this mean we should all be vegetarians? Is it possible to enjoy meat in more sustainable ways? How? Are there more sustainable approaches to raising livestock than current practices? What might those look like?

Some tools are designed specifically to help consumers make more sustainable purchases. One example is the GoodGuide, a computer application that allows consumers to access detailed ratings for health, environment, and social responsibility for over 50,000 products. GoodGuide compares data in over 300 databases relating to over a thousand criteria in areas like chemical ingredients, factory conditions, industrial-sector performance, and national laws and regulations. The GoodGuide methodology uses a wide variety of metrics including:

- absolute measures, which account for the total impacts of company or product, such as total tons of carbon emissions or total dollars donated to humanitarian relief;
- relative measures, which grade performance on interval scales such as one-to-ten or bad-to-excellent; and

FIGURE 6-4 Eco-footprint measures help demonstrate the relative impacts of lifestyles in different cultures. In the United States, it takes 12.2 acres to supply the average person's basic needs; in the Netherlands, 8 acres; in India, 1 acre. The Dutch ecological footprint covers 15 times the area of the Netherlands, whereas India's footprint exceeds its area by only about 35%. Most strikingly, if the entire world lived like North Americans, it would take three planet Earths to support the present world population.

**Chad was oblivious to the fact that he
had a very large carbon footprint.**

- binary (yes/no) measures, which indicate whether or not a product or company exhibits specific characteristics or practices, such as particular third-party certifications or policies regarding animal testing.

From its many measures, GoodGuide creates standardized ratings so that consumers can compare them meaningfully across products and brands (see Figure 6-5). Plans for the service also include features that will allow users to create personal ratings based on their own values and priorities.[53]

CRITICAL THINKING ACTIVITY

Calculate Your Own Carbon Footprint

Calculate your own carbon footprint using one of the calculators commonly found on the Internet. Check out www.safeclimate.net, http://www.carbonfootprint.com/calculator.aspx, http://www.climatecrisis.net/takeaction/carboncalculator/, or any other sites you find.

Now, find a different a Web site calculator and recalculate your footprint. Is it the same? Why or why not? (Hint: Compare the questions for depth and variety.) Calculate your carbon footprint once more, using a different calculator you found on the Web. Does it match one of the other two you used? How can you reconcile the difference? How does your consumption compare with the national average? Finally, what could you do to reduce your own carbon footprint?

Chapter Summary

The superior use of information is an important source of competitive advantage. Better information use leads to more effective strategies, more efficient processes, and more sustainable products and operations. Sustainable, effective marketing strategies benefit from research and metrics in several ways. Appropriate metrics help managers to assess market opportunities, select target markets, develop effective marketing programs, and monitor performance. Internal reporting of metrics helps organizations improve. External reporting assists stakeholders in making decisions regarding investment and collaboration. This chapter points to a wide range of secondary sources for sustainability information and metrics, and it highlights the importance of primary research. Finally, it discusses some of the most widely used metrics for benchmarking and assessing the sustainability of entire organizations and of individual products from design and manufacture through marketing, distribution, use, and final disposition.

FIGURE 6-5 There's an app for that. Good Guide creates standardized sustainability ratings so that consumers can make meaningful comparisons.

Review of Chapter Objectives

- The importance of measurement
- Principles for measurement in sustainable marketing
- Uncovering information
- Uses and types of sustainability metrics

Key Concepts

Research	Internal Reporting	Performance Indicators	Scorecard
Measurement	External Reporting	Substantive Information	Life-Cycle Assessment
Metrics	Higher-Order Scales	Methodological Information	Carbon Footprint Calculators
Baseline Performance	Benchmarks	Sustainability Audits	

Endnotes

1. *Reuters* (2009), "EU to Introduce New Indicator to Complement GDP," September 8, http://www.wSebcsd.org/plugins/DocSearch/details.asp?type=DocDet&ObjectId=MzU2MDE, accessed September 17, 2009.

2. Gross National Happiness, The Centre for Bhutan Studies, http://www.grossnationalhappiness.com/, accessed September 25, 2010.

3. Cobb, Clifford, Gary Sue Goodman, and Mathis Wackernagel (1999), *Why Bigger Isn't Better: The Genuine Progress*

Indicator—1999 Update, San Francisco, CA: Redefining Progress.

4. Meadows, Donella (1998), "Indicators and Information Systems for Sustainable Development," A report to the Balaton Group, published by the Sustainability Institute, http://publications.ksu.edu.sa/Conferences/Sustainable%20Development%20Strategies%202002/Donella.pdf, accessed August 12, 2009.

5. Porter, Michael E. (1998), *Competitive Advantage: Creating and Sustaining Superior Performance*, New York: Simon & Schuster.

6. Epstein, Marc J. (2008), *Making Sustainability Work: Best Practices in Managing and Measuring Corporate Social, Environmental, and Economic Impacts*, San Francisco, CA: Berrett-Koehler Publishers.

7. Epstein, Marc J. (2008), *Making Sustainability Work: Best Practices in Managing and Measuring Corporate Social, Environmental, and Economic Impacts*, San Francisco: Berrett-Koehler Publishers (p. 24).

8. Sony Ericsson, 2008 Sustainability Report, http://www.sonyericsson.com/cws/download/1/647/105/1247572946/Sony_Ericsson_Sustainability_Report_2008.pdf, accessed February 26, 2010.

9. Jaeger, William K. (2005), *Environmental Economics for Tree Huggers and Other Skeptics*, Washington D.C.: Island Press (p.1).

10. World Business Council for Sustainable Development (2008), Case Study: IBM Enterprise Energy Management System, http://www.wbcsd.org, accessed August 11, 2009.

11. Kurani, Ken (2007), "Impact of In-Car Instruments on Driver Behaviour," IEA, ITF Eco-Drive Workshop, Paris, November, http://www.internationaltransportforum.org/Proceedings/eco-driving/4-02Kurani.pdf, accessed August 13, 2009.

12. Epstein, Marc J. (2008), *Making Sustainability Work: Best Practices in Managing and Measuring Corporate Social, Environmental, and Economic Impacts*, San Francisco, CA: Berrett-Koehler Publishers (p. 36).

13. GE Citizenship, Priorities and Engagement, Commitments and Progress, 2008 Commitments, http://www.ge.com/citizenship/priorities_engagement/energy_and_climate_change_cp.jsp.

14. Research databases typically are available online through libraries at universities or other institutions. Check your school library's Web site and see what databases are available to you.

15. U.S. Environmental Protection Agency, Sustainability, http://www.epa.gov/Sustainability/, accessed August 12, 2009.

16. World Business Council for Sustainable Development, http://www.wbcsd.org, accessed August 12, 2009.

17. Hartman Group, http://www.hartman-group.com/, accessed August 12, 2009.

18. RiskMetrics Group, ESG Analytics, http://www.riskmetrics.com/sustainability, accessed August 12, 2009.

19. Quick MBA, Marketing, Conjoint Analysis, http://www.quickmba.com/marketing/research/conjoint/, accessed August 12, 2009.

20. Hartman Group Publications, "Sustainability: The Rise of Consumer Responsibility," http://www.hartman-group.com/publications/view/81, accessed September 23, 2009.

21. Werbach, Adam (2009), *Strategy for Sustainability: A Business Manifesto,* Boston, MA: Harvard Business Press (p. 78).

22. CERES, http://www.ceres.org/Page.aspx?pid=416, accessed August 6, 2009.

23. Global Reporting Initiative, Reporting Framework Downloads, http://www.globalreporting.org/ReportingFramework/ReportingFrameworkDownloads/, accessed August 6, 2009.

24. Global Reporting Initiative, Reporting Framework Downloads, http://www.globalreporting.org/ReportingFramework/ReportingFrameworkDownloads/, accessed August 6, 2009.

25. U.S. Army, Sustainability, News & Events, http://www.sustainability.army.mil/news/news.cfm, accessed August 6, 2009.

26. U.S. Army, Sustainability, News & Events, http://www.sustainability.army.mil/news/news.cfm, accessed August 6, 2009.

27. U.S. Army, Sustainability, News & Events, http://www.sustainability.army.mil/news/news.cfm, accessed August 6, 2009.

28. GRI Reporting, http://www.esprojects.net/attachment/f884d384a217c98c4bfa49875a2f02d9/97bfb39f57e0da93671d8416d729d695/presentation_GRI_nina.doc, accessed August 12, 2009.

29. International Organization for Standards, http://www.iso.org/iso/about.htm, accessed August 6, 2009.

30. Wasik, John F. (1996), *Green Marketing and Management: A Global Perspective,* Cambridge, MA: Blackwell Publishers, Inc.

31. D' Souza, Clare (2004), "ISO 14000 Standards: An Environmental Solution or a Marketing Opportunity?" *Electronic Green Journal,* 1 (20), Article 4.

32. EU Eco-Management and Audit Scheme (EMAS), http://ec.europa.eu/environment/emas/index_en.htm, accessed August 6, 2009.

33. European Parliament (2009), Regulation of the European Parliament and of the Council on the Voluntary Participation by Organisations in a Community EcoManagement and Audit Scheme (EMAS), Repealing Regulation (Ec) No 761/2001 and Commission Decisions 2001/681/Ec and 2006/193/Ec.

34. Wasik, John F. (1996), *Green Marketing and Management: A Global Perspective,* Cambridge, MA: Blackwell Publishers, Inc.

35. Ottman, Jacquelyn A. (1998), *Green Marketing: Opportunity for Innovation,* New York: J. Ottman Consulting, Inc.

36. Epstein, Marc J. (2008), *Making Sustainability Work: Best Practices in Managing and Measuring Corporate Social, Environmental, and Economic Impacts*, San Francisco, CA: Berrett-Koehler Publishers (p. 236).

37. Esty, Daniel C. and Winston, Andrew S. (2006), *Green to Gold: How Smart Companies Use Environmental Strategy to Innovate, Create Value, and Build Competitive Advantage*, New Haven, CT: Yale University Press (p. 118).

38. NikeBiz, Nike Responsibility, Considered Design, The Considered Index, http://www.nikebiz.com/responsibility/considered_design/considered_index.html, accessed February 27, 2010.

39. Business for Social Responsibility and IDEO (2008), "Aligned for Sustainable Design: An A-B-C-D Approach to Making Better Products, " http://www.bsr.org/reports/BSR_Sustainable_Design_Report_0508.pdf accessed June 2, 2008.

40. Werbach, Adam (2009), *Strategy for Sustainability: A Business Manifesto,* Boston, MA: Harvard Business Press (p. 107).

41. Wal-Mart, Corporate, Press Room, "Wal-Mart Unveils Packaging Scorecard to Suppliers," http://walmartstores.com/FactsNews/NewsRoom/6039.aspx, accessed February 27, 2010.

42. Wal-Mart, Corporate, Press Room, "Wal-Mart Unveils Packaging Scorecard to Suppliers," http://walmartstores.com/FactsNews/NewsRoom/6039.aspx, accessed September 23, 2009.

43. Rosenbloom, Stephanie (2009), "At Wal-Mart, Labeling to Reflect Green Intent," *New York Times,* July 15, http://www.nytimes.com/2009/07/16/business/energy-environment/16walmart.html?_r=3, accessed August 12, 2009.

44. GreenBiz, Green Confidence Index, http://www.greenbiz.com/greenconfidence, accessed December 27, 2009.

45. Kleiner, A. (1991), "What Does It Mean To Be Green?" *Harvard Business Review*, 69 (5): 38–47.

46. Keoleian, G., & Menerey, D. (1993), *Life Cycle Design Guidance Manual*, Cincinnati, OH: Environmental Protection Agency.

47. Hart, Stuart L. (1995), "A Natural-Resource-Based View of the Firm," *Academy of Management Review*, 20 (4): 986–1015.

48. Scientific Applications International Corporation (SAIC) (2006), "Life Cycle Assessment: Principles and Practice," http://www.epa.gov/NRMRL/lcaccess/pdfs/600r06060.pdf, accessed August 12, 2009.

49. Schenck, Rita (2008), "Life Cycle Assessment and Sustainable Food Systems," Institute for Environmental Research and Education, http://www.iere.org/index.html

50. The Nature Conservancy, "Our Initiatives, Get Started, Carbon Footprint Calculator," http://www.nature.org/initiatives/climatechange/calculator/, accessed August 12, 2009.

51. *National Geographic*, Features, "The Big Thaw: How to Help" http://ngm.nationalgeographic.com/2007/06/big-thaw/how-to-help, accessed August 12, 2009.

52. Knickerbocker, Brad (2007), "Humans' Beef with Livestock: A Warmer Planet," *Christian Science Monitor*, http://www.csmonitor.com/2007/0220/p03s01-ussc.html, accessed August 5, 2009.

53. "Green Marketing in the Age of Transparency," GreenBiz.com February 09, 2010 http://www.greenbiz.com/video/2010/02/09/green-marketing-age-transparency#ixzz0kdcebKNk http://www.greenbiz.com/video/2010/02/09/green-marketing-age-transparency, and GoodGuide's Methodology, GoodGuide, http://www.goodguide.com/about/methodology, accessed September 10, 2010.

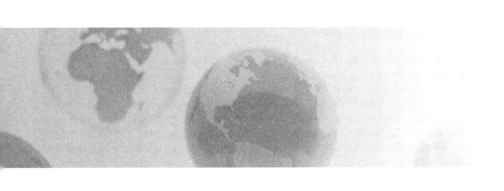

Market Segmentation, Targeting, and Positioning for Sustainability

INTRODUCTION: LEGOMANIACS

In 2003, LEGO was the first (and until 2008 it remained the only) toy company to have signed on to the United Nations Global Compact,[1] which is described as "a strategic policy initiative for businesses that are committed to aligning their operations and strategies with ten universally accepted principles in the areas of human rights, labour, environment and anti-corruption."[2] A key component of LEGO's mission is building human capital globally through child development.

If someone were to ask the question, "Who is the market for LEGO building blocks?" the fast and easy answer would be children. But that answer would be at best partially right. And in many important ways it would be utterly wrong. LEGO owes much of the vitality and profitability of its products and company to adult users.[3] In the early 1990s, adult fans of LEGO went from being a mostly invisible market segment to an organized, trademarked, and influential market force.[4] Currently, adult fans manage entire online communities (e.g., LUGNET)[5] and local clubs (e.g., Tucson LEGO Club)[6] all over the world.

LEGOfan.org sponsors official LEGO ambassadors, who are expected "to be active contributors to the LEGO world-wide community"[7] by engaging in activities such as fan-to-fan support in online forums, active participation with local LEGO clubs, new club formation, leadership in online communities, article writing and publication online and offline, and presentations at LEGO-related events and conferences.

At this point, we might conclude that the market is segmented into two demographic groups, children and adults, right? Not so fast. It turns out that the adult market is fragmented into smaller segments based on special interests as diverse as trains,[8] medieval life,[9] modern architecture[10] and zombies![11] To better experience the remarkable range of interests of LEGO users, visit YouTube and search LEGO.

THINK ABOUT IT

Market Fragmentation and the Internet

According to Chris Anderson, editor in chief of *Wired* and author of *The Long Tail*,[12] the power of the Internet to provide virtually anything to anybody anywhere has allowed markets to fragment into millions of tiny niches. Market niches (such as train-loving fans of LEGO) can become profitable for marketers because they can be identified and reached with very specific products, services, and messages with relative ease and little cost.

What does this fragmentation mean for traditional assumptions about market segmentation and market potential? Will Internet-based businesses, such as Amazon, with their ability to offer an unlimited variety of goods, ultimately make traditional marketers, such as bookstores, obsolete? Why or why not? What kinds of marketing ventures are possible now that couldn't have survived before the Internet? What kinds of opportunities does the Internet provide for more sustainable marketing? Are there implications for reduced waste? Reduced energy use? Product reuse or recycling?

CHAPTER OBJECTIVES

Devising a marketing strategy typically involves segmentation, targeting, and positioning. Companies segment markets in order to account for different customer wants and needs. Companies then choose to target one or more market segments that they can serve competitively. Finally, companies position their offerings by crafting marketing mixes and communicating to appeal distinctively to their target segments. In this chapter, you will explore:

- The emerging green market
- Segmenting the green market
- Positioning for sustainability
- Taking the green position in the business-to-business sector

THE EMERGING GREEN MARKET

As businesses desire to improve the sustainability of their products and practices, they often seek to identify customers who will be receptive to more sustainable products and, if possible, who will pay a premium for them. The term **green market** is commonly used to distinguish sustainability-oriented consumers and the businesses that serve them.

One of the most powerful cultural trends driving branding today is a worldwide shift in consumers' attitudes toward environmental sustainability. This is true the world over. Citing major studies from 2007 and 2008,[13] the World Business Council for Sustainable Development reports that:

> 96% of Europeans say that protecting the environment is important for them personally. Two-thirds of this group say that it is "very important". . . . Consumers in most countries are becoming more aware and willing to act on environmental concerns. The US had the largest rise of all, from 57% in 2007 to 80% in 2008. Chinese consumers also showed increased willingness to act on their concerns about climate change.[14]

The size of the green market is debatable and depends on definitions. One fact, however, is not debatable: The green market is growing. The Hartman Group is a research firm that tracks consumer sustainability trends. Its 2008 report[15] noted, among other things, that over 90 percent of consumers want to participate in sustainability; that only about half of them believe they understand what sustainability is; and that they expect companies to take leadership and responsibility for it. In addition, the Hartman report found that sustainability matters most to consumers when it affects them closely and personally, such as in food or personal care items.

Another research firm, GfK Roper, creates an annual Green Gauge report for businesses interested in tracking the attitudes and behaviors of the green market. Its 2008 report[16] also confirmed continued growth in the numbers of Americans that are concerned about sustainability. Among other things, it found that 72 percent of Americans (an annual increase of 10%) claimed a fair amount of knowledge about environmental issues; 28 percent (a 20% increase from 2007) said they seek out environmental information; green purchases were most common when they resulted in money savings; increasing percentages of consumers were buying more sustainable products even though they cost more; and almost a third of all Americans felt they should be doing more for the environment. The 2008 Green Gauge report also found that environmental concerns and green behaviors have become a primary topic of conversation in a majority of U.S. households, and that the information flows not only from parents to children, but also from children to parents.

THINK ABOUT IT

In your household, how often do environmental issues enter into discussion? Which members of your household are most likely to initiate such discussions? From where do they get their information?

SEGMENTING THE GREEN MARKET

Segmenting markets allows firms to target marketing programs directly to those who are most likely to buy. This also holds true for the green market. Consumers who are interested in more sustainable goods and services are far from being homogeneous. Understanding the differences among them requires various approaches to market segmentation.

Traditional market segmentation relies on a variety of assumptions. One such assumption is that individuals who share common **demographic** characteristics, such as age, sex, and ethnicity, will desire similar products. Unfortunately, except in terms of very broad tendencies, demographics are limited for identifying target segments for sustainable marketing. Imagine two people of the same age, sex, and race who live next door to each other. Demographically they are identical. Now imagine that one of them favors country music and Wrangler jeans, cares deeply about wilderness issues, and has no real awareness of global poverty. The neighbor listens to progressive punk, collects body piercings, is passionate about social equality, and hates the very idea of being stranded outside of a metropolitan area. In some product categories they may have similar preferences, but in others, they will be vastly different. How and why they relate to sustainability will also vary widely.

Within any demographic group, the range of psychological needs, values, attitudes, lifestyles, and aesthetic preferences is potentially enormous. Such variations are better captured with **psychographic** measures. Psychographic criteria tend to be more useful than demographics for identifying differences in consumers' environmental and social priorities.[17] In fact, the majority of published segmentation schemes are based on psychographic measures.

Lifestyle segmentation, one form of psychographics, focuses on overall patterns of consumer choices and behavior. One of the simplest forms of lifestyle segmentation divides the green market into two broad categories. **Primary conservationists** are people who make major changes in their lives in an effort to reduce consumption. **Secondary conservationists** don't change their basic consumption patterns, but they seek to offset their impact through reusing, recycling, and the use of developing technologies.[18]

THINK ABOUT IT

Who Buys What?

What kinds of goods and services are most likely to appeal to primary conservationists? What kinds of products are more appropriate for secondary conservationists? Why?

In a 2009 report,[19] the Hartman Group presented another psychographic segmentation scheme for the green market. Hartman described four segments of "The World of Sustainability," which differ based on their levels of concern for social and environmental issues and the frequency and intensity of their pro-sustainability behaviors (see Figure 7-1). The "core" consumer segment displays the highest levels of involvement in a sustainability lifestyle, including such behaviors as purchasing environmentally friendly products and the strictest adherence to pro-sustainability attitudes. The "inner mid-level" and "outer mid-level"

FIGURE 7-1   The Hartman Group's "World of Sustainability" segments consumers according to their knowledge of and commitment to sustainability principles.

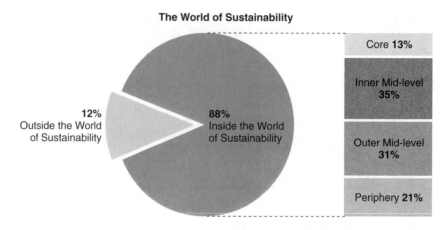

segments demonstrate progressively less commitment to sustainability and fewer related behaviors. The segment Hartman calls the "periphery" displays only minimal concern for social and environmental sustainability. The 12 percent of consumers who live outside of Hartman's "world of sustainability" say that they rarely, if ever, factor social or ecological factors into their purchase decisions.

GfK Roper is another organization that conducts segmentation research in the area of consumers and environmental sustainability. Roper's 2008 Green Gauge report divided the population into the following six segments:

- Genuine Greens (17%)—environmental activists, committed to pro-environmental behavior. They perceive no barriers to action.
- Not Me Greens (21%)—environmental believers, daunted by the perception that most issues are too big to handle. Their behaviors lag behind their attitudes and tend to be limited to convenient actions like recycling.
- Go-With-the-Flow Greens (16%)—environmental moderates, likely to do easy things, like curbside recycling, but without much real concern. They tend not to relate to problems like global warming.
- Dream Greens (13%)—environmentally friendly but naïve. They would behave more sustainably if they knew how and why to do so.
- Business First Greens (21%)—environmentally indifferent. They tend to think that the environment is somebody else's problem, to the extent that there is a problem, and that somebody else should deal with it.
- Mean Greens (11%)—environmental cynics and skeptics. They are likely to think environmentalism is a sham or a political conspiracy.[20]

Most segmentation schemes focus on common purchase and consumption behaviors. At least one, however, focuses on attitudes and behaviors associated with product disposition and disposal. In other words, different segments treat products differently once they are done with them. The Disposition Decision Taxonomy[21] (see Figure 7-2) shows the range of choices consumers make when disposing of a product.

Most of the common schemes for identifying sustainability-related market segments make some use of psychographics. However, other bases of segmentation, such as benefits sought, are also useful and may be combined with demographics and psychographics.

All of the above psychographic segmentation schemes attempt to categorize major chunks of the American population. In so doing, they may be too broad and general to be very useful for an individual firm, especially considering the trend toward market fragmentation described by *Wired*'s Chris Anderson (see "Think About It: Market Fragmentation and the Internet"). More accurate and relevant segmentation may well depend on a firm conducting its own research.

When companies desire to identify market segments more finely and narrowly than demographics and psychographics allow them to do, they often turn to benefit segmentation. **Benefit segmentation** identifies groups based on the combinations of benefits they desire from a particular purchase or product category.

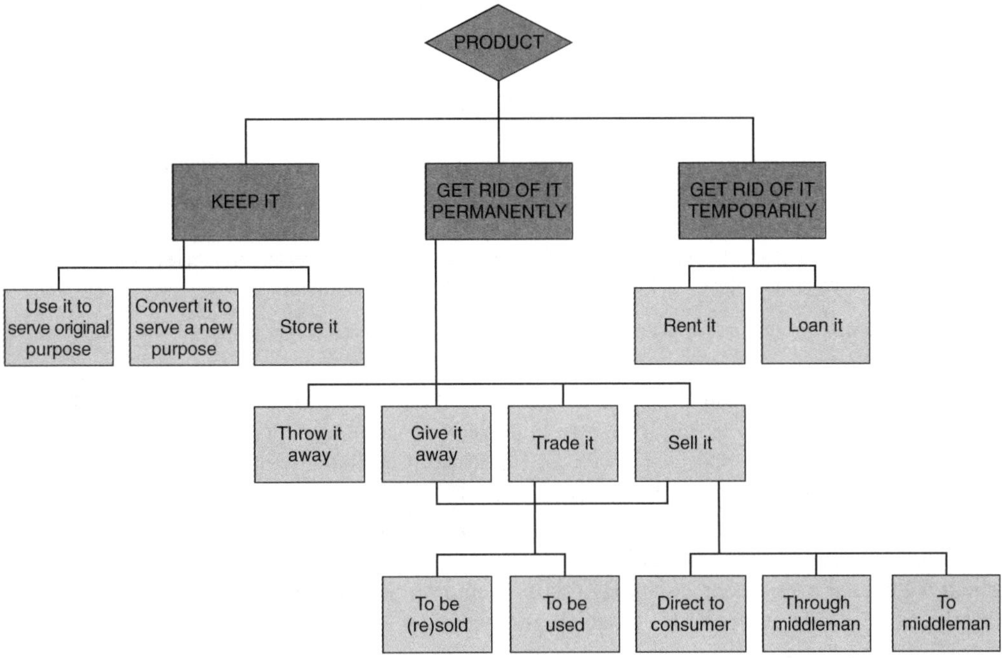

FIGURE 7-2 The Disposition Decision Taxonomy.

When consumers purchase products or services, what we are really doing is purchasing certain solutions or benefits. There are three general classes of benefit, and consumers' desire for them in different forms and combinations helps to define market segments. We value **utilitarian** or **functional benefits**[22] because they help us solve problems. We value **symbolic** or **self-expressive benefits** because of what they communicate about us to others and to ourselves. **Hedonic** or **experiential benefits**[23] are important for the qualities of the experiences they deliver.

The automobile industry uses benefit segmentation. Functional benefits include things like fuel efficiency, safety ratings, reliability, and the capacity to carry passengers and possessions. Symbolic benefits include vehicle styling and brand associations with different lifestyles or levels of status. For example, a sports car, a four-door sedan, and a pickup truck all make different kinds of statements about their owners. Even two different sedans may express very different personalities or priorities. Experiential benefits include different levels of creature comforts, audio experiences, visual stimulation, or acceleration and handling characteristics. Every vehicle has a certain **benefits profile** with respect to the three benefit categories. Benefit segmentation helps match automotive design with complex customer needs.

The market success of the Toyota Prius owes much to its benefits profile. Functionally it doesn't perform any better (and arguably worse) than many other compact cars. Symbolically, however, it became a badge of environmental awareness and action. In 2007, the *New York Times* commented on the Prius as a status symbol: ". . . buyers of the Prius want everyone to know they are driving a hybrid. . . . The Prius has become, in a sense, the four-wheel equivalent of those popular rubber "issue bracelets" in yellow and other colors—it shows the world that its owner cares."[24]

It turns out that the Prius also delivers unexpected experiential benefits. One product reviewer sums it up like this: ". . . the Prius is probably the closest you'll come to playing a video game while driving. The constant goal of maximizing your MPGs quickly makes the Prius a fun car to drive in possibly the least traditional sense of the word 'fun.' Well, get comfy in that video game chair because the Driving Mode buttons make the Prius go from being an Atari to a Wii."[25]

Other products, including very simple and mundane ones, also have identifiable benefits profiles that can be matched with appropriate market segments. For example, the functional benefits (i.e., cleaning power) of Clorox Green Works cleaners are emphasized clearly in the brand advertising. Symbolically, the product communicates caring for health and the environment, and that, in turn, may result in a consumer experiencing a heightened feeling of satisfaction. Other details, like fragrance, can add further to the experiential benefits of using the product.

THINK ABOUT IT

Sustainability and Benefit Segmentation

Can sustainable products and services be appealing to consumers at a utilitarian or functional level? If yes, how so? What problems can be solved for them? Do sustainable products or consumer behaviors provide symbolic or self-expressive benefits? Are there certain segments for which this is especially true? Can living more sustainably yield experiential benefits? What kinds of positive experiences or feelings might come from it?

As we've seen, sustainability means different things to different people, if it means anything at all, and successful benefit segmentation requires companies to understand those differences. For some people, the most important sustainability-related benefit is personal safety or family health, which motivates the purchasing of organic foods and nontoxic personal care and household items. For others, the most important benefit is saving money and living more frugally, which leads to energy conservation and waste reduction. Many consumers are passionate about nature and the outdoors, and they focus on environmental benefits for the sake of preserving the world's wild places. Others place higher priorities on humanitarian issues, leading them to seek out products from companies that provide fair pay and healthy working conditions to their workers. Still others prioritize the humane treatment of animals, which may lead them to vegetarian or vegan lifestyles that in turn create lower carbon footprints.

In 2008, a collaborative study by Boston College researchers Juliet Schor, Amory Starr, and Margaret Willis, and the Center for a New American Dream, a nonprofit organization that helps people consume more sustainably, surveyed over 1,800 affiliates of the center about what they had done to reduce their consumption, what motivated them to do so, and what they were doing in their communities to promote increased sustainability. Eighty-seven percent reported having made changes to live more sustainably. Common areas of change included reduced energy use, reduced driving, reduced use of plastic water bottles, and reduced meat consumption (see Tables 7-1 and 7-2).[26]

TABLE 7-1 Conscious Consumer Practices

	CNAD Survey Percentage[†]
Have you done anything to change your lifestyle to make it more environmentally sustainable?	
Yes	87
No	2
Not sure	11
Of those who answered yes to the above question, people who:	
Change light bulbs	97
Reduce utility use (energy efficient house/windows, unplug appliances, wood heat, etc.)	93
Drive less (combine errands, walk more, etc.)	90
Discontinue purchases of plastic water bottles	88
Conserve water	87
Buy green household products	81
Have considered/have become a vegetarian	78
Take fewer airplane flights	64
Commute to work in a way other than an automobile	44
Purchase a hybrid car	14

†Data for the first question (change in lifestyle) are based on 2,164 responses. Data for subsequent questions are based on the 87 percent of respondents who answered "yes" to the first question, 1,890 respondents. Percentages for different consumption practices are based on those who answered from 4 to 7 on a scale of "1 = very inconsistently" and "7 = very consistently" engage in the practice.

TABLE 7-2 Percentage of Those Rating Various Motivations for Consumer Decisions As "Very Important"

	Percentage[†]	Number of Respondents
Living life in accordance with their values	64	2,195
Reusing, recycling, secondhand	57	2,201
Reducing overall consumption	56	2,202
Addressing ecological issues	51	2,233
Promoting personal health and product safety	50	2,196
Seeking quality products, craftsmanship	47	2,205
Addressing climate change	45	2,222
Promoting the well-being of the next generation	43	2,223
Supporting the local economy	43	2,225
Supporting alternatives to the dominant consumer culture	43	2,184
Living simply	41	2,208
Promoting fair wages and incomes for workers and producers	38	2,225
Enjoyment	30	1,796
Serving as a model for other people to see	25	2,197
Being avant-garde	6	1,730

[†]Percentage includes those who answered 7 on a scale from 1 = "Not very important" to 7 = "Very important."

Table 7-2 lists the values and goals that motivated respondents to change their consumption patterns or lifestyles. The most common motivation was, "living in accordance with my values." Other important factors included improving personal health and supporting local businesses.

LOHAS and the Cultural Creatives

One of the most successful and widely recognized segments in the green market is the self-described **Lifestyles of Health and Sustainability (LOHAS).** LOHAS is an organization of businesses that monitors the changing U.S. marketplace for goods and services focused on health, the environment, social justice, personal development, and sustainable living.[27] In reality, the LOHAS market can itself be segmented in a wide variety of ways, including lifestyle segmentation, benefit segmentation, or **usage segmentation**, which identifies market segments according to the amounts or quantities consumers purchase within a given product category.

The diverse and growing community of LOHAS businesses provides goods and services largely to consumers identified as **cultural creatives.**[28] These are educated consumers who make conscientious purchasing and investing decisions based on social and cultural values. Around one in four adult Americans is part of this group. These consumers will wield significant influence on the future of business and also on the future of progressive social, environmental, and economic change. Formally identified in 2000, the LOHAS market in the United States in 2006 was conservatively estimated at $209 billion and is growing fast.[29] One business that capitalizes on the growing LOHAS market is the Green Microgym, a gym that harnesses the energy of members' workouts with power generators hooked up to cardio machines.[30] In a "burn and earn" program, gym members receive a dollar for each hour of electricity they generate, helping power the facility and reducing their membership fees while they strengthen their bodies.

LOHAS businesses classify themselves according to six general sectors or product categories (see Table 7-3). At first glance, it may appear that the six LOHAS sectors have little in common. For example, a manufacturer of recycled plastics or an automaker working on next-generation, energy-efficient vehicles may not appear to have much in common with an ecotour operator or a retailer of organic clothing. But 30 million consumers believe there is a commonality that transcends any operational and structural differences.[31]

The interconnections between global economies, cultures, environments, and political systems play a large role in the holistic worldview of the typical LOHAS consumer. LOHAS businesses and customers emphasize the interconnections of mind, body, and spirit within individuals. The focus on personal development, with the ultimate goal of achieving one's full human potential, is of utmost concern to cultural creatives. The current growth in this market group strongly supports the notion that spirituality is no longer relegated to churches or to the New Age periphery. It is migrating to the center of mainstream cultural awareness. The LOHAS segment is a values-driven segment that tends to "vote its values with its dollars."

TABLE 7-3 LOHAS Product Categories

Personal Health	**Natural Lifestyles**
Natural, organic products	Indoor and outdoor furnishings
Nutritional products	Organic cleaning supplies
Integrative health care	Compact fluorescent light bulbs
Dietary supplements	Social change philanthropy apparel
Mind-Body-Spirit products	*U.S. market—$10.6 billion*
U.S. market—$118.03 billion	
Green Building	**Alternative Transportation**
Home certification	Hybrid vehicles
Energy Star appliances	Biodiesel fuel
Sustainable flooring	Car sharing programs
Renewable energy systems	*U.S. market—$6.12 billion*
Wood alternatives	
U.S. market—$50 billion	
Ecotourism	**Alternative Energy**
Ecotourism travel	Renewable energy credits
Eco-adventure travel	Green pricing
U.S. market—$24.17 billion	*U.S. market—$380 million*

THINK ABOUT IT

Are You a Cultural Creative?

Check off the statements you agree with. If you agree with 10 or more, you probably are one—and a higher score increases the odds. You are likely to be a cultural creative if you . . .

1. . . . love nature and are deeply concerned about its condition;
2. . . . are strongly aware of the problems of the whole planet (global warming, destruction of rain forests, overpopulation, lack of ecological sustainability, and exploitation of people in poorer countries) and want to see more action on them;
3. . . . would pay more taxes or pay more for consumer goods if you knew the money would go to clean up the environment and to stop global warming;
4. . . . place a lot of importance on developing and maintaining your relationships;
5. . . . value helping other people bring out their unique gifts;
6. . . . volunteer for one or more good causes;
7. . . . care intensely about psychological and spiritual development;
8. . . . see spirituality or religion as important in your life but are also concerned about the role of the religious right in politics;
9. . . . want more equality for women at work and want more women leaders in business and politics.
10. . . . are concerned about violence and the abuse of women and children around the world;
11. . . . want our politics and government spending to put more emphasis on children's education and well-being, on rebuilding our neighborhoods and communities, and on creating an ecologically sustainable future;
12. . . . are unhappy with both the left and the right in politics and want to find a new way that is not in the mushy middle;
13. . . . tend to be optimistic about our future and distrust cynical and pessimistic views;
14. . . . want to be involved in creating a new and better way of life in our country;
15. . . . are concerned about what big corporations are doing in the name of making more profits, for example, downsizing, creating environmental problems, and exploiting poorer countries;
16. . . . have your finances and spending under control and are not concerned about overspending;

17. . . . dislike all the emphasis in modern culture on success and "making it," on getting and spending, and on wealth and luxury goods; and

18. . . . like people and places that are exotic and foreign, and like experiencing and learning about other ways of life.[32]

Alternative Consumption Segments

Within the category of primary conservationists, there are several segments engaged in **alternative consumption**, meaning that they reject **consumerism**, or the notion that happiness and well-being are derived from the accumulation of material goods. One form of alternative consumption is **voluntary simplicity** or simple living,[33] the option to live with less, reducing one's material consumption by choice.[34] This choice often entails changing jobs or lifestyles in an effort to achieve more free time and a richer life.[35] Another segment, referred to as **locavores**,[36] stresses the environmental, social, and economic value of eating products grown close to home.

VIRTUAL FIELD TRIP

Dee Williams's Dream House

For a warm-hearted look at one person's adventure in alternative consumption, watch this short video on You Tube (http://www.youtube.com/watch?v=eZM2G-PfEbc&feature=player_embedded) in which Dee Williams downsizes to a tiny house on wheels. What lessons does she learn from her experiment? What aspects, if any, of her lifestyle would work for you?

Some consumers attempt to opt out of the dominant consumption culture entirely. They embrace **anti-consumption**, a socio-political movement against consumerism.[37] Motives for anti-consumption include resistance to commodity culture and corporate brands,[38] a desire to feel more authentic through one's consumption behavior,[39] and a desire to demonstrate love of the natural world.[40] For some consumers, the move toward anti-consumption is a direct response to corporate efforts to gain a share of the green market. For example, as mainstream marketing developed an interest in the organic food movement, early adopters of organic foods actively resisted this effort to co-opt the values of organic food production and consumption. Rather than becoming customers of the corporation, these consumers engaged in actively oppositional behaviors.[41] One of the most radical anti-consumption segments calls itself Freegans.[42] As accomplished "dumpster divers," their pride and hallmark is living from other people's waste, including food waste from restaurant and grocery stores, and clothing and household items from residential trash.[43] Freegans and other especially frugal consumers around the world network online[44] and face-to-face in order to trade free and found items.

POSITIONING FOR SUSTAINABILITY

Positioning a product or brand entails the use of marketing communication to create a distinctive identity for it in the minds of consumers. To position themselves for success in the growing green market, firms need to examine the benefits provided by their products and services and match those benefits with target customers' core sustainability values. Herman Miller is one example of a company that has achieved a unique and powerful position in the office furniture industry while leading the industry in both environmental and social sustainability. Combining emphases on design and holistic human experience, its market position reads almost like a mantra for the cultural creatives: "Herman Miller, Inc., works for a better world around you. We do this by designing furnishings and related services that improve the human experience wherever people work, heal, learn, and live."[45]

VIRTUAL FIELD TRIP

Walk, Run or Float a Mile in My Shoes

KEEN first made a splash in the footwear market in 2003 by inventing a sandal with toe protection. In 2004 the fledgling firm donated its entire marketing budget to relief for the victims of the Indian Ocean Tsunami. Explore the KEEN website (www.keenfootwear.com) and then read about the company from other online sources. What is KEEN's market position? What sets KEEN apart from its competitors? Now compile the description of a "poster person" for KEEN's target market. Who is this person demographically? What are the person's core values? What is his or her occupation? What unmet needs would drive this person to KEEN?

One way to position for sustainability is to create a line of products that are demonstrably green. Let's return to the example of the automotive industry. Both Toyota and Honda have sought to claim a sustainability position through the introduction of hybrid models. The race to sustainability has Honda and Toyota neck and neck with the finish line still far in the distance. In 2007, Honda was named the greenest car company by the Union of Concerned Scientists.[46] In 2009, Toyota received the same honor from BusinessCar in the United Kingdom.[47] In its bid for a position of sustainability in the office products industry, Office Depot produces an entire catalog dedicated to its most sustainable products[48] (see Photo 7-1). The same positioning strategy hasn't worked for Chrysler, however. Chrysler designed and marketed hybrid-power versions of both the Dodge Durango and the Chrysler Aspen. According *Los Angeles Times* reporter Ken

PHOTO 7-1 Office Depot targets businesses that are trying to operate more sustainably with its Green Book catalog.

Bensinger, Chrysler discontinued production of its hybrids even before they had hit the dealer showrooms.[49]

In successful segmentation, targeting, and positioning, the key is to discover and resonate with the meanings and values that target customers hold most strongly. Advertisements illustrate different sustainability-related positioning strategies. Mythic Paint, for example, appeals to a segment concerned with health and safety with ads that say, "Safe for people; safe for pets; and safe for the Earth" and emphasize the nontoxic nature of the product (www.mythicpaint.com). YOLO Colorhouse, another marketer of nontoxic paints, chooses to emphasize the aesthetic or artistic qualities of its product with the tag line, "Created by artists with nature in mind" (www.yolocolorhouse.com).

Another common positioning strategy for more sustainable products is an emphasis on economy or money savings. This is the strategy Energy Star uses to promote CFLs. Its ad states that, "An ENERGY STAR qualified compact fluorescent light bulb (CFL) will save about $30 over its lifetime and pay for itself in about 6 months" (www.energystar.gov).

Backpacker Magazine, (see image below) which urges people to adopt more sustainable practices and lifestyles, uses a positioning strategy that emphasizes an appreciation for nature with the slogan, "The outdoors at your doorstep" (www.backpacker.com). Yet another common market position for more sustainable products is an emphasis on humanitarian goals and benefits. Brilliant Earth diamond jewelry advertises "Luxury with a conscience" for its Conflict-Free Diamonds (www.brilliantearth.com).

Striving to become sustainable does not necessarily require a company to position its products as green or sustainable. For example, as we learned in Chapter 2, Nike's positioning strategy has nothing to do with sustainability and everything to do with athletic performance, even though the company is an industry leader in both environmental and social issues. Similarly, Sprint Nextel appears to be serious about environmental sustainability,[50] having, among other things, instituted an ambitious cell phone take-back and recycling program.[51] However, Sprint's market position focuses primarily on the functional attributes of its wireless network, such as speed, reliability, and mobility.

Ultimately, at the heart of a company's market position is its reputation, and reputation arises not only from what the firm says about itself, but also, and perhaps primarily, from what others say. In the era of free-flowing information on the Internet, it is more important to act sustainably than to proclaim sustainability as a virtue.

Backpacker Magazine: "The outdoors at your doorstep."

Brilliant Earth diamonds are positioned as a more humanitarian choice.

TAKING THE GREEN POSITION IN THE BUSINESS-TO-BUSINESS SECTOR

Business-to-business sustainable segments include businesses that sell sustainable products and services to other businesses. And these businesses are finding increasing interest in sustainability among their customers. A multi-billion dollar "environmental services industry" (ESI) provides both products and services to the business-to-business (B2B) sector.[52]

Some products in the ESI category meet the need for employee health and safety in the workplace. For example, AFM developed Safecoat and Safechoice paints, a nontoxic line of paints and cleaners. AFM's customers include companies such as Herman Miller, Gap, and Banana Republic, which are looking to safeguard their employees by creating more sustainable workplaces.[53]

Other services help companies become more sustainable in their own operations. For example, one service company identified a need for better chemical management among large- and medium-sized companies. Many companies use "between 5,000 and 50,000 different chemicals" in their maintenance, repair, and operations. And for many toxic chemicals, safer and more sustainable options are available.[54]

In some cases, the impetus to become a sustainable supplier comes directly from the business customer. For example, Ford Motor Company works with its suppliers to increase recycling and waste reduction. As a result, less waste goes into the environment, and costs are lower for Ford.[55] In the supply chain for casual and athletic clothing, post-consumer recycled polyester fleece made from polyethylene terephthalate (PET) plastic bottles is becoming increasingly popular.[56] Outdoor clothier Patagonia, working with fabric manufacturer Malden Mills, refined the fabric into a finer, softer version called Synchilla. As a result, "Sales exploded, and the company became known for the 'fleece jacket.'"[57]

Sustainability-minded suppliers can offer innovative solutions to customers' problems, such as the age-old problem of waste disposal. Consider the story of Rocky Mountain Recycling in the mini case study.

Mini Case Study

Rocky Mountain Recycling

Retail stores generate tons of waste, much of which is highly recyclable,[58] including loose plastic and plastic bags, corrugated cardboard, aluminum cans, plastic hangers, plastic beverage bottles, office paper, and paperback books.[59] Traditionally, however, stores have lacked the processes to make most of the recycling financially feasible. It simply took too much effort to separate and consolidate the various waste items into quantities worth dealing with. As a result, stores typically recycled cardboard, which they could compress in their balers, and paid to have the rest hauled away.

In 2006, former garbage truck driver Jeff Ashby saw the solution. What if other recyclables, such as plastics and aluminum, could be sandwiched in bulk between layers of cardboard in balers at the retail site? Recyclers could easily separate the layers and end up with marketable quantities of the various commodities. Enter Rocky Mountain Recycling with a new idea, the Super Sandwich Bale™ (see Photo 7-2). The recipe for the sandwich is as follows: "First, add a bottom layer of cardboard, then add the filler layer of shrink wrap and hangers, plastic bottles and cans, and office paper and crush it into a two- to three-foot high midsection. Top it off with cardboard and serve to a material recovery facility (MRF)."[60]

The Super Sandwich Bale was originally designed for Wal-Mart. Other organizations, including retail competitors and the U.S. military are now looking into the process.[61] According to Ashby, Wal-Mart now recycles "more than 25 percent of what once was tossed into the trash compactor." And recyclables are valuable. Manufacturing from virgin polyethylene resin is "almost twice as expensive as using recycled plastic"; thus "What was once an expense for W-M has now become an income source."[62] Rocky Mountain Recycling now employs over 200 people in 11 states and recycles over 50,000 tons per month.[63]

In what ways does Rocky Mountain Recycling help its customers to address the four system conditions of The Natural Step Framework? How does the Super Sandwich Bale facilitate closed-loop or cradle-to-cradle manufacturing?

PHOTO 7-2 Jeff Ashbey with Super Sandwich Bales.

In the B2B sector, even more than in consumer marketing, there is a growing green market. Businesses see the strategic advantages of sustainability, and they are moving rapidly to make changes. They are building greener buildings, working to eliminate waste and emissions, seeking renewable sources of power and materials, and providing safer and more rewarding workplaces. B2B market segments are different in that they are aligned with specific industries, materials, and processes, but the need for sustainability is universal.

CRITICAL THINKING ACTIVITY

Talkin' 'bout My Generation (Apologies to the Who)

Echo Boomers. Millennials. The Net Generation. Generation Y. Generation Y the Hell Not! No matter what you call the current generation of young adults, born between 1981 and 2000, the fact is they have inherited and grown up in a very different world—culturally, politically, technologically, and in practically every other way—than any generation before them. And more than any previous generation, they have a stake in creating a sustainable society.

Think about generation Y in terms of distinct lifestyle segments. (Hint: Every large high school has readily identifiable cliques or social groups that reflect different values, tastes, styles, attitudes, and behaviors.)

1. List and name as many segments as you can. If you aren't a member of generation Y, interview someone who is.
2. For each segment, try to identify at least one core value (more if possible) that resonates with environmental or social sustainability.
3. Now put yourself in the position of a clothing marketer with multiple brands, one for each segment, and all of which are environmentally and socially sustainable. Craft a marketing message to position a clothing brand to each segment, such that the message taps into that segment's core values.

Chapter Summary

Research points to a large and growing market for sustainable products and services in both business-to-consumer and B2B sectors. So-called green products used to be targeted to small and specialized market segments, or niches. Now, the green market is so large, complex, and mainstream that it requires segmentation. Green segments include the LOHAS customers, anti-consumerists, and alternative consumers of all kinds.

Consumers have different personal priorities with respect to sustainability. Effective segmentation requires attention to demographics, psychographics, and benefits desired by consumers. Choosing which segments to target has implications for product positioning. And, as we shall see in coming chapters, it also affects every aspect of the marketing mix.

Review of Chapter Objectives

- The emerging green market
- Segmenting the green market

- Positioning for sustainability
- Taking the green position in the business-to-business sector

Key Concepts

Green Market   90
Demographics   91
Psychographics   91
Lifestyle
    Segmentation   91
Primary Conservationists   91
Secondary
    Conservationists   91
Benefit Segmentation   92

Functional Benefits (also
    known as Utilitarian
    Benefits)   93
Symbolic Benefits (also
    known as Self-Expressive
    Benefits)   93
Hedonic Benefits (also
    known as Experiential
    Benefits)   93

Benefits Profile   93
Lifestyles of Health
    and Sustainability
    (LOHAS)   95
Usage Segmentation   95
Cultural Creatives   95
Alternative Consumption   97
Consumerism   97

Voluntary Simplicity   97
Locavores   97
Anti-Consumption   97
Positioning   97
Business-to-Business
    Sustainable
    Segments   100

Endnotes

1. Lego Group, Progress Report 08, http://cache.lego.com/downloads/info/Progress_Report_2008.pdf, accessed March 6, 2010.

2. United Nations Global Compact, Latest News, http://www.unglobalcompact.org/, accessed March 6, 2010.

3. Antorini, Yun Mi (2007), "Brand Community Innovation: An Intrinsic Case Study of the Adult Fans of LEGO Community," Doctoral dissertation, Department of Intercultural Communication and Management, Copenhagen Business School.

4. Moon, Jae Yun and Lee Sproull (2001), "Turning Love into Money: How Some Firms May Profit from Voluntary Electronic Customer Communities," unpublished manuscript, Stern Business School, New York University.

5. Lugnet, http://www.lugnet.com/, accessed August 23, 2009.

6. Tucson Lego Club, http://www.tlclub.org/, accessed August 23, 2009.

7. LEGO Fan, Overview, http://www.legofan.org/ambassadors/ambassadors.html, accessed August 23, 2009.

8. North Georgia LEGO Train Club, http://www.ngltc.org/, accessed August 23, 2009.

9. Bones' Medieval LEGO Page, http://necrobones.com/legos/medieval/, accessed August 23, 2009.

10. The Brothers Brick, LEGO Architecture Space Needle and Empire State Building, http://www.brothers-brick.com/2009/02/08/lego-architecture-space-needle-and-empire-state-building-news/, accessed August 23, 2009.

11. I09, The Zombie Apocalypse, http://io9.com/5059315/the-zombie-apocalypse—in-legos, accessed August 23, 2009.

12. Anderson, Chris (2006), The Long Tail: Why the Future of Business Is Selling Less of More, New York: Hyperion.

13. European Commission, Directorate General Environment/Eurobarometer 295, *Attitudes of European Citizens towards the Environment*, March 2008; National Geographic Society/GlobeScan, Greendex 2008: Consumer Choice and the Environment—A Worldwide Tracking Survey; Synovate/Aegis, 2007; Synovate/BBC World, 2008.

14. World Business Council for Sustainable Development (2008), "Sustainable Consumption Facts and Trends from a Business Perspective," http://www.wbcsd.org/DocRoot/I9Xwhv7X5V8cDIHbHC3G/WBCSD_Sustainable_Consumption_web.pdf, accessed December 8, 2009.

15. Hartman Report (2008), Presentation made during the Northwest Sustainability Discovery Tour in Portland, Oregon. Also see Chan, Kara (1999), "Market Segmentation of Green Consumers in Hong Kong," *Journal of International Consumer Marketing*, 12 (2): 7–24; Laroche, M., J. Bergeron, and G. Barbaro-Forleo (2001), "Targeting Customers Who Are Willing to Pay More for Environmentally Friendly Products," *Journal of Consumer Marketing*, 18 (6): 503–520.

16. GfK Roper Consulting (2008), "Green Gets Real . . . Current Economic Environment Subduing Green Enthusiasm but Driving Practical Action," http://www.gfkamerica.com/newsroom/press_releases/single_sites/003698/index.en.html, accessed October 13, 2009.

17. Straughan, Robert D. and James A. Roberts (1999), "Environmental Segmentation Alternatives: A Look at Green Consumer Behavior in the New Millennium," *Journal of Consumer Marketing*, 16 (6): 558–575.

18. DeGrandpre, R.J., and W. Buskist (1991), "Culture, Contingencies and Conservation," *Psychological Record*, 41: 501–522.

19. The Hartman Group (2009), "Sustainability: The Rise of Consumer Responsibility, Executive Summary," http://www.Hartman-Group.Com/Publications/View/81, accessed September 23, 2009.

20. GfK Roper Consulting (2008), "Green Gets Real . . . Current Economic Environment Subduing Green Enthusiasm but Driving Practical Action," http://www.gfkamerica.com/newsroom/press_releases/single_sites/003698/index.en.html, accessed October 13, 2009.

21. Jacoby, Jacob, Carol K. Berning and Thomas F. Dietvorst (1977), "What About Disposition?," Journal of Marketing 41 (4): 22–28

22. Batra, Rajeev and Olli T. Ahtola (1990), "Measuring the Hedonic and Utilitarian Sources of Consumer Attitudes," *Marketing Letters*, 2 (2): 159–70.

23. Batra, Rajeev and Olli T. Ahtola (1990), "Measuring the Hedonic and Utilitarian Sources of Consumer Attitudes," *Marketing Letters*, 2 (2): 159–70. Also see Dhar, Ravi, and Klaus Wertenbroch (2000), "Consumer Choice between Hedonic and Utilitarian Goods," *Journal of Marketing Research*, 37 (1): 60–71.

24. Maynard, Micheline (2007), "Say 'Hybrid' and Many People Will Hear 'Prius,'" *New York Times*, July 4, http://www.nytimes.com/2007/07/04/business/04hybrid.html, accessed March 7, 2010.

25. Prius Chat, Prius Chat's In-Depth Review and First Drive, http://priuschat.com/news/priuschats-2010-prius-in-depth-review-and-first-drive, accessed March 7, 2010.

26. Center for a New American Dream, Conscious Consumer Survey, http://www.newdream.org/consumption/survey.php, accessed June 25, 2010.

27. "The LOHAS Marketplace: $209 Billion Strong (And Growing)," *Lifestyles of Health and Sustainability*, http://www.lohas.com/, accessed May 27, 2008.

28. See Ray, Paul H. and Sherry Ruth Anderson (2000), *Cultural Creatives: How 50 Million People Are Changing the World*, New York: Harmony Books.

29. "The LOHAS Marketplace: $209 Billion Strong (And Growing)," *Lifestyles of Health and Sustainability*, http://www.lohas.com/, accessed May 27, 2008.

30. The Green Microgym, http://thegreenmicrogym.com/, accessed August 24, 2009.

31. "The LOHAS Marketplace: $209 Billion Strong (And Growing)," *Lifestyles of Health and Sustainability*, http://www.lohas.com/, accessed May 27, 2008.

32. See Ray, Paul H. and Sherry Ruth Anderson (2000), *Cultural Creatives: How 50 Million People Are Changing the World*, New York: Harmony Books.

33. Luhrs, Janet (1997), *The Simple Living Guide*, New York: Broadway Books.

34. Murray, Jeff B. (2002), The Politics of Consumption: A Re-Inquiry on Thompson and Haytko's (1997) 'Speaking of Fashion,'" *Journal of Consumer Research*, 29 (December): 427–440.

35. Ottman, Jacquelyn A. (1998), *Green Marketing: Opportunity for Innovation*, New York: J. Ottman Consulting, Inc. (p. 43).

36. Locavores, http://www.locavores.com/, accessed August 24, 2009.

37. Lee, Michael S.W., Karen V. Fernandez, and Michael R. Hyman (2009), "Anti-Consumption: An Overview and Research Agenda," *Journal of Business Research*, 62 (2): 145–147.

38. Fischer, Eileen (2001), "Revolution in Rhetorics of Resistance: An Analysis of the Emergence of the Anti-Brand Movement," *Advances in Consumer Research*, 28: 123–124.

39. Zavestoski, Stephen (2002), "The Social-Psychology Bases of Anticonsumption Attitudes," *Psychology and Marketing*, 19 (2): 149–165.

40. Dobscha, Susan (1998), "The Lived Experience of Consumer Rebellion against Marketing," *Advances in Consumer Research*, 25: 91–97.

41. Thompson, Craig J. and Gokcen Coskuner-Balli (2007), "Countervailing Market Responses to Corporate Co-optation and the Ideological Recruitment of Consumption Communities," *Journal of Consumer Research*, 34 (2): 135–152.

42. Freegan.info, "What Is a Freegan," http://freegan.info/?page_id=2, accessed August 24, 2009.

43. Kurutz, Steven (2007), "Not Buying It," *New York Times*, June 21, http://www.nytimes.com/2007/06/21/garden/21freegan.html, accessed August 24, 2009.

44. Freecycle, Portland, Group Info, http://www.freecycle.org/group/United%20States/Oregon/Portland, accessed August 24, 2009.

45. Herman Miller, "About Us, About Herman Miller, The Basics," http://www.hermanmiller.com/About-Us/About-Herman-Miller/The-Basics, accessed August 24, 2009.

46. Honda, News and Views, News Releases, "Honda Named Greenest Automaker by Union of Concerned Scientists," http://corporate.honda.com/press/article.aspx?id=200704033945, accessed August 24, 2009.

47. Autoblog, Green, "Business Car: Toyota Still the World's Greenest Automaker," http://green.autoblog.com/2009/04/14/business-car-toyota-still-the-worlds-greenest-automaker/, accessed August 24, 2009.

48. Esty, Daniel C. and Andrew S. Winston (2006), Green to Gold: How Smart Companies Use Environmental Strategy to Innovate, Create Value, and Build Competitive Advantage, New Haven, CT: Yale University Press (p. 131). Environmental Leader (2008), Office Depot Launches Green Product Line, April 8, http://www.environmentalleader.com/2008/04/08/office-depot-launches-green-product-line/, accessed August 23, 2009.

49. Bensinger, Ken (2008), "Chrysler Ends Hybrid Adventure Before It Can Begin," *Los Angeles Times*, October, 29, http://articles.latimes.com/2008/oct/29/business/fi-speedblog29, accessed March 7, 2010.

50. Sprint, Company Info, Corporate Responsibility, http://www.sprint.com/responsibility/index.html accessed March 7, 2010.

51. Sustainable Life Media (2009), "Sprint Targets 90% Cellphone Takeback Rate," February 16, http://www.sustaiablelifemedia.com/content/story/strategy/sprint_targets_90_percent_cellphone_takeback_rate, accessed August 24, 2009.

52. Wilson, David N. (1994), *Marketing Environmental Services*, Rockville, MD: Government Institutes Inc.

53. Ottman, Jacquelyn A. (1998), *Green Marketing: Opportunity for Innovation*, New York: J. Ottman Consulting, Inc. (p. 75).

54. Dolphin Safe Source, http://www.dolphinsafesource.com/, accessed August 24, 2009.

55. Greene, Jay (2009), "Crain's Detroit Business," August 2, http://www.crainsdetroit.com/article/20090802/SUB01/308029989#, accessed August 24, 2009.

56. Bookrags, Polar Fleece, http://www.bookrags.com/research/polar-fleece-woi/ accessed April 21, 2009.

57. Casey, Susan (2007), "Blueprint for Green Business," *Fortune*, May 29, http://money.cnn.com/magazines/fortune/fortune_archive/2007/04/02/8403423/index3.htm, accessed April 21, 2009.

58. CalRecycle, "Business Waste Reduction: Waste Reduction at Retail Stores," http://www.ciwmb.ca.gov/BIZWASTE/factsheets/Retail.htm, accessed August 24, 2009.

59. Wal-Mart Corporate, "Zero Waste: Waste," http://walmartstores.com/Sustainability/9176.aspx, accessed August 24, 2009.

60. Rocky Mountain Recycling, http://www.rockymountainrecycling.com, accessed April 21, 2009.

61. Jarvik, Elaine (2008), Super Sandwich Bale—Utah Man's Idea Nets Wholesale Recycling, *Deseret News*, April, 22, http://www.deseretnews.com/article/1,5143,695272741,00.html, accessed April 21, 2009.

62. Rocky Mountain Recycling, http://www.rockymountainrecycling.com, accessed April 21, 2009.

63. Rocky Mountain Recycling, http://rockymountainrecycling.com/, accessed August 24, 2009.

Global Problems, Global Opportunities

INTRODUCTION: TRANSOCEANIC TOXINS

Poisons, such as mercury, lead, cadmium, and dioxins along with other pollutants, are international travelers, and no passport is required.

> Fumes and dust from industrial factories, coal-powered energy plants and privately owned cars in China are crossing the ocean and polluting the air in the United States. . . . On some days, nearly 25% of polluting matter above Los Angeles can be traced to Asia, according to the US Environmental Protection Agency. . . . Ozone, carbon monoxide, mercury and polluting matter from Asia have been detected on Mount Bachelor in Oregon and Cheeka Peak in Washington State, says Dan Jaffe, an atmospheric scientist at the University of Washington.[1]

In a recent NASA study using satellite sensor technology, researchers measured the impact of East Asian air pollution on North America. For the period from 2002 to 2005, they found that "18 teragrams—almost 40 billion pounds—of pollution aerosol was exported to the northwestern Pacific Ocean and 4.5 teragrams—nearly 10 billion pounds—reached North America annually from East Asia."[2]

THINK ABOUT IT

Global Systems

What happens to chemicals like dioxins and metals like lead after they enter the atmosphere? Do they disappear? Where do they go? When pollution runs into the ocean, does it remain local? Have you ever looked at canned seafood, such as shrimp and crab? Where do these foods originate? What do you know about pollution controls in those countries' coastal areas? As you learned in Chapter 2, sustainable marketing requires a whole-system perspective. To what extent are the major environments of marketing global as opposed to local systems?

To an extent never before experienced on planet Earth, all humans are interconnected. We breathe the same atmosphere. We eat from the same oceans. Our communication and transportation systems are linked, and our economies are interdependent. And now, more than ever, we want the same kinds of lifestyles and material goods. For all these reasons, the needs for sustainable marketing and a sustainable society are global as well. This chapter examines the challenges and opportunities for sustainable marketing in a global business environment.

CHAPTER OBJECTIVES

In this chapter, you will learn about the global scope of sustainable marketing including:

- Global environmental challenges
- Global economic challenges
- Global government and regulatory challenges
- Global consumers and sustainable marketing
- Sustainability in global business-to-business markets

GLOBAL ENVIRONMENTAL CHALLENGES

The natural capital and ecosystem services that provide the basis for all human activity are part of a system that knows no national boundaries. Airflows, ocean currents, wildlife migrations, and intercontinental travel turn localized phenomena like pollution and disease into multinational or global phenomena.

There have been success stories in dealing with global environmental problems. For example, dangerous depletion of the ozone layer, which protects the Earth from potentially deadly levels of ultraviolet radiation, was discovered in the 1970s, reached its peak in the 1980s, and has since been successfully reversed. The reversal was made possible because scientists, lawmakers, and businesses worked together on a global level. Compounds called chlorofluorocarbons (CFCs), prevalent in consumer goods using aerosol sprays and integral to cooling and air-conditioning systems, were the culprits. A worldwide ban on CFCs, coupled with innovations in product design, turned out to be the solution.

Currently, humanity faces even more difficult challenges in the forms of climate change and drastic shortages of clean water. These are global threats to the natural environment, and thereby to humanity, which can only be addressed successfully at a global level. Governments, scientists, businesses, and consumers must all play their parts. As the communicative interface between business and society, marketing has a particularly important role to play (see Photo 8-1).

World Water

Arguably the world's most pressing environmental and humanitarian issue is the decreasing supply of safe, drinkable water. Fresh water, although consumed and managed locally or regionally, depends on systems that are global.

PHOTO 8-1 The earth is in our hands. Sustainable marketing is a global concern.

According to the World Health Organization, more than 3,500,000 people die every year from water-related diseases; 84 percent of those deaths occur among children aged 0–14; and 98 percent occur in the developing world.[3] Already dire in much of Africa, a growing **water crisis** also threatens the rest of the planet, thanks in part to global warming. According to British journalist and climate change investigator Mark Lynas, "Glacier and snow-melt in the world's mountain chains depletes freshwater flows to downstream cities and agricultural land. Most affected are California, Peru, Pakistan and China. Global food production is under threat as key breadbaskets in Europe, Asia and the United States suffer drought, and heat waves outstrip the tolerance of crops."[4]

However, climate change isn't the only cause of water shortages. Some of the problem lies in unsustainable personal and industrial consumption. For example, "Golf courses in the US Southwest use more water than any other part of the country, about 88 million gallons per year, per course. The water needed for just one Arizona golf course could fill 12,000 swimming pools or provide for all the water needs for about 1,500 Americans (or 20,000 Africans)."[5] Two big Texas reservoirs, Lake Travis and Lake Buchanan, provide drinking water for 1 million people, and in 2009, Lake Travis was down 54 percent.[6]

Water isn't just for drinking and watering lawns. Industrial uses are varied and intensive. For example, semiconductor fabrication is extremely water intensive. According to engineering researcher Farhang Shadman, "One manufacturing plant uses anywhere between two to four million gallons of very, very pure water, we call it ultra-pure water, per day, and that, on the average, is roughly equivalent to the water usage of a city of maybe 40 or 50,000 people."[7]

Agriculture, the world's largest industry, accounts for 69 percent of all the freshwater used by people on the planet.[8] As you can see in the table below, with current technologies, our food supply takes a tremendous amount of water.

The extraordinary amounts of water reported in Table 8-1 reflects **embedded water**, also called virtual water; that is, all the water used in the production of the product. For example, most of the water embedded in a hamburger comes from irrigation to grow the grain the cattle eat.[9] One of the greatest challenges to sustainable marketing in the coming years will be to help businesses and consumers to value water differently and use it more wisely and efficiently.

Currently two issues stand out as major controversies around water and marketing. One is bottled water, and the other is water privatization.

Bottled Water

In Sacramento, California, Nestlé is building a water bottling plant, and an interesting and familiar debate ensues. According to Nestlé Waters North America:

> To better serve our customers in Northern California we will be opening a new bottling facility in Sacramento in early 2010. We are looking forward to becoming part of the Sacramento community as an employer and as a neighbor.[10]

Meanwhile, a Sacramento news blogger offers this perspective:

> Nestlé will pay the city's industrial rates for water: $.9854 for every 748 gallons. . . . Down at the local Safeway, a 24-pack of half-liter bottles of their water-flavored water fetches $3.99. That works out to about $38 million paid by consumers for about $37,000 worth of tap water, with some packaging, shipping and press releases thrown in.[11]

TABLE 8-1	Water usage for food and beverage production
Product	**Water Usage**
1 latte	55 gallons
Glass of orange juice	45 gallons
Glass of milk	53 gallons
Glass of beer	20 gallons
1 egg	53 gallons
Apple	16 gallons
Hamburger	630 gallons[12]

Critics of Nestlé claim that the corporation not only profits hugely from what are essentially free ecosystem services, but also that the company does irreparable harm to local aquifers by drawing out large amounts of water and transporting it to places where the water, once consumed, can't replenish the aquifer from which it came.[13] There are, of course, other sustainability issues around bottled water. One is plastic bottles. Although recyclable, most are not recycled. Citing government and NGO sources, Earth911 reports that, "Americans buy an estimated 29.8 billion plastic water bottles every year" and that "Nearly eight out of every 10 bottles will end up in a landfill."[14] Another issue is purity. Numerous studies, including one by the Natural Resources Defense Council,[15] have shown that bottled water is no safer to drink than tap water in the United States, and that testing requirements for tap water actually exceed those for bottled water.

Globally and domestically, bottled water can save lives, especially when natural disasters disrupt or contaminate normal flows. In a show of innovation for sustainability, a group called United Bottle has developed interlocking plastic water bottles that, when emptied of water and refilled with local materials, turn into a building blocks suitable for building temporary or even long-term shelters.[16]

Water Privatization

The scope of the marketing opportunities around global water became clear in 2000 with the publication of a *Fortune* magazine article, which proclaimed that water was the new oil. According to author Shawn Tully, "From Buenos Aires to Atlanta to Jakarta, the liquid everybody needs—and will need a lot more of in the future—is going private, creating one of the world's great business opportunities. The dollars at stake are huge. Supplying water to people and companies is a $400-billion-a-year industry. That's 40% of the size of the oil sector and one-third larger than global pharmaceuticals. And this is just the beginning."[17]

According to Tully, large municipalities have been turning over their water utilities to companies like France-based Suez, because the governments lack either the money or the will to upgrade facilities. For the authorization to make a profit from their services, private companies invest in water treatment and distribution facilities. In the case of Buenos Aires, Suez was able to deliver more and cleaner water throughout the city, including to its poorest areas, at lower prices than the government had.

Not all communities embrace privatized water utilities. In the developing world, water-for-profit models have made clean water inaccessible for many poor populations. Critics of privatization claim that in developing nations, "the World Bank has been quietly imposing a for-profit system of water delivery, leaving millions of people without access to water."[18] In Bolivia, South America's poorest (and the world's eighth poorest) nation, citizen groups have engaged in heated battle with major corporations controlling and making huge profits from diminishing supplies of fresh water.[19] According to Jorge Cuba, a Bolivian journalist writing for UNESCO, "The conflict erupted in January 2000 when the price of drinking water was tripled in the central Bolivian city of Cochabamba, and peasants in the surrounding arid region suddenly found that the water they had been drawing freely for generations no longer belonged to them. City-dwellers accustomed to subsidized water supplies were confronted by the true market price, while the peasants—mostly Quechua Indians who had owned the water for centuries—involuntarily found themselves customers of Aguas del Tunari, a subsidiary of the British firm International Water."[20]

The conflict lasted 10 months and cost at least a dozen lives. The government gave in and rescinded its contract with the private provider. However, Cuba writes, "Cochabamba's basic problems have not been solved. The city has no more than five hours of water a day, and only 40 percent of farmers in the surrounding area have access to clean water." In addition, the financial damages incurred by Aguas de Tunari served as a red flag to other companies considering investment in Bolivia.

THINK ABOUT IT

Evidence shows that businesses may often be better suited (in terms of experience, efficiencies, and capital) to develop and operate water utilities than governments are, and yet the very notion of letting a firm make a profit from a public resource strikes many people as wrong. Critics of privatized water systems stress that clean water is a human right, and not a commodity to be bought and sold. What do you think? Should companies like Suez and Nestlé be allowed to profit from local water supplies? How might better marketing practices avert the kinds of situations that might lead to backlash against businesses?

The Global Greenhouse

The most obviously shared natural system on Earth is its atmosphere. In addition to containing life-supporting air, shielding the Earth from deadly ultraviolet radiation, and functioning as the planet's temperature-control system, the atmosphere also acts as the sink for all of humanity's gaseous waste. For businesses and societies in general, the costs of using that sink have typically been regarded as externalized costs, or "externalities," meaning that they have used the sink for free, or very cheaply, and that the real costs are borne by society in many forms, including taxes, illness, drought, flooding, and a host of others.

Dumping waste gases, such as sulphur dioxide (responsible for acid rain) or greenhouse gases (GHGs, responsible for some level of global climate change), into the atmosphere is one example of an externalized cost. Many countries have restrictions on sulphur dioxide emissions, which have the effect of charging the costs of cleanup to the polluters. To date, GHGs have been less regulated. However, the privilege of dumping carbon into the atmosphere may soon get more expensive in the United States, which currently is moving toward regulating carbon emissions. A White House statement says:

> We must take immediate action to reduce the carbon pollution that threatens our climate and sustains our dependence on fossil fuels. We have had limits in place on pollutants like sulfur dioxide, nitrogen dioxide, and other harmful emissions for some time. After decades of inaction, we will finally close the carbon pollution loophole by limiting the amount of carbon polluters are allowed to pump into the atmosphere.[21]

One scenario for curbing GHGs is a carbon **cap and trade** program. Cap and trade is a policy that sets legal limits on emissions and then allows organizations that pollute less than the limit to sell allowances to those that pollute more. According to the U.S. Environmental Protection Agency:

> Cap and trade is an environmental policy tool that delivers results with a mandatory cap on emissions while providing sources flexibility in how they comply. Successful cap and trade programs reward innovation, efficiency, and early action and provide strict environmental accountability without inhibiting economic growth."[22]

It appears likely that the U.S. Senate is moving in the direction of passing some kind of price-on-carbon legislation, either a cap and trade scheme or a straight tax on GHG

Savage Chickens

emissions.[23] The United States is not alone, nor even a leader, in putting a price on GHGs. The European Union (EU) put a price on GHGs in 2005 with the **European Union Emissions Trading Scheme**.[24] The policy was revised and strengthened beginning in 2008 and is currently undergoing more revisions for a new trading period beginning in 2013. A 2009 directive of the European Parliament and Council outlines EU's commitment to reducing GHGs and, at the same time, emphasizes that the effort must be made worldwide: "The European Council . . . made a firm commitment to reduce the overall greenhouse gas emissions of the Community by at least 20% below 1990 levels by 2020, and by 30% provided that other developed countries commit themselves to comparable emission reductions and economically more advanced developing countries contribute adequately according to their responsibilities and respective capabilities."[25]

When discussing global climate change, the elephants in the room are China, India, and the United States. The United States famously refused to ratify the Kyoto Protocol to reduce global warming, and congressional battles make any headway on carbon reductions difficult, especially as economic competitors like China and India refuse to participate at meaningful levels. China has overtaken the United States as the world's largest GHG producer with 23 percent of global emissions. India trails with 5 percent, but its rate is growing rapidly. Both countries acknowledge the need to reduce emissions, but they resist committing to firm agreements that might hamper their economic growth.[26] Recently, both the Chinese and Indian governments have begun to view sustainable development as a source of both economic growth and global competitiveness through innovation. For example, China intends to lead the world in the development of electric cars[27] and solar power;[28] and for its part, India is developing its own domestic cap and trade program.[29]

GLOBAL ECONOMIC CHALLENGES

Just as we all share in the state of Earth's ecosystems, we also participate in and are affected by the global economy. The magnitude of global trade is stunning. In 2008, the United States alone imported over $2.5 trillion in goods and services[30] and exported over $1.8 trillion.[31] In 2008, Atlanta-based Coca-Cola, operating in over 200 countries, reported revenues of over $31 billion.[32] In that same period, Swiss-based Nestlé made over $89 billion from its multinational operations. Global trade moves products and capital around the world in enormous quantities with remarkable efficiencies.

However, as we can see in the example of e-waste recycling, global trade can also shift the burdens of environmental harm from affluent populations to those that are poor and powerless by comparison. According to Greenpeace, "Inspections of 18 European seaports in 2005 found as much as 47 percent of waste destined for export, including e-waste, was illegal. In the UK alone, at least 23,000 metric tonnes of undeclared or 'grey' market electronic waste was illegally shipped in 2003 to the Far East, India, Africa and China. In the United States, it is estimated that 50–80 percent of the waste collected for recycling is being exported in this way."[33]

A recent CBS *60 Minutes* investigation[34] into U.S. e-waste recycling tracked illegally exported computer monitors to Hong Kong and then on to China. There they were being "recycled" by impoverished workers, paid by crime bosses protected by local police and government. The workers boil off lead over open coal fires, recover precious metals with acids in open barrels, incinerate plastic cases releasing highly toxic fumes, and dump mountains of refuse leading to rivers of poison where children play.

Multinational businesses have sometimes viewed the global marketplace in terms of opportunities to sidestep local environmental and labor regulations. This industrial-era thinking assumes that social and environmental concern constrains economic activity. Research suggests, however, that "pro-environmental countries fare better in terms of economic growth, investment and size of the industrial and service sectors."[35] The global marketplace does, in fact, provide a wealth of opportunities for marketing sustainably. One of those opportunities lies in building human capital in the global workforce.

Global Workforce

Global marketing organizations have traditionally outsourced labor, or moved production to countries where labor is cheaper than it is in domestic markets, in order to reduce costs and remain competitive in the global marketplace. Many factories in those countries were notorious for their exploitive and abusive practices with respect to workers. Historically, that has led to human rights protests and heavy public relations repercussions for high-profile companies and brands. According to a 2010 investigative report in the *Oregonian*, working conditions in some of those factories, especially those that supply international brands, are not only improving, they are helping to transform lives and reduce extreme poverty: "Years after activists accused Nike and other Western brands of running Third World sweatshops, the issue has taken a surprising turn. . . . Workers who stitched shoes for Nike Inc. and apparel for Columbia Sportswear Co. . . . are fueling a wave of prosperity in rural China. The boom has a solid feel, with villagers paying cash for houses."[36]

The article goes on to report that, despite wages that are miniscule by Western standards, workers are saving, investing, educating their children, and building the economies in their home communities. For example, a 31-year-old textile factory worker has saved enough to purchase a six-unit apartment building in his home community; a 40-year-old migrant construction worker has returned home and built a small fishing resort; and a former chemical plant worker has purchased a van and started a taxi service in his hometown.

THINK ABOUT IT

Building Human Capital

Naturally, issues of outsourcing and the cheap mass production of consumer goods are complex and controversial, especially from a sustainability standpoint (see Photo 8-2). However, focusing on the issue of human capital reveals some interesting questions. If workers from poor, rural villages can accumulate sufficient wealth to fuel economic development in their hometowns, what does that mean for marketing opportunities? As people emerge from poverty, what happens to their standards of living? How do their expectations change? If millions of people begin demanding consumer goods at higher levels, what is the effect on the overall demand for resources? How, if at all, can marketing organizations meet that increased demand sustainably?

PHOTO 8-2 Exploitation or opportunity? What determines the difference for these young women working in a garment factory?

Sustainable Marketing and Levels of Development

The opportunities and challenges for marketing firms in the global marketplace differ according to the levels of national and regional **economic development** in the places where they do business. Marketing education has traditionally prioritized the interests of **developed nations**, which include nations in North America, Europe, and parts of Asia, and treated **emerging nations**, including the nations of China, India, Brazil, and Mexico, and **developing nations**, mostly in the Global South (nations in Africa, Central and Latin American, and much of Asia) as potential sources of customers, labor, and resources.

A more productive and sustainable approach to global marketing is one that seeks to grow human capital, rather than exploit human resources in less developed regions, and to preserve and replenish natural capital throughout the world, assuring that future generations can survive and thrive as ours has. An important part of sustainable international marketing is the use of **appropriate technology**, meaning technology that is designed to be ideally suited to the environmental, economic, and social situations in the community in which it is employed.

Let's examine how the opportunities for sustainable marketing differ according to levels of economic development. First, however, let's clarify something important about the designations of developed, emerging, and developing nations. These labels are assigned on the basis of per capita gross domestic product. As such, they represent averages of income and affluence. In reality, averages can be misleading. Many developing nations have large populations of people that are deeply poor, ruled by a minority that is very rich, and with a small middle class. Most emerging nations also exhibit wide gulfs between the very rich and the very poor, but they also tend to have substantial or growing middle class populations.

Developed Nations and Sustainable Marketing

The world's most developed economies have the advantages of well-developed capital markets, stable governments, mature business institutions, and high levels of educational attainment and opportunity. However, much of the developed world's infrastructure is old, inefficient, and wasteful. Developed nations also consume disproportionate shares of the world's energy resources and have contributed disproportionately to the accumulation of GHGs that exacerbate global climate change.

Much of the real opportunity for sustainable marketing in the developed world lies in problem mitigation; that is, eliminating wastefulness, updating infrastructure, and reducing negative social and environmental impacts of current practices. One example of more sustainable marketing through waste reduction is called backhauling. Rather than returning with empty trailers, truckers instead load up with other companies' merchandise that can be delivered on their return trips. Macy's, a department store, and Schneider, a trucking company, have piloted such programs, and have lowered costs, increased revenue, and reduced emissions.[37] Similarly, the easiest, cheapest, and most effective ways to achieve dramatic reductions in GHG production lie in the areas of increased energy efficiency and conservation.

Beyond efficiencies such as backhauling and energy conservation, new technologies in the developed world will probably need to focus on radical innovation to make affluent consumer lifestyles sustainable. The necessary educational resources, capital, and technology are in place to make dramatic improvements in transportation, housing, and industrial infrastructures, and to develop more sustainable sources of energy.

Developing Nations and Sustainable Marketing

Life in the world's developing nations defines the opposite end of the spectrum from that in the developed nations. The greatest challenges to human life, health, and well-being persist in the developing nations, where millions of people face severe environmental degradation and a daily struggle for the most basic resources, such as food, water, and fuel. Unemployment, illness, malnutrition, and lack of education are widespread. And yet, it is in developing nations that the opportunities for sustainable marketing are in some ways the greatest.

The general lack of development in many African, Latin American, and Asian countries provides the opportunity to avoid the sustainability missteps of the developed nations. Rather than investing in the kinds of wasteful and unsustainable technologies that have evolved in the developed nations, developing nations have a chance to build infrastructures that are sustainable from the beginning. For example, countries that were slow to create landline-based telephone systems have leapfrogged ahead to develop excellent wireless systems. South Africa's mobile phone service currently reaches 83 percent of its population,[38] which is roughly equal to that of the United States.[39] Likewise, the poor state of traditional, grid-based electrical service to African villages provides excellent opportunities to develop local systems based on solar power.[40] In rural Nepal and about 25 other countries, the nonprofit Light Up the World Foundation has specialized in providing safe, long-lasting LED lighting to villages to replace kerosene lamps or wood fires, which create serious health and fire hazards. The LED lights operate on low voltages from batteries that are recharged by renewable power sources such as solar cells, human-pedaled generators, or small wind turbines.

If necessity is, indeed, the mother of invention, then developing nations offer enormous opportunities for innovation in sustainable marketing. One example of ingenuity and entrepreneurship can be found at the University of Nairobi, Kenya. Cell phone use in Kenya is widespread, but electricity is unreliable and expensive. To address this issue, two Nairobi engineering students have designed and built a cell phone charger that draws power from the motion of a bicycle. They built their pocket-sized prototype chargers from junkyard scraps, and they hope to mass-produce them with assistance from the university.[41]

Among the very poor in developing nations, appropriate technologies tend to rely more on labor, which is abundant, and less on financial capital, which may be scarce. Labor-intensive technologies employ more people and tend to work better when infrastructure is limited or unreliable. For example, a road crew of many manual laborers can do the same work as large road-building equipment, but without the need for expert maintenance, spare parts, or massive capital outlays. Among the poorest of the world's poor, trash pickers, scavengers who sort through trash seeking items of value, have emerged as an important force in reclaiming and reusing recyclable materials. Jack Chang of *McClatchy Newspapers* writes, "The unsung heroes are the impoverished trash pickers who fill the streets of countless cities around the developing world, searching garbage for cardboard, plastic bags and other treasure that can be sold and recycled. Every day, they rescue hundreds of thousands of tons of material from streets and trash dumps that get reprocessed into all kinds of products. That not only cuts back on the resources used by industries but also lightens the load on dumps that are quickly reaching capacity."[42]

Emerging Nations and Sustainable Marketing

Emerging nations exhibit many of the characteristics of both developing and developed nations. In the industrialized cities, all the trappings of an affluent consumer society are evident. Elsewhere, deep poverty is more reminiscent of the developing world. In nations like China, India, and Brazil, rapid industrialization using abundant, cheap labor has led to enormous growth, not only in wealth and infrastructure, but also in consumer demand.

This is a double-edged sword. Exploding demand means new customers for consumer goods and services, and new growth opportunities for the businesses that provide them. But with the growth in consumption and production come huge demands for energy resources and the potential for huge waste streams. For example, "The number of cars in China and India is predicted to rise from about 17 million to 1.1 billion by 2050. The addition of hundreds of millions of working, middle-class people in the developing world, all seeking a Western quality of life, will shake up nearly every industry."[43]

With outdated industrial and consumption practices, like dirty, coal-fired power plants and traditional waste disposal, such rapid growth could lead to global environmental catastrophe. On the other hand, if the hundreds of millions of consumers coming online in emerging economies can be supplied with sustainable products, distributed through efficient and sustainable infrastructures, then they could become the economic engine that drives global sustainable marketing. Brazil, for example, has become a world leader in biofuels, derived from its abundant crops of sugarcane.[44] The Brazilian city of Curitiba is widely hailed to be one of the world's most sustainable. Some interesting facts:

- Curitiba has the highest recycling rate in the world—70 percent.
- Curitiba has bus system that is so good that car traffic decreased by 30 percent while the population tripled in a 20-year period.
- Curitiba has the largest downtown pedestrian friendly shopping area in the world.
- Curitiba has built large numbers of beautiful parks to control floods rather than concrete canals. So many that they use sheep to cut the grass as it's cheaper than lawnmowers.
- Curitiba is a city where 99 percent of its inhabitants want to live. In comparison, 70 percent of Sao Paolo's residents want to live in Curitiba.
- Curitiba's average income per person has gone from less than the Brazilian average in the 1970s to 66 percent greater than the Brazilian average.[45]

Mini Case Study

A Sustainable Rural Village

In Huangbaiyu, Liaoning Province, a joint China-U.S. Center for Sustainable Development team is "advising local developers on the planning and construction of a sustainable rural village that the government hopes will serve as a prototype for improving the lives of 800 million rural Chinese."[46] Local builders are erecting model homes with environmentally friendly materials and technologies such as: recyclable polystyrene roof panels and insulation produced by BASF; compressed earth and straw walls created with machines made by Vermeer, a U.S. company; and 1,000-watt solar panels from BP. "BASF sees a huge market in China for superinsulating polystyrene as a possible alternative to resource-intensive building materials like coal-fired brick, which was recently banned in many cities under new Chinese environmental regulations. And if BP can accelerate China's move into the mass production of solar collectors, we will see a rapid, cost-efficient expansion of the global solar marketplace."[47]

What advantages do emerging nations have over developed nations as laboratories and marketplaces for sustainable technologies? What opportunities do the growth in emerging nations offer to firms in developed nations?

In another emerging economy, the Chilean forestry and wood manufacturing company, Masisa, sees social and environmental responsibility as key parts of its competitive strategy. Masisa's own research found that "our products' final consumers—people remodeling their kitchens or buying new furniture—consider a company's impact on the environment to be their second priority, right behind product design and durability."[48] The company is encouraging others in its supply chain to improve their own carbon footprints by offering basic education on emissions and energy savings.

GLOBAL GOVERNMENT AND REGULATORY CHALLENGES

Differences in environmental and social laws and regulations among countries can create both challenges and opportunities for marketers. In some cases, regions with minimal regulation and enforcement have been targeted by multinational corporations as markets, as labor pools, or as dumping grounds. For example, in the 1990s, facing increasing tobacco regulation in developed nations, large tobacco companies pumped up their marketing in less-regulated developing and emerging markets.[49] The exportation, often illegal, of electronic waste also targets regions where regulations are weak or unenforced.

Many corporations would prefer to follow uniform, worldwide sustainability standards, but they find it difficult to balance such standards with widely varying local regulations, traditions, and competitive pressures.[50]

THINK ABOUT IT

Is it possible for a company with high standards for environmental and social practices to compete successfully with a company that takes advantage of lax regulations to cut corners and reduce costs? Why or why not? What roles should world governments play in influencing the competitive environment?

Increasingly, the regulations that most influence international marketing are not primarily enacted by governments but, rather, by intergovernmental agreements and organizations. International trade agreements, such as **NAFTA** (North American Free Trade Agreement); common markets, such as the EU; and organizations, such as the **WTO** (World Trade Organization) and **World Bank**, have grown in scope and power over the years, presumably in order to provide member nations with fair and equitable trade rules, to adjudicate international disputes, and to promote economic development. On balance, such agreements have benefited international marketing and increased the volume of global trade; however, the benefits may accrue mostly to large international corporations, with adverse consequences to already disadvantaged populations and to the natural environment.

VIRTUAL FIELD TRIP

NAFTA

The North American Free Trade Agreement was controversial before it was signed by the leaders of Canada, Mexico, and the United States in 1992, and it remains controversial. Do an Internet search on "NAFTA pros and cons." What benefits has NAFTA had, and for whom? Who has been disadvantaged, and why? What have been some of the unintended social and environmental consequences? Do you think NAFTA should be rescinded, expanded, renegotiated, or kept as is?

The WTO, successor to the General Agreement on Tariffs and Trade (GATT) and one of the most powerful organizations on the planet, has over 150 member nations[51] and governs policies that affect virtually all the world's international trade. GATT and the WTO have without a doubt succeeded in increasing global commerce. Nevertheless, ethicist Peter Singer cites four criticisms of the WTO: first, that it consistently places economic considerations ahead of the environment and human rights; second, that it undermines national protections and sovereignty; third, that it is undemocratic, allowing a few members to override the will of a majority; and fourth, that it enriches the world's richest people at the expense of its poorest.[52] In his book, *Blessed Unrest*, Paul Hawken criticizes the WTO for facilitating "the corporatization of the commons,"[53] by which he means the privatization of ownership of formerly public property such as fresh water, the human genome, seeds, and airwaves.

Because sustainability is linked directly to issues of trade, the WTO has the power, if not the will, to be a major force for positive change. For example, in the case of rapidly declining world fisheries, made worse by fishing subsidies by individual governments, one group of fisheries experts has declared that, "... the WTO, which has in place mechanisms to enforce its agreements, is the only institution that can tackle the global problem of overfishing subsidies."[54]

As the importance of climate change has become clearer to global leaders, other organizations and agreements have gained power and prominence. The most well-known intergovernmental efforts include treaties, such as the United Nations Framework Convention on Climate Change,[55] and agreements, such as the Kyoto Protocol[56] and the more recent United Nations Summit on Climate Change held in Copenhagen.[57]

Public fears about health and safety have led to the ban of **genetically modified** (GM) **foods** in many European countries. This is meant to preserve the original genetics and biodiversity of food crops and animals, but does it increase sustainability? Robert B. Shapiro, CEO of Monsanto, has a different viewpoint: "If companies genetically code a plant to repel pests, farmers don't have to spray with pesticides."[58] Naturally, if the relevant genes are patented, then genetic modification can lead to competitive advantage and enormous profits for companies like Monsanto.

THINK ABOUT IT

Is it possible for companies to approach GM food production sustainably? Does reduced use of pesticides offset potential risks to health and food safety? Why or why not? Can biodiversity be preserved in the food supply if GM crops become widespread? How? What is the role of sustainable marketing?

The EU has developed a series of environmental directives related to electronic and chemical wastes. These include the **Restriction of Hazardous Substances Directive** (RoHS) adopted in February 2003, which restricts the use of specific hazardous materials found in electrical and electronic products.[59] WEEE is the acronym for the **Waste from Electrical and Electronic Equipment** directive, which "mandates the treatment, recovery and recycling of electric and electronic equipment . . . for all applicable products in the EU market after August 13, 2006. . . . WEEE compliance aims to encourage the design of electronic products with environmentally safe recycling and recovery in mind. RoHS compliance dovetails into WEEE by reducing the amount of hazardous chemicals used in electronic manufacture."[60] **REACH** is EU's regulation on the manufacture and use of chemicals. The acronym stands for Registration, Evaluation, Authorization and Restriction of Chemical substances. Its purpose is "to improve the protection of human health and the environment through the better and earlier identification of the intrinsic properties of chemical substances."[61] The European Commission believes that REACH will enhance the innovative capability and competitiveness of the EU chemicals industry.

One impact of such regulations is that they force suppliers to develop more sustainable products for the large European market. This, in turn, makes the same products available for other markets as well. Wal-Mart, for example, has decided voluntarily to bring RoHS-compliant products to the U.S. market.[62]

GLOBAL CONSUMERS AND SUSTAINABLE MARKETING

All across the world consumers' attitudes toward sustainable products and lifestyles are growing stronger and more positive. One arena where this shift shows up is that of social and environmental activism. Paul Hawken estimates that the number of the world's environmental and social-justice organizations exceeds 100,000.[63] According to Hawken, this constitutes a global social movement on a scale never seen before.

A worldwide study by GfK Roper reveals that concern for environmental sustainability is rising worldwide. However, the same study shows that "less than one third of the total population (29%) feel they can personally do a 'fair amount' or 'a lot' to improve the environment."[64]

A 2009 global tracking study by National Geographic and GlobeScan, called Greendex, measures both attitudes and actual consumer behaviors:

This quantitative consumer study of 17,000 consumers in a total of 17 countries (14 in 2008) asked about such behavior as energy use and conservation, transportation choices, food sources, the relative use of green products versus traditional products, attitudes towards the environment and sustainability, and knowledge of environmental issues.[65]

Greendex research shows that both attitudes and consumer behavior are greening. Perhaps surprisingly, the populations living most sustainably by Greendex measures are China, India, and Brazil. Citizens of more affluent nations, such as the United States, Canada, and members of the EU, have larger environmental footprints, suggesting that affluence alone may constitute a barrier to sustainable living.

In the affluent, developed nations, there is great market potential for more sustainable products and lifestyles. For example, the LOHAS market, discussed in Chapter 7, is also prevalent in Japan.[66] Green consumers in Europe continue to grow both in their numbers and in their diversity.[67] In some parts of the world and in some industries, the push toward sustainability is becoming such a dominant force that whole regions can be identified as target markets. The U.S. Department of Commerce identifies the Nordic countries of Denmark, Finland, Norway, and Sweden as a prime target for sustainable marketing.[68] In Bangkok, Thailand, where population density and high traffic volume created a severe air quality problem, Shell Oil Company successfully markets a cleaner burning fuel. Called Pura, it's a blend of natural-gas-converted zero-sulfur liquid mixed with regular diesel, and it's promoted as a way to reduce pollution and help keep engines cleaner and lasting longer. The same formula is sold in Holland as V-Power, and is promoted as a fuel that enhances engine power.[69]

Despite global improvement in the sustainability of consumer behaviors, there remains a significant gap between attitudes and actions. A 2008 study out of Stanford University[70] documents this gap and identifies five major barriers to more sustainable consumer behavior:

1. Lack of awareness and knowledge—Many consumers claim they don't know how to reduce their social and environmental impacts.
2. Negative perceptions—Many consumers tend to believe that more sustainable products are inferior with respect to actual performance.
3. Distrust—Many consumers don't believe marketers' sustainability claims, and rightfully so because of the level of false and misleading claims.
4. High prices—Many consumers believe, often correctly, that more sustainable products carry higher prices, which they are unwilling to pay.
5. Low availability—Many consumers have a hard time even finding more sustainable products, such as organic foods, renewable power, or environmentally friendly apparel or home furnishings.

The corresponding solutions, according to the Stanford study, all derive from sustainable marketing. They include (1) educating consumers, (2) designing and building better products, (3) communicating honestly, (4) offering a clearer value proposition and (5) distributing products more widely.

SUSTAINABILITY IN GLOBAL BUSINESS-TO-BUSINESS MARKETS

Global progress in sustainability reaches well beyond governmental regulation and individual consumption practices. Core values of social, economic, and environmental sustainability are also evident in much of the business-to-business (B2B) market. U.S. managers looking to increase their global business markets need to consider the sustainability values of their target market as closely as they consider the cultural traditions, regional and local laws, and business customs.

Financial services companies may not be the first industry that comes to mind when one thinks about combating global warming. But the insurance company, Swiss Re, which operates in the B2B market insuring other firms, is doing just that. Swiss Re sees the "potentially catastrophic effects of climate change as major risk[s] to its industry and its customers"[71] The company uses incentives to encourage employees to drive hybrid cars, use energy-efficient appliances, and install solar panels. By reducing their own carbon footprint, Swiss Re wants, in part, to raise risk awareness among its clients.

As industries of all kinds attempt to become more sustainable, they exert pressure throughout their supply chains to provide more environmentally and socially positive products and services. In B2B marketing, even more than in consumer marketing, sustainable practices are becoming an obvious and important competitive advantage in the global marketplace.

PHOTO 8-3 Robert Swan in Antarctica.

CRITICAL THINKING ACTIVITY

One Man: Global Effort

In 1986, Robert Swan (see Photo 8-3) became the first person to walk to the South Pole. He spent five years raising funds for the adventure. Swan and two companions walked for 70 days over 900 miles from the Jack Hayward base on the Antarctic coast to the South Pole. They walked without radio communications or back-up support and hauled 350-pound sledges. While walking, Swan noticed that his eye color changed. He later learned he'd been walking under the hole in the ozone layer without adequate protection against ultraviolet radiation. The party arrived at the South Pole on January 11, 1986. This adventure was followed by an expedition to the North Pole, and on May 14, 1989, Swan and his team of eight people from seven nations reached their destination, making Robert Swan the first man to walk to both poles.[72]

Swan had promised supporters he would get the word out about the global environmental crisis. And for years, that's exactly what he's done. In 1992, he was a keynote speaker at the first United Nations Conference on Environment and Development, and he committed to furthering his mission of global and local environmentalism. His accomplishments include One Step Beyond, The South Pole Challenge, where he brought 35 young adventurers from 25 nations together to remove and recycle 1,500 tons of waste that had been left at the Bellinghausen Base in Antarctica after decades of scientific research. When the adventurers finished, native penguins returned to the beach for the first time in 47 years. Swan again participated in another international event, the 2002 World Summit for Sustainable Development in Johannesburg, South Africa. He traveled around the country with his sailboat, 2041, reaching over 750,000 young South Africans with his message of sustainability and AIDS prevention. The name of Swan's boat honors the year when the Antarctic Treaty, which now bans mining and mineral exploration in Antarctica and protects the continent as "a Natural Reserve Land for Science and Peace," comes up for debate. In 2003, Swan took corporate leaders to Antarctica to witness firsthand the effects of climate change and charged them with the responsibility of becoming sustainability leaders in their industries. In March 2008, Swan and a small team lived for two weeks at the Antarctic E-base, "the world's first education station in Antarctica to be used as a resource for teachers and young people from around the world," relying solely on renewable energy.[73]

Think about the power of his financial backers' demands and Swan's own individual efforts. What could be accomplished if multinational corporations assumed similar responsibility for the environment? Should businesses use their economic power to demand social and environmental progress? How might their stakeholders respond? How would this affect their global competitive advantage? What impact would this have on global markets for their products and services?

Chapter Summary

In our interconnected world, where every nation and virtually every person is affected by global trade, sustainable marketing also is global in scope. Different levels of economic development create different challenges and opportunities for sustainable marketing. In the most affluent nations, where consumer demand is already increasing for sustainable products and services, the call is for less waste, greater efficiencies, and the conversion of unsustainable systems and infrastructures to more sustainable and renewable models. In emerging economies, the challenge for sustainable marketing is to harness explosive growth in consumer demand and industrialization so that rising standards of living among huge populations can be provided without destroying the environment in the bargain. In the poorer, developing nations, sustainable marketing must focus on providing for basic human needs, such as clean water, adequate food, and necessary medicines, and also on building human capital through education and work opportunities. Because communication, power, and transportation infrastructures are still poorly developed, there are huge opportunities to leapfrog over outdated technologies and establish sustainable options from the beginning. National government regulations and international trade agreements can either help or hinder efforts to improve social and environmental sustainability. Sustainable marketing, if practiced by the world's largest corporations, could effectively focus the efforts of both governments and businesses on building human capital, creating new and more affluent markets, and serving those markets with sustainable goods and services.

Review of Chapter Objectives

- Global environmental challenges
- Global economic challenges
- Global government and regulatory challenges
- Global consumers and sustainable marketing
- Sustainability in global business-to-business markets

Key Concepts

Water Crisis   107
Embedded Water   107
Cap and Trade   109
European Union
   Emissions Trading
   Scheme   110
Economic Development   112

Developed Nations   112
Emerging Nations   112
Developing
   Nations   112
Appropriate
   Technology   112
NAFTA   115

WTO   115
World Bank   115
Genetically Modified (GM)
   Foods   116
RoHS (Restriction of
   Hazardous Substances
   Directive)   116

WEEE (Waste from
   Electrical and Electronic
   Equipment)   116
REACH (Registration,
   Evaluation, Authorization
   and Restriction of Chemical
   Substances)   116

Endnotes

1. *Asia News* (2006), "China's Air Pollution Hits United States," July 31, http://www.asianews.it/view.php?l=en&art=6843, accessed September 3, 2009.

2. Physorg.com (2008), "Satellite Measures Pollution from East Asia to North America," March 17, http://www.physorg.com/news124991552.html, accessed September 3, 2009.

3. World Health Organization (2008), "Safer Water, Better Health," http://www.who.int/quantifying_ehimpacts/publications/saferwater/en/index.html, accessed September 6, 2009. See also, http://water.org/facts.

4. Lynas, Mark (2009), "Climate Change Explained: The Impact of Temperature Rises," Written for the *Guardian*, April 14, 2009. A slightly updated precis of Six Degrees, http://www.marklynas.org/2009/5/5/climate-change-explained-the-impact-of-temperature-rises, accessed September 5, 2009.

5. Esty, Daniel C. and Andrew S. Winston (2006), *Green to Gold: How Smart Companies Use Environmental Strategy to Innovate, Create Value, and Build Competitive Advantage*, New Haven, CT: Yale University Press (p. 160).

6. McFarlan, John (2000). "In a Hot Summer, Liquid Gold in Texas Isn't oil—It's Water." The Associated Press. July 26, *Oregonian*, A-7.

7. Water Footprint of a Chip Fabrication Plant, http://www.vertatique.com/water-footprint-chip-fabrication-plant, accessed March 1, 2010.

8. World Wildlife Fund (2009). *Focus*, 31(3).

9. Alter, Alexandra (2009), Yet Another 'Footprint' to Worry About: Water, *Wall Street Journal*, February 17, http://online.wsj.com/article/SB123483638138996305.html, accessed October 15, 2009.

10. Nestle Waters, http://www.nestlewatersca.com/sacramento/, accessed October 15, 2009.

11. Garvin, Cosmo (2009), "Something in the Water," *NewsReview.com*, July 30, http://www.newsreview.com/sacramento/content?oid=1050642, accessed August 10, 2009.

12. World Wildlife Fund (2009). *Focus*, 31(3).

13. Stop Nestle Waters, http://stopnestlewaters.org/ accessed August 10, 2009.

14. Earth911, "Plastic: Facts about Plastic Bottles," http://earth911.com/recycling/plastic/plastic-bottles/facts-about-plastic-bottles/, accessed March 12, 2010.

15. Natural Resources Defense Council, "Bottled Water: Pure Drink or Pure Hype," http://www.nrdc.org/Water/Drinking/Bw/bwinx.asp, accessed March 12, 2010.

16. Arc Space, Exhibition, http://www.arcspace.com/exhibitions/louisiana2/green-architecture-for-the-future.html, accessed March 12, 2010.

17. Tully, Shawn (2000), "Water, Water Everywhere," *Fortune*, May 15, http://money.cnn.com/magazines/fortune/fortune_archive/2000/05/15/279789/index.htm, accessed March 12, 2010.

18. Barlow, Maude and Tony Clarke (2004), "Water Privatization," *Global Policy Forum*, http://www.globalpolicy.org/component/content/article/209/43398.html, accessed September 8, 2009.

19. *CBC News*, "Sell the Rain: How the Privatization of Water Caused Riots in Cochabamba, Bolivia," http://www.cbc.ca/news/features/water/bolivia.html, accessed September 8, 2009.

20. Cuba, Jorge (2000), "Free or Foreign: The Water Battle in Bolivia," *UNESCO Courier*, December, http://www.unesco.org/courier/2000_12/uk/planet2.htm, accessed March 12, 2010.

21. The White House, "Issues, Energy and Environment," http://www.whitehouse.gov/issues/energy_and_environment/, accessed October 15, 2009.

22. Environmental Protection Agency, "Cap and Trade," http://www.epa.gov/captrade/, accessed October 15, 2009.

23. Lutzy, Rebecca (2009), "Senators Gear Up to Ditch Cap-and-Trade This Year and Focus on Energy," *Energy Collective*, August 15, http://theenergycollective.com/TheEnergyCollective/46351, accessed October 15, 2009.

24. Emission Trading System (EU ETS), http://ec.europa.eu/environment/climat/emission/index_en.htm, accessed October 15, 2009.

25. Office Journal of the European Union, http://eur-lex.europa.eu/LexUriServ/LexUriServ.do?uri=OJ:L:2009:140:0063:0087:en:PDF, accessed October 15, 2009.

26. Goldenberg, Suzanne and Jonathan Watts (2009), "US Aims for Bilateral Climate Change Deals with China and India," guardian.co.uk, October 14, http://www.guardian.co.uk/environment/2009/oct/14/obama-india-china-climate-change, accessed October 15, 2009.

27. Bradsher, Keith (2009), "China Vies to Be World's Leader in Electric Cars," *New York Times*, April 1, http://www.nytimes.com/2009/04/02/business/global/02electric.html, accessed October 15, 2009.

28. Watts, Jonathan (2009), China Puts Its Faith in Solar Power with Huge Renewable Energy Investment," guardian.co.uk, May 26, http://www.guardian.co.uk/world/2009/may/26/china-invests-solar-power-renewable-energy-environment, accessed October 15, 2009.

29. Goldenberg, Suzanne and Jonathan Watts (2009), "US Aims for Bilateral Climate Change Deals with China and India," guardian.co.uk, October 14, http://www.guardian.co.uk/

environment/2009/oct/14/obama-india-china-climate-change, accessed October 15, 2009.

30. "U.S. Total Import Trade in Goods and Services," http://www.census.gov/foreign-trade/statistics/historical/gandsimp.pdf, accessed September 6, 2009.

31. "U.S. Total Export Trade in Goods and Services," http://www.census.gov/foreign-trade/statistics/historical/gandsexp.pdf, accessed September 6, 2009.

32. Yahoo Finance, "Investing, Industry Center, Beverages, Soft Drinks, The CocaCola Company Profile," http://biz.yahoo.com/ic/10/10359.html, accessed September 6, 2009.

33. Green Peace, "Where Does E-Waste End Up," http://www.greenpeace.org/international/campaigns/toxics/electronics/where-does-e-waste-end-up, accessed September 5, 2009.

34. CBS *60 Minutes* (2009), "The Wasteland," August 30, http://television.aol.com/show/video/partner/cbs/60-minutes/60-minutes-083009/SbbEMEmNKcY7CWz9i1e91MNvKXyLKStc, accessed September 5, 2009.

35. Schofer, Evan and Francisco J. Granados (2006) "Environmentalism, Globalization and National Economies," 1980–2000, *Social Forces*, 85 (2, December): 965–991.

36. Read, Richard (2010), "Chinese Factory Workers Cash in Sweat for Prosperity," *Oregonian*, March 7, pp. A1, A12.

37. Sustainable Life Media (2009), "Schneider & Macy's Save on Empty Containers," October 15, http://www.sustainablelifemedia.com/content/story/design/schneider_and_macys_save_on_empty_containers, accessed October 15, 2009.

38. "Tech Crunchies, Internet Statistics and Numbers: South Africa's Mobile Phone Penetration," http://techcrunchies.com/south-africas-mobile-phone-penetration/, accessed September 7, 2009.

39. Gearlog, "U.S. Cell Phone Penetration Tops 82 Percent," http://www.gearlog.com/2007/11/us_cellphone_penetration_tops.php, accessed September 7, 2009.

40. "Africa Renewal: Solar Power," http://www.un.org/ecosocdev/geninfo/afrec/vol20no3/203-solar-power.html, accessed September 7, 2009.

41. Upham, BC (2009), "Kenyan Entrepreneurs' Bike Powered, Phone Charging Dynamo," *Triplepundit*, August 21, http://www.triplepundit.com/2009/08/african-entrepreneurs-bike-powered-phone-charging-dynamo/, accessed August 28, 2009.

42. Chang, Jack (2008), "Scorned Trash Pickers Become Global Environmental Force," *McClatchy*, March 24, http://www.mcclatchydc.com/2008/03/24/31468/scorned-trash-pickers-become-global.html, accessed March 11, 2010.

43. Esty, Daniel C. and Andrew S. Winston (2006), *Green to Gold: How Smart Companies Use Environmental Strategy to Innovate, Create Value, and Build Competitive Advantage*, New Haven, CT: Yale University Press (p. 16).

44. Plummer, Robert (2006), The Rise, Fall and Rise of Brazil's Biofuel, *BBC News*, Jan 24., http://news.bbc.co.uk/2/hi/business/4581955.stm, accessed March 11, 2010.

45. Cities for People, Curitiba, Brazil, http://www.citiesforpeople.net/cities/curitiba.html, accessed March 11, 2010.

46. McDonough, William (2006), "China as a Green Lab," *Harvard Business Review*, 84 (2, February).

47. McDonough, William (2006), "China as a Green Lab," *Harvard Business Review*, 84 (2, February).

48. Correa, Maria Emilia (2007), "Leading Change in Latin America," *Harvard Business Review*, 85 (10): 40–42.

49. Makary, Martin A. and Ichiro Kawachi (1998), "The International Tobacco Strategy," *Journal of the American Medical Association*, 280, 1194–1195, http://jama.ama-assn.org/cgi/content/full/280/13/1194, accessed September 7, 2009.

50. Epstein, Marc J. (2008), "Making Sustainability Work: Best Practices in Managing and Measuring Corporate Social, Environmental, and Economic Impacts," San Francisco, CA: Berrett-Koehler Publishers.

51. World Trade Organization, "Understanding the WTO, Members and Observers," http://www.wto.org/english/thewto_e/whatis_e/tif_e/org6_e.htm, accessed September 8, 2009.

52. Singer, Peter (2002), *One World: The Ethics of Globalization*, New Haven, CT: Yale University Press.

53. Hawken, Paul (2007), *Blessed Unrest*, New York: Penguin Group.

54. Sumaila, Ussif Rashid, Ahmed Khan, Reg Watson, Gordon Munro, Dirk Zeller, Nancy Baron, and Daniel Pauly (2007), "The World Trade Organization and Global Fisheries Sustainability," *Fisheries Research*, 88 (p. 1–4).

55. UNFCCC, Essential Background, http://unfccc.int/essential_background/items/2877.php, accessed March 13, 2010.

56. UNFCCC, Kyoto Protocol, http://unfccc.int/kyoto_protocol/items/2830.php, accessed March 13, 2010.

57. United Nations, Summit on Climate Change, http://www.un.org/wcm/content/site/climatechange/lang/en/pages/2009summit, accessed March 13, 2010.

58. Magretta, Joan (1996). "Growth through Global Sustainability: An Interview with Monsanto's CEO, Robert B. Shaprio," *Harvard Business Review*, 75 (1): 78–88.

59. RoHS & WEEE—Information Guide to RoHS Compliance, http://www.rohsguide.com/rohs-faq.htm, accessed August 27, 2009.

60. RoHS & WEEE—Information Guide to RoHS Compliance, http://www.rohsguide.com/rohs-faq.htm, accessed August 27, 2009.

61. Environment, Reach, "What Is Reach," http://ec.europa.eu/environment/chemicals/reach/reach_intro.htm, accessed August 27, 2009.

62. "Recycling Today, Wal-Mart to Market ROHS Compliant Laptops," http://www.recyclingtoday.com/news/news.asp?ID=9220, accessed September 8, 2009.

63. Hawken, Paul (2007), *Blessed Unrest*, New York: Penguin Group (p. 2).

64. Corporate Social Responsibility Newswire, CSR Press Release, http://www.csrwire.com/press/press_release/15419-Global-Environmental-Concerns-Growing-as-Population-Looks-to-Government-to-Lead-Charge-Reports-GfK-Roper-Consulting, accessed August 27, 2009.

65. National Geographic, "Greendex: What is Greendex," http://www.nationalgeographic.com/greendex/, accessed March 13, 2010.

66. "Lifestyles of Health and Sustainability: LOHAS Takes Japan," http://www.lohas.com/journal/japan.html, accessed September 8, 2009.

67. Food Navigator, "Green Consumer Shifts in Attitude," http://www.foodnavigator.com/Financial-Industry/Green-consumer-shifts-in-attitude, accessed September 8, 2009.

68. Export, Articles, Market of the Month-Nordics, http://www.export.gov/articles/marketofmonth/eg_main_019703.asp, accessed September 8, 2009.

69. Esty, Daniel C. and Andrew S. Winston (2006), *Green to Gold: How Smart Companies Use Environmental Strategy to Innovate, Create Value, and Build Competitive Advantage*, New Haven, CT: Yale University Press.

70. Bonini, Sheila and Jeremy Oppenheim (2008), *Stanford Social Innovation Review*, Fall, http://www.ssireview.org/articles/entry/cultivating_the_green_consumer/, accessed March 13, 2010.

71. Way, Mark and Britta Rendlen (2007), "Walking the Talk at Swiss Re," *Harvard Business Review*, 85 (10): 42.

72. Swan, Robert with Gil Reavill (2009), *Antarctica 2041: My Quest to Save the Earth's Last Wilderness*, New York: Broadway Books.

73. Swan, Robert, Public Presentation, University of Portland, 2008; Personal Communication, 2008; Responsibility Alliance http://www.responseabilityalliance.com/html/robert_swan_obe.html, accessed September 7, 2009; "2041" http://www.2041.com/about-2041/, accessed September 7, 2009.

Sustainable Products and Services

INTRODUCTION: HOW DO YOU LIKE MY MEDICINE?

According to writer Susan Stranahan, you may well be "drinking water laced with minute quantities of drugs, including antibiotics, steroids, antidepressants and hormones."[1] In 2008, the Associated Press conducted an investigation of drinking water in 24 major U.S. metropolitan areas and found measurable amounts of pharmaceuticals. The study revealed that, "Drugs get into the drinking water supply through several routes: some people flush unneeded medication down toilets; other medicine gets into the water supply after people take medication, absorb some, and pass the rest out in urine or feces. Some pharmaceuticals remain even after wastewater treatments and cleansing by water treatment plants."[2] Stranahan adds that, at their current quantities, drugs in the water system don't appear to pose human health risks, but that no one really knows what the consequences might be to humans or to aquatic life of long-term exposure.[3]

THINK ABOUT IT

How do you feel about the news that your drinking water, streams, and rivers may be contaminated with prescription drugs? Who shares in the responsibility for controlling the amounts of pharmaceutical waste being introduced to the environment? Does a marketer have any responsibility for a product once it has been sold?

A major function of marketing is the development and management of the **product mix**, which includes all of the goods and services a company offers to its customers, along with the packaging that accompanies them. The product mix has impact on numerous stakeholders, which include the company, its customers, and society, both current and future. A product's impact is felt throughout its life cycle, which begins with strategy and design and continues through manufacturing, marketing, consumption, and final disposition. In the product mix, we also include the brand, which is integral to how customers and society perceive and understand the product mix. This chapter focuses on products as goods and services. We deal with packaging and branding separately in Chapter 10.

CHAPTER OBJECTIVES

In this chapter, you will learn principles of sustainable product strategy, including:

- Product stewardship
- Service-dominant logic
- Product sustainability
- Developing sustainable new products
- Sustainable services

PRODUCT STEWARDSHIP

For the product mix to be sustainable often requires a company to take increased responsibility for its product offerings. This concept, known as **product stewardship**, is defined as "understanding, controlling, and communicating a product's environmental, health, and safety related effects throughout its life cycle, from production (or extraction) to final disposal or reuse."[4] Advantages of product stewardship to a business include reductions in overall life-cycle costs.[5] Kodak practices product stewardship with respect to its one-time-use cameras, which are used once and then returned in their entirety by the consumer to Kodak for film development and camera recycling. The cameras are shipped to Kodak manufacturing facilities, where they are inspected and remanufactured with fresh film to be sold again. Plastic parts that can't be reused are shipped to a recycling center, where they are ground up into pellets and remolded into cameras or other products.[6] Because a product migrates through an entire supply chain on its way to consumers and beyond, many of the issues around product stewardship come up again in Chapter 11 about marketing channels.

This chapter stresses the importance of sustainability in the product mix and discusses some of the ways marketing firms are assuming greater responsibility for their products' social and environmental impacts. The job of making products more sustainable begins with rethinking the **product strategy**, which can be defined as a firm's decisions concerning the best combination of goods and services to deliver value to its target market. In the coming age, however, product strategies can't be concerned only with customer satisfaction and business profits. They must also recognize society's other stakeholders, both present and future.

SERVICE-DOMINANT LOGIC

Consumers meet many of their needs by purchasing a variety of goods and services. Since the industrial revolution, the guiding logic of marketing has been one of manufacturing and selling products, which in turn provide service to consumers. As we look for ways to create sustainable product strategies, we can often identify more direct means for meeting the needs of consumers. Rather than focusing primarily on the sale of goods, with certain services as ancillary or complementary features, **service-dominant logic** (SDL)[7] focuses on what needs people are trying to meet rather than what products they will buy. In other words, consumers don't necessarily want more products; they want the services or benefits the products provide. For example, in buying or leasing a DVR (digital video recorder), a consumer doesn't want primarily a box full of hardware and software. She wants a convenient, reliable source of quality in-home entertainment. The DVR, cable, and satellite dish are only valuable as means of delivering the service.

SDL revolves around the question: "What benefits or services are our customers seeking?" The key to a sustainable product strategy is to offer the benefits in a way that is competitive as well as socially and environmentally responsible. SDL offers a more sustainable way of thinking about marketing, "one in which service provision rather than goods is fundamental to economic exchange."[8]

One path to greater product sustainability is called **dematerialization**, which "occurs when fewer resources are used to create the same or equivalent benefits."[9] Bob Willard describes dematerialization as "the ultimate in environmental sensitivity, since product take-back is automatic."[10] In other words, once a dematerialized service is delivered, the only thing left behind is the benefit. Donald Fuller describes three ways to dematerialize:

- Limit the quantities of materials used in packaging,
- Move from disposable goods to higher quality durable goods, and
- Convert traditional ownership of durable goods to shared ownership, shared use, or rental programs.[11]

The philosophy of Natural Capitalism, presented in Chapter 2, also uses SDL. According to its authors, "The business model of traditional manufacturing rests on the sale of goods. In the new model, value is instead delivered as a flow of services—providing illumination, for example, rather than selling light bulbs."[12] To be competitive, a firm must make sure that its customers can use its services as easily or conveniently as if they owned and used the products themselves.[13]

One advantage of selling services rather than products is that it eliminates the need for product guarantees.[14] By retaining ownership and control of service-delivery products, the firm frees itself from the costs of replacement or repair due to misuse by the consumer. At the same time, customers are relieved of the burdens and costs of purchasing, storing, handling, and disposing of the same products. A traditional example would be a housecleaning service. The service provider uses cleaning products and equipment, but maintains control over them. Customers receive the benefit of cleanliness without the need of dealing with chemicals, containers, and machinery (not to mention spending prime weekend time on housekeeping). There is less waste overall, and possibly greater satisfaction. Zen Home, in New York City, is a home-cleaning business that competes on the basis of luxury service and eco-friendly products.[15] A less traditional example of a service provider is Zipcar, which provides the benefit of automobile transportation without the need for car ownership, maintenance, storage, insurance, or resale.[16]

In the world of business-to-business (B2B) marketing, Xerox demonstrates the advantages of SDL. Xerox has reinvented itself as a provider of documentation services rather than a manufacturer and seller of copiers. Xerox leases, maintains, and refurbishes copiers, including technology updates, and in general, provides whatever a customer requires in order to reproduce documents. The SDL strategy yields "higher customer satisfaction, lower energy usage, and 91 percent rate of recycling of printers, demonstrating that you can minimize resource usage while maximizing service."[17]

THINK ABOUT IT

What other products could be replaced in our lives with services? Could kitchens and all their supplies be replaced with food service? What kinds of waste and expense could be eliminated? What other benefits could it have for health and enjoyment? Under what circumstances would it work? What would be lost in the bargain? What about housing? Could home ownership be replaced by a high-quality service? What expenses and burdens could be removed from the consumer? In what ways could it enhance sustainability? What would potentially be sacrificed? If, over the course of your life, you could spend less money for greater housing value, would you forego owning a home?

The marketing opportunities employing SDL are practically limitless. To explore other imaginative examples of SDL marketing, check out the Oakland Public Library's "Tool Lending Library,"[18] or Avelle's Bag Borrow or Steal.[19]

PRODUCT SUSTAINABILITY USING THE NATURAL STEP FRAMEWORK

As you've learned previously, The Natural Step Framework (TNSF) provides a highly useful, science-based means for understanding sustainability. Developing and marketing sustainable products requires an understanding of the entire life cycle of a company's goods and services. This includes not only the products, but also their packaging. It begins with product strategy and design, includes production processes and the sourcing of materials, and extends through the sale to the product's use and its end-of-life disposition by the customer. From the perspective of TNSF, a sustainable product is one that doesn't violate the four conditions of a sustainable system. Let's reexamine the system conditions and apply them to product strategy.

System Conditions One and Two

A sustainable product does not contribute to increasing concentrations of substances from the Earth's crust or of synthetic substances in the ecosphere. In other words, it doesn't pollute or poison the environment with toxic metals, fossil carbon, or synthetic materials. The kinds of pollutants covered by these two system conditions include gasoline, coal, mercury, chromium, plastics, pesticides, flame retardants, solvents, and other materials the Earth is incapable of reabsorbing, breaking down, or neutralizing in human time.

Part of achieving the right balance of goods and services to provide competitive customer benefits occurs in the design process. Product design, as part of the overall product strategy, is full of opportunities to enhance sustainability along with other important product attributes, such its functional, aesthetic, and experiential qualities. Here are some ways product design can improve sustainability by keeping in mind the first two system conditions of TNSF.

1. Design products to be manufactured with renewable, reclaimed, nontoxic and organic materials—for example, Seventh Generation has led the household-cleaning products industry in the design and development of effective, eco-friendly products.
2. Design products for more efficient, carbon-neutral storage and transportation—for example, all® Small and Mighty laundry detergent, formulated with only a third of the water contained in standard detergents, reduces both shipping and storage costs, saving both energy and water along the way.
3. Design products for safe, carbon-neutral operation—for example, Burley bicycles fitted with trailers for hauling kids, pets, or gear.[20]
4. Design products for disassembly, remanufacturing, and materials recovery.

Design for disassembly (DfD) is an important part of cradle-to-cradle design and manufacturing. Consider the experience described by consultant Jonathan Larson, "In one DfD project

All that's left behind is clean.
Seventh Generation. Free & Clear

Protecting Planet Home™

Absolutely free of dyes, fragrances, and masking agents – developed for those with asthma, allergies, sensitive skin, or chemical sensitivities.

Stop by for a visit: **seventhgeneration.com**

Seventh Generation has led the industry in eliminating toxic and synthetic substances from household cleaning products.

G-Diapers are designed to biodegrade completely, helping solve the problem of 50 million disposable diapers entering landfills every day.

I worked on, production costs were cut by over 50%, service calls and consumer relations were greatly simplified, toxic processes were eliminated, and so much solid waste was removed and so much recycled material was introduced into the production systems that this manufacturer became a net consumer of waste products."[21]

There are significant opportunities to increase sustainability in the manufacturing process as well. They include:

- replacing fossil fuels and nuclear power with renewable energy sources;
- replacing or reusing petroleum-based hydraulic fluids and lubricants;
- eliminating the use of pesticides, inorganic fertilizers, and chemical solvents; and
- reducing or eliminating the use of virgin (nonrecycled) materials.

Examples of firms reducing their impacts on the first two system conditions are abundant. For example, Toyota Logistics Services (TLS), which prepares imported automobiles for North American distribution, uses a large number of hydraulic machines. It has replaced all the petroleum-based hydraulic fluids with a vegetable-based fluid called Safe Lube. When hydraulic lines occasionally rupture, spilling hydraulic fluid, it no longer results in a toxic event. TLS also purchases 100 percent renewable wind power for the operation of its Portland, Oregon, facility. The cost is offset by numerous energy saving innovations, and the net effect is a reduction of the ecological footprint of every Toyota vehicle that passes through the facility.

As an example of reducing the use of virgin materials (produced with high levels of energy from raw petroleum), the apparel-marketing firm, Patagonia, has helped popularize the use of recycled polyester in its Synchilla fleece and Capilene fabrics, effectively reducing the carbon footprints of its products. Compared to virgin aluminum from bauxite ore, recycled aluminum can be fabricated with a 95 percent savings in energy consumption.[22] The aluminum industry has recently begun producing recycled aluminum foil for household use.

THINK ABOUT IT

What product manufacturers have changed their processes and materials to create more sustainable finished goods? Consider products you use every day, such as personal care products, foods, electronics, and clothing (see Photo 9-1). Which brands, if any, offer a more sustainable alternative?

PHOTO 9-1 For many consumers, the Whole Foods brand has become synonymous with more sustainable products.

Finally, in accordance with principles of product stewardship, companies should take greater responsibility for product take-back. This allows them to retain sources of reusable and recyclable materials, which in turn leads to more stable supply chains and long-term cost reductions. Patagonia has instituted its Common Threads Garment Recycling program, which allows customers to return "worn out Capilene® Performance Baselayers . . . Patagonia® fleece, Polartec® fleece clothing (from any maker), Patagonia cotton T-shirts, and now some additional polyester and nylon 6 products that come with a Common Threads tag"[23] for recycling into new fabric. Nike's Reuse-a-Shoe program, which turns used shoes into athletic play surfaces and consumer products, has recycled more than 24 million pairs of shoes since it began in 1990.[24]

Some firms are moving toward creating more sustainable products, but their customers are not always aware of these efforts. For example, premier Oregon wine maker Sokol Blosser was one the first to begin wine production in the Willamette Valley. Its website home page touts its quality wines, its location as an event venue, and its tasting room and special offers. These all constitute important information for consumers looking for quality wine or an outdoor venue for a special event. Customers have to look much deeper into the website to learn about Sokol Blosser Winery's commitment to sustainability through principles of TNSF.

Sokol Blosser Winery uses The Natural Step Framework to enhance the sustainability of its products and its production processes.

THINK ABOUT IT

To Tell, or Not to Tell?

Sokol Blosser Winery is one of many companies that focus on the social and environmental sustainability of its products and processes, but without talking too much about it. Firms like Nike and Wal-Mart also are working hard to become more sustainable, and yet they put little effort into advertising their achievements on that front. Why might a company choose not to advertise about its sustainability efforts? Are there any advantages from a public relations standpoint of not telling one's own sustainability story? (Hint: Think about issues like source credibility, stakeholder expectations, and market positioning.) Under what circumstances would it make the most sense to actively promote a product's sustainability?

System Condition Three

According to system condition three, a sustainable product does not contribute to the increasing degradation of the Earth's systems. In other words, a sustainable product builds natural capital rather than depleting it. Here, too, it is possible to increase a product's sustainability at every step of the life cycle from cradle to cradle, that is, from design and manufacture to reclamation and recycling or remanufacture.

One of the most important ecosystem services, and one of the most endangered, is the Earth's supply of fresh water. Sustainable products must be manufactured or grown with as little use of fresh water as possible. Manufacturing and agricultural wastes should never be allowed to contaminate streams, rivers, oceans, or water tables. Products should also be designed to conserve water as they are used in both consumer and industrial applications. Examples are low-flow showerheads and faucets, dual-flush and composting toilets, and drought-resistant native landscaping.

Industries that rely on ecosystem services, such as forest products, fisheries, farming, and ranching, need to limit their harvests to sustainable levels and find new ways to generate products without destroying the systems that produce them. While it may not be immediately obvious, paper products, which come from forests, offer many opportunities for innovation and conservation. For example, customers enjoying their Big Macs and fries may not know that the napkins they use today are more sustainable than those of just a few years ago. McDonalds, looking to reduce packaging and shipping, asked its paper-products supplier to make some packaging changes, but the supplier went further, and showed the fast-food giant how a change in the "dimpling" pattern on the napkins allowed the supplier to pack 25 percent more napkins in each box, allowing more product to be shipped with less energy.[25] In another example, the Canadian nonprofit organization, ForestEthics, reports that:

> FedEx Office . . . avoids paper sourced from delicate caribou habitat, Indonesian forests and has "just made a major shift away from tree plantations in the US South". The company also was the first to express a "solid preference" for FSC (Forest Stewardship Council) certified paper and has said that most of the paper used in its copy centers will be from FSC-certified sources.[26]

System Condition Four

System condition four holds that a sustainable product does not undermine people's ability to meet their own needs. In other words, a sustainable product builds human capital rather than exploiting human resources. Many of the negative social impacts of products occur in the manufacturing process. For example, workers in developing nations may be subjected to inhumane working conditions for very low compensation, simply because the demand for jobs is so high. Similarly, entire communities may suffer when industrial facilities pollute their air, water, and soils. We discuss these manufacturing issues more fully in Chapter 11 in our discussion of marketing channels.

Products can undermine consumers' well-being to the extent that they create persistent problems such as health hazards or excessive debt. Harmful or dangerous products frequently encounter regulatory actions, such as consumer protection laws; legal actions, such as lawsuits; or market reactions, such as boycotts. Such societal responses are costly to companies' budgets and reputations, and tend to be avoided by enlightened managers. The issue of excessive consumer debt became especially notable during the global recession of 2008–2009. In addition to repercussions throughout the financial products industries, the recession has caused many people to reassess their actual material needs.[27]

A concern with the effects of products on human capital need not function solely on reducing negative effects. Sustainable products should actually enrich human experience rather than encumbering it with junk. As it does for workers in manufacturing processes, a sustainable product should also increase consumers' overall well-being in such areas as:

- Health,
- Literacy and intellectual growth,
- Creative expression,
- Productivity,
- Leisure,
- Relationships.

LEGO group, with its philosophy of "lifelong play"[28] exemplifies the human well-being side of product sustainability. With products designed for people from preschoolers to professionals, LEGO products are revered by customers the world over for their quality, precision, consistency, and longevity. More than that, LEGO building systems have been shown to foster creativity, critical thinking, and community among fans of all ages and nations.[29]

DEVELOPING SUSTAINABLE NEW PRODUCTS

As if there weren't enough good reasons to develop more sustainable products, a joint report from Business for Social Responsibility and IDEO[30] cites a number of external factors that are driving the need for more sustainable product design, including increasing threats of regulation, product recalls, supply-chain pressure, consumer rejection, and bad press. The same report goes on to underscore several advantages of engaging in sustainable product design, including better product quality, resource efficiency, market positions, operational agility and adaptability, and serendipitous innovation. In short, developing more sustainable new products helps companies to stay out of hot water and become stronger competitors.

Consumer Products

Developing new consumer products that are more environmentally and socially sustainable can expand existing markets and open up new ones.[31] For example, Clorox, by introducing its Green Works line of cleaning products, claims to have captured 45 percent of the growing "natural cleaning" category, overtaking the long-time market leader, Seventh Generation.[32]

Designing sustainable products requires firms to be aware of future trends, engage environmental systems thinking, and develop an understanding of new manufacturing techniques, materials, and impacts.[33] One way businesses create more sustainable products is to reformulate or redesign them in order to reduce use of synthetic compounds (see Photo 9-2). In agriculture, for example, the most popular way to reduce the use of synthetic chemicals is to become organic. Downsides to organic growing may include lower crop yields; however, the upsides include better prices for farmers and healthier soil, water, workers, and consumers.

In the cleaning-products industry, SC Johnson is moving deliberately toward greater sustainability across all its brands (which include Pledge, Mr. Muscle, Windex, Scrubbing Bubbles, Glade, Raid, OFF!, Saran, Drano, and Ziploc). In 2001, the company established its Greenlist™, which classifies product ingredients according to their effect on the environment. The list continues to grow and evolve, and it currently covers over 95 percent of the ingredients used by SC Johnson in all its products. Most recently, it reformulated Windex to decrease its toxicity and increase its cleaning power. SC Johnson has submitted its Greenlist for scientific review to agencies such as World Wildlife Fund and the Green Chemistry

PHOTO 9-2 K2 Eco inline skates. Not only are the boots and laces made from recycled plastic bottles but the wheel frame is made from bamboo.

Institute, and it has made it available to other companies, including competitors, free of charge.[34]

Finding innovative solutions to product design and development while making progress toward increased sustainability means thinking about familiar products in new ways. Forward-thinking firms are connecting the design function to other parts of their firms (such as sales and marketing) in order to draw on the competencies and innovations from multiple groups. For example, Nike took on the problem of sustainable footwear with a cross-functional team in the development of their Considered line. The Considered design team began as a "small group of chemists, biologists, material specialists, designers and product developers. . . ."[35] Begun as a pilot program, Considered designed a shoe that reduces material waste by 61 percent, energy use by 35 percent, and solvents and adhesives by 89 percent. The shoe is also designed to take better advantage of recycling in Nike's Reuse-a-Shoe program. Nike continues to work toward more sustainable designs. By 2011, Nike plans to have all footwear meeting the baseline for sustainability pioneered by the Considered line.[36]

Recently, Nike teamed with environmentalist and NBA All-Star guard Steve Nash to create Nike Trash Talk, the first performance basketball shoe made from manufacturing waste. The Nike Trash Talk is made with an upper pieced together from leather and synthetic leather waste from the factory floor using zigzag stitching. The midsole uses scrap-ground foam from factory production. The outsole uses environmentally preferred rubber that reduces toxins and incorporates Nike Grind material, made from footwear outsole manufacturing waste. Shoelaces and sockliners are made from environmentally preferred materials. Shoes are packaged in a fully recycled cardboard shoebox.[37]

Mini Case Study

Interface

Interface, the Atlanta-based floor covering company, exemplifies sustainability in its product mix throughout the life cycle. In striving to achieve "Mission Zero,"[38] its goal to have zero impact on the planet, Interface has reexamined and redesigned virtually every aspect of its business. In doing so, it has turned one of the dirtiest industries in the world into one of the most progressive. Below are some highlights from its 2008 Ecometrics™ report:[39]

- *Environmental impacts are down.* Interface's net greenhouse gas emissions are down 71 percent from its 1996 baseline, 34 percent from reductions, and 37 percent from offsets. Energy consumption per unit of production is down 44 percent since 1996, and 28 percent of the company's global energy supply is from renewable sources. Notably, 89 percent of electricity is renewable, including three factories that are operating on 100 percent green electricity. Water intake per unit of production is down 72 percent from 1996 levels.
- *Sustainability continues to drive innovation.* Interface's continued focus on closing the loop on

product manufacture through the ReEntry® program resulted in the diversion of 43 million pounds of carpet and carpet scrap from the landfill in 2008, bringing the totals for this program to 175 million pounds since 1995. ReEntry 2.0, introduced in 2007, is an innovative technology that allows the company to recover carpet backing and face fiber and use them in making new products.
- *Closing the Loop.* Recycled and bio-based materials make up 24 percent of the raw materials used in Interface operations, a critical piece in the company's progress away from virgin materials.
- *Waste Reduction Continues.* Total waste sent to landfills since 1996 has been reduced 67 percent across company operations. Additionally, the focus on reducing process and material waste through Interface's QUEST (Quality Using Employee Suggestions and Teamwork) program has produced impressive results, netting the company $405 million in cumulative, avoided waste costs since 1996.

The lessons of Interface are too numerous and profound to describe in full here. To learn more about Interface's ongoing journey toward sustainability, browse the Web for what has been said and written by and about the company's pioneering leader, Ray Anderson.

Giant Opportunities: Designing Products for Business and Government

It's tempting to focus on consumer products in a book like this, because as consumers, we're all pretty familiar with the examples. However, many of the richest opportunities for profit and sustainability gains lie in creating products for the business and government sectors.

Businesses, more than consumers or governments, depend for their success on keeping waste, costs, and risks to a minimum. Chapter 2 presented the business case for sustainability, which includes improvements in the areas of waste and efficiency as well as others, such as employee satisfaction and turnover. For all these reasons, businesses are embracing the principles of sustainability faster than consumers. Businesses make good customers for sustainable products. Not only do they often have a better grasp than consumers of the advantages of sustainable products, but they also tend to buy in much larger quantities. For example, it takes a lot of households to buy as much hand soap, toilet paper, or window cleaner as are used in the typical office building or by the typical company. We'll focus more on business customers when we examine the marketing channels in Chapter 11.

In many ways, government is an even more important sector than business for the development and marketing of sustainable products. Consider the following statement from the Government Purchasing Project:

> The government is the largest consumer in the United States, representing 20 percent of the gross national product. This purchasing leverage can be an enormously effective tool, which can save taxpayers money, set the standard for private industries, expand the marketplace for "green" technologies, and consequently make these technologies and environmentally preferable products more available to consumers as a whole.[40]

Certain problems require government-scale solutions, which in turn, provide huge opportunities for product innovators. One such problem, with implications for both the economy and

PHOTO 9-3 There is market opportunity in reversing environmental damage. Invasive species, like zebra and quagga mussels, threaten ecosystems and create enormous economic harm.

the environment, is that of invasive mollusks. Two species of freshwater mussels, zebra and quagga, have created billions of dollars worth of damage to dams, ports, boats, and ecosystems since their accidental introduction in the mid-1980s by ships from Eastern Europe. Removing the mussels has typically required either scraping, which involves costly shutdowns and excessive wear and tear on machinery, or poisoning with chlorine, which kills the mussels but also kills all the other fish and aquatic life in the area. This massive problem created an equally massive opportunity for the development of an environmentally friendly and equipment-friendly solution.

Answering the call was Marrone Bio Innovations, a company known for effective organic pesticides and herbicides. In June 2007, at a Canadian power plant on Lake Ontario, Marrone tested a new product, Zequanox, which is based on bacteria that occur naturally in soil, and which kills invasive mussels while being safe for mammals and native aquatic species.[41] Zequanox is a green product that solves a huge environmental problem (see Photo 9-3). For Marrone Bio Innovations, it's a potential gold mine, and its customers are primarily government agencies.

SUSTAINABLE SERVICES

Eco-efficient Services are those that are either closely related to products, or substitute for products,[42] thereby reducing the use of material and energy.[43] There are four general types:

- **Product Services** extend the life of a product through maintenance, upgrading, repair, guarantees, and product take-backs. The maintenance service for an office photocopier is an example. Firms can be motivated to adopt this eco-efficient manufacturing model by the possibility of increased profitability through service contracts and supplies, such as copier toner.

- **Use Services** allow the benefit of use without the need to buy the product. Common exchange models for use services are leasing, renting, sharing, and pooling. For example, U-haul allows movers to rent the service of safe, convenient, personal property moving. The more people sharing one durable product, the fewer resources are extracted from the Earth, and less waste is produced in the manufacturing process.
- **Intangible services** substitute systems, often technology based, for products. For example, online banking with automated bill paying takes the place of writing checks. Voice mail on your home phone replaces the answering machine.
- **Result services** work toward satisfying customer needs while reducing the need for material products altogether.[44] Public transportation is one example. "In the case of result services, the product is owned and run by the supplier, who therefore has an incentive to intensify and optimize the product's operation, and to increase its service life. In addition, developing and offering a result instead of a pre-specified product or service can facilitate the incorporation of environment factors from scratch."[45]

Services have both front-stage and backstage components. The front stage is where the customer experiences the service delivery—receiving the haircut, picking up the clean clothing, or signing for a package delivery. The backstage encompasses all the people, processes, and products required to produce the service. The biggest opportunities for sustainability gains in services typically lie in the backstage. For example, UPS's customers may or may not notice changes in UPS's sustainability, but behind the scenes, the company is pioneering change. In the area of social sustainability, UPS focuses on building human capital both within the firm and in communities where it operates.

Through employee volunteerism and some monetary support, the UPS Foundation provides assistance to communities around the world, focusing on areas such as literacy, nonprofit effectiveness, diversity, and community safety.[46] On the environmental front, the company is also an innovator. UPS claims the world's largest fleet of alternative fuel trucks, including new hydraulic hybrid technology (see Figure 9-1). It has switched to paperless electronic systems for delivery recording and billing.[47]

Sustainable Business-to-Business (B2B) Services

Sustainable B2B services are flourishing in virtually every commercial and industrial sector. For example, in the area of architecture and building, private architecture firms, contractors, nonprofits, and customers all work together to improve building technologies and practices. The U.S. Green Building Council's **LEED (Leadership in Energy and Environmental Design)** rating program, which evaluates a building's environmental sustainability, has provided guidance leading to huge strides in energy and water conservation, the reduction of building waste, and the use

FIGURE 9-1 Brown is the new green. UPS is an industry leader in making shipping services more sustainable.

of renewable and nontoxic materials. Green buildings save organizations money, have less negative environmental impacts, and make better, healthier workplaces. In *Harvard Business Review*, Charles Lockwood writes, "LEED buildings, for both white-collar and blue-collar workers are increasing. In 2000 just 46 white-collar buildings earned LEED certification. There were 1,632 such workplaces in 2006 and 5,417 of them in 2007—that's a 232% increase. . . . Now let's look at the blue-collar numbers: Just one blue-collar facility in the United States registered for LEED certification in 2000. In 2006, 40 of them registered for or received certification, and in 2007 that figure climbed to 111—a 178% increase."[48]

Other B2B firms have begun to identify niche professional services opportunities. For example, Shorebank Pacific markets financing for sustainable business ventures. In order to maximize triple-bottom-line benefits, Shorebank bundles sustainability consulting with its financing services.[49] The legal firm Tonkon Torp LLP offers specialized legal council to businesses in the renewable energy industry. Its work includes wind, ethanol, biomass, wind power, solar power, and wave energy projects throughout the western United States.[50]

Opportunities for sustainability also are increasing in day-to-day B2B services such as janitorial maintenance. For example, Pacific Building Care (PBC) Janitorial Services "provides Commercial Janitorial Services to a portfolio of 110 million square feet in Central & Southern California, Denver, Colorado and Phoenix, Arizona. Customer sites include prominent headquarters facilities situated on large corporate campuses."[51] In early 2009, this firm earned a Green Seal Certification for its green cleaning programs and practices.[52] You'll learn more about the Green Seal program and other third-party certification programs in Chapter 10.

Many large corporations provide onsite cafeteria services for their workers. This is yet another area making real gains in sustainability. For example, Sodexo food services focuses on offering food that is:

- organically grown without the use of synthetic pesticides and fertilizers;
- humanely raised to protect the health and well-being of livestock and minimize the use of antibiotics and other chemicals;
- sustainably caught from properly managed wild fisheries and aquaculture facilities operated to protect natural fish populations and the surrounding environment;
- fairly traded, contributing to an improved quality of life in agricultural regions; and
- sustainably grown using agricultural practices that protect natural habitat, conserve energy, restore soil health, and protect water quality.[53]

Consumers don't often hear about sustainability gains in the B2B services sector. In many cases, even workers may not be fully aware of their companies' sustainability efforts. However, the services provided to the B2B sector have significant economic, human, and environmental impact. The same is true for services in the government sector.

Sustainable Consumer Services

The drive to sustainability has also led to innovation in the area of consumer services. One example is the fast-growing green power industry. Utilities companies routinely offer customers energy packages that help in the development of renewable energy sources such as wind, solar, and biomass. Oregon electric supplier, Portland General Electric, describes its Green Source program:

> Green Source allows you to purchase 100 percent of your electricity from renewable sources and reduce reliance on fossil fuels. In 2008, approximately 85 percent of the electricity came from new wind sources and 15 percent from new biomass (wood waste).[54]

The laundry and dry-cleaning industry hasn't been known for its innovation. The drive to sustainable marketing is changing that. Dry cleaning has traditionally relied on perchloroethylene, a chemical that can, over long-term exposure, cause liver and kidney damage, memory loss and confusion, and irritation of the skin, eyes, nose, and throat.[55] Ecomat-Cleaners has "achieved a 100 percent reduction of hazardous-waste emissions compared to traditional dry cleaning by adopting their own brand of multiprocess wet cleaning. It involves a combination of water, natural soaps and oils, steam and labor skilled at targeting tough spots and stains."[56] This service performs as well or better than traditional dry cleaning.

Another major consumer-service category, tourism, has been making strides in sustainability. A prime example of result services, tourism delivers relaxation, stimulation, and other desirable experiences while maintaining almost complete control over the products involved. Ecotourism is one of the most rapidly growing and dynamic sectors of the tourism market. In the United States, ecotourism is defined by seven characteristics:

- It involves travel to natural destinations;
- It minimizes impact on the destination environment;
- It builds environmental awareness;
- It provides direct financial benefits for conservation;
- It provides financial benefits and empowerment for local people;
- It respects local culture; and
- It supports human rights and democratic movements.[57]

In some areas, especially those with fragile ecosystems, ecotourism may be a double-edged sword. On the one hand, the ability to bring in tourism revenues may save an area from devastating agricultural or industrial development. On the other hand, even ecotourism requires development, which has the potential of degrading or polluting ecosystems. The Galapagos Islands illustrate this problem. According to ecotourism experts:

- Development of the tourist industry has attracted workers, which have nearly tripled the islands' permanent population, creating new sources of pollution and new pressure on fisheries;
- Tourists from around the world have brought not only money, but also have introduced invasive animal and insect species, threatening the islands' unique biodiversity;
- Relatively little tourist income (about 15%) directly benefits the Galapagos economy, with the rest accruing to foreign-owned airlines and tour boat operators;[58] and
- The majority (80%) of revenues generated by the National Park are diverted to the Ecuadorean government's general revenues rather than being reinvested in conservation.[59]

The development of parks and preserves for ecotourism can also displace native populations, creating a problem called "conservation refugees,"[60] wherein traditional cultures lose access to their homes and livelihoods. Attention to the pros and cons of ecotourism has led to oversight by third-party agencies. There reportedly exist over one hundred ecotourism certification agencies worldwide, including:

- The Certification for Sustainable Tourism (CST) in Costa Rica;
- The Nature and Ecotourism Accreditation Program (NEAP) in Australia;
- Blue Flag in Europe, South Africa, and the Caribbean;
- The Protected Area Network (PAN) in Europe;
- Committed to Green in Great Britain; and
- Smart Voyager in the Galapagos.[61]

For consumers wishing to minimize the negative impacts (or maximize the positive impacts) of their tourism dollars, certification programs can be useful. However, it pays to do one's homework, because not all programs focus on the same levels or areas of sustainability.

VIRTUAL FIELD TRIP

Or Maybe Not So Virtual

Identify an eco-destination you'd like to visit. Perhaps you've always wanted to go to Africa or India, Alaska, Costa Rica, or the Peruvian Andes. Use the Internet to find accommodations, activities, and transportation. Search for firms that specialize in ecotourism. How well does each supplier embody the seven ecotourism characteristics? Are any practices that claim to be "ecotourism" actually defeating sustainability efforts?

PHOTO 9-4 Building human capital through sport at the 2010 World Cup in South Africa –The theme of the world's largest sporting event was "Say no to racism."

THINK ABOUT IT

Consider the case of SDL in the music industry. How has the industry dematerialized its product mix? Is the industry more sustainable because of it? Think about the changes in TNSF system conditions. What is the net effect on atmospheric carbon? On heavy metals? On ecosystems? On people? How has dematerialization affected the profitability of music sales? Which parts of the industry have benefited? Who, if anyone, has been harmed? Has it been good or bad for musicians?

CRITICAL THINKING ACTIVITY

A Balance Sheet for Human Capital

Pick any consumer product. Divide a sheet of paper into two columns, labeled "liabilities" and "assets." In the liabilities column, list all the ways you can think of that the product wastes or reduces consumers' ability to experience well-being. In the assets column, list the ways it builds people's ability to live fuller lives. How favorable is the balance? How can the balance be shifted toward the positive? (See Photo 9-4).

Chapter Summary

A major function of marketing is the development of the product mix, which includes all of the goods and services a company offers to its customers. A sustainable product mix delivers value and service to its target customers, makes a profit for the firm that provides it, and also preserves or builds natural and human capital. Product sustainability cannot be assessed only at the point of sale. Sustainability must be built in throughout the life cycle, from concept through design, manufacturing, distribution, sale, consumption, and final disposition. This chapter presented the concepts of product stewardship and SDL. It revisited TNSF to explore the meaning of product sustainability. Finally, it discussed issues of sustainable new product development and sustainable services, in the consumer sector as well as in the B2B and government sectors.

Review of Chapter Objectives

- Product stewardship
- Service-dominant logic
- Product sustainability

- Developing sustainable new products
- Sustainable services

Key Concepts

Product Mix   122
Product
   Stewardship   123
Product Strategy   123

Service-Dominant Logic   123
Dematerialization   123
Eco-Efficient
   Services   132

Product Services   132
Use Services   133
Intangible services   133
Result services   133

LEED (Leadership in
   Energy and Environmental
   Design)   133

Endnotes

1. Stranahan, Susan Q. (2009), "Drugs in Our Drinking Water: What Do We Do with Unused Medicines?" *AARP Bulletin Today*, February 27, http://www.productstewardship.us/associations/6596/files/Drugs%20in%20Our%20Drinking%20Water%20-%20AARP%20Bulletin%20Today%202.3.09.pdf, accessed September 20, 2009.

2. Doheny, Kathleen (2008), "Drugs in Our Drinking Water?" *WebMD Health News*, http://www.medicinenet.com/script/main/art.asp?articlekey=87742, accessed September 20, 2009.

3. Stranahan, Susan Q. (2009), "Drugs in Our Drinking Water: What Do We Do with Unused Medicines?" *AARP Bulletin Today*, February 27, http://www.productstewardship.us/associations/6596/files/Drugs%20in%20Our%20Drinking%20Water%20-%20AARP%20Bulletin%20Today%202.3.09.pdf, accessed September 20, 2009.

4. Business Dictionary, Product Stewardship, http://www.businessdictionary.com/definition/product-stewardship.html, accessed September 20, 2009.

5. Hart, Stuart. L. (1995), "A Natural-Resource-Based View of the Firm," *Academy of Management Review*, 20 (4): 986–1015.

6. Kodak, Corporate Citizenship, "One-Time Use Camera," http://www.kodak.com/US/en/corp/HSE/oneTimeUseCamera.jhtml?pq-path=7225, accessed September 20, 2009.

7. Vargo, Stephen L. and Robert F. Lusch (2004), "Evolving to a New Dominant Logic for Marketing," *Journal of Marketing*, 68 (June): 1–17.

8. Vargo, Stephen L., and Robert F. Lusch (2004), "Evolving to a New Dominant Logic for Marketing," *Journal of Marketing*, 68 (June) (p. 1).

9. Fuller, Donald, A. (1999), *Sustainable Marketing: Managerial-Ecological Issues*, Thousand Oaks, CA: Sage (p. 81).

10. Willard, Bob (2002), *The Sustainability Advantage: Seven Business Case Benefits of a Triple Bottom Line*, Gabriola Island, BC, Canada: New Society Publishers (p.117).

11. Fuller, Donald A. (1999), *Sustainable Marketing: Managerial-Ecological Issues*, Thousand Oaks, CA: Sage (p. 82).

12. Hawken, Paul, Amory B. Lovins, and L. Hunter Lovins (1999), "A Road Map for Natural Capitalism," *Harvard Business Review* (May –June) (p.146).

13. Halme, Minna, Gabriele Hrausa, Christine Jasch, Jaap Kortman, Helga Jonuschat, Michael Scharp, Daniela Velte and Paual Trindale (2005), *Sustainable Consumer Services: Business Solutions for Household Markets*, Sterling VA: Earthscan.

14. Halme, Minna, Gabriele Hrausa, Christine Jasch, Jaap Kortman, Helga Jonuschat, Michael Scharp, Daniela Velte and Paual Trindale (2005), *Sustainable Consumer Services: Business Solutions for Household Markets*, Sterling VA: Earthscan.

15. Zen Home Cleaning, http://www.zenhomecleaning.com/index.htm, accessed September 20, 2009.

16. Zipcar, http://www.zipcar.com/, accessed September 20, 2009.

17. Werbach, Adam (2009), *Strategy For Sustainability: A Business Manifesto*, Boston, MA: Harvard Business Press (p. 23).

18. Oakland Public Library, "Tool List and Tool Library Guidelines," http://www.oaklandlibrary.org/Branches/tll_toolsched.html, accessed September 21, 2009.

19. Avelle, http://www.bagborroworsteal.com/ui/howitworks, accessed September 21, 2009.

20. Burley, http://www.burley.com/, accessed November 25, 2009.

21. Jonathan Larson, "The Philosophy of Design for Disassembly," http://www.me.mtu.edu/~jwsuther/erdm/dfd_paper.pdf, accessed October 7, 2009.

22. Fuller, Donald A. (1999), *Sustainable Marketing: Managerial-Ecological Issues*, Thousand Oaks, CA: Sage (p. 82).

23. Patagonia, "Environmentalism: Common Threads Garment Recycling," http://www.patagonia.com/web/us/patagonia.go?assetid=1956, accessed September 20, 2009.

24. Nike, "Reuse a Shoe," http://www.nikereuseashoe.com/, accessed September 20, 2009.

25. Ottman, Jacquelyn A. (1998), *Green Marketing: Opportunity for Innovation*, New York: J. Ottman Consulting Inc. (p.179).

26. Forest Ethics, "Green Grades 2009," http://forestethics.org/green-grades-09, accessed November 30, 2009.

27. Barbaro, Michael and Louis Uchitelle (2008), "Americans Cut Back Sharply on Spending," *New York Times*, January 14, http://www.nytimes.com/2008/01/14/business/14spend.html, accessed December 1, 2009.

28. Lego, About Us, http://www.lego.com/eng/info/default.asp?page=lifelong, accessed September 20, 2009.

29. Antorini, Yun Mi (2007), "Brand Community Innovation: An Intrinsic Case Study of the Adult Fans of LEGO Community," doctoral dissertation, Department of Intercultural Communication and Management, Copenhagen Business School.

30. Business for Social Responsibility and IDEO (2008), "Aligned for Sustainable Design: An A-B-C-D Approach to Making Better Products," http://www.sustainablelifemedia.com/files/documents/bsrsustainabledesign.pdf, accessed November 29, 2009.

31. Willard, Bob (2002), *The Sustainability Advantage: Seven Business Case Benefits of a Triple Bottom Line*, Gabriola Island, BC, Canada: New Society Publishers (p.114).

32. Ottman, Jacquelyn (2009), "Green Marketing Really Has Gone Mainstream," *Leading Green*, July 21, Harvard Business Press, http://blogs.harvardbusiness.org/leadinggreen/2009/07/green-marketing-has-come-a-lon.html, accessed October 6, 2009.

33. Richardson, J., T. Irwin, and C. Sherwin (2005). "Design & Sustainability: A Scoping Report for the Sustainable Design Forum, Design Council," http://www.britishdesigninnovation.org/new/dd/images/reports/3_Design_&_Sustainability_Design_Council_Scoping_Report.doc, accessed October 3, 2009.

34. SC Johnson, "Integrity, Sustainability, Improving Our Products, Our Greenlist Process," http://www.scjohnson.com/en/commitment/focus-on/greener-products/greenlist.aspx, accessed October 6, 2009.

35. Business for Social Responsibility and IDEO (2008), "Aligned for Sustainable Design: An A-B-C-D Approach to Making Better Products," page 31, http://74.125.155.132/search?q=cache:HUtZWL8cMBQJ:www.sustainablelifemedia.com/files/documents/bsrsustainabledesign.pdf+Aligned+for+Sustainable+Design:+An+A-B-C-D+Approach+to+Making+Better+Products&cd=1&hl=en&ct=clnk&gl=us, accessed October 7, 2009.

36. Holmes, Stanley (2005), "Green Foot Forward," *Business Week*, November 28, pg. 24.

37. "Steve Nash and Nike Turn Garbage Into Trash Talk" (2008) February 13, http://www.nikebiz.com/media/pr/2008/02/13_Nash.html, accessed October 3, 2009.

38. Interface Flor, "Mission Zero," http://www.interfaceflor.eu/internet/web.nsf/webpages/528_EU.html, accessed September 22, 2009.

39. Interface Global, "Sustainability, News, Interface Reports Annual Ecometrics," http://www.interfaceglobal.com/Sustainability/News—Articles/Interface-Reports-Annual-Ecometrics.aspx, accessed September 22, 2009,

40. Government Purchasing Project, http://www.gpp.org/, accessed November 30, 2009.

41. Marrone Bio Innovations, http://marronebioinnovations.com/pdf/Decemberewceremonypressreleasefinal.pdf, accessed November 30, 2009.

42. Van der Zwan, F. and T. Bhamra (2003), "Services marketing: Taking up the Sustainability Development Challenge," *Journal of Services Marketing*, 17(4): 341–356 (p. 355).

43. Halme, Minna, Gabriele Hrausa, Christine Jasch, Jaap Kortman, Helga Jonuschat, Michael Scharp, Daniela Velte and Paual Trindale (2005), *Sustainable Consumer Services: Business Solutions for Household Markets,* Sterling VA: Earthscan.

44. Ottman, Jacquelyn A. (1998), *Green Marketing: Opportunity for Innovation*, New York: J. Ottman Consulting Inc. (p. 99). Also see Van der Zwan, F. and T. Bhamra (2003), "Services Marketing: Taking up the Sustainability Development Challenge," *Journal of Services Marketing*, 17(4): 341–356 (p. 355).

45. Van der Zwan, F. and T. Bhamra (2003), "Services Marketing: Taking up the Sustainability Development Challenge," *Journal of Services Marketing*, 17(4): 341–356 (p. 355).

46. UPS, "Community, Corporate Responsibility, Everyone Matters," http://www.community.ups.com/, accessed October 7, 2009.

47. UPS, Pressroom, Fact Sheets, Ten Things, http://pressroom.ups.com/Fact+Sheets/Ten+Things+You+May+Not+Know+About+UPS%27s+Environmental+Initiatives, accessed October 7, 2009.

48. Lockwood, Charles (2006), "Building the Green Way," *Harvard Business Review*, 84 (June, 6): 129–137.

49. ShoreBank Pacific, http://www.eco-bank.com/, accessed September 21, 2009.

50. Tonkon Torp LLP brochure. *Renewable Energy Practice.*

51. Pacific Building Care, http://www.pbcare.com/index.asp, accessed November 27, 2009.

52. Pacific Building Care, News, PBC Janitorial Services Certified by Green Seal, http://www.pbcare.com/content.asp?id=75&t=1, accessed November 27, 2009.

53. Sodexo, Sustainability, Food Services, http://www.sodexousa.com/usen/citizenship/sustainability/foodservices/foodservices.asp, accessed November 27, 2009.

54. Portland General, Products, Renewable Power, http://www.portlandgeneral.com/home/products/renewable_power/default.aspx, accessed September 21, 2009.

55. Office of Pollution Prevention and Toxics, U.S. Environmental Protection Agency (1994), "Chemicals in the Environment: Perchloroethylene OPPT Chemical Fact Sheet," August, http://www.epa.gov/chemfact/f_perchl.txt, accessed September 9, 2009.

56. Ottman, Jacquelyn A. (1998), *Green Marketing: Opportunity for Innovation*, New York: J. Ottman Consulting Inc. (p. 76).

57. Honey, Martha (2008), *Ecotourism and Sustainable Development: Who Owns Paradise?* 2nd edition, Washington, D.C.: Island Press.

58. Honey, Martha (2008), *Ecotourism & Sustainable Development: Who Owns Paradise?* 2nd Edition, Washington, D.C.: Island Press.

59. Sweeting, James, Aaron Bruner, and Amy Rosenfeld (1999), "The Green Host Effect: An Integrated Approach to Sustainable Tourism and Resort Development," Conservation International Policy Paper. Washington, DC: Conservation International.

60. Conservation Refugees, http://www.conservationrefugees.org/, accessed December 1, 2009.

61. Tourist Travel, Ecotourism Certificate, http://www.touristtravel.com/ecotourism_certification.htm, accessed December 1, 2009.

Sustainable Branding and Packaging

INTRODUCTION: BEHIND GREAT BRANDS

Interbrand, a global consulting firm, produces an annual list of the 100 best global brands.[1] Their top ten, Coke, IBM, Microsoft, General Electric, Nokia, McDonald's, Google, Toyota, Intel, and Disney, also reads like a list of some of the most sustainable large companies as measured by Global 100.[2] At number five, Nokia was ranked by the Dow Jones Sustainability Index[3] as the most sustainable technology company of 2009.[4] Is it coincidence? Interbrand thinks it isn't. A study by Interbrand finds a correlation between corporate social responsibility and brand value. The results suggest, "that for the companies in the analysis, 13 cents out of every dollar of brand value is linked to CSR efforts."[5]

THINK ABOUT IT

Brand Value

What might explain a connection between efforts to become sustainable and the strength of a brand? What makes a brand strong? What's the role of consumer emotions, such as trust? What's the importance of a brand's consistency with its consumers' values? What's the role of innovation? How are these affected by a company's commitment to become sustainable?

This chapter unpacks the meaning of sustainable branding. It defines "sustainable brand" and highlights the main keys to making a brand economically, socially, and ecologically viable. As major parts of the product mix that contribute to both sustainability and branding, packaging and labeling are also addressed.

CHAPTER OBJECTIVES

In this chapter, you will learn additional principles of sustainable product strategy, including:

- Sustainable branding
- Sustainable packaging
- Sustainable labeling

SUSTAINABLE BRANDING

A **brand** consists of the identifying trademarks of a product or company and all the meanings invested in those trademarks by its stakeholders. A brand is a product of communication, and increasingly, the relevant communication comes from customers and critics as well as from marketers. Once upon a time, a brand was considered to be little more than the name, the logo, and whatever slogans and messages marketers attached to their products. That notion is fully discredited. At a 2009 meeting of BrandBase in Denmark company executive Tormod Askildsen said of the LEGO brand, "We control the trademark, but we can't control the brand." In other words, a trademark is the property of a company, but its meanings are created and reside in the minds of people both inside and outside the firm. In many ways, a brand is public property. Whether companies like it or not, their brands, or their reputations, are built from the shared experiences of customers and other stakeholders.

Consumers typically have a lot to say about products and services. They also have a lot of credibility with other consumers, and on the Internet they have easy forums for sharing their opinions. A 2006 study by Nielsen BuzzMetrics found that over a quarter of all search results on Google for the world's 20 largest brands are links to consumer-generated content.[6] Also weighing in on a brand's meaning are the countless watchdog groups that monitor business practices for their social and environmental performance.

Given that a brand's meaning is essentially a shared idea of what a product or company stands for, what then constitutes a **sustainable brand**? Using the logic of Triple Bottom Line, a sustainable brand is economically enduring, and its associations in the minds of customers and other stakeholders rightfully include social justice and ecological sustainability (see Photo 10-1).

Brands are not economically sustainable when they lose relevance to customers or acquire negative associations. Forces such as cultural and technological change affect a brand's relevance. One brand that has struggled to remain relevant is RadioShack. In 2009, the company began to refer to itself simply as "The Shack" in an attempt to update a brand suffering from a negative association with obsolete technology. In 2009, General Motors killed off its Pontiac brand, and Kodak retired the Kodachrome brand.[7] In GM's case, auto experts agree that Pontiac management destroyed the brand's value by producing poor quality cars that failed to live up to consumers' expectations.[8] Kodak gave Kodachrome a hero's funeral for its importance to the history of color photography, but in the end, Kodachrome was made obsolete by newer, better films and by the advent of digital photography.[9] For a truly unsustainable brand, consider Enron.

PHOTO 10-1 Sustainability is becoming an important part of the brand message.

Associated with one of the largest frauds in American business history, Enron is unlikely ever to return as a viable brand.

As we know from Chapter 5, one of the most powerful cultural trends driving branding today is a worldwide shift in consumers' attitudes toward environmental sustainability. Brands associated with exploitive treatment of people or the planet lose traction with consumers and other stakeholders. Good managers avoid risking their brands' value through irresponsible corporate behavior, and as global demand for socially and ecologically sustainable products continues to increase, brands will need to adapt accordingly to remain relevant and desirable. Coca-Cola appears to be doing that. According to author Jared Diamond:

> Coca-Cola's survival compels it to be deeply concerned with problems of water scarcity, energy, climate change and agriculture. One company goal is to make its plants water-neutral, returning to the environment water in quantities equal to the amount used in beverages and their production. Another goal is to work on the conservation of seven of the world's river basins, including the Rio Grande, Yangtze, Mekong and Danube—all of them sites of major environmental concerns besides supplying water for Coca-Cola.[10]

Principles of Sustainable Branding

Citing the consumer trend toward greater concern about society and the environment, Raphael Bemporad and Mitch Baranowski of BBMG[11] suggest five principles of sustainable branding:[12]

1. Align brand practice with the brand promise.
2. Engage stakeholders in value creation.
3. Deliver value at practical, social, environmental, and cultural levels.
4. Share an authentic brand story.
5. Empower customers and society to be better.

First, companies must align their practice with their promise. Thanks to the Internet and social media, companies can't hide behind marketing slogans and advertising campaigns. They must match their actions with their claims. Sustainable branding grows from integrity. Conflicting stories, manipulations, and hypocrisy weaken a brand by eroding consumers' trust.

Consider how the operations, products, and services at Aveda, a personal care company, reflect its corporate values: "Our mission at Aveda is to care for the world we live in, from the products we make to the ways in which we give back to society. At Aveda, we strive to set an example for environmental leadership and responsibility—not just in the world of beauty, but around the world."[13] Nice sentiments, but how do these values relate to company practices? First, the mission of the company is evident in its products. In the "world of beauty," where Aveda competes, the company provides in-store and online product advice based on individual hair and skin profiles to determine which products are right for customers. The firm provides detailed descriptions of product ingredients including sourcing information, an ingredient glossary, a link to its efforts to use organics, and its green ingredient policy. Aveda "sets an example for environmental leadership and responsibility . . . around the world" in part through its programs in Nepal. Company collaboration with NGOs in Nepal has helped to increase household income among some of the Nepalese poor by 318 percent. During the 2009 holiday season, the wrapping paper for Aveda gift sets was sustainably sourced from the Nepalese lokta shrub in a process that does not destroy the plant stock.[14]

Second, companies must engage stakeholders to create value. For obvious reasons, companies aren't completely credible in telling their own stories. A sustainable brand embraces the contributions of customers and other stakeholders in building the brand's reputation. For better or worse, engaged customers, employees, watchdog groups, and members of the communities where companies operate all have potentially powerful stories to tell. And those stories ring truer than any advertising or corporate sponsored public relations.

Companies can benefit greatly by supporting communities of loyal customers.[15] LEGO has done a brilliant job of engaging customers in this way. The independent user community, LEGOFan.org, actually sponsors LEGO ambassadors, "a community based program made up of adult LEGO hobbyists who share their product and building expertise with the world-wide LEGO community . . . and the public . . . LEGO Ambassador's mission is to help provide inspiration for LEGO builders of all ages and from all parts of the world."[16] Company employees are another key stakeholder group in telling the brand story. Says Ogilvy & Mather CEO, Shelly Lazarus, "The most overlooked segment of potential brand building is the internal audience—all the employees of the company. They're out in the world interacting with people every day."[17] Companies can also work with nongovernmental organizations (NGOs) to create value. For example, the influential Marine Stewardship Council, which certifies sustainable fisheries, originally formed out a partnership between Unilever and the World Wildlife Fund.[18]

Third, companies must deliver benefits on three levels. Sustainable brands need to offer (1) practical or utilitarian benefits such as quality, value, and convenience; (2) benefits to society and the natural environment; and (3) benefits that allow stakeholders to feel like they belong to a larger community that shares their values.

Honda Motors is a good example of a firm that has managed to deliver benefits at multiple levels. Honda has long enjoyed the perception of excellent value and, with that, deep customer loyalty. Honda has delivered consistent reliability at a reasonable price.[19] Among Honda owners, the brand communicates intelligence and fiscal responsibility. And now Honda is making headway in the green auto market with the hybrid version of the popular Civic,[20] the Fit,[21] which was named a 2010 Top 10 Green Car by Kelley Blue Book, and its hydrogen-fueled, zero-emission FCX Clarity, which was declared the 2009 World Green Car. To understand the sense of community felt by some Honda owners, visit the website: www.hondaclub.com.

Fourth, companies must share an authentic brand story. Unsubstantiated social and environmental claims tend to get exposed to the detriment of the company making the claims. A sustainable brand should foster transparency about its environmental and social impacts. Transparency builds trust among stakeholders, who in turn will promote and support the brand.

The term **radical transparency**, referring to an organization's complete and public openness about its practices, is gaining widespread appreciation among marketing organizations as business and society shift to a culture of sustainability. According to a 2007 *Wired* article: "Radical forms of transparency are now the norm at startups—and even some Fortune 500 companies."[22] Author Daniel Goleman cites a trend toward greater transparency in the marketplace regarding the environmental and health impacts of products. According to Goleman, "Companies are already responding to this sea change in attitudes toward product transparency. In recent months, both Clorox and S.C. Johnson have done what was once unthinkable: revealed the ingredients of their consumer products. Despite years of arguments that ingredients are proprietary and should be a closely held secret, the new transparency climate awards major points in reputation and image to companies willing to be more open—and penalizes those that dig in their heels."[23] An authentic brand story is one that arises from real and verifiable organizational actions and customer experiences.

THINK ABOUT IT

The Transparent Classroom

To underscore the importance of transparency, think about your various professors' grading policies. How well do you understand the criteria on which your work is evaluated? Is the process clear and open? How would you feel if the criteria were kept secret and unexplained (especially if your term grade turned out to be surprisingly low)?

Fifth, the brand must empower customers and society. Sustainable brands do more than simply communicate their image and position in the marketplace. According to BBMG, sustainable brands also help their customers to live better, more fulfilling lives and to contribute more to society. This lofty objective is achieved when a brand engages a customer's deeper needs and desires and provides a platform for action.

For example, the active wear company Nau provides a platform for action by asking customers to choose how the company will spend its charitable contribution from each purchase. On a personal website called "John's Swoosh Page,"[24] a Nike fan features his own runs for charity and invites readers to pledge charitable contributions.

A brand is the sum of the stories society tells about a company and its products. For a brand to be sustainable, such stories must reflect real and substantial value to consumers and to society in general. A sustainable brand grows from an organization's integrity and its authentic efforts to contribute to a better world. It inspires customers and other stakeholders not only to tell its story but also to participate actively in its efforts. It's open and transparent, not only about its successes, but also about its challenges.

Mini Case Study

Stonyfield Farms

What started out as an organic farming school has become one of the best known brands in the sustainable food industry. Stonyfield Farms is now the world's leading organic yogurt maker. Over the years, the company branched into organic smoothies, soy-yogurts, ice cream, and milk. Education is still a guiding corporate value. The company strives to be a model of a profitable sustainable business, providing "a healthful, productive and enjoyable work place for all employees" and providing an excellent return on investment for stakeholders. Photos and bios of farm families and their cows are profiled on the company webpage. Internet visitors are invited to "Have a Cow" and learn about life on the farm through the eyes of Hershey, Libby, Spiffy, or Viper. Human connections are offered through familiar FAQ options, but you can also blog with a farmer or watch a video of the Varney family at work at Nezinscot Farm.[25]

How does Stonyfield Farms embody the five principles of sustainable branding as presented by BBMG? Do its actions speak as loudly as its words? Does it invite other stakeholders to participate in building the brand? What practical benefits does it deliver? What social benefits? Is it helping create a feeling of community among its stakeholders? Is it open and transparent about its products and processes? Does it somehow empower others to do and be better?

In a study for the World Wildlife Fund, Anthony Kleanthous and Jules Peck set out to understand sustainable brands.[26] They conclude that mainstream consumers want the brands they choose to have environmental and social responsibility built in, and they will reward sustainable brands with their loyalty. Based on interviews and a survey of leading marketing professionals, Kleanthous and Peck discovered ten keys to sustainable branding. They're consistent with BBMG's five principles, but they also add additional dimensions of research, measurement, and management for innovation.

Ten Keys to Sustainable Branding

1. *Understand your brand.* The WWF report suggests using a "brand perception audit" to understand the meanings of the brand to all stakeholders, including customers and employees.
2. *Understand your consumers.* The report advocates the use of "anthropological" techniques to learn about present and potential customers' social and environmental values and practices, and how those are manifested in their brand choices.
3. *Get your own house in order.* Clean up your business's internal operations. Get serious about reducing waste and energy use. Find ways to use materials more efficiently and sustainably. Stress your concern and expectations for sustainability with your suppliers.
4. *Integrate CSR.* The corporate social responsibility function should be embedded in everything the business does, and it should drive innovation in every aspect of the company. Core business functions should develop key performance indicators to track and reward sustainable practices.
5. *Innovate.* Identify new and better ways that your brand can help customers feel like they are contributing to a more sustainable society.
6. *Motivate.* Incorporate sustainability goals into the performance reviews of sales and marketing professionals. Reward people for behaviors that exemplify a company's triple-bottom-line values.
7. *Collaborate.* Create multi-functional teams or networks. People from different backgrounds and with different skills within your organization can drive creativity and innovation while making sure all stakeholder groups benefit from increased sustainability.
8. *Communicate.* Tell the story of your journey to sustainability openly and honestly. Invite outsiders to observe and report as well.

9. *Enlist your customers in achieving your sustainability goals.* Happy customers are a business's best marketers. Make sure that every interaction between customers and your brand helps to build customers' sense of belonging to something worthwhile.

10. *Measure, monitor, and report.* The move to sustainability is a journey that requires measurement, benchmarking, and continuous improvement in all the products and processes that contribute to brand value. Look for the same attention to improvement in supplier companies.

THINK ABOUT IT

Reinvigorating a Brand

Because sustainability drives creativity and innovation, the move toward more sustainable products and services can revitalize a brand. Consider a brand that you think is growing tired. Does it have a reputation for social and environmental responsibility? What could be done to make it more sustainable? How might increased sustainability reinvigorate the brand? Consider the ten keys described earlier.

The Internal Brand

In the prior discussions of sustainable branding, you may have noticed that many of the keys refer to processes and activities that are internal to a company rather than external. **Internal branding** refers to the development of a culture that values and supports the brand story among employees. In the words of Starbucks chairman Howard Schultz, "If we want to exceed the trust of our customers, then we first have to build trust with our people. Brand has to start with the culture and naturally extend to our customers."[27]

Employees function, for good or ill, as ambassadors of the brand.[28] The keys to sustainable branding—integrity, authenticity, stakeholder engagement, transparency, and value for both customers and society—all depend on developing an organizational culture that is committed to principles of sustainability. Companies like Patagonia realize the importance of building a sustainable brand from the inside out. Patagonia was founded by people with a deep respect for nature, and the company continues to build its culture of sustainability through the hiring process. Consider this statement about jobs from the company website: "We're always looking for motivated people to join us. . . . We're especially interested in people who share our love of the outdoors, our passion for quality and our desire to make a difference."[29]

Wal-Mart also understands the importance of corporate culture to the brand, but it hasn't always been a sustainability-minded culture. It faces the much more difficult task of engineering a major cultural change. It has tackled the problem with a multi-pronged approach.[30] First, it exerted leadership from the highest levels of the company, the CEO and the chairman of the board. Next it cultivated and hired sustainability champions to begin the hard work of change. It developed volunteer sustainable value networks, which elicited grassroots participation from employees who were already concerned about environmental and social issues. Finally, it linked progress on sustainability goals to employee performance evaluations and made it clear that advancement within the company would require attention to sustainability.[31]

VIRTUAL FIELD TRIP

Examining Brand Sustainability

Pick a major brand that has been featured in the news for its sustainability efforts (hint: several are mentioned in this chapter), and explore its practices more broadly and deeply via Internet searches. What claims does the company make about social and environmental responsibility? What evidence does it offer to back up its claims? What do watchdog agencies have to say about the company's practices? Does the company appear to operate from a culture of sustainability?

SUSTAINABLE PACKAGING

A sustainable brand can only exist as an honest representation of sustainable products and practices. There remains one important aspect of the product mix that we haven't yet covered: packaging. Packaging is a major part of a customer's experience with a product. It also communicates marketers' messages about the brand. And, unfortunately, packaging is a major contributor to environmental pollution and degradation. The U.S. Environmental Protection Agency (EPA) reports that we currently send 90 percent of all fossil-fuel-based plastic packaging to landfills.[32] In 2007, U.S. residents and institutions produced over a quarter trillion tons of trash.[33] For marketing to be sustainable, packaging and labeling must also be sustainable (see Figure 10-1).

Packaging is an integral and tangible part of the product mix. As you've probably already learned, packaging serves a multitude of important functions. It helps protect products from damage and theft. It facilitates storage and transport. It communicates brand identity, promotional messages, and important consumer information. It can also perform important consumer services, such as organizing, measuring, and dispensing a product. However, packaging also contributes enormously to the waste that clogs the world's landfills, stokes its incinerators, and pollutes its oceans and rivers. The keys to **sustainable packaging** lie in maximizing the benefits of packaging while striving not to violate the Natural Step's four system conditions of a sustainable society.

THINK ABOUT IT

Pick a package from a product you've purchased recently. Perhaps it's a molded plastic clamshell or the aluminum cans and plastic rings from a six-pack of soda. How does the packaging potentially violate the system conditions of a sustainable society? How might it contribute to increased environmental levels of toxic metals, synthetic substances, and atmospheric carbon? How might it contribute to the increased degradation of ecosystems such as forests and watersheds? What kinds of steps could minimize its negative effects? Which of those steps could reduce a company's overall costs? Can any of them improve the essential functions of the package? Could they improve the customer experience?

FIGURE 10-1 If clothing is packaging for people, then Adam and Eve may have created the original sustainable packaging: completely renewable and biodegradable.

The Sustainable Packaging Coalition (SPC) is a nonprofit organization that advocates for more environmentally friendly packaging and innovation in the supply chain. According to the SPC definition, sustainable packaging:

- is beneficial, safe, and healthy for individuals and communities throughout its life cycle;
- meets market criteria for performance and cost;
- is sourced, manufactured, transported, and recycled using renewable energy;
- maximizes the use of renewable or recycled source materials;
- is manufactured using clean production technologies and best practices;
- is made from materials healthy in all probable end-of-life scenarios;
- is physically designed to optimize materials and energy;
- is effectively recovered and utilized in biological and/or industrial cradle-to-cradle cycles.[34]

Timberland is working to make shoeboxes more sustainable in an innovative way. On its Earthkeeper line, it includes an ingredients label, much like you'd find on packaged foods. The label reports the environmental impacts of the shoe's production. IKEA, in a constant battle against excessive packaging, uses employees as "air-hunters" to identify wasted space in its shipping containers.[35]

Packaging and the Triple Bottom Line

Of all aspects of a product, packaging often has the most immediate financial payback for sustainability efforts. One company getting serious about packaging sustainability is Sprint. As is often the case for packaging changes, Sprint's efforts have more than paid for themselves. In 2009, *GreenBiz* reported that Sprint's greener packaging would save the company about $2 million a year and reduce its waste output by over 600 tons. Packing innovations include compostable air pillows in shipping cartons, new clamshell-style packages that are recyclable and significantly smaller, paper products that are Forest Stewardship Council (FSC) certified, and the phasing out of PVC and petroleum-based inks.[36]

In addition to being more environmentally friendly and saving money, sustainable packaging should also be customer friendly. In other words, it should provide the benefits of being relatively easy to open and to reuse or recycle. Amazon has developed new packaging that is both greener and easier for customers to use. According to a 2009 article in *Triple Pundit*, an online publication dedicated to triple-bottom-line issues, Amazon's "products are housed in recycled cardboard boxes that are easy to open without the use of a knife or box-cutter! The eco-conscious program also cuts down on excess and wasteful packaging. A specialized software program determines the proper proportions needed for each product, ensuring the items are shipped in a correctly-sized box, reducing excess waste. And finally, products are shipped in one box, instead of several."[37] The remainder of this chapter deals with specific contributions of sustainable packaging and labeling to the triple bottom line.

Remove, Reduce, and Recycle

The principles of dematerialization and service-dominant logic covered in Chapter 9 apply as much to packaging as they do to the core product. Says sustainable marketing consultant Jacquelyn Ottman, "In packaging a key to simplicity is source reduction—using designs that require less material in the first place. Since source reduction means the elimination of the very bells and whistles that make some types of packing so convenient, this can be tricky."[38] Tricky, but not impossible.

Improving the sustainability of packaging requires creativity and innovation, and, as in the case of Amazon, it can yield bonus rewards in both cost savings and customer satisfaction. In some cases, this is as simple as removing excess packaging. For example, underarm deodorant used to come packaged in plastic containers, which, in turn, were packaged in paper boxes. Wal-Mart buyers, always on the lookout for ways to cut costs, began to question both the necessity and the extra cost of the boxes. By simply removing the boxes, marketers were able to reduce consumer waste, save money on packaging materials and processes, and save money and fuel by shipping more products in the same amount of space.[39]

Another approach to reduced packaging is to reduce the overall bulk of a product. This is especially useful if the product contains significant volumes of water or air. For example, the trend in super-concentrated laundry detergents started by Unilever's, all® Small and Mighty and championed by former Wal-Mart CEO Lee Scott is a case in point.[40] By reducing the amount of water in the product, Unilever is able to use smaller containers, requiring less plastic, enabling more detergent to be shipped in less space, and reducing its storage footprint. This saves significant amounts of fuel, energy, and money for marketers, and it benefits consumers by providing a product that is easier to lift and easier to store. Also driven by Wal-Mart, General Mills reformulated its Hamburger Helper product by simply making the noodles flatter. This reduced the amount of air trapped in a package, allowed the product to fit in a smaller box, and saved money on both energy and materials.[41]

When the size or bulk of a product can't be reduced, sometimes significant sustainability gains are possible through merely changing other aspects of the packaging such as shape and overall dimensions. For example, redesigning the shape of the familiar gallon milk jug increased its sustainability. The new, square jugs use fewer resources, are cheaper to ship, and cost less.[42] Cost efficiencies extend to costs of labor and water to clean old-fashioned milk crates (the new jugs ship in recyclable cardboard and shrink wrap), to increasing the number of jugs on each pallet, and eliminating the needed travel to the dairy with empty crates. However, some consumers initially complained about the new jugs, citing spilled milk and difficulty in pouring. In an example of service-dominant logic, warehouse retailer Sam's Club brought in staff to show customers how to pour easily from the new jugs.[43]

Where packaging can't be avoided or reduced, to be sustainable it needs to be fully and easily recyclable. Here, too, the call for sustainability drives innovation. For example, Tom's of Maine has improved the sustainability of its deodorant packaging by using recycled content and creating a deodorant tube made entirely of one type of plastic.[44] Typical deodorant tubes are made of multiple plastics, making recycling difficult. In the electronics industry, many manufacturers are replacing Styrofoam with recyclable corrugated cardboard in their protective packaging.[45]

THINK ABOUT IT

What do you expect from your packaging? Minimal material? Construction from recycled and recyclable content? Ease of opening and use? Clear product information? What if you got just a bit more? Like a lovely little flower garden. Cargo Cosmetics' PlantLove lipstick comes in tubes made of corn and boxed in packages with wild flower seeds embedded in the biodegradable paper and ready to plant.[46] A competitor, Origins cosmetics, offers customers the option of bringing in any brand of empty cosmetic containers with the promise that the company will figure out how to recycle them.[47] What other unexpected, value-added design elements could be added to packaging?

SUSTAINABLE LABELING

Labeling is an important part of packaging. It conveys important information for customers as well as for shippers and handlers. Labeling also presents challenges to sustainability. Trace amounts of metals or toxic substances hidden in product labels might seem inconsequential. However, when multiplied millions, or even billions of times, tiny amounts add up to meaningful quantities. If those quantities end up in the air, water, and soil, they can be problematic. For example, a glass beverage bottle may seem sustainable from the standpoint that glass is endlessly recyclable, and recycling takes far less energy and water than producing glass from raw materials.[48] But if the bottle carries a paper label, the label must be removed and disposed of in the recycling process. Conventional labels are attached with adhesives that contain zinc, which, when concentrated, is toxic to the liver, kidneys, heart, brain, and other organs.[49] Henkel, a German company, has introduced new labeling adhesives that are "manufactured entirely from renewable raw materials in the form of casein and starch. That renders them entirely biodegradable, particularly as they contain no added zinc whatsoever. . . ."[50]

Stressing its environmental credentials, Vodka360 is bottled in glass with 85 percent recycled content, 70 percent of which is post-consumer waste. Its labels are made from 100 percent post-consumer, chlorine-free waste paper and printed with nontoxic water-based inks.

Not all labeling ends up on a package. Some goes directly on the product itself. Fresh fruit routinely gets labeled for sale in supermarkets. The sticky plastic labels convey information about the fruit and its origin, but they can be a nuisance, they can damage delicate fruit, and they eventually end up in the trash. As a more sustainable alternative, fruit labels may soon be replaced by laser tattoo technology. According to the Institute of Food Technologists, "A carbon dioxide laser beam was used to etch information into the first few outer cells of the fruit peel. The mark can't be peeled off, washed off, or changed, offering a way to trace the fruit back to its original source."[51] Testing has shown that the laser tattoos don't damage the fruit and are impenetrable to organisms that cause decay.

Third-Party Certifications: Telling the Sustainability Story

Through labeling, packages play an important role as communication media. Labels can underscore the environmental attributes of a product and a firm. They can be used to reassure consumers with descriptions of product testing and purity. One positive trend in labeling is the inclusion of **third-party certifications**. Created primarily by governments or nonprofits, third-party certifications are seals that indicate a product meets certain standards for social or environmental performance. Such certifications can be a source of competitive advantage. According to Christine Meisner Rosen, in Europe in the 1990s, eco-certifications drove rapid growth in the demand for more sustainable products. The certifications allowed firms with superior environmental performance to make their case to the consuming public with the added credibility of impartial, third-party endorsers. The increased demand at the consumer level was soon felt throughout the industrial supply chains as suppliers and manufacturers hurried to meet standards set by the certifying agencies.[52]

Third-party certification is a form of **co-branding**, wherein two organizations combine their brands to benefit both brands.[53] The certification brand lends credibility to the product brand, and, in turn, a sustainable product supports the value of the certification.

For example, Green Seal is an independent, nonprofit organization that provides science-based environmental certification of standards for a variety of products and services including institutional cleaners, soaps, cleaning supplies and paints, and for business operations including hotels and meeting venues (see Figure 10-2). Green Seal is currently in the pilot stage of a certification for product manufacturers based on requirements in five areas:

1. Transparency and accountability at the corporate level, including publicly available company-wide social and environmental policies; an effective environmental management system; identification of social and environmental roles and responsibilities; compliance; and publicly available annual reporting.
2. Aggressive goals, actions, and achievements in major social and environmental impact areas, including workplace conditions; expanded opportunities for local communities; indigenous peoples' rights; biological diversity; social and environmental assessment; and reductions in greenhouse gases, water use, waste, and toxic chemicals.
3. Effective and accountable supplier management practices to ensure sustainable sourcing of product raw materials, ingredients, and components.

FIGURE 10-2 Green Seal is an independent, nonprofit organization that provides science-based environmental certification of standards for a variety of products and services.

4. Scientific life-cycle assessments on key product lines coupled with aggressive actions to reduce environmental and health impacts. Includes requirements for reducing or eliminating impacts from raw materials; manufacturing; packaging; transport; product use; and the end-of-product life.

5. Ambitious requirements for third-party certification of the company's products to verify social and environmental responsibility of products and to make it easier for consumers to reduce the negative impacts—and increase the social and environmental benefits—of their purchases.[54]

For many marketers, third-party certification for sustainability is a necessity for doing business with some customers. For example, Grand Central Baking in the Pacific Northwest recently decided to source all its white flour from Shepherd's Grain,[55] a local alliance of family farms committed to sustainable practices such as no-till farming and direct seeding. Shepherd's Grain, in turn, requires its members to be inspected and certified by Food Alliance, an organization that provides comprehensive third-party certification for the production, processing, and distribution of sustainable food.[56]

Some third-party certifications come from community-based programs such as Alaska's Green Star and extend to a wide variety of local businesses. "Green Star® is a non-profit organization, based in Anchorage, Alaska, that encourages businesses to practice waste reduction, energy conservation and pollution prevention through education, technical assistance, and an award-winning voluntary 'green business' certification program."[57]

Other certification programs are widespread, even global, but limited to specific industries. For example, the Marine Stewardship Council (MSC) is a global organization that administers a seafood certification and labeling program that recognizes and rewards sustainable fishing. MSC works with all stakeholders in the fishing industry including seafood companies, scientists, conservation groups, and the public as it promotes sustainable seafood production and consumption.[58]

Whereas some certifications apply primarily to production processes, others focus on the impacts of product usage. For example, in 1992, the EPA and the U.S. Department of Energy developed the Energy Star program to help consumers save on energy costs and to protect the environment through energy efficient products and practices. Energy Star is a "voluntary labeling program designed to identify and promote energy-efficient products to reduce greenhouse gas emissions."[59] Energy Star labeling can be found on major appliances, office equipment, heating and air-conditioning systems, lighting, home electronics, and more. The EPA has even extended the certification to cover new homes and commercial buildings.

In any given industry, multiple certification programs may exist, reflecting different areas of concern. For example, consumers buying coffee can choose from beans that are verified as organic, Fairtrade, Smithsonian Bird Friendly, and Rainforest Alliance approved. Wines may be designated as organic, biodynamic, salmon-safe, or LIVE (for Low Input Viticulture & Enology) (see Figure 10-3). Such certifications may be mutually supportive of

FIGURE 10-3 Salmon Safe certification assures West Coast consumers that products come from more sustainable agricultural practices.

sustainability goals, as they tend to be in the wine industry, or they may conflict. The forestry industry has seen such interest in sustainable practices that competing third-party certification programs have developed. The Sustainable Forests Initiative (SFI) has been criticized by FSC for condoning, "environmentally harmful practices including large-scale clearcutting and chemical use, logging of old growth and endangered forests, and replacement of forests by ecologically degraded tree plantations. And there's no guarantee that many products marketed as SFI have any connection to SFI certified forests."[60] For its part, SFI notes that its certification process has been "subject to rigorous independent assessments by respected academic and conservation groups, and is accepted by international organizations and governments around the world."[61] While the debate continues, marketers and consumers who want products and materials from sustainable sources will have to choose.

Truth in Labeling

While most third-party certifications are fairly straightforward and rigorous, some may actually be used to misrepresent a product's true impacts on health, well-being, or the environment. For example, a 2009 controversy over a food-labeling campaign called Smart Choices, which is backed by many large food manufacturers, revolves around a green checkmark that supposedly is "designed to help shoppers easily identify smarter food and beverage choices."[62] The problem is that the standard for "smarter" is so low that even sugary products like Kellogg's Froot Loops and Cocoa Krispies carry the label, much to the dismay of many nutritionists.

Among its many activities, the food-oriented advocacy group, Sustain, monitors food labeling in order to keep companies honest. For example, the organization called out Heinz "for hijacking the phrase *farmers' market* for its tinned soup, whose ingredients bear little relation to what would be on sale in a real farmers' market—i.e. fresh, local, seasonal food sold by the grower themselves."[63]

The magazine *Fast Company* cited **sustainability labeling** as the top sustainability trend for 2009. The goal of sustainability labeling is to communicate information such as carbon footprints and chemical contents, thereby enabling consumers to make more informed purchase decisions.[64]

CRITICAL THINKING ACTIVITY

How Much Information Is Too Much Information When It Comes to Product Labeling?

How much information is too much information when it comes to product labeling? What are the advantages to consumers of including information about environmental and social sustainability on labels? Are there any potential advantages for marketers as well? Are there problems associated with trying to put too much information on a label? Are there potential problems with trying to condense too much information into a single score or symbol?

Chapter Summary

Sustainable brands are economically viable and associated in the minds of stakeholders with positive social and ecological practices. To be sustainable, a brand must develop and retain stakeholders' trust and respect. The keys to sustainable branding are integrity, authenticity, stakeholder engagement, transparency, and value for both customers and society. More than ever before, consumers want products to be sustainable, including in their packaging and labeling. Improving the sustainability packaging is often a quick win with respect to triple-bottom-line goals, saving money on both materials and shipping while also reducing negative impacts. Sustainable packaging begins with principles of dematerialization, which involves removing, reducing, and reusing materials whenever possible and making everything safe and recyclable. Sustainable labeling follows the same principles and includes information that informs consumers honestly about a product's environmental and social impacts.

Review of Chapter Objectives

- Sustainable branding
- Sustainable packaging
- Sustainable labeling

Key Concepts

Brand 140	Radical Transparency 142	Sustainable Packaging 145	Co-Branding 148
Sustainable Brand 140	Internal Branding 144	Third-Party Certifications 148	Sustainability Labeling 150

Endnotes

1. Interbrand, Best Global Brands 2009 rankings http://www.interbrand.com/best_global_brands.aspx, accessed October 11, 2009.
2. Global 100, 2010 Global 100: The Definitive Corporate Sustainability Benchmark http://www.global100.org/, accessed October 12, 2009.
3. Dow Jones, Dow Jones Sustainability Indexes, http://www.sustainability-index.com/07_htmle/assessment/overview.html, accessed October 12, 2009.
4. Arghire, Ionut (2009), "Nokia Named the World's Most Sustainable Technology Company by Dow Jones Sustainability Indexes," September 21, 2009 http://news.softpedia.com/news/Nokia-Named-the-World-039-s-Most-Sustainable-Technology-Company-122235.shtml, accessed October 12, 2009.
5. Silverman, Greg (2009), "Uncovering the Link between CSR and Brand Value: Developing a New Methodology," http://www.interbrand.com/paper.aspx?paperid=77&langid=1000, accessed October 12, 2009.
6. Media BuyerPlanner, "26% of Search Results Link to Consumer Generated Content," December 14, 2006 |http://www.mediabuyerplanner.com/entry/38283/26-of-search-results-link-to-consumer-generated-content/, accessed September 21, 2009.
7. PSFK, "Dead Brands of 2009," http://www.psfk.com/2009/07/dead-brands-of-2009.html, accessed October 11, 2009.
8. Zenlea, David (2009), "Jim Wangers on the Death of Pontiac Excitement," *Automobilemag.com*, April 30, http://blogs.automobilemag.com/6507316/editors-soapbox/jim-wangers-on-the-death-of-pontiac-excitement/index.html, accessed October 11, 2009.
9. Kodak (2009), "A Tribute to Kodachrome: A Photography Icon," June 22, http://homepage.1000words.kodak.com/default.asp?item=2388083, accessed October 1, 2009.
10. Diamond, Jared (2009), "Will Big Business Save the Earth?" *New York Times*, December 5, http://www.nytimes.com/2009/12/06/opinion/06diamond.html?_r=1&pagewanted=2, accessed December 7, 2009.
11. BBMG, http://www.bbmg.com/, accessed September 21, 2009.
12. Bemporad, Raphael and Mitch Baranowski (2009), "The Five Principles of Sustainable Branding," http://www.sustainablelife-media.com/content/column/brands/five_principles_of_sustainable_branding, accessed September 21, 2009.
13. Aveda, "Mission," http://aveda.aveda.com/aboutaveda/mission.asp, accessed December 1, 2009.
14. Aveda, "What's New," http://www.aveda.com/whatsnew/nepal.tmpl, accessed December 2, 2009.
15. McAlexander, James H., John W. Schouten, and Harold J. Koenig (2002), "Building Brand Community," *Journal of Marketing*, 66 (January): 38–54.
16. LEGO Fan, http://www.legofan.org/ambassadors/ambassadors.html, accessed December 8, 2009.
17. Shinn, Sharon (2008), "Brand Evangelist," *Biz Ed*, March/April (p. 18).
18. World Wildlife Fund http://www.worldwildlife.org/who/media/press/2004/WWFPresitem728.html, accessed March 22, 2010.
19. Jensen, Cheryl (2009), "Honda and Toyota Top Reliability Survey, but Ford Closes Gap," *New York Times*, October 27 http://wheels.blogs.nytimes.com/2009/10/27/honda-and-toyota-top-reliability-survey-but-ford-closes-gap/, accessed December 2, 2009
20. Honda, http://automobiles.honda.com/civic-hybrid/, accessed December 2, 2009
21. Honda, http://automobiles.honda.com/fit/, accessed December 2, 2009
22. Thompson, Clive (2007), "The See-Through CEO," *Wired*, 15, 4 (March), http://www.wired.com/wired/archive/15.04/wired40_ceo.html, accessed December 10, 2009.
23. Goleman, Daniel (2009), "Winning in an Age of Radical Transparency," *Harvard Business: Leading Green*, May 7, http://blogs.harvardbusiness.org/leadinggreen/2009/05/radical-transparency.html, accessed December 10, 2009. See also: Goleman (2009), *Ecological Intelligence: How Knowing the Hidden Impacts of What We Buy Can Change Everything*, New York: Broadway Books.
24. John's Swoosh Page, http://www.trizera.com/jsp/, accessed December 10, 2009.
25. Stonyfield Farm, http://www.stonyfield.com, accessed October 7, 2009
26. Kleanthous, Anthony and Jules Peck (2006), *Let Them Eat Cake: Satisfying the New Consumer Appetite for Responsible Brands*, World Wildlife Fund, p. 6, http://www.wwf.org.uk/filelibrary/pdf/let_them_eat_cake_abridged.pdf accessed October 3, 2009.
27. Holmes, Stanley (2001), "Starbucks: Keeping the Brew Hot," *Business Week*, August 6.
28. Vallaster, Christine and Leslie de Chernatony (2006), "Internal Brand Building and Structuration: The Role of Leadership," *European Journal of Marketing*, 40 (7/8): 761–784.
29. Patagonia, http://www.patagonia.com, accessed December 10, 2009.
30. Martin, Diane M. and John W. Schouten (2009) "Engineering a Mainstream Market for Sustainability: Insights from Wal-Mart's Perfect Storm," in *Explorations in Consumer Culture Theory*, edited by John F. Sherry, Jr., and Eileen Fisher, 150–167, London, UK: Routledge.
31. Martin, Diane M. and John W. Schouten (2009), "Engineering a Mainstream Market for Sustainability: Insights from Wal-Mart's Perfect Storm," in *Explorations in Consumer Culture Theory*, edited by John F. Sherry, Jr., and Eileen Fisher, 150–167, London, UK: Routledge.
32. Pkg Stuff, http://pkgstuff.blogspot.com/2009/04/do-we-understand-biodegradable.html, accessed October 7, 2009.
33. U.S. Environmental Protection Agency, "Non-Hazardous Waste," http://www.epa.gov/waste/basic-solid.htm, accessed October 7, 2009.
34. Sustainable Packaging Coalition, http://www.sustainablepackaging.org/pdf/Definition%20of%20Sustainable%20Packaging%2010-15-05%20final.pdf, accessed October 7, 2009.

35. Werbach, Adam (2009), *Strategy for Sustainability: A Business Manifesto*, Boston, MA: Harvard Business Press (p. 109).

36. Staff (2009), "Cadbury and Sprint to Save Tons of Waste with New Greener Packaging," *GreenBiz News*, November 4, http://www.greenbiz.com/news/2009/11/04/cadbury-and-sprint-save-tons-waste-new-greener-packaging, accessed December 10, 2009.

37. Shoemaker-Galloway, Jace (2009), "It's a Wrap: Amazon Launches Frustration-Free Packaging Certification Program," *Triple Pundit*, November 20, http://www.triplepundit.com/2009/11/it's-a-wrap-amazon-launches-frustration-free-packaging-certification-program/, accessed December 10, 2009.

38. Ottman, Jacquelyn A. (1998), *Green Marketing: Opportunity for Innovation*, New York: J. Ottman Consulting Inc (p. 102).

39. Fishman, Charles (2006), The Wal-Mart Effect: How the World's Most Powerful Company Really Works—And How It's Transforming the American Economy, New York: The Penguin Press.

40. "Sustainability Is Good," http://www.sustainableisgood.com/blog/2007/09/concentrated-la.html, accessed September 20, 2009.

41. Kistler, Matt (2009), "Save More. Live Better," white paper, Wal-Mart, http://www.awarenessintoaction.com/whitepapers/Wal-Mart-Supply-Chain-Packaging-Scorecard-sustainability.html, accessed October 8, 2009.

42. Rosenbloom, Stephanie (2008), "Solution or Mess? A Milk Jug for a Green Earth," June 30, *New York Times*, http://www.nytimes.com/2008/06/30/business/30milk.html?_r=3&ex=1215489600&en=42e2b3ac232d00f7&ei=5070, accessed September 14, 2009.

43. Rosenbloom, Stephanie (2008), "Solution or Mess? A Milk Jug for a Green Earth," June 30, *New York Times*, http://www.nytimes.com/2008/06/30/business/30milk.html?_r=3&ex=1215489600&en=42e2b3ac232d00f7&ei=5070, accessed September 14, 2009.

44. Tom's of Maine, http://www.tomsofmaine.com/Default.aspx?cid=s-090001, accessed September 22, 2009.

45. CalRecycle, http://www.ciwmb.ca.gov/Packaging/CaseStudies/, accessed July 22, 2009.

46. Cargo Cosmetics, http://www.cargocosmetics.com/plantlove.html, accessed October 8, 2009.

47. Origins, http://www.origins.com/about/index.tmpl?page=recycle, accessed October 8, 2009.

48. Environment Green, http://www.environment-green.com/Glass_Recycling.html, accessed October 10, 2009.

49. Taban, C. H., M. Cathieni, and P. Burkard (1982), "Changes in Newt Brain Caused by Zinc Water-Pollution," *Cellular and Molecular Life Sciences*, 38 (June 6): 683–685.

50. http://www.henkel.com/cps/rde/xchg/SID-0AC8330A-6E8028DB/henkel_com/hs.xsl/12169_20090914-sustainable-labeling-solutions-22852_COE_HTML.htm, accessed October 10, 2009.

51. Institute of Food Technologists (2009), "Laser Etching Puts Label on Fruit," September , http://www.ift.org/news_bin/news/news_home.shtml, accessed October 10, 2009.

52. Rosen, Christine Meisner (2001), "Environmental Strategy and Competitive Advantage: An Introduction," *California Management Review*, 43 (1-Spring): 8–17.

53. Blackett, Tom and Bob Boad (1999), *Co-Branding: The Science of Alliance*, London, UK: MacMillan.

54. Green Seal, http://www.greenseal.org/index.cfm, accessed November 27, 2009.

55. Sustainable Food News (2009), "Grand Central Baking Transitions to Sustainable Flour Supply," September 1, http://www.foodalliance.org/newsroom/articles/2009/GrandCentral-ShepsGrain-SFN-1Sep09.pdf, accessed October 8, 2009.

56. Food Alliance, http://foodalliance.org/, accessed March 19, 2010.

57. Green Star, http://www.greenstarinc.org/ accessed September 11, 2009.

58. Marine Stewardship Council, http://www.msc.org/, accessed September 11, 2009.

59. Energy Star, http://www.energystar.gov/index.cfm?c=about.ab_history, accessed September 11, 2009.

60. Forest Stewardship Council, http://credibleforestcertification.org/, accessed September 11, 2009.

61. Sustainable Forest Initiative, http://www.sfiprogram.org/join-SFI/sfi-recognition.php, accessed September 11, 2009.

62. Neuman, William (2009), "For Your Health, Froot Loops," *New York Times*, September 4, http://www.nytimes.com/2009/09/05/business/05smart.html, accessed September 6, 2009.

63. SustainWeb, http://www.sustainweb.org/labelling/, accessed December 10, 2009.

64. Chaudhuri, Saabira (2009), "Top 3 Sustainability Trends for 2009," *Fast Company*, December 5, http://www.fastcompany.com/articles/2008/12/top-sustainability-trends.html?page=0%2C1, accessed December 10, 2009.

Marketing Channels: Sustainability in the Value Chain

INTRODUCTION: SELL YOUR TRASH

When we think of recycling, liquefied worm poop packaged in reused soda bottles isn't usually the first thing that comes to mind. But it was the first product TerraCycle founder, Tom Szaky, brought to market.[1] Szaky's story doesn't end with worm excrement; he's found other ways to turn waste into consumer goods. Among other things, TerraCycle now makes backpacks and messenger bags out of Capri Sun drink pouches, gift-wrap bows out of Clif Bar wrappers, and flowerpots out of e-waste.[2] TerraCycle's supply chain includes those who would prefer to get paid two cents per item for their trash rather than send it to a landfill. And TerraCycle's customer base, in addition to its direct, online consumers, now includes retailers such as Target and Wal-Mart.

THINK ABOUT IT

In what ways does TerraCycle alter the traditional value chain? In what ways does this encourage consumers to take on new roles or behaviors? Is the TerraCycle model sustainable? Why or why not? What social or environmental advantages does the company create? What do you suppose happens to the TerraCycle products when they are no longer desired or usable?

This chapter examines how marketing channels can become more sustainable and contribute to triple-bottom-line goals. Following principles of sustainability, members of the marketing value chain can enhance business performance and deliver value to customers, while also building environmental and human capital. This chapter challenges and expands the concept of marketing channels and the value chain. It presents the concept of sustainable value circles and explores what this concept means for roles, relationships, and processes in the marketing channels.

CHAPTER OBJECTIVES

In this chapter, you will learn about:

- Converting value chains to sustainable value circles
- Building sustainable channel relationships: communication and collaboration

TerraCycle turns consumer waste into consumer goods.

- Developing sustainable channel operations
- Sustainability in retailing

MARKETING CHANNELS: FROM VALUE CHAINS TO SUSTAINABLE VALUE CIRCLES

Marketing channels are the means whereby goods, services, and value move between producers and consumers or between buyers and sellers. A marketing channel is made up of firms, such as manufacturers, wholesalers, agents, brokers, and retailers, all working together to deliver products and services to customers.[3] Each of these firms forms a link in what is commonly called a **value chain**, which is the chain of activities and institutions that add value to a product on its way from manufacturing to an end consumer. Each link adds some kind of value to the products that move through the channel. Some firms in a value chain add tangible benefits to a product, whereas others provide service, such as facilitating its distribution.

Each channel member is a marketing firm; that is, it has customers that it must serve and satisfy. Likewise, each firm is a customer in that it purchases goods and services from suppliers in order to perform its functions. For example, a trucking company sells distribution services to manufacturers, wholesalers, and/or retailers. In turn, it purchases trucks, fuel, office supplies, and the services of drivers, who may be independent contractors.

As is the case with every other marketing activity, achieving sustainability and competitive advantage in marketing channels requires innovation from a whole-system perspective. Failure to consider the effects of a marketing action throughout entire economic and ecological systems often leads to unintended consequences and undesirable trade-offs. What makes achieving a whole-system perspective particularly challenging is that marketing channels tend to have multiple members performing many different functions. Channel members may even be partners and competitors at the same time. As John Elkington put it as early as 1994, "The challenge facing companies is to work out ways of co-operating with their suppliers, customers, and other stakeholders . . . while ensuring that they benefit not only in corporate citizenship terms, but also in terms of competitive advantage."[4]

Decisions made anywhere in the marketing channels have consequences for the overall sustainability and profitability of a product. When multiple firms are making the decisions, overall impact can be harder to assess and control. Important metrics, such as life-cycle assessments, may require input from all partners in the value chain from raw materials suppliers to end users and beyond.

You may have seen examples of marketing channels, or value chains, that are basically linear, with goods and services flowing from manufacturers to consumers and money flowing from consumers back through the channels toward manufacturers, with each member of the chain taking payment along the way. Conventionally, a marketing channel has been viewed as a **throughput system**, meaning a system in which materials come in and materials go out, with no real accounting for their ultimate origination or destination. In sustainable marketing, however, as in nature, there are no throughput systems. The often-neglected ends of the value chain all link to something, somewhere. For example, the raw materials that eventually make up a computer don't appear out of nowhere. They all originate from the Earth, and the Earth exacts a price for them in terms of ecosystem services. Similarly, the computer monitor that goes to a landfill doesn't disappear there. It eventually cycles back into the Earth's ecosystems, along with all its toxic components. The conventional, linear model of marketing channels is unsustainable for a number of reasons.

Linear Flows and Waste

Waste is a major cause of costs and problems in marketing channels. Waste of some kind is generated at every link in the value chain. As independent operators, channel members historically have disposed of their waste in the simplest and cheapest ways possible. This typically meant dumping airborne wastes into the atmosphere; pouring liquid wastes into rivers, lakes, oceans, or soil; and paying someone to haul solid wastes off to landfills or incinerators. The most obvious problem with waste is that it pollutes. In terms of The Natural Step Framework, linear throughput systems increase concentrations of toxic substances in the biosphere; they destroy or reduce the effectiveness of natural systems; and they create problems for human health and well-being (see Figure 11-1).

Another problem for business is that waste is expensive. It costs money to create waste, and it costs money to dispose of it. However, if managed properly, waste can be eliminated or converted into a source of revenue. Shipping pallets provide a prime example of turning waste to revenue. Most products are shipped on pallets, which traditionally have been made of wood. Wooden pallets cause numerous expensive and sometimes devastating problems. First, they require wood, which depletes forests. Because wooden pallets are heavy and difficult to move, they contribute to relatively high levels of worker injuries. Nails in pallets cause damage to facilities, requiring maintenance and repair, and to products and packaging, contributing to even greater waste. Wood pallets can also be infested with insect pests that are transported to foreign ecosystems where they cause enormous harm. Finally, someone ultimately has to pay to have the pallets hauled away and destroyed. By switching to pallets made of corrugated cardboard or recycled plastic, companies can be spared much of the expense and waste associated with wood.

FIGURE 11-1 Every link in the value chain contributes to a product's environmental impact. This diagram depicts the total carbon footprint of a can of cola.

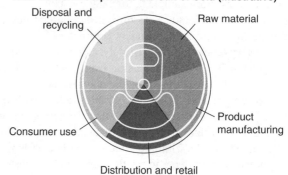

Such pallets are made from recycled materials rather than from virgin wood. They are much lighter than wooden pallets, resulting in fewer worker injuries. They don't damage surfaces or carry pests. And at the end of their lives, they can be reused or recycled.[5]

Cradle to Cradle

Every waste product in the natural world serves as a vital input to other organisms and processes. Plants create food and oxygen to sustain animal life, and animal waste creates fertilizer and builds soil that allows plants to thrive. Following principles of biomimicry, in which industrial processes are modeled after biological processes, the cradle-to-cradle philosophy, championed by Michael Braungart and William McDonough,[6] holds that all industrial waste can and should be eliminated by making sure that all of it either serves as biodegradable nutrients for natural systems (the biosphere) or is reclaimed for reuse in human technological systems (the **technosphere**). **Cradle-to-cradle certification** helps companies design products that can be reabsorbed harmlessly by nature or reintroduced to the technosphere through recycling. Cradle-to-cradle manufacturers produce products with renewable energy, use water efficiently, and treat people responsibly. Aveda, the beauty products company, has several products that are cradle-to-cradle certified[7] (see Photo 11-1).

PHOTO 11-1 Aveda was the first company in the beauty products industry to receive cradle-to-cradle certification for some of its products.

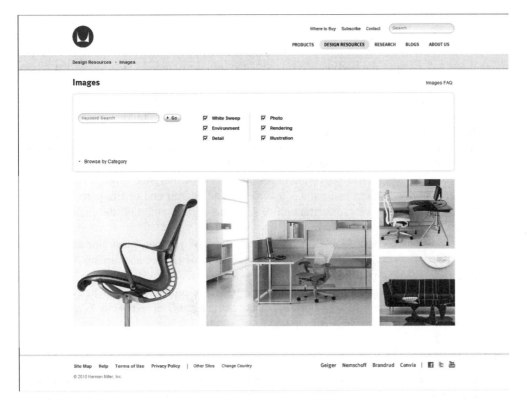

PHOTO 11-2   The Herman Miller chair, Celle, is MBDC Gold and Silver Cradle to Cradle certified, depending on configuration. This means that it is composed of environmentally safe and healthy materials, is designed for material reuse in a closed-loop system, such as recycling or composting, and is assembled using 100% renewable energy. This Herman Miller chair was designed to be disassembled rapidly into components that are easy to reuse or recycle.

Cradle-to-cradle thinking results in marketing channels wherein waste is reduced dramatically and consumers become suppliers of many of the raw materials required for manufacturing. The ability to reclaim recyclables from products begins with product design. **Design for disassembly** (DfD) allows products to be more easily and safely reduced to their component materials at end of life. According to author Alex Steffen, "Major consumer electronics companies—from Panasonic to Phillips—are re-vamping their lines to make disassembly for recycling, and the remaining disposal as easy, cheap, and safe as possible. Features like low or no-lead solder, modular electronics boards, snap-fit rather than glued joints, and included instructions for disassembly make it easier for the dead product to have a new life."[8]

Other companies that have embraced DfD include Herman Miller and Steelcase, both of which make office furniture that can be broken down easily and quickly into recyclable components (see Photo 11-2). Nike's Considered line of footwear also exemplifies design for disassembly.

VIRTUAL FIELD TRIP

Waste = Food

The documentary video, Waste = Food, is available for viewing online or as a DVD in many libraries. Watch the video and discuss how cradle-to-cradle design and manufacturing can be a source of competitive advantage for members of a marketing channel.

Reversing Flows of Materials, Money, and Ideas

Since the early 1970s, the marketing literature has recognized the need for **reverse logistics**, that is, the systematic movement of waste back through marketing channels, in order to convert it back into usable raw materials. In a 1971 *Journal of Marketing* article, Zikmund and Stanton wrote, "The recycling of solid wastes is a major ecological goal. Although recycling is technologically feasible, reversing the flow of materials in the channels of distribution—marketing trash through a 'backward' channel—presents a challenge. . . . The consumer must be motivated to undergo a role change and become a producer—the initiating force in the reverse distribution process."[9]

One way for reverse logistics to work is for retailers, or other channel members, to take back and consolidate recyclable materials such as plastic bags, packaging, and used products. For example, since July 2007, major retailers in California have been required to collect used plastic bags for recycling.[10] Best Buy has become a receiver and consolidator for electronic waste.[11] Metro Paint accepts unused house paints from consumers or contractors and recycles them into new, high-quality, low-cost paint in several colors.[12] Caterpillar offers its customers an exchange program for engines and parts. Customers trade in their end-of-life parts and receive like-new remanufactured parts for a fraction of new-parts prices and with the same new-parts warranties.[13]

For marketing to be sustainable, such backward flows of materials must ultimately become viewed as normal, forward flows, turning value chains into **value circles**, and turning consumers or end users into suppliers of raw materials and component parts for manufacturers (see Figures 11-2 and 11-3). In keeping with the principles of cradle-to-cradle production and The Natural Step Framework, value circles help to keep synthetic and toxic materials isolated in closed technological loops and out of the natural environment.

Secondary Markets

Even prior to recycling, many products can continue to provide value through **secondary markets**, which provide used or surplus goods at prices that are usually well below initial retail prices. For example, organizations such as thrift shops collect and resell used clothing and

FIGURE 11-2 A traditional value chain depletes natural capital, converting it into waste. At each step, resources are consumed, value is added, and waste is produced.

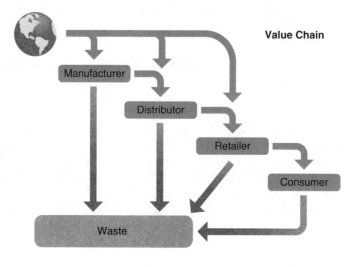

FIGURE 11-3 In a value circle waste materials that are not immediately biodegradable are captured and reconverted to raw materials. Value is still added at each step, but natural capital remains intact.

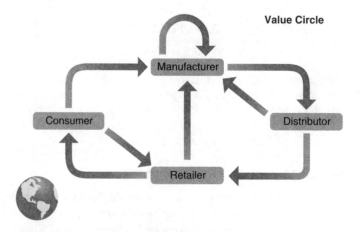

household goods while providing jobs for disadvantaged persons.[14] Ultimately, most garments can be recycled at the ends of their useful lives, especially since 90 percent or more of all textile waste can be recovered as usable fiber.[15] With some fibers, like polyester, it's already less expensive to produce textiles from recycled materials than from virgin materials.[16]

Mini Case Study

The ReBuilding Center

In 1998, a group of volunteers started a construction salvage organization called the ReBuilding Center,[17] which became the nation's largest nonprofit center for the reuse of salvaged construction and remodeling materials. The center's inventory includes sinks, tubs, tile, lumber, doors, windows, trim, and more. These materials are ready to be reused in new construction and remodeling projects. They come in part from contractors and home remodelers, who earn tax deductions for their contributions.

Perhaps the ReBuilding Center's most innovative and important function is its DeConstruction Services, a more sustainable alternative to conventional demolition. Traditional building demolition involves wrecking balls, bulldozers, and dump trucks to remove debris to a landfill. Alternatively, the ReBuilding Center uses skilled work crews to dismantle buildings by hand, at costs that are comparable to those for standard demolition. The crews salvage up to 85 percent of buildings' materials for reuse. Huge amounts of material are diverted from landfills, and

the value of the salvaged material is enough to provide jobs for about eight times as many people as would be employed in a standard demolition. According to ReBuilding Center estimates, the dismantling of a 2,000 square-foot house preserves 2,400 gallons of clean water, saves 33 mature trees, provides 907 additional hours of work at a living wage, and reduces greenhouse gas (GHG) emissions by as much as taking three cars off the road for a year.[18]

View the time-lapse movie of DeConstruction Services at: http://rebuildingcenter.org/deconstruction-services/.

In what ways does the ReBuilding Center turn a value chain into a value circle? How does the organization increase environmental sustainability? How does it improve social sustainability within the community where it operates? What other complex products can be deconstructed for reuse or remanufacturing following a similar model? What can builders and manufacturers do to make their products easier to de-manufacture and return to the value cycle?

As materials are kept in closed value circles, becoming resources instead of waste, their value increases. This allows consumers and other members of the value circle to benefit financially from conserving them, consolidating them, and returning them to the marketing channels. As we noted at the beginning of the chapter, TerraCycle is a small-scale example of a company that pays consumers to reclaim certain kinds of products and packaging. In many cases, consumers don't require direct monetary compensation for the service of recycling packaging waste or spent products. It may be enough for them to save money on trash pickups or hazardous-waste disposal fees. This is especially true for electronics, compact fluorescent light bulbs (CFLs), and toxic substances such as used paint, motor oil, or batteries, which require special handling in order to be recycled safely.

Marketing Opportunities

Reclaiming materials and facilitating their flows in value circles has become a profitable business sector. For example, in Chapter 7 we learned that Rocky Mountain Recycling expanded its business through the innovative use of cardboard balers to incorporate and consolidate a broader range of recyclables. In another interesting example, Xstrata, a global mining company, has also become a major player in the recycling of electronic waste. Essentially treating spent consumer electronics as if they were mineral deposits, Xstrata reclaims precious metals, which are then reused in both consumer and industrial products. According to company information, in 2009 15 percent of its Horne Smelter's annual production came from recycling. At the company's CCR refinery, recycling contributes 15 percent of the copper, 20 percent of the gold, 10 percent of the silver, and 85 percent of the platinum/palladium refined there.[19]

As we've discussed, closing the loop on a value circle has many advantages. It helps keep harmful waste out of the environment; it can convert waste and disposal costs into sources of revenue; it can provide industry with stable supplies of raw materials without depleting natural capital; and it can help build human capital by providing living-wage jobs for more people. Many businesses and industries get it, and are moving voluntarily in the direction of creating value circles. For example, Dell's Asset Recovery & Recycling Services helps its small-business customers deal with the disposal of old computers by going to the customer's workplace, eliminating all data on storage drives, and dismantling the machines.[20] This isn't just an example of corporate largess. Dell, along with other electronic manufacturers, has learned to mine old electronics for usable parts and materials.

In some cases, governments pass legislation to speed up the transition. Dell has worked on the legislative front to encourage more regulations governing manufacturers to take back Dell equipment.[21] The European Union has enacted a law requiring auto manufacturers to take back their vehicles at end of life, at no additional cost to car owners, and to disassemble and recycle the components.[22]

Overlapping Value Circles: Cooperation across Industries

Often, the materials generated as waste in one industry are best suited for uses outside that industry's value circle. In such cases, sustainability is improved through cross-industry collaboration. Recyclers such as Xstrata perform the functions of intermediaries between industries by reclaiming materials from some industries, such as gold and platinum from electronic waste, and turning them into valuable resources for other industries, such as jewelry.

In cases where less processing is needed to convert waste to resources, members of one value circle can trade materials directly with members of other industries. An article in the *Academy of Management Review* written over 15 years ago cited an example from the Danish community of Kalundborg where several companies found ways to use each other's waste products as their own raw materials. Author Paul Shrivastava wrote, "The coal-fired power plant sells its excess steam to the city, the fishery, the enzyme plant, and the refinery, instead of discarding it. These organizations use it as a heating source. It sells its fly ash to the cement company and its limestone sludge to the wall-board plant. Statoil refinery supplies the power plant with treated wastewater for cooling and desulphurized gas for fuel, saving 30,000 tons of coal a year."[23] Although not a completely closed loop, the Kalundborg network of value circles demonstrates how companies in different marketing channels can collaborate to reduce costs and decrease their overall environmental footprints.

BUILDING SUSTAINABLE CHANNEL RELATIONSHIPS: COMMUNICATION AND COLLABORATION

Marketers don't have to go it alone when it comes to developing new, more sustainable practices. Marketing channels exist and thrive because they add value for customers. Naturally, at each step of the way, channel members attempt to maximize their own profits, and those firms with the most **channel power** have distinct advantages in doing so. However, the competition for profits within the marketing channels is not necessarily a zero-sum game. Through cooperation, channel members can innovate, create synergies, and build value that benefits everyone. A 2009 study emphasized the importance of marketing firms forming close partnerships with customers and other channel members in order to achieve gains in innovation, product design, manufacturing, and supply chain management.[24] Value circles work best when relationships among channel members are open and collaborative.

Collaboration can involve people and organizations both upstream and downstream in the marketing channels, and it can benefit all members of a value circle. The primary requirements for channel collaboration are common or complementary goals and communication. For example, in order to foster better communication and greater environmental sustainability among its suppliers, Wal-Mart sponsored a packaging fair for its **upstream channel members**, that is, its suppliers and its suppliers' suppliers. At the event, packaging companies met with product companies to learn more about their needs, including more sustainable packaging options. In turn, product suppliers learned about packaging innovations such as waterproof coatings for cardboard boxes that are made from recycled plastic, instead of petroleum, and will break down again in a landfill, unlike traditional laminates.[25]

The focus on channel sustainability is not strictly environmental. Marketers can also influence other channel members to be more socially sustainable. For example, as author Marc

Epstein reports, "H&M (Hennes & Mauritz), a Scandinavian-based global clothing manufacturer and retailer, focuses its social responsibility efforts on monitoring the working conditions of its suppliers. H&M (like many others) has established a code of conduct that suppliers must follow. To monitor compliances, H&M has more than 30 auditors who report to local offices as well as to corporate CSR departments. The manager of the CSR department reports directly to the managing director (CEO) of the company."[26] Nike, adidas, and other sportswear companies follow similar practices of establishing, monitoring, and enforcing rules of conduct for worker treatment as well as for environmental practices in suppliers' manufacturing facilities. Nike's code of conduct has been in place since 1991 and has been updated regularly since then.[27]

Marketers also may attempt to engage **downstream channel members**, that is, their customers and their customers' customers, on down to end users. For example, SC Johnson, a family-owned manufacturer and wholesaler of household cleaning products, has sponsored numerous consumer education initiatives, including high school student-produced videos, to teach consumers how to live more sustainably.[28] When critics targeted Dell for unsustainable use of paper in its catalogs, Dell increased the recycled paper content and also challenged its customers to explore recycled paper options.[29]

Transparency and Chain of Custody

Transparency, or the extent to which an organization's operations and practices are open and visible to outside observers, is a key element in sustainable marketing. As discussed in Chapter 3, transparency is required for accountability, and accountability is required for truly ethical and responsible conduct. Transparency makes it possible for all stakeholders, including other channel members, investors, and customers to evaluate the relative sustainability of a product as it moves through the marketing channels.

An important function of marketing channel transparency is the ability to establish the **chain of custody** of a product or its components. Chain of custody refers to the documented ability to trace the movement and possession of materials from their current places back to their origins. Consumers and retailers often rely on third-party certifications to verify that products meet certain standards of environmental and social stewardship. Third-party certifiers are especially attentive to chains of custody. For example, in the quest to improve forestry practices and to promote more sustainable wood products, the Forest Stewardship Council (FSC) tracks FSC-certified material through the production process—from the forest to the consumer, including all successive stages of processing, transformation, manufacturing, and distribution.[30] The Marine Stewardship Council (MSC) has established similar chain of custody requirements for its seafood certification process: "Once a fishery has been certified, before its seafood can carry the MSC ecolabel, all companies in the supply chain—from boat to plate—must have MSC Chain of Custody certification. This way every link is checked to make sure the MSC label is only displayed on seafood from a MSC certified sustainable fishery."[31] Examples of other industries that are attempting to establish reliable chain of custody certification processes are diamond mining (where blood diamonds are a particular concern),[32] gold mining,[33] meat,[34] and organic foods.[35]

One method of assuring channel transparency is the use of **external audits**, wherein third-party certifiers observe and document business practices for compliance with standards that are typically voluntary. For example, Worldwide Responsible Accredited Production (WRAP) is an independent, nonprofit organization dedicated to the certification of lawful, humane, and ethical manufacturing throughout the world.[36] WRAP certifies factories, which may manufacture many different brands, in the apparel and footwear industries. It conducts audits of working conditions and certifies factories for a period of six months at a time.

Recognizing that the food system is responsible for one-third of all GHGs and the largest share of Earth's fresh water supply, agricultural production is making a significant shift toward more sustainable products and practices.[37] Transparency in food channels includes information about food growing (including soil treatment, animal treatment, worker treatment, and the use of water and chemicals), food transportation (including food miles and methods of transport), and food handling (which can lead to contamination with life-threatening food pathogens).

Mini Case Study

Bon Appétit Management Company

Some food service companies are working to make their supply chains more sustainable. Bon Appétit Management Company, which runs more than 400 on-site custom restaurants in 29 states, wants to be known for its socially responsible food sourcing and business practices.[38] At its University of Portland facility in Portland, Oregon, Bon Appétit Management Company first partnered with the Food Alliance, a nonprofit organization that certifies farms, ranches, and food handlers for sustainable agricultural and facility management practices[39] in their efforts to source local, sustainable food. The company soon built numerous relationships directly with local growers and processors on the forefront of sustainable practices. Local suppliers include Truitt Brothers[40] in Salem, Oregon, for canned fruits and vegetables; Shepherd's Grain[41] in central Oregon and Washington for flour; and Sauvie Island Organics[42] for fresh vegetables. Bon Appétit Management Company improved its disposal of food wastes by replacing garbage

disposals with high-capacity pulpers, which reduce liquid and solid waste—including food scraps, placemats, napkins, and straws to 85 percent of their original volume.[43] This makes the waste useful to a local composter, saves the company 350,000 gallons of water over the five-month long academic semester, and keeps food waste out of the landfill. Finally, Bon Appétit Management Company takes its educational mission seriously. Signage in on-campus cafés reminds students of the origins and sustainability of their food. Once a semester, the company sponsors its Eat Local Challenge, (see Figure 11-4) where students are challenged to eat lunch made entirely of foods grown within 150 miles of the café.

Do you know where your food comes from? How can you find out? How sustainable is food service on your campus? What local foods are available for your home cooking? Which retailers in your area offer the best choices for a sustainable diet?

FIGURE 11-4 Food service provider, Bon Appétit Management Company educates customers about the benefits of eating foods that are locally produced and sourced.

Building Sustainable Channel Capacity

One common barrier to sustainable marketing is a lack of production capacity among more sustainable suppliers. For example, the growing demand for organic cotton currently outstrips the world supply, forcing companies to use nonorganic cotton. Cotton farmers have incentives to grow organically. Organic cotton brings higher prices than conventional cotton; organic farming is safer and healthier for workers; and organic practices are better for soils, water usage, and water quality than chemical-intensive conventional practices. However, there is an economic disincentive for switching to organic methods. It takes about three years for a conventional farm to be certified organic. During that time, the crops cannot be sold as organic and, therefore, command only the lower prices associated with conventional cotton. The problem for the farmer is intensified because during the transition to organic growing, production costs increase and crop yields typically fall off, leaving less cotton to sell. Wal-Mart, seeing the need for an increased supply of organic cotton, decided to help build production capacity at the farm level. First, it entered into long-term agreements with cotton farmers, and then it agreed to pay the higher organic prices for cotton from fields that were in transition from conventional to organic cotton. The net result is that farmers get better prices, healthier workers, and healthier soils while Wal-Mart gets a growing and reliable supply of organic cotton that it can make available to its clothing and textile suppliers.[44]

Another important aspect of increasing sustainable channel capacity is building human capital throughout the value circle. Building human capital involves education, training, nutrition, health care, and access to technologies that enhance sustainable practices and productivity. Healthy workers are more stable and productive; they create better products and services; and they create fewer burdens on families and society. In addition, more prosperous workers can buy more goods and services, adding to the overall size and strength of global markets. A combination of transparency, training, and collaboration can create stronger channel relationships, which in turn build human capital in ways that benefit every member of the value circle.

Sustainable Harvest Coffee (SHC), a U.S. importer of organic and Fairtrade-certified coffee beans, provides an excellent example of increasing sustainable channel capacity by building human capital. Whereas most coffee is bought and sold anonymously on global commodities markets, SHC has developed a business model that cultivates long-term relationships between coffee farmers and the companies that roast, package, and brand the coffee for consumer markets.[45] According to the company's website, "The communication between a roaster, Sustainable Harvest, and farmers creates a forum for roasters to explain their needs, specifications, and quality expectations directly to farmers. By bringing the supply chain partners together on a regular basis, Sustainable Harvest is also able to tackle industry challenges and lead innovation within the specialty coffee sector."[46]

In addition to facilitating communication and collaboration between channel members, SHC contributes directly to farmer development. SHC provides over 180,000 farmers in Mexico, Tanzania and Peru, with training, management systems, trade credit, peer-to-peer sharing of best practices, and improved technology, all of which allows them to produce consistently higher quality beans and earn more than double the industry average for their product. Higher earnings translate to higher standards of living, including better education and health care for the growers' families. The roasters, for their part, benefit from a stable supply of high-quality beans that are traceable through chain of custody back to their sources. A key to the Relationship Coffee model is complete transparency both up and down the marketing channels. Customers can be assured they are buying products that are environmentally and socially responsible, and suppliers can learn more effectively what their customers need and how to best provide it. Starbucks, which pioneered the modern coffee-shop business in the United States, also emphasizes a relationship model in managing its supply chain.[47]

DEVELOPING SUSTAINABLE CHANNEL OPERATIONS

The marketing-channel functions of transportation and logistics provide place and time utility. In other words, these functions get products where they need to be, when they need to be there. Distribution, including transportation and storage, contributes greatly to a product's ecological footprint. **Sustainable distribution** emphasizes efficiency and carbon neutrality, and it tends to prioritize local production wherever possible. Beyond improvements in the downward flows of products and services, sustainable distribution also incorporates material backflows from consumers to manufacturers. As discussed earlier in the chapter, reverse material flows in the marketing channels can help convert refuse to resources, allowing manufacturers to replace virgin materials with recyclables more easily.

Greener Facilities and Warehousing

One of the biggest opportunities for increasing the sustainability of product distribution lies in the area of green building. Distribution functions such as storage, bulk-breaking, and assortment, and the management of these functions, occur in buildings ranging from factories to warehouses to distribution centers to retail stores to office buildings. According to data from the U.S. Energy

Information Administration, buildings are responsible for nearly half of all energy consumption and GHGs in the United States, and of that, about four-fifths is commercial and industrial.[48] In addition to generating staggering amounts of atmospheric carbon, industrial and commercial buildings also use enormous amounts of fresh water; they replace trees, grasses, and soils (which purify air and water) with polluting concrete and asphalt; and they concentrate toxic substances in the form of building materials.

Many of the environmentally damaging aspects of buildings and parking lots can be offset by more sustainable building practices, such as those that are advocated by the U.S. Green Building Council and monitored in its LEED (Leadership in Energy and Environmental Design) certification programs. Greener buildings also contribute to the health and well-being of workers, as we shall see in the following example.

Toyota Logistic Services (TLS), which operates a vehicle distribution center in Portland, Oregon, illustrates many of the ways that product distribution facilities can be made more sustainable. The Portland VDC processes approximately a quarter-million Japanese-manufactured Toyota, Lexus, and Scion vehicles for the U.S. market every year. To do so requires a facility with over 100,000 square feet of buildings on over 100 acres of land along the Willamette River. Some of the features that improve the sustainability of the site and its operations include:[49]

Buildings:

- Seventy-five percent of the building materials (by weight) have recycled content.
- Forty-three percent of building materials were produced regionally (within 500 miles).
- No CFC refrigerants are used in the heating, ventilation, air-conditioning, and return equipment.
- One hundred percent clean wind energy is purchased for the facility.
- Low emitting materials were used in construction. Low volatile organic compounds (VOCs) materials include adhesives and sealants, paints and coatings, carpets, and composite woods (containing no urea-formaldehyde resins).

Human activity:

- Variable lighting is tied into natural lighting (from skylights) and occupancy/motion sensors.
- Openable windows provide fresh air and reduce heating/cooling loads.
- Shower facilities encourage bicycle commuting; all employees receive free bus/light-rail passes.
- Ninety percent of all regularly occupied spaces have direct views to the outside.

Landscaping:

- Self-sustaining native plants are used in landscaping, requiring no landscape irrigation.
- Mechanical filtering and bio-swales (see Chapter 2) clean, clear, and cool run-off water prior to draining into the Willamette River.

Waste:

- Ninety-five percent of all facility waste is recycled (including composting of food waste).
- Rainwater is harvested for toilet flushing.
- All hydraulic fluid is nonpetroleum based, made from vegetable oil.
- Ninety-nine percent of construction waste was diverted from landfills.

THINK ABOUT IT

Consider a building with which you are familiar. It may be your classroom building, dormitory, apartment, or home. How could it be updated to emit fewer GHGs? What infrastructure, maintenance, or operations changes could be implemented to achieve results closer to the ones TLS enjoys? What system or process would you seek to improve first? Why? Who has the authority to make those improvements? Describe your first step toward making the building more sustainable.

Greener Transportation

The other aspect of product distribution that offers huge opportunities for increased sustainability is transportation. Airplanes, ships, trains, and trucks are the major modes of product transport. It turns out that the mode of product transportation is much more relevant to its sustainability than the number of miles traveled. Air transport produces by far the most GHGs per weight of product. One recent study reports that shipping fresh food, such as fish, is a massive source of GHGs. Most of the world's salmon fillets are consumed fresh, and have never been frozen. The same fillets, if flash-frozen at the source, retain all their freshness and can be shipped in much more environmentally friendly ways, such as container ships.[50]

Although not as polluting as air freight, truck transport is also a major source of GHG emissions. According to the firm Sustainable Logistics LLC, "Commercial trucks are the source of 25% of the smog-forming pollutants and over 50% of the soot derived from all highway vehicles; yet they make up less than 2 percent of the vehicles on the road and drive less than 6% of the total miles driven. To put this in greater perspective, trucks emit three times more soot and smog-forming pollutants than a coal-fired power plant, for every unit of energy they burn."[51] One way to improve the sustainability (and costs) of trucking, or any other form of transport, is to reduce the size and weight dimensions of the product being shipped. This is a key part of the rationale behind many of the product design decisions discussed in Chapter 9 and the packaging decisions discussed in Chapter 10.

The global transportation and logistics giant, United Parcel Service (UPS), is taking the lead in innovation to reduce the environmental impacts of shipping. In its 2008 Corporate Social Responsibility (CSR) report, UPS reports: "In 2008, shifts from ground to rail and air to ground together prevented absolute emissions of 3 million metric tonnes of CO_2."[52]

UPS operates the world's largest fleet of alternative-fuel delivery trucks, experimenting with bio-fuels, battery-powered electrics, hydrogen fuel cells, and other technologies to reduce the use of fossil fuels. Another area of potential improvement lies in the routing of delivery trucks. For example, drivers learn to minimize the numbers of left turns in a route and to turn off trucks during deliveries, both of which reduce idling, which in turn reduces fuel consumption, costs, and carbon emissions.[53] The company's 2008 CSR report states that, "In 2008, Package Flow Technology enabled us to reach our cumulative goal, set in 2003, of eliminating 100 million miles driven."[54] Package Flow Technology achieves distribution efficiencies through constant innovation of hardware, software, and processes. It allows the company to optimize the number of trucks in use on a daily basis, load vehicles according to the order of deliveries, minimize waiting and idling time through routing, identify stopping locations that permit multiple deliveries, and keep drivers updated and on route with handheld computers.

THINK ABOUT IT

UPS has made a strategic decision to innovate its package delivery processes to be more sustainable and improve its bottom line. Did you know about UPS Package Flow Technology program before reading about it here? What does this mean to you as a consumer? How important are the sustainability efforts of a transportation company in your decision of which package delivery company to use?

Shorter Channels

Another way some marketers are making channels more sustainable is by shortening and simplifying them (see Figure 11-5). The process, called **disintermediation**, entails reducing the numbers or roles of intermediaries in a marketing channel or, in more common terms, cutting out the middleman. Market intermediaries, or channel members, exist because they add something of value to the overall system. However, as times and circumstances change, the value of certain intermediaries may decrease to the point that they add more cost and/or waste than their services can justify.

The rise of CSAs (community-supported agriculture) provides a good example. CSAs deliver farm products directly to consumers either at the farm or at points of distribution such as

FIGURE 11-5 Equal Exchange reduces the number of profit-taking channel intermediaries and provides better earnings to producers.

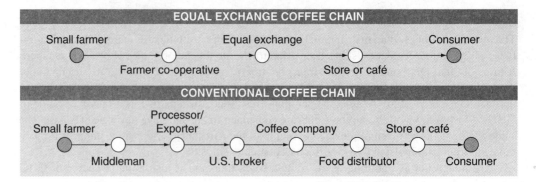

churches, schools, or community centers. Because the produce never passes through conventional wholesale and retail institutions, certain channel functions, such as packaging, labeling, and merchandising are unnecessary. The savings from disintermediation—which accrue from labor, materials, and waste—can then be spent in other ways, such as increasing the amount of produce grown organically and improving farm conditions. Other examples of disintermediation are Fairtrade channels for coffee[55] and eBay.[56]

SUSTAINABILITY IN RETAILING

Retailing has a special place in the marketing channel. It is the primary interface between consumers and the rest of the value circle. This privileged and influential position has earned retailing its nickname as the big middle of the value chain.[57] Retailers can play many roles in moving us toward a more sustainable society. They include influencing their suppliers to provide more sustainable products; educating consumers through merchandising and signage; and providing consumers with take-back sites for reusable and recyclable materials.

Influencing Suppliers

Retailers are, by their nature, customers for all their upstream channel members. As customers, they choose the kinds of product and service assortments that they will offer to their own customers. Small retailers, serving socially or environmentally conscious target markets, thrive by featuring sustainable products. For example, Hot Lips Pizza, a family-owned company in Portland, Oregon, operates five restaurants, a mobile pizza kitchen, and a soda brewery that cater to a specific segment of Portland's relatively young, sustainability-minded population. Hot Lips Pizza supports a large number of local farms and ranches, which practice organic and natural agricultural methods.

In contrast, large mass-market retailers like Target and Wal-Mart don't cater to niche markets that demand sustainable products. Theirs is a mainstream market made up of people from all walks of life. The size and buying power of these and other mega-retailers give them a great deal of power to influence the products and practices of their suppliers, whether those suppliers are small companies or huge corporations. Wal-Mart, the world's largest retailer, has begun to demand more sustainability from all its suppliers. At the same time, the company has been helping its suppliers to reach ambitious sustainability goals. For example, Dana Undies, a supplier of cotton underwear and clothing for children, received help from Wal-Mart to reduce its energy consumption. Wal-Mart engineers conducted an energy audit and provided Dana Undies with a plan for capital improvements and operational changes that made the factory more sustainable, paid for themselves in the first year, and netted the company a 52 percent savings in electricity costs.[58]

Educating Consumers

One of the most important ways retailers can help bring about a more sustainable society is by educating their customers about the advantages of buying more sustainable goods and services. Retailers around the world serve millions of customers every day, people who are deliberately seeking information, forming opinions, and making purchases. Retailers communicate with customers through **merchandising** methods, including product displays, signage, sampling, and décor. Such in-store marketing communication has the advantage of a relatively attentive and motivated audience, and as such, it has the power to deliver sustainability messages.

It's likely that many, if not most, American consumers don't know or care very much about sustainability. They do, however, care about things like saving money and living healthy lives. Retailers can help to shape consumer knowledge and attitudes about sustainability by drawing connections to their customers' deeply held values. For example, when Wal-Mart undertook the goal of selling energy-efficient CFLs, it did so with prominent in-store displays featuring the bulbs' energy savings and lower long-term costs. It also gave CFLs prime shelf space and price promotions. Some supermarkets now post signs in their parking lots reminding customers to bring their reusable shopping bags into the store.

Another area where retailers can educate consumers is that of the price–value proposition of more sustainable products. Consumers generally have the perception that green products are more expensive than their less sustainable counterparts, and that is often the case. Through merchandising efforts, retailers can help customers to more fully understand and appreciate the extra value associated with buying and living sustainably. Consumers regularly pay more for products that deliver more value. Through merchandising, retailers can stress greater value in a number of ways. For example, they can emphasize the long-term savings provided by products that use less energy (e.g., CFLs or energy-efficient appliances) or are higher in quality and durability (e.g., LEGO toys, which last virtually forever and never become obsolete). Or they can stress benefits to human health (e.g., pesticide-free produce, hormone-free milk, or nontoxic house paints).

Taking Back Recyclables

Finally, as we discussed earlier in the chapter, retail stores can provide ideal sites for consumers to return used products and packaging, thus keeping them in the value circle. Because consumers are going to stores already, with space in their vehicles reserved for their purchases, it's convenient to carry along reclaimable waste. Retailers can then consolidate recyclables into quantities that have commercial value. For example, Staples credits customers $3 each for returning used ink and toner cartridges and recycles tens of millions of cartridges in the United States alone.[59]

In summary, retailers can reduce many of the barriers to living more sustainably. They can increase consumers' access, in terms of price and assortment, to products that are more sustainable. They can help consumers understand the importance and the increased value of more sustainable living. And they can help provide the infrastructure or systems that make it easier for consumers to make more sustainable choices.

CRITICAL THINKING ACTIVITY

Identify a favorite possession. It may be something you bought for yourself or it may be something you received as a gift. Using what you've learned in this chapter, consider the value circle of your favorite item. Think about the materials that went into the item's manufacturing. Was it made with cradle-to-cradle or design for disassembly in mind? How did it get to you? Who were the upstream value circle members? Who will be the downstream members? Is the process transparent and can you learn the origins of all the materials included in your item? In other words, what can you learn about the chain of custody? Finally, what resources are available to you, as the consumer, to practice sustainable disposition?

Chapter Summary

Supply chains and value circles work best when each member of the chain takes a whole-system perspective. As you've learned in this chapter, decisions made by one member of the value circle can have consequences for other members. Secondary markets and reverse flows are often good options for moving goods through the value circle. In many cases, one industry's waste can be another's fuel. Credibility as a sustainable firm means maintaining transparency throughout the chain of custody. Creating greener facilities and transportation, providing for human capital, and educating consumers all work to the benefit of overall greener logistics.

Review of Chapter Objectives

- Converting value chains to value circles
- Building sustainable channel relationships: communication and collaboration
- Developing sustainable channel operations
- Sustainability in retailing

Key Concepts

Marketing Channels   154
Value Chain   155
Throughput System   155
Technosphere   156
Cradle-to-Cradle
    Certification   156

Design for
    Disassembly   157
Reverse Logistics   157
Value Circles   158
Secondary Markets   158
Channel Power   160

Upstream Channel
    Members   160
Downstream Channel
    Members   161
Transparency   161
Chain of Custody   161

External Audits   161
Sustainable
    Distribution   163
Disintermediation   165
Merchandising   166

Endnotes

1. *Environmental Network News* (2009), "Earthworm Family-Safe Products Achieve National Distribution," September 3, http://www.enn.com/press_releases/3084, accessed October 22, 2009. See also, Szaky, Tom and Paul Hawken (2009), *Revolution in a Bottle: How TerraCycle Is Redefining Green Business*, New York: Penguin.
2. TerraCycle, http://www.terracycle.net/, accessed October 21, 2009.
3. Christopher, Martin (2005), Logistics & Supply Chain Management: Creating value-adding networks, 3rd edition, New Jersey: FT Press.
4. Elkington, John (1994), "Towards the Sustainable Corporation: Win-Win-Win Business Strategies for Sustainable Development," *California Management Review*, 36 (2, Winter): 90–100 (p. 90).
5. Wise Geek, http://www.wisegeek.com/what-is-a-cardboard-pallet.htm, accessed November 17, 2009. Also see Wise Geek, http://www.wisegeek.com/what-are-the-advantages-of-plastic-pallets.htm, accessed November 17, 2009.
6. McDonough, William and Michael Braungart (2002), *Cradle to Cradle: Remaking the Way We Make Things*, New York: North Point Press.
7. Chua, Jasmin Malik (2009), "Aveda Gets Cradle-to-Cradle Certification for 7 Products: a Beauty Industry First," *Treehugger*, April 28, http://www.treehugger.com/files/2009/04/aveda-cradle-to-cradle.php, accessed November 17, 2009.
8. Steffen, Alex (2005), "Design for Disassembly: Zero Waste and Sustainable Prosperity," *World Changing*, January 26, http://www.worldchanging.com/archives/002005.html, accessed November 17, 2009.
9. Zikmund, William G. and William J. Stanton (1971), "Recycling Solid Wastes: A Channels-of-Distribution Problem," *Journal of Marketing*, 35 (3, July): 34–39.
10. Cal Recycle, http://zerowaste.ca.gov/PlasticBags/default.htm, accessed November 14, 2009.
11. Consumer Reports (2008), "Best Buy Ups the Ante for Retailer Recycling Programs," June 4, http://blogs.consumerreports.org/electronics/2008/06/best-buy-ups-th.html, accessed October 29, 2009.
12. Metro, http://www.oregonmetro.gov/index.cfm/go/by.web/id=521, accessed October 29, 2009.
13. Caterpillar, http://www.cat.com/parts/remanufactured-products, accessed January 6, 2010.
14. Goodwill, http://www.goodwill.org/page/guest/about, accessed October 29, 2009.
15. Donohue, Michele (2009), "Clothes Sense: Revenue Generated Even if Clothing Can't Be Worn," *Non-Profit Times*, January 1, http://www.allbusiness.com/society-social/philanthropy-grants-gifts-major/11773470-1.html, accessed October 29, 2009.
16. Alibaba.com, http://www.alibaba.com/product-gs/258526763/0_9D_Recycled_Polyester_Staple_Fiber.html, accessed November 18, 2009.
17. The Rebuilding Center, http://www.rebuildingcenter.org, accessed October 29, 2009.
18. The Rebuilding Center, http://www.rebuildingcenter.org/deconstruct/, accessed October 29, 2009.
19. Noranda Recycling, http://www.norandarecycling.com/doc/xrec_brochure_2008.en.pdf, accessed November 18, 2009.
20. Environmental Leader, September 20, 2007, http://www.environmentalleader.com/2007/09/20/dell-launches-new-asset-recovery-recycling-program-for-small-businesses/, accessed September 29, 2009. Also see Esty, Daniel C. and Andrew S Winston (2006), *Green to Gold: How Smart Companies Use Environmental Strategy to Innovate, Create Value, and Build Competitive Advantage*, New Haven, CT: Yale University Press.
21. Werbach, Adam (2009), *Strategy for Sustainability: A Business Manifesto*, Boston, MA: Harvard Business Press.
22. Epstein, Marc J. (2008), *Making Sustainability Work: Best Practices in Managing and Measuring Corporate Social, Environmental, and Economic Impacts*, San Francisco: Berrett-Koehler Publishers, (p. 204). Also see Power, S. (2006), "Take It Back: Where Do Cars Go When They Die? In Europe, They Have Little Choice." *Wall Street Journal*, April 17, R6.
23. Shrivastava, Paul (1995), "The Role of Corporations in Achieving Ecological Sustainability," *Academy of Management Review*, 20 (4): 936–960.
24. Harris, Simon, Brad Mackay, Floyd D'Costa, and Victoria Eavenson (2009), "The Global Networked Value Circle: A New Model for Best-in-Class Manufacturing," Capgemini and the University of Edinburgh.

25. "Wal-Mart Launches Suppliers Package Tool," March 13, 2007, http://www.abcmoney.co.uk/news/13200737997.htm, accessed October 1, 2009.

26. Epstein, Marc J. (2008), Making Sustainability Work: Best Practices in Managing and Measuring Corporate Social, Environmental, and Economic Impacts, San Francisco, CA: Berrett-Koehler Publishers, p. 89.

27. Nike, "Workers & Factories: Improving Conditions in Our Contract Factories," http://www.nikebiz.com/responsibility/workers_and_factories.htmlv, accessed October 29, 2009.

28. Georgeson, Cynthia (2000) "Partnerships for Progress: A Case Study from SC Johnson," *Education for a Sustainable Future: A Paradigm of Hope for the 21st Century*, ed. Keith A. Wheeler and Anne Perraca Bijur, 247–252, New York: Plenum.

29. Esty, Daniel C. and Andrew S. Winston (2006), Green to Gold: How Smart Companies Use Environmental Strategy to Innovate, Create Value, and Build Competitive Advantage, New Haven, CT: Yale University Press.

30. Forest Stewardship Council, FSC Chain of Custody Certification, http://www.fsc.org/134.html, accessed November 19, 2009.

31. Marine Stewardship Council, MSC Chain of Custody Standard for Seafood Traceability, http://www.msc.org/about-us/standards/standards/msc-chain-of-custody-standard, accessed November 19, 2009.

32. The Conflict-Free Diamond Council, http://www.conflictfree-diamonds.org/wheretobuy/certificationprograms.html, accessed November19, 2009.

33. Mammoth Tusk Gold, http://www.mammothgold.com/faq.html, accessed November 19, 2009.

34. New Zealand Business Council for Sustainable Development, http://www.nzbcsd.org.nz/supplychain/content.asp?id=265, accessed March 20, 2010.

35. People's Food Co-op, http://www.peoplesfoodcoop.com/organic_farmtoyou.html, accessed November 19, 2009.

36. Worldwide Responsible Accredited Production, http://www.wrapcompliance.org/certification-program, accessed November 1, 2009.

37. Bon Appetit Management Company Foundation, http://www.eatlowcarbon.org/, accessed March 20, 2010.

38. Bon Appetit Management Company Information Sheet, obtained August, 2008. See also Bon Appetit Management Company, http://www.bamco.com/.

39. Food Alliance, http://www.foodalliance.org/, accessed October 30, 2009.

40. Truitt Brothers, http://www.truittbros.com/familyfarms/index.html, accessed November 19, 2009.

41. The Shepherd's Grain, http://www.shepherdsgrain.com/, accessed November 19, 2009.

42. Sauvie Island Organics, http://www.sauvieislandorganics.com/, accessed January 6, 2010.

43. In Sink Erator, http://www.insinkerator.com/Pulper_Systems.html

44. Reuters (2008), "Wal-Mart to Boost Supply of Organic Cotton," April 7, http://www.reuters.com/article/environment News/idUSN0727133420080407, accessed November 24, 2009.

45. Sustainable Harvest Specialty Coffee Importers, http://sustainableharvest.com/our_model, accessed November 24, 2009.

46. Sustainable Harvest Specialty Coffee Importers, http://sustainableharvest.com/our_model/advantages_of_relationship_coffee/, accessed November 24, 2009.

47. Starbucks, http://www.starbucks.com/sharedplanet/ethical Sourcing.aspx, accessed January 6, 2010.

48. http://www.architecture2030.org/current_situation/building_sector.html, accessed November 28, 2009.

49. This information was obtained directly from Ron Corbin, the site manager of the Portland Vehicle Distribution Center.

50. Haight, Abby (2009), "Frozen Salmon over Fresh? Why, It's Better for the Planet That Way," *Oregonian*, November 22.

51. Sustainable Logistics LLC, http://www.sustainablelogistics.us/, accessed November 28, 2009.

52. UPS, http://www.community.ups.com/sustainability/index.html, p. 62, accessed November 28, 2009.

53. "Fuel Conservation No Idle Matter at UPS" (2006), *Multi-Channel Merchant*, June 14, http://multichannelmerchant.com/opsandfulfillment/advisor/fuel_conserve/ accessed November 1, 2009.

54. UPS, 2008 CSR Report, 7.0 Environmental Stewardship, http://www.responsibility.ups.com/community/Static%20Files/sustainability/2008_CSR_PDF_Environ.pdf, pp. 62–63, accessed June 27, 2010.

55. Equal Exchange, http://www.equalexchange.coop/fair-trade, accessed March 25, 2010.

56. Gunther, Marc (2010), "Why eBay Is a Green Giant," *GreenBiz.com*, February 16 http://www.greenbiz.com/blog/2010/02/16/why-ebay-green-giant, accessed March 25, 2010.

57. Arnould, Eric (2005), "Animating the Big Middle," *Journal of Retailing*, 81(2): 89–96.

58. Wal-Mart, http://walmartstores.com/sites/sustainabilityreport/2007/environmentSupplyEnergy.html, accessed November 28, 2009.

59. Staples, http://www.staples.com/sbd/cre/products/3dollar_inkrecycle/, accessed January 6, 2010.

Sustainable Pricing

INTRODUCTION: THE VALUE OF A HEALTHY PLANET

In 1997, a landmark study by an international team of scientists and economists attempted to put an economic value on ecosystem services. They concluded that, "For the entire biosphere, the value (most of which is outside the market) is estimated to be in the range of US$16–54 trillion per year, with an average of US$33 trillion per year. Because of the nature of the uncertainties, this must be considered a minimum estimate. Global gross national product total is around US$18 trillion per year."[1]

The value described above refers to the ecosystem services provided by the Earth, including:

- purification of air and water,
- mitigation of droughts and floods,
- generation and preservation of soils and renewal of their fertility,
- detoxification and decomposition of wastes,
- pollination of crops and natural vegetation,
- dispersal of seeds,
- cycling and movement of nutrients,
- control of the vast majority of potential agricultural pests,
- maintenance of biodiversity,
- protection of coastal shores from erosion by waves,
- protection from the sun's harmful ultraviolet rays,
- stabilization of the climate,
- moderation of weather extremes and their impacts, and
- provision of aesthetic beauty and intellectual stimulation that lifts the human spirit.[2]

What does this have to do with the price of goods and services you buy in the store or online? The Earth has no way to exact a cash payment from each of us, so these ecosystem services traditionally have been regarded as free for the taking. However, every violation of the ecosystem reduces the Earth's ability to provide these free services. When that happens, we humans incur real economic costs. For example, overlogging forests inhibits their ability to filter and cool and clean water, which in turn hurts fish populations in streams and rivers, which in turn increases the price of fish. On the other hand, the same logging practices may produce cheaper wood products, at least in the short term.

THINK ABOUT IT

One of the main criticisms of marketing and consumerism is that the retail prices of goods and services fail to reflect the true costs of their manufacturing and marketing. Would a fair price for a product also include a premium for its impact on the environment and human health? Why or why not?

This chapter explores the question: What is a sustainable price? Or in other words, how can pricing help a company to achieve its sustainability goals while also remaining competitive in the marketplace?

CHAPTER OBJECTIVES

In this chapter, you will learn more about the influences on pricing as they relate to social and environmental sustainability, including:

- Sustainable pricing: real product cost
- Barriers to sustainable pricing
- Sustainable pricing strategies
- Complementary currencies

As you already know, price is a major part of the marketing mix and an important element in the marketer's tool kit. A **price** is basically the monetary value of a product as agreed upon between a seller and a buyer. Put more simply, price equals perceived value. It's what the customer pays. A price differs from a **cost**, which refers to the sum of money, time, and resources associated with a purchase or activity. The price of a quart of milk may be less than $2 at a retail store; however, the cost to the purchaser includes a portion of the shopping and travel time, and of the travel expenses required for the purchase. The cost of that same quart of milk to the dairy producer is entirely different and includes, among other things, a portion of the expenses required for the production, packaging, and marketing of the milk.

Pricing is a strategic activity that marketers use to achieve desired outcomes such as market position, market share, profit margins, and volume of sales. Factors that affect pricing decisions include supply and demand, costs of production and marketing, competitor actions, and government regulations. Each of these factors is susceptible, in turn, to global economic forces.

SUSTAINABLE PRICING: RECOVERING THE REAL PRODUCT COST

Although many factors other than costs influence a pricing decision, costs do matter. A **sustainable price** accounts fully for the economic, environmental, and social costs of a product's manufacture and marketing while providing value for customers and a fair profit for business (see Figure 12-1). Pricing, like any other aspect of marketing, business, or life, is not sustainable if it violates the four system conditions outlined in The Natural Step Framework:

1. A price that fails to include the costs of eliminating or offsetting greenhouse gas emissions, or that fails to include the recovery and reuse of metals and plastics, violates the first system condition.
2. A price that is kept low through the systematic use and disposal of new synthetic compounds violates the second system condition.
3. A price that relies on the systematic degradation of the Earth's natural systems, such as forests, rivers, and fisheries, violates the third system condition.
4. A price that can only be achieved through the exploitation and mistreatment of workers violates the fourth system condition.[3]

Take the price of coal-powered electricity, for example. Cheap power generated by burning coal has fueled industrial revolutions in Europe, the United States, and China, and it continues to subsidize American lifestyles. But the real cost of coal power far exceeds its price at the electric meter. Coal power violates at least two of the system conditions. First, it takes minerals, such as carbon and

FIGURE 12-1 Pricing is affected by market factors. From a systems perspective, those must also include social and environmental costs. Heal, Geoffery (2000) Nature and the Marketplace: Capturing the Value of Ecosystem Services, Washington, D. C.: Island Press, (p. 29).

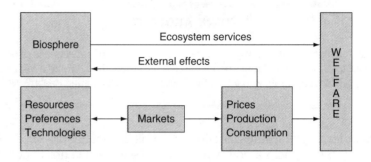

sulphur, from the Earth's crust and transports them, through combustion, into the atmosphere. Part of the economic costs of global climate change should be charged to coal power, as should the costs attributed to acid rain. Second, much of the coal mining in the United States, achieved economically through a practice called mountaintop removal, devastates entire local ecosystems through deforestation, topsoil removal, and the dumping of vast amounts of waste into valleys and streams. These actions have led to irreparable damage to biodiversity and watersheds.[4] Coal power's affects on the ability of people to meet their needs is arguable. Many communities in Appalachia, for example, currently rely on coal mining to support local economies. On the other hand, several studies suggest that the environmental destruction has led to more economic harm than good.[5]

THINK ABOUT IT

Deferred Costs and Downstream Problems

For each of the four system conditions, think of an example of a product cost that isn't covered by the price to the consumer. Who pays for it? What are the likely long-term consequences of perpetually deferring that cost? What would be the likely consequences of paying the cost up front and pricing the product more sustainably?

There are certain well-known realities associated with selecting a price for a product. First, the price must be sufficient to recover all the costs of manufacturing and marketing. Next, it must also generate a sufficient profit to provide a satisfactory return on investment. Finally, it must contribute to the survival of the company in a competitive marketplace.

Other, lesser-known realities are also becoming clearer to businesses, governments, and consumers. First, the real costs of products are seldom reflected in the actual prices that consumers pay at the register. Second, all costs, even incidental or external costs to the environment or to human welfare, ultimately get paid by someone. And third, as demonstrated in a study called the "U.S. Economic Impacts of Climate Change and the Costs of Inaction,"[6] real costs to people and the environment that are dodged or deferred in the marketing process inevitably come due later with heavy interest and penalties.

Externalized costs

When a consumer buys a product, such as a music system or a new pair of shoes, the tendency is to assume that all the costs of manufacturing and marketing that product are somehow included in the price. As you learned in the beginning of this chapter, there are also unpaid social and economic costs, called **externalized costs**, which are associated with most goods and services. When it sustains damage, the Earth has no system for demanding payment from firms such as product manufacturers and transportation companies. According to author Donald Fuller, ". . . not requiring products to pay their ecological way sends false signals that distort the functioning of the market mechanism, and it fails to self-correct."[7] Or as the marketing scholar Paul Shrivastava put it, "Existing economic systems make many polluting and wasteful goods seem alluringly inexpensive because they do not incorporate the full ecological costs of their production or use. These costs are passed on to future generations, transferred to nonusers of products as taxes, or exported to less environmentally regulated countries."[8]

The difference between retail prices and the real costs of products can be enormous. This isn't exactly news. A 1998 study by the International Center for Technology Assessment determined that the real cost of a gallon of gasoline at that time was about $15 per gallon.[9] Actual at-the-pump prices in the United States during 1998 peaked at around $1.30 per gallon.[10] In its calculation of real costs, the study included direct government subsidies; the costs of protecting oil supplies; and environmental, health, and social costs. All told, the externalized costs amounted to more than a trillion dollars per year, or a little over $24,000 for a family of four.

THINK ABOUT IT

The Four-Hundred-Dollar Fill-Up

Imagine if all the externalized costs for gasoline were included in the price per gallon to the consumer. Filling the tank of a car or SUV could cost somewhere between $300 and $400. How would that affect your driving habits? What alternatives would you consider for transportation? How might it influence your choice of where to live?

Gasoline isn't the only product whose price hides huge externalized costs. Practically every product's price does. Some externalized costs, such as government subsidies, are paid out of current funds, like tax revenues, in order to manage prices for political or strategic reasons. Those costs are economically sustainable if they are paid as they are incurred. However, as we've seen, many of the social and environmental costs of bringing products to market have not been included in the price. They are not "charged" to businesses, but instead have been externalized into "a river, a town, a single patient or a whole generation."[11]

Life-Cycle Costing

Total product costs are determined by using full-cost accounting (FCA), which "allocates all direct and indirect costs to a product or product line for inventory valuation, profitability analysis, and pricing decisions."[12] Uncovering all the costs of a product requires us to examine the complete picture of the product life cycle. **Life-cycle costing** attempts to identify all costs—internal and external—associated with a product throughout its entire journey from manufacturing to eventual disposition.[13] Life cycle assessments (LCAs) can be used to identify all the financial, social, and environmental costs of bringing a product to market, and FCA integrates those costs into the balance sheet.

Some portion of the full life-cycle cost of a product already is borne by consumers. In addition to the price of a product, consumers also incur other costs of purchasing, use, and disposition. **Purchase costs** include all the costs associated with searching for products, gathering and comparing information about choices, and transporting the product home. **Product-use costs** include any costs of switching from another product as well as the costs of maintenance, wear and tear, and any energy and supplies needed to use the product. Finally, **Disposition** or **postuse costs** include fees for garbage, recycling, and other postuse collection, such as transportation to a thrift store donation center. Finally, between use and disposal, many consumers also incur **storage costs** with the rental of commercial self-storage units. The self-storage industry reported that in 2007 Americans spent over $20 billion for additional storage space.[14]

VIRTUAL FIELD TRIP

The Price of Food

According to a 2008 report by a Pew Charitable Trusts commission, ground beef from grass-fed cattle costs about $1 more per pound than ground beef from a factory-farmed cow. Another investigation in 2009[15] compared factory-farm beef from Costco with grass-fed, free-range beef from Colorado's Best Beef. The comparison, for half a cow with identical cuts and identical weights, was Costco: $922.30; Colorado's Best Beef: $1,303.70.

The price for the grass-fed beef is 41 percent higher. Now take YouTube on a virtual field trip to explore some factory farms (search *factory farm*), and another to a ranch that raises grass-fed livestock. Which model of agriculture has higher externalized costs to the society and the environment? Which would you rather support with your dollars?

The Pew commission reports that "our meat is cheap only because we don't count all the costs: Taxpayers spend $4.1 billion cleaning up livestock sewage leaks and $2.5 billion treating salmonella. All told . . . [factory farms] may be costing taxpayers $38 billion a year—costs that aren't reflected in the retail price of meat."[16]

It's not always true that prices are higher for more sustainable products. In many cases, long-term savings and benefits offset a higher purchase price. For example, solar or photovoltaic panels are currently expensive, and their price is a major barrier to homeowners. However, once installed, they use free energy from the sun to run electric appliances and to light, heat, or cool a home. Solar energy is generated during the day, when conventional electricity is the most expensive. On sunny days, solar panels can produce more power than is needed, returning electricity to the power company, making the electric meter run backwards, and reducing the homeowner's electric bill.

Another price problem with solar power for consumers is that it can take several years for a system to pay for itself in energy savings. Homeowners who might otherwise be interested in solar power resist making the investment for fear that they will move before realizing the financial benefits. One innovative payment system has solved this problem by assigning the costs of solar systems not to the individual consumer but, rather, to the home itself. PACE (Property Assessed Clean Energy) programs are administered through partnerships between private companies, such as Renewable Funding,[17] and city governments. The cost of a solar system or other energy improvement project is added to the property tax bill and amortized over 20 years. If the homeowner sells before that time, the remaining price of the improvement and the benefits of using it are transferred to the new owner.

BARRIERS TO SUSTAINABLE PRICING

Sustainable pricing, if it could be achieved, would help to assure that no generation or nation of consumers lives beyond its means, and that the price of overconsumption would not be passed on as inherited debt to future generations. The reality of sustainable pricing is that there are significant barriers to its implementation. The common barriers are competitive, political, and cultural, and they are all interrelated.

Competitive Barriers

To price a product voluntarily in such a way as to internalize, rather than externalize, environmental and social costs is market suicide if competitors are not willing or obliged to do the same thing for equivalent products. Given two products that are perceived to be basically the same, consumers will choose the less-expensive alternative under most conditions. Exceptions tend to be limited to niche markets of exceptionally values-driven and activist consumers, who will pay a price premium to reward conscientious marketers. However, even ultra-green consumers will look for additional points of product differentiation to justify the extra expense. For example, many consumers will spend the extra $0.10 to $0.20 per pound for organic bananas if they believe they are deriving health benefits, improving the conditions for agricultural workers, or helping protect fragile tropical environments. However, if both banana options are organic, but one is priced higher in order to internalize additional environmental or social costs, those same consumers may balk at paying more, particularly if the price premium is substantial.

Political Barriers

Competitive barriers to sustainable pricing can be minimized or eliminated through legislation that requires higher levels of corporate responsibility for social and environmental costs. The political barrier lies in the fact that democratic governments tend to lack the will to enact any legislation that raises consumer prices. Return to the example of beef prices. Part of the reason beef from factory farms is so much cheaper than beef from free-ranging cattle is that, in factory farms, cows are fed hormones to make them grow faster and fatter, and constant streams of antibiotics to keep them from spreading diseases despite being crowded together in unsanitary conditions. Laws forbidding such additives would force corporate farms to raise cattle in healthier conditions and produce beef that would be healthier for people to eat. However, it would also raise the prices of beef and allow smaller ranching operations to compete more effectively, all of which is counter to the short-term economic interests of big corporate agriculture.

Taxes on corporate by-products such as pollution, water use, energy use, and carbon emissions theoretically can help cover externalized costs, if they are applied to programs of social and environmental support and reparation. Taxes have the added benefit of providing incentives for conducting business more sustainably. The political barrier is, of course, that taxes are no more popular with voters than price increases at the register. Increased taxes on global corporations have the added disadvantage of encouraging them to outsource more jobs and processes offshore to countries with lower taxes. Moreover, smaller businesses that don't have offshore options can become less competitive.

Yet another way governments can encourage, or discourage, sustainable pricing is through subsidies. Current federal subsidies on corn play a huge role in the price of beef—factory farms depend on cheap corn as feed for cattle—as well as on formulations and practices throughout the food industry. Think back to the petroleum example. Gasoline, without the many federal subsidies for oil companies, would more than triple in cost to consumers. Imagine, however, if even half of the trillion-plus dollars in annual subsidies to oil companies were used instead as incentives for developing alternative energy sources and the infrastructure to provide and use them conveniently. The barrier, once again, lies in the lack of political will to divert subsidies from the massive corporations that fund campaigns and maintain current economic power structures.

Cultural Barriers

To some extent, the political and competitive barriers to sustainable pricing are rooted in cultural barriers. Current lifestyles, values, and expectations are deeply ingrained and difficult to change. Most people don't voluntarily reduce their levels of consumption, and the ones who do are rare enough and notable enough to prove the point. Sustainable pricing seems to imply higher prices for everything. If that's the case, then sustainable prices also imply less of everything for all but the poorest consumers, who should stand to gain materially from a more sustainable society.

If, as a part of sustainable marketing, sustainable pricing is necessary to the sustainability of businesses, the economy and, ultimately, society, then our global consumer culture must somehow learn to embrace the principle of paying the full costs of our consumption. Short of economic collapse, which everyone hopes to avoid, how can people be persuaded to regulate and, in the case of developed nations like the United States, reduce our ecological footprints to sustainable levels? The answers are not crystal clear, but here are some possibilities worth exploring. None are sufficient by themselves to overcome the political, competitive, and cultural aspects of barriers to sustainable pricing, but in combination, they might be.

1. Change pricing, if necessary, in gradual and structured ways. In 2008, with the burst of the American housing bubble and mortgage-backed securities, we saw what can happen when prices are realigned rapidly.
2. Use government subsidies as incentives, rather than disincentives, to develop more sustainable technologies, such as electric cars, and infrastructure, such as in-road electrical power or widespread battery-swapping stations. In other words, reward good business behavior, rather than bad, with the ability to keep prices lower on more sustainable products.
3. Use marketing techniques to promote a shift in values from quantity to quality. There are several ways to connect this shift to values people already hold, such as health and attractiveness. For example, American consumers would be healthier, fitter, and more attractive eating smaller quantities of more wholesome foods.
4. For necessities like food and clothing, keep prices low for more sustainable options, such as organic produce and cotton, by building supply-chain capacity and achieving economies of scale. Eventually sustainable production practices would be the norm, the natural growing capacity of soil would increase, and producers would save on such costs as pesticides, fertilizers, and worker illnesses.
5. Shift marketing strategies from a product focus to a service and benefits focus. Demonstrate that consumers can enjoy the same lifestyle benefits while consuming fewer material resources and, therefore, spending less. For example, rather than every household

with occasional needs owning a pickup truck or SUV, a community or neighborhood could operate a trucks-on-demand service with a small pool of communally owned vehicles. Same benefit, but at lower price to the individual.

6. Begin a marketing-aided, national or global dialog on the nature of happiness and well-being. Most of us know intuitively that amassing more material goods does not make people happier, but we often doubt or ignore that intuition, if for no other reason than to be on the safe side. Once consumers no longer believe they can buy happiness, they may stop trying so hard to do it. The key is learning and sharing nonmaterial solutions, bringing the price for well-being into more people's grasp.

7. Emphasize the inherent well-being to be found in clean, healthy, and productive communities, and support communities in building their human capital. People with the resources and skills to be productive and contribute to their families and society are less likely to abuse drugs, vandalize property, and victimize people. Money saved on law enforcement and poverty abatement could instead be used to bring down prices on services that build health, skills, and relationships.

In summary and in general, the keys to sustainable pricing are to account for the real life-cycle costs of products; reduce those costs by developing more sustainable processes and practices; support and reward sustainable practices by realigning government subsidies; and use marketing techniques to help break society's addiction to abundant and cheap, but unhealthy and unsustainable products (see Figure 12-2). As you learned in The Natural Step Framework, operating more sustainably reduces waste, which in turn saves an organization money, which can be reinvested strategically, including in maintaining competitive prices for its products. Companies like Sainsbury's, IKEA, and Wal-Mart understand these principles. These companies are striving to bring more sustainable products, such as organic produce and toxin-free home furnishings, to middle-class and working-class customers at affordable prices.

Occasionally, customer innovation provides the key to reducing the prices to consumers of more sustainable products. For example, LED lighting for housing is currently the most efficient and sustainable solution, but the prices of LED lights are still prohibitive. Now check out this reader tip from the Inhabitat website, regarding a way to utilize cheap holiday lights: "A string of LED holiday lights, combined with a two-dollar socket adapter from your local home-improvement store, can transform a lamp or overhead light into an eco-friendly light source. A 50-bulb string uses less than 5 watts of electricity, and, this time of year, they can be had for a fraction of the price of a commercial LED bulb."[18]

FIGURE 12-2 Northwest Natural Gas offers customers a choice of sustainable pricings: The Average Option and the Climate Neutral Option.

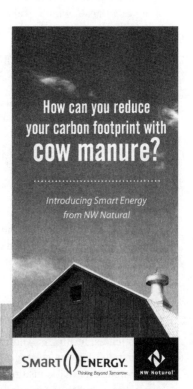

Climate Change Challenge

The concentration of carbon dioxide – a key greenhouse gas – in the atmosphere has increased more than 30 percent since industrialization, which most in the scientific community believe is causing global temperatures to rise.

While natural gas is the cleanest-burning fossil fuel, NW Natural believes we all must participate in finding ways to tackle the global warming challenge. Along with using energy as efficiently as possible, we think participating in Smart Energy is a step in the right direction. We invite you to join us.

We wouldn't ask you to do something we aren't doing

NW Natural is offsetting the emissions from the natural gas used to heat our facilities for the next five years, resulting in the removal of more than 6,100 tons of carbon dioxide. With additional contributions from customers like you, together we can eliminate millions of pounds of carbon dioxide emissions.

Getting the most from your energy dollar

We believe Smart Energy can support our state's ambitious greenhouse gas emission reduction goals. But we also believe that nothing can serve as a substitute for the wise use of energy through efficient appliances and conservation.

Find energy-saving tips and details about incentives for high-efficiency equipment at **nwnatural.com or energytrust.org.**

About the Climate Trust

To implement Smart Energy, NW Natural partnered with The Climate Trust, a Portland-based non-profit organization created to develop high-quality offset projects that reduce greenhouse gas emissions.

In 1997, Oregon became the first state in the nation to create a carbon emission standard. The Climate Trust was founded to supply offsets using the guidelines of the new law. Since its founding, The Climate Trust has invested $9 million in projects expected to offset 2.6 million metric tons of carbon dioxide, and has been recognized as one of the leading providers of high-quality offsets in the US. Learn more about The Climate Trust at **climatetrust.org.**

Smart Energy Investments

NW Natural will not profit from Smart Energy. Nearly 70 percent of all Smart Energy contributions will be used by The Climate Trust to fund offset projects including project identification, development, monitoring and operational support. The remaining 30 percent will be used for overall program administration and to educate Oregonians about Smart Energy and climate change.

Smart Energy Commitments

When biogas or other clean energy projects are launched, you'll receive carbon offsets equal to the amount of CO_2 associated with your gas use from the time you signed up for the program. Each year, NW Natural will send you a report on Smart Energy investments and the resulting carbon offsets.

How can you reduce your carbon footprint with **cow manure?**

Introducing Smart Energy from NW Natural

SMART ENERGY. *Thinking Beyond Tomorrow.* NW Natural

BEYOND COSTS: SUSTAINABLE PRICING STRATEGIES

The road from cost to price can have a few twists and turns. Product costs, whether complete or limited, are only one factor used in determining price. Product attributes, product benefits, brand value, and a firm's competitive strategy all have a role in the final price decision. The desire to move toward the recovery of full product costs does not mean the firm has to give up other useful pricing strategies. Cost-based pricing, value-based pricing, promotional pricing, prestige pricing, and others all have their place in sustainable marketing.

Cost-based pricing, in which a marketer sets a price by adding a fixed amount or percentage to the product's cost, can help keep consumer prices at a minimum, which can make products affordable for huge populations of very poor consumers, the so-called bottom of the pyramid,[19] and at the same time generate high volumes of sales for a company. For example, Hindustan Unilever in India employs a very low cost-based pricing structure that allows the very poor in the country access to affordable soap. In the last few years, manufacturers of generic AIDS drugs have used cost-based pricing to deliver more affordable medicines to vast numbers of HIV sufferers in Africa, Brazil, and India.[20] In order to maintain low bottom-of-the-pyramid (BotP) prices, companies may prefer to cover externalized costs from profits in more affluent segments of the market. In some cases, governments may also subsidize BotP prices for strategic or humanitarian reasons, helping to offset externalized costs.

BotP subsidies often come in the form of **tiered pricing**, which refers to charging different prices in different countries or markets according to consumers' ability to pay. The pharmaceutical industry has begun to use tiered prices for potentially life-saving drugs in poor nations. Companies that manufacture AIDS drugs charge high prices (called **market-skimming pricing**) for patent-protected drugs in wealthy nations, arguing that they need their massive profits to support research and development. In poorer countries, they charge less, at least in part, to fend off competition from generic drug manufacturers that tend to find loopholes in international patent laws. The tiered pricing also allows large pharmaceutical companies to lay some claim to social responsibility.[21]

Fair-trade products use a form of cost-based pricing that begins with a stable, living wage for farmers and other producers.[22] Often fair-trade products end up being more expensive than comparable conventional products, but that isn't always the case. Channel members, such as importers, that are dedicated to fair-trade practices may take smaller markups in order to keep retail prices competitive. Other fair-trade marketers organize themselves as nonprofit organizations in order to keep prices competitive while yielding sufficient profits to reinvest in their operations and to cultivate additional human capital in the marketing channels. Consider this statement from fair-trade importer, Ten Thousand Villages: "As an importer, wholesaler and retailer, Ten Thousand Villages is a successful nonprofit enterprise. We use sales profits to increase purchases from artisan partners and to expand our distribution channels. In the past fiscal year, we increased purchases from artisans by more than one million dollars."[23] Other companies, such as Sustainable Harvest Coffee (see Chapter 11), help manage the retail price of fair-trade products by shortening the supply chain and reinvesting the savings.

Value-based pricing is set according to the value customers perceive a product to have. As you learned in Chapter 5, increasingly large segments of consumers will pay premiums for brands or products they believe to be environmentally or socially responsible. Some are motivated by concern about problems like global climate change, others by problems of air or water quality in their own communities, and still others by concern for their health or that of their children. One study found that married women with at least one child are more likely to pay more for environmentally friendly products.[24]

A 2001 study by the Future Energy Research Corporation, a UK manufacturer of fuels from biowaste, found that 71 percent of homeowners would prefer to buy their electricity from renewable sources, and that as many as 45 percent would pay some kind of premium to do so.[25] We might wonder if the worldwide recession that began in 2008 had some affect on individual's willingness to pay. A 2009 World Bank survey provides some insights (see Figure 12-3). The survey, conducted internationally, asked respondents in each country whether they would be willing to pay an additional 1 percent (of per capita GDP) for all their purchases in order to take steps against climate change. Of those who said no, 10 to 25 percent said they would be willing to pay an additional one-half of 1 percent. Higher-income respondents were only marginally more willing to pay extra than low-income respondents.[26]

FIGURE 12-3 A World Bank study surveyed consumers around the world about their willingness to help pay for climate change efforts.

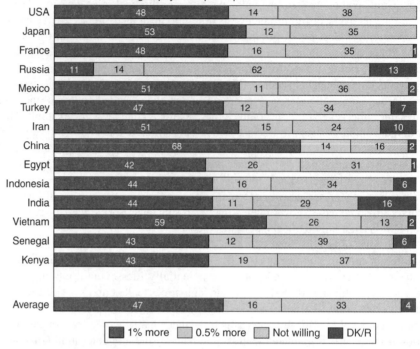

Willingness to Pay for Climate Policy

Would you be willing to pay [1% per capita GPD month more for energy and other products] as part of taking steps against climate change? Those not willing then asked if willing to pay 0.5% per capita GDP

Despite opportunities for value-based pricing in certain "green" segments, research shows that few firms actually use it; instead they default to cost-based or competitor-matching approaches.[27] Reasons companies cite include difficulties in assessing consumer value perceptions and in communicating product value. A report by McKinsey & Company argues that companies routinely set prices too low for new product offerings. In doing so, they give up significant revenues and profits, and they establish public perceptions of "correct prices" at unnecessarily low levels.[28] Proponents of value-based pricing point out that (1) a higher price often helps communicate higher product value, and (2) if a company finds that it needs to make a price correction, customers are much more willing to accept a price decrease than an increase.

Author Marc Epstein argues for value-based pricing strategy as a way to recover externalized costs. The logic is that if consumers understood the real-life trade-offs for low prices, they might well be willing to pay extra for the added value of more sustainable offerings. For example, if electricity users in a community knew that relatively cheap power had direct negative consequences for public health (measured in costs of medical treatment, lost work, etc.), they might see the value in paying a little more every month for cleaner power production.[29]

One clear example of consumer willingness to help pay externalized costs is the market for so-called voluntary carbon offsets. A carbon offset is basically an investment in greenhouse gas reduction, which may be achieved through such means as the planting of forests or developing renewable energy sources. Offsets are commonly sold to consumers who wish to reduce the impact of personal consumption, such as air travel. According to one report, voluntary purchases of carbon offsets in 2008 exceeded about $700,000 or the equivalent of more than 120 million metric tons of CO_2 reduction.[30]

Discounts and Promotions in Sustainable Pricing

Sometimes, companies may choose to discount products temporarily to levels that aren't profitable to achieve other strategic objectives. **Market-penetration pricing** sets initial prices artificially low in order to speed up sales of a new product. This is especially useful for encouraging market acceptance for a new green product. For example, when Toyota first introduced the Prius hybrid to the United States in 2001, its under-$20,000 price tag was said to be lower than Toyota's cost of manufacture and marketing (even without considering externalized costs). Part of Toyota's objective was to improve market acceptance of the new technology and establish itself as an environmental leader in the auto industry. Soon after the car hit showrooms, there were long waiting lists of people who wanted them. State and federal governments added to the discounting by offering tax breaks to buyers. Eventually, as demand grew, government subsidies decreased and retail prices increased.

Many retailers also used market-penetration pricing to speed the acceptance of CFLs. For high-volume consumer goods, such as CFLs, manufacturing costs drop over time due to economies of scale, leaving more margin from which to allocate both profits and payment of externalized costs. In the case of CFLs, some retailers are addressing externalized costs by cooperating in the collection and recycling of the bulbs.

Mini Case Study
Traverse City Light & Power

Writing in 1998, sustainable marketing consultant Jacquelyn Ottman noted that customers in Traverse City Light & Power's Green Rate program paid a 1.58 cent-per-kilowatt-hour premium for wind power generated by a locally installed wind generator. Those same customers also agreed to multiyear contracts for which they received locked-in rates.[31] In March of 2009, TCL&P canceled its Green Rate program. Jim Carruthers, a board member and early proponent of renewable power, said he'd "like to see us not charge people extra just to do green things. . . . We're becoming more sustainable and more green in energy production at Light & Power, so let's just have everybody pay the same rate and do progressive things." A 2008 Michigan state law requires that 10 percent of the state's electricity come from renewable energy sources by 2015. TCL&P exceeds the state mandate with its goal of generating 30 percent of its power through renewable energy resources by 2020. Proposed projects include a wind farm and four biomass plants.[32]

What do you think of TCL&P's decision to cancel its Green Rate pricing strategy? What strategic purpose did the Green Rate pricing achieve? What changes in TCL&P's business environment prompted it to cancel the program? What message does the new 'same rate for everybody' send to TCL&P's customers and other stakeholders?

Prestige Pricing

Sometimes, a price is more than just a price. In the case of **prestige pricing** it's a message, not only about the product but also about the owner. One envy-producing green product with a prestige-oriented price tag is the Tesla Roadster[33] (see Photo 12-1). Ever since its introduction in 2007, the limited-production, all-electric Roadster has been turning heads and snapping necks in the automotive world. High-profile early buyers include Google founders Larry Page and Sergey Brin, Arnold Schwarzenegger, and George Clooney.

Prestige pricing isn't necessarily limited to exclusive, big-ticket items. Starbucks Coffee Company has made a good business out of taking a commodity and turning it into a prestige brand. The company could rely on coffee quality alone to sustain its premium price position, but it has demonstrated that the move toward sustainability is also compatible with its quality mission. Working with the nongovernmental organization, Conservation International, Starbucks

PHOTO 12-1 Tesla's Roadster, the company's first electric vehicle, came to market with a prestige-pricing strategy.

developed the C.A.F.E. (Coffee and Farmer Equity) program, "a comprehensive set of measurable standards, including 24 criteria supported by more than 200 environmental and social indicators."[34] C.A.F.E. is used to set the prices the coffee giant pays growers. The company stresses that coffee quality is the primary price driver, but once quality concerns are met, growers can earn extra price consideration for adherence to C.A.F.E. practices. By achieving certain sustainability milestones, growers receive $0.05 per pound price premiums. In 2008, C.A.F.E. growers' price premiums totaled $1.9 million, money that "helps farmers offset the out-of-pocket investments they may have made to improve their agronomy practices and/or enhance the working conditions on the farm."[35]

COMPLEMENTARY CURRENCIES AND EXCHANGE SCHEMES

Sustainable marketing often emphasizes the value of building and maintaining local economies. Products that are grown or produced locally often have much smaller ecological footprints than those that come from great distances and as a result of mass production. Services that are produced and delivered locally tend to keep local money circulating locally. One problem for consumers of supporting local businesses is the perception, or the reality, of higher costs for goods and services that lack large-scale efficiencies.

Some market segments "vote with their dollars," choosing to pay more for local and more sustainable products. Other consumers elect to bypass the conventional money economy altogether in favor of **complementary currencies**, or nonmonetary means of paying for goods and services. **Bartering**, or the direct trading of goods and services without using money as an exchange medium, may be the best-known form of complementary currency. Bartering and other noncash exchange relationships tend to be limited to smaller geographic regions. Choosing to trade in skills, talents, and labor, people who use complementary currencies are participating in what author Gill Seyfang describes as "the wealth of contemporary alternative exchange systems which exist alongside mainstream money. A wide range of complementary currencies have been springing up in developed and developing countries since the 1990s as a response to social, economic and environmental needs, in the form of skills-exchanges, modern-day barter, green versions of supermarket reward schemes, and even notes and coins."[36]

Complementary currencies remain in a local area, bound to people and what they offer the community. Currency or credit earned in the community is exchanged locally for goods and services, which helps to build and sustain the community. In contrast, the mobility of mainstream currency, coupled with the dominance of large corporations, promotes the flight of capital away from smaller communities and into the pockets of distant investors.[37] One of the oldest complementary currencies in the United States, Ithaca Hours, started in 1991 in Ithaca, New York. The organization's website states that, "Ithaca Hours help to keep money local, building the Ithaca economy. It also builds community pride and connections. Over 900 participants publicly accept Ithaca Hours for goods and services. Additionally some local employers and employees have agreed to pay or receive partial wages in Ithaca Hours, further continuing our goal of keeping money local."[38]

Other kinds of exchange schemes also allow members to exchange items of value without the necessity of mainstream currencies. Some exchange schemes elevate bartering to a community level. A **local exchange trading scheme (LETS)** is a community-based network of people who trade goods and services, often by listing "wants" and "offers" in local directories. For example, a plumber may need a painter; a painter may need haircuts; and a stylist may need a new kitchen faucet installed. LETS facilitates coordinating "offers" with "wants" in order to satisfy each person's needs. One advantage of LETS and other complementary currencies is that, by allowing credit to be stored in the system, they allow people to make trades without having a perfect "value match."

Time banks, also called service exchanges, are similar to other barter systems, except that they use time as a currency. Time bank participants voluntarily provide services to others in a community. For their services, they "deposit" hours that they can withdraw later and spend for services they need. Home maintenance projects, elder care, childcare, gardening, dog walking, and providing transportation to shops are all examples of common time bank activities.[39]

RecycleBank offers yet another means of exchange outside of mainstream currencies. Households earn RecycleBank Points for various activities, and the Points can be used to shop at selected local and national businesses. The scheme rewards members for "all kinds of green actions like using renewable energy, reusing products, digital downloads and recycling electronic waste."[40] RecycleBank even makes the disposition of electronics easy. You provide the make, model, and condition of your unwanted cell phone, laptop, or music player. RecycleBank provides a printable packing slip and a mailing label so you can send your device to one of its partners. Once the device is received and inspected, you are awarded RecycleBank Points. RecycleBank Points can be used for local and national goods and services from over 1,500 companies such as Kohls, GNC, Office Depot, Albertsons, Origins, and Ruby Tuesday. RecycleBank also offers the "Gconomy Visa Card," which gives a cardholder points for each purchase and gives a percentage of one's annual charges to an NGO of the cardholder's choice. During his April 2009 acceptance speech for the Champion of the Earth award presented by the United Nations Environment Program, CEO Ron Gonen stated that, "Today, RecycleBank serves over one million people in 20 states across the United States, and that number continues to increase every week. We will launch our service in Europe this summer. To date, the material recycled by the households we service has enabled RecycleBank to save cities tens of millions of dollars annually in landfill disposal fees, save over 1.5 million trees, and save millions of gallons of oil."[41]

CRITICAL THINKING ACTIVITY

Different Pricing Strategies

Donald Fuller identifies several pricing strategies that are compatible with the design and manufacture of environmentally friendly products.[42] Read about the different pricing strategies described here and see if you can come up with at least one example for each:

1. Meet-the-competition pricing: Maintain price at "look-alike" competitor levels, allowing positive eco-attributes to serve as the "tie-breaker."
2. Premium green pricing: Target customers who will pay a premium to obtain "green" benefits.
3. Bulk pricing: Provide products in larger quantity packages at per-unit discounts that reflect savings in packaging material.
4. Service-life pricing: Compare the price over time between environmentally preferable products with long life spans and those with short life spans.
5. Take-back pricing: Price durable goods so as to facilitate the recovery of materials and future costs of disposal.
6. Rent/lease pricing: Retain ownership of the product and charge consumers only for actual use.

Chapter Summary

Sustainable pricing accounts fully for the economic, environmental, and social costs of a product's manufacture and marketing while providing value for customers and a fair profit for a business. Understanding and recovering the full cost of a product's manufacture and marketing requires a life-cycle assessment and full-cost accounting. Several pricing strategies are useful in making marketing more sustainable. They include cost-based and value-based pricing; price skimming and tiered pricing; market-penetration pricing and economies of scale;

voluntary subsidies or offsets; and prestige pricing. In each case, pricing is designed to make a product competitive while yielding adequate financial resources to reinvest in previously externalized human or environmental resources. Finally, in attempts to increase sustainability by building local markets, several nonmonetary pricing schemes, or complementary currencies, have been developed. They include barter, local exchange trading schemes, time banks, and RecycleBank.

Review of Chapter Objectives

In this chapter, you learned about the influences on pricing as they relate to social and environmental sustainability, including:

- Sustainable pricing: real product cost
- Barriers to sustainable pricing
- Sustainable pricing strategies
- Complementary currencies

Key Concepts

Price   171
Cost   171
Sustainable Price   171
Externalized
   Costs   172
Total Product Costs   173
Life-Cycle Costing   173

Purchase Costs   173
Product-Use
   Costs   173
Disposition or Postuse
   Costs   173
Storage Costs   173
Cost-Based Pricing   177

Tiered Pricing   177
Market-Skimming
   Pricing   177
Value-Based
   Pricing   177
Market-Penetration
   Pricing   178

Prestige Pricing   179
Complementary
   Currencies   180
Bartering   180
Local Exchange Trading
   Scheme (LETS)   180
Time Banks   180

Endnotes

1. Costanza, Robert, Ralph D'arge, Rudolf De Groot, Stephen Farber, Monica Grasso, Bruce Hannon, Karin Limburg, Shahid Naeem, Robert V. O'Neill, Jose Paruelo, Robert G. Raskin, Paul Sutton, and MarJanuary Van Den Belt (1997), "The Value of the World's Ecosystem Services and Natural Capital," *Nature,* 387 (May): 253–260.

2. Daily, Gretchen C. (1997), Nature's Services: Societal Dependence on Natural Ecosystems, Washington, DC: Island Press.

3. The Natural Step, http://www.thenaturalstep.org/the-system-conditions, accessed May 19, 2009.

4. Palmer, M. A., E. S. Bernhardt, W. H. Schlesinger, K. N. Eshleman, E. Foufoula-Georgiou, M. S. Hendryx, A. D. Lemly, G. E. Likens, O. L. Loucks, M. E. Power, P. S. White, and P. R. Wilcock (2010), "Mountaintop Mining Consequences," *Science*, 327 (5962): 148–149.

5. Hendryx, M. (2008), "Mortality Rates in Appalachian Coal Mining Counties: 24 Years Behind the Nation," *Environmental Justice*, 1 (1): 5–11. Available at http://www.sludgesafety.org/health/Mortality_Coal.pdf; Hendryx, M. and M. Ahern (2009), "Mortality in Appalachian Coal Mining Regions: The Value of Statistical Life Lost," Public Health Reports, 124 (Jul–Aug). Available at http://wvgazette.com/static/coal%20tattoo/Mortality%20AppCoalRegions.pdf; Konty, M.F., and J. Bailey (2009), "The Impact of Coal on the Kentucky State Budget," Report prepared for the Mountain Association for Community Economic Development. Available at http://www.maced.org/coal/documents/Impact_of_Coal.pdf;Mountain Association for Community Economic Development (2009), "The Economics of Coal in Kentucky: Current Impacts and Future Prospects." Available at http://www.maced.org/coal/documents/Economics_of_Coal.pdf; Napoleon, A. and Schlissel, D. (2009), "Economic Impacts of Restricting Mountaintop/Valley Fill Coal Mining in Central Appalachia," Report by Synapse Energy Economics, Inc. Available at http://www.sierraclub.org/coal/factsheets.aspx

6. Ruth, Matthias, Dana Coelho, and Daria Karetnikov (2007), "The U.S. Economic Impacts of Climate Change and the Costs of Inaction," Center for Integrative Environmental Research (CIER), University of Maryland.

7. Fuller, Donald, A. (1999), *Sustainable Marketing: Managerial-Ecological Issues,* Thousand Oaks, CA: Sage (p. 33).

8. Shrivastava, Paul (1995) "The Role of Corporations in Achieving Ecological Sustainability," *Academy of Management Review*, 20 (4, October): 936.

9. International Center for Technology Assessment (1998), "Real Price of Gasoline Report Reveals Actual Cost of Gas to Consumers Is as High as $15.14 per Gallon,"

http://www.icta.org/press/release.cfm?news_id=12, accessed January 30, 2010.

10. U.S. Department of Energy, http://www.eia.doe.gov/emeu/international/gas1.html, accessed January 30, 2010.

11. Hawken, Paul (2007), *Blessed Unrest,* New York: Penguin Group (p. 62).

12. Epstein, Marc J. (2008), Making Sustainability Work: Best Practices in Managing and Measuring Corporate Social, Environmental, and Economic Impacts, San Francisco, CA: Berrett-Koehler Publishers (p. 111).

13. Epstein, Marc J. (2008), Making Sustainability Work: Best Practices in Managing and Measuring Corporate Social, Environmental, and Economic Impacts, San Francisco, CA: Berrett-Koehler Publishers (p. 111).

14. Self Storage Blog, http://www.selfstorageblog.com/vital-statis-tics-of-the-self-storage-industry/, accessed March 26, 2010.

15. Free Agriculture Restore Markets, http://www.fa-rm.org/blog/2009/04/price-of-grass-fed-vs-grain-fed-beef.html, accessed January 30, 2010.

16. Roberts, Paul (2008), "The Cost of Steak," *Los Angeles Times*, August 23, http://articles.latimes.com/2008/aug/23/news/OE-ROBERTS23, accessed January 30, 2010.

17. Renewable Funding, http://www.renewfund.com/, accessed December 14, 2009.

18. Inhabitat, http://www.inhabitat.com/2010/01/13/reader-tip-how-to-put-your-led-holiday-lights-to-use-year-round/, accessed June 27, 2010.

19. Prahalad, Coimbatore K. (2004), *The Fortune at the Bottom of the Pyramid: Eradicating Poverty through Profits*, Upper Saddle River, NJ: Wharton School Publishing and Pearson Education.

20. Avert, http://www.avert.org/generic.htm, accessed December 14, 2009.

21. UNAIDS, 2008 Report on the global AIDS epidemic, http://www.avert.org/generic.htm, accessed December 14, 2009.

22. Fairtrade Labeling Organizations International, http://www.fairtrade.net/impact, accessed July 16, 2009.

23. Ten Thousand Villages, http://www.tenthousandvillages.com/php/fair.trade/index.php, accessed December 14, 2009.

24. Laroche, Michale, Jasmin Bergeron, and Guido Barbaro-Forleo (2001), "Targeting Consumers Who Are Willing to Pay More for Environmentally Friendly Products," *Journal of Consumer Marketing*, 18(6): 503–520.

25. Willard, Bob (2002), The Sustainability Advantage: Seven Business Case Benefits of a Triple Bottom Line, Gabriola Island, BC, Canada: New Society Publishers (p. 112).

26. World Bank, http://blogs.worldbank.org/climatechange/do-you-think-it-costs-earth-willingness-pay-climate-policies-results-our-multi-country-poll, accessed January 18, 2010.

27. Hinterhuber, Andreas (2008), "Customer Value-based Pricing Strategies: Why Companies Resist," *Journal of Business Strategy*, 29 (4): 41–50.

28. Marn, Michael V., Eric V. Roegner, and Craig C. Zawada (2003), "Pricing New Products," *McKinsey Quarterly*, 3 (August):26–39.

29. Epstein, Marc J. (2008), Making Sustainability Work: Best Practices in Managing and Measuring Corporate Social, Environmental, and Economic Impacts, San Francisco, CA: Berrett-Koehler Publishers (p. 152).

30. Ecosystem Marketplace and New Carbon Finance (2009), "Fortifying the Foundation: State of the Voluntary Carbon Markets 2009," available at http://ecosystemmarketplace.com/documents/cms_documents/StateOfTheVoluntaryCarbonMarkets_2009.pdf, accessed March 29, 2010.

31. Ottman, Jacquelyn A. (1998), *Green Marketing: Opportunity for Innovation,* New York: J. Ottman Consulting Inc. (p. 107).

32. Domsic, Melissa (2009), "Light & Power Cancels Green Rate Program," March 26, http://www.record-eagle.com/local/local_story_086070144.html accessed October 31, 2009.

33. Tesla Motors, http://www.teslamotors.com/, accessed December 14, 2009.

34. Starbucks, http://www.starbucks.com/sharedplanet/ethicalinternal.aspx?story=sspprinciples, accessed December 14, 2009.

35. http://www.starbucks.com/SharedPlanet/ethicalInternal.aspx?story=pricesAndQuality, accessed December 14, 2009.

36. Seyfang, Gill (2009), The New Economics of Sustainable Consumption: Seeds of Change, New York: Palgrave Macmillan (p. 141).

37. Seyfang, Gill (2009), The New Economics of Sustainable Consumption: Seeds of Change, New York: Palgrave Macmillan (p. 142).

38. Ithaca Hours, http://www.ithacahours.org/about.php, accessed March 20, 2010.

39. Seyfang, Gill (2009), The New Economics of Sustainable Consumption: Seeds of Change, New York: Palgrave Macmillan (p. 149).

40. RecycleBank, http://www.recyclebank.com/how-it-works, accessed December 14, 2009.

41. RecycleBank, http://www.recyclebank.com/about, accessed December 14, 2009.

42. Fuller, Donald A. (1999). "Marketing Mix Design-for-Environment (Dfe): A Systems Approach," *Journal of Business Administration & Policy Analysis*, 27–29; 309–336.

Sustainable Marketing Communication

INTRODUCTION: BEYOND PETROLEUM OR BACKPEDALING?

A 2007 article in the British newspaper, *The Guardian,* pointed out some specifics about what most of us already believe in general, namely that what companies say and what they do are sometimes miles apart: "Shell, the oil company that recently trumpeted its commitment to a low carbon future by signing a pre-Bali conference communiqué, has quietly sold off most of its solar business. The move, taken with rival BP's decision last week to invest in the world's dirtiest oil production in Canada's tar sands, indicates that Big Oil might be giving up its flirtation with renewables and going back to its roots."[1] An article in TreeHugger was less gentle with the giant British Petroleum: "What does BP stand for these days? Beyond Propaganda? ByeBye Planet? Bad Pollution? We just aren't certain anymore, now that it is spending $3 billion to buy into the stupid fuel, oil from the Alberta Tar Sands, global warming's new Ground Zero."[2] And WebEcoist added, in a post on the world's worst greenwashers: "BP's ad campaign with the theme 'Beyond Petroleum' led the public to believe the company was headed in the direction of cleaner, renewable fuels. But, it turned out the company was spending more money on advertising than on green efforts...."[3]

When nonmarketers think about marketing, they often think primarily about marketing communication. When they think about marketing communication, they think about advertising. So, what do people think about advertising? It turns out that they mainly don't trust it. A 2007 worldwide Nielsen study found that people around the world trust media advertising only about half the time.[4] A 2009 Advertising Association study in the United Kingdom revealed that in its markets, "fewer than one in six people trust advertisers."[5]

THINK ABOUT IT

Trust and Marketing

As a consumer, how much do you trust marketing messages? Is it the same for all companies and brands? What do you think causes consumer skepticism? What effect did it have for BP to make environmental claims and then fail to live up to them? Is it possible for a company to make credible social and environmental claims? Can a company like BP gain consumer trust? How would BP do it, especially after being responsible, in 2010, for the Gulf of Mexico catastrophe involving the Deepwater Horizon oil spill, the largest environmental disaster in U.S. history?

In order to understand and to practice sustainable marketing, we must understand how marketing communication can be done more sustainably and in ways that promote a more sustainable society.

CHAPTER OBJECTIVES

In this chapter, you will learn:

- The nature of sustainable marketing communication
- The keys to sustainable marketing communication
- Barriers to sustainable marketing communication
- Cardinal sins of sustainable marketing communication: greenwashing, astroturfing, and other green lies

Marketing communication—also called marcom, the promotion mix, or integrated marketing communication (IMC)—is a critical element of the marketing mix and, more broadly, of a marketing strategy. Like any other aspect of the marketing mix, marketing communication is created and implemented with specific target markets and strategic objectives in mind. Marketing communication serves many goals and objectives. At various times and in various situations, organizations use marketing communication to achieve any or all of the following:

- Create awareness of the product or service
- Educate or provide information about the product, brand, or company
- Remind or reassure customers about the brand
- Persuade potential customers to try the brand
- Reward buyers for purchasing the brand
- Improve the company or brand image
- Improve or maintain employee morale

The effort to make an organization more sustainable places additional demands on marketing communication. Author Donald Fuller suggests two additional objectives: (1) establishing and maintaining the environmental credibility of a firm, its brands, and its products; and (2) educating a broad range of stakeholders about environmental issues.[6]

Many firms have taken such objectives seriously, as demonstrated by an increasing number of consulting firms and advertising agencies dedicated to sustainability-related marketing communication. This chapter introduces and explores the concept of sustainable marketing communication.

THE NATURE OF SUSTAINABLE MARKETING COMMUNICATION

For an organization striving to become sustainable, marketing communication, like everything else, must be done in a sustainable fashion, and it should contribute to building a more sustainable society. We define **sustainable marketing communication (SMC)** as messages and media directed to any of an organization's stakeholders for the purpose of achieving the organization's marketing and sustainability objectives. Based on the understanding of sustainability established in the first three chapters, marketing communication is sustainable to the extent that it meets the following conditions:

1. It contributes to triple-bottom-line value for the organization, that is, it helps build financial, natural, and human capital.
2. It takes a whole-system perspective and considers all the organization's legitimate stakeholder interests.
3. It facilitates transparency, accountability, and integrity in the organization.
4. It helps move an organization forward with respect to the four conditions for sustainability as laid out in The Natural Step Framework.

In the pursuit of sustainable marketing, we must hold communication to the same standards as we do other aspects of marketing strategy and tactics. The rest of this chapter explores what that means and how it can be accomplished.

THE KEYS TO SUSTAINABLE MARKETING COMMUNICATION

Marketing communication is a strategic endeavor, and in order to be successful, marcom managers must begin with a clear set of objectives. In addition to the standard marketing objectives of creating awareness, informing, persuading, reminding, and rewarding, SMC pursues additional goals related to sustainability. One aspect of sustainability stressed in Natural Capitalism (see Chapter 2) is radical resource productivity; in other words, achieving maximum benefit from the fewest possible resources. SMC achieves radical resource productivity in part through two additional principles—integration and leverage.

Integration

SMC is integrated. The concept of **integrated marketing communication (IMC)** holds that all the messages from an organization, in all media, should work together holistically to convey the organization's desired image or market position. Think of IMC like a rope. Its strength and effectiveness come from the fact that many individual strands of fiber are integrated into a single cord. Without proper integration, all you have is a pile of fibers. Marketing communication that lacks integration may just be a hodgepodge of different messages going in different directions to different audiences. Without integration, marketing messages may contradict each other, thereby undermining the credibility of the firm or the brand and confusing audiences.

Consistent with The Natural Step Framework (see Chapter 2), SMC requires a whole-system perspective that includes all organizational stakeholders. This implies that SMC also needs to be integrated across external and internal audiences. **External marketing communication** helps maintain connections or relationships with customers and other external stakeholders, such as potential customers, investors, suppliers, government, and nongovernmental organizations (NGOs).[7] **Internal marketing communication** helps to maintain employee morale and to teach and motivate employees to be effective ambassadors for the organization and its brands. Some of the best spokespersons for an organization's sustainability efforts are members of the organization who feel pride and ownership regarding those efforts.

Integrating across messages, media, and audiences is, by itself, not enough to ensure the effectiveness or the sustainability of marketing communication. The message must also be built on a foundation of **integrity**. In an information-rich society, the truth about marketing claims or business practices is difficult to hide indefinitely. Anything less than honesty is simply not sustainable. For reasons we shall soon discuss, SMC also helps to assure that messages *about* an organization are consistent with messages coming *from* the organization. In other words, we'll see that SMC influences third-party communication in ways that enhance an organization's marketing and sustainability objectives.

Leverage

Another source of radical resource productivity in marketing communication is **leverage**, or the ability to have the greatest possible impact using the least necessary resources. Leverage in SMC comes from using the communication power of communities and networks. If an organization's marketing message gets picked up and disseminated by customers, product reviewers, or other influential stakeholders, that additional communication activity can accelerate the marketing message at great benefit and at no cost to the organization. Messages may be transmitted face-to-face among such groups as friends, families, neighbors, and coworkers. Messages may also travel virally through virtual communities by such means as email or social networking (see Chapter 15); or they may be spread by traditional mass media such as newspapers, television, and radio.

For an example of leveraging social networks, consider the case of Naked Juice reported in Mobile Marketing Daily from *MediaPost*. Soon after announcing that it had become the first national brand to use a 100 percent post-consumer recycled polyethylene bottle, Naked

PHOTO 13-1 Naked Juice's sustainability initiatives become topics for blogs and social networking—good, cheap marketing communication.

Juice ". . . launched a campaign asking consumers to do their bit for the environment by passing along a 'Naked Message in a Bottle.' Facebook users can 'drink' Naked Juice and pass virtual bottles and their messages along to friends. For every bottle passed (up to 400,000), Naked Juice will donate five cents (up to $20,000) to Keep America Beautiful and its recycling education initiatives."[8] The Naked Juice story not only spread through Facebook networks, but was also picked up and passed along by dozens of other online publications and blogs, including "eco" sites (e.g., Green Lifestyles and GoGreen), industry sites (such as FoodBev.com and SolidWasteMag.com) and mainstream business sites (e.g., Fast Company) (see Photo 13-1).

Brand Community

Communities are important as more than merely sources of communication leverage. Another objective of SMC should be to create stronger, more trusting relationships with customers. In 2002, an influential article in the *Journal of Marketing* established a new metric of customer loyalty: integration in a brand community.[9] A brand community is a web of people and relationships that share dedication to a brand and its success in the marketplace.[10] Companies build brand communities by cultivating meaningful, positive relationships with their customers and by facilitating the same kinds of relationships among customers. Brand communities actively help companies achieve their marketing goals. They are more likely to engage in repeat purchases and to buy other products in the brand family. They are often less price sensitive, easier to reach with marketing programs, and more receptive to those programs, meaning that they provide higher profit margins for the company. And most importantly from a marketing communication standpoint, enthusiastic members of a brand community tend to act as ambassadors or missionaries for the brand, actively promoting it to others.

Members of a brand community are also more likely than other customers to get behind a company's social and environmental goals. For example, loyal Harley-Davidson customers have been an important part of that company's long-time support for the Muscular Dystrophy Association (MDA). According to the Harley-Davidson website: "Support for MDA began in 1980 and since then, the Harley-Davidson family of customers, dealers, suppliers and employees has raised more than $65 million to aid research and program services for children and adults with muscular dystrophy."[11] A hallmark of the Harley-Davidson/MDA connection is the level of integration and interaction among Harley-Davidson stakeholders in events to raise money for the charitable organization.

THINK ABOUT IT

The Power of Friendship

Consider the following questions:

1. What are the most important features of a good friendship?
2. How does a good friendship develop? What does it take to maintain?
3. What kinds of behaviors can strain a friendship?

Did your answers to question #1 include things like trust? Generosity? Real concern for each other's well-being? The willingness to stand up for each other? Did your answers to question #2 include things like open and truthful communication? Common values and interests? Shared experiences? And did your answers to question #3 include things like betrayal of trust? Taking unfair advantage? Deception?

Now put yourself in the position of a marketing communication manager. How could you apply the principles of friendship to your company's relationships with its stakeholders? What benefits would come from that? How would you accomplish that?

It's valuable for a business to cultivate a brand community among its customers. It's equally important to build goodwill and community among other stakeholders as well. We should point out that different stakeholder categories often have considerable overlap. For example, a woman who supplies materials or services to a clothing company may also be a company stockholder as well as one of the company's loyal customers. That same woman may influence the attitudes and behaviors of people in her other social and business circles, spreading goodwill and credible information about the company.

Communities of Purpose

Previous chapters have discussed the importance of collaboration with stakeholders on the journey to sustainability. Such collaborations can result in **communities of purpose**, groups of people united by common or overlapping goals and working collaboratively to achieve specific outcomes.[12] In his 2007 book *Blessed Unrest*, Paul Hawken describes a global web of "coherent, organic, self-organized congregations involving tens of millions of people dedicated to change."[13] By Hawken's estimate, there are over a million organizations in the world devoted to ecological sustainability and social justice.

Communities of purpose may be managed by businesses or nonprofit organizations, and while members of the managing organization may receive financial compensation, members of the broader community commonly receive no remuneration. Instead, they work for personal satisfaction and other positive emotional outcomes. Examples of communities of purpose include different groups within the growing "natural health movement"[14] wherein people with shared physical, mental and spiritual goals have organized themselves into a multi-billion-dollar market for "lifestyles of health and sustainability."[15] The for-profit LOHAS group is one organizational hub for natural health communities.

Community-supported agriculture (CSA) is another manifestation of a community of purpose that links small-scale farmers directly with consumers. Consumers in the CSA pay at the beginning of a season for weekly allotments of a farm's produce. They may visit the farm, meet the growers, and even contribute occasional farm labor as part of their payment (see Photo 13-2). According to one study, in 2007, over 1,500 CSAs operated in North America.[16] Each CSA is managed by an individual farm. LocalHarvest, an organization that maintains a database of CSAs, cites advantages for both farmers and consumers. Farmers receive early-season payment, which helps their cash flow, and they have the opportunity to get to know their customers. Consumers get a steady supply of ultra-fresh and usually organic foods, exposure to new vegetables and uses, and a clear sense of where their food is coming from.[17]

Yet another example of a community of purpose is Carrotmob, the organization profiled in Chapter 5 that promotes sustainable business practices by arranging consumer "buycotts." Using social media such as Facebook and Twitter, Carrotmob mobilizes consumer flash mobs to

PHOTO 13-2 Community supported agriculture (CSA) provides consumers with fresh, local foods.

converge on a particular store that has agreed in advance to invest its earnings during a specified time period into some kind of sustainability project. The mob makes purchases, the store earns many times its usual revenue, and it becomes more sustainable.[18]

THINK ABOUT IT

Your Very Own Mob

Take a moment to consider a goal that's particularly dear to your heart. Now try to think of everything you could do personally to make that goal a reality. Could you pull it off? Next, think of all the people you know who have some stake, however small, in that same goal. Imagine what it would be like if you could get all of them to think and interact creatively to find ways to achieve the goal. How much easier would it be? If the group were successful, how would they feel about their success?

Marketing organizations can leverage the creative resources of communities of purpose if they are willing to serve as catalysts or sponsors for the communities. Communities are formed of people and relationships. Relationships are built through communication. Effective communication is more likely when the stakeholder relationships are characterized by trust, mutual respect, and a desire to help each other succeed.

Accountability and Transparency

Loyal stakeholders are typically willing forgive many of an organization's mistakes or shortcomings,[19] if for no other reason than they appreciate the organization and trust its intentions. However, not all stakeholders are equally inclined to grant an organization the benefit of the doubt with respect to environmental and social issues. NGOs and watchdog groups in particular are notoriously (and many would say rightfully) skeptical of corporate motives and behaviors.

Even consumers find companies' sustainability claims hard to swallow. An international study of consumers found that only about 10 percent trust what companies say about climate change, and only about 25 percent trust what companies claim regarding energy-efficient products and services. About 70 percent say they want third-party verification of climate change claims.[20]

The surest path to good relations with skeptical stakeholders is for a company to be openly accountable for its actions. Let's look at an example from the world of interpersonal relationships. Suppose someone you barely know accidentally damages your car while it's parked on the street. In one scenario, the person comes to you, admits the accident, and offers to make it right. In the second scenario, the person leaves the scene and says nothing to you; however, a witness later presents you with a cell-phone video of the incident. In which scenario do you end up having more respect for the person who damaged your car? In which scenario are you most inclined to go after that person for damages? Finally, after which scenario would you be more inclined to do business with the person who damaged your car?

Transparency is an important element of accountability. To some marketing managers, the thought of exposing marketing practices to outside observers might cause a fair amount of anxiety. They might ask: Why invite criticism? Alternatively, author Adam Werbach suggests that "transparency and openness are business opportunities." He asks, "Why not engage critics and ask them to help make the company better?"[21] In that way, if they find problems, they will be inclined to help with solutions rather than just criticize. Scholar Stuart Hart similarly suggests that "transparency would not jeopardize a competitive advantage. On the contrary, it may enhance the image, reputation, and legitimacy of the firm."[22] The fast-food giant McDonald's believes in transparency. Consider these words from a blog by McDonald's VP Bob Langert: "I observed this first-hand. . . . In the height of the anti-globalization movement, French farmer, Jean Bove, used McDonald's as a symbol of his movement. The McDonald's France business did not hide from the issue. Rather, it started an 'Open Doors' campaign, inviting the public into their offices, their restaurants, and their suppliers. They had nothing to hide. They were proud of their people and suppliers. Instead of cowering, they were very transparent. Today, our business in France is one of our most successful markets, with this transparency strategy as a key part of their success."[23] Langert goes on to describe several innovations that McDonald's has achieved through direct collaboration with NGOs such the Environmental Defense Fund, Conservation International, and Greenpeace.

In 1998, author Pierre McDonagh developed four "building blocks" for sustainable communication: trust, access, disclosure, and dialogue. From this perspective, trust begins with access or openness to stakeholders' questions and concerns about environmental and social issues. A more proactive form of communication is disclosure, which often takes the form of voluntary reporting and audits of environmental and social performance. Perhaps the most productive form of communication, however, is **stakeholder dialogue**, or an on-going and meaningful exchange between a firm and its stakeholders. By actively engaging its stakeholders in dialogue, an organization builds trust and gains broader perspectives of its impacts on the environment and society.[24]

Credibility

Credibility is the stock in trade of marketing communication. However, more often than not, consumers don't regard companies' claims as credible. Most marketing messages are probably honest and well intended, but those that are overblown or downright deceptive cause the whole enterprise to be suspect. Think of it as a "bad neighborhood." The majority of residents are good, hard-working people operating on a thin margin of economic survival. It only takes the occasional mugging to give the whole place a bad name. The neighborhood of marketing communication has had more than its share of muggings. A study published by the ad agency J. Walter Thompson in 1991 found that only 9 percent of surveyed consumers viewed a manufacturer's self-declared warranty/claims to be as credible as an approval from an environmental group, an independent lab's findings, or a scientist's testimonial.[25] And there's no reason to believe consumers have become any more trusting of corporate claims since then.

THINK ABOUT IT

The Lies That Blind

Here are a couple of common words in marketing communication:

- **Puffery**—marketing messages that rely on exaggeration or ungrounded opinion; empty claims of superiority
- **Spin**—highly biased or distorted portrayal of a situation or set of facts, often considered deceptive or manipulative.

Puffery and spin are legal in marketing, as long as they aren't proven to be technically false. What does this mean for the public perception of marketing communication? If puffery and spin are sanctioned in marketing, then how does that affect the credibility of the marketing communication profession?

One rule for establishing credibility in the marketplace is simple: Let someone else tell your story. That "someone else" may be the press, NGOs, or academic researchers. When the authors of this book were researching the early sustainability efforts of Wal-Mart in the spring of 2006, there was a lot of excitement among Wal-Mart employees about the environmental gains the company was making on several fronts. The excitement was well deserved; success stories were abundant and impressive. A common question we heard was, "How can we best tell this story?" Our answer was, "You can't. Who would believe you? All you can do is continue to do the right thing. Others will notice. Let them tell the story." Wisely, the company showed restraint, and its story is being told, including in the pages of this textbook, and also in any number of other books, magazines, newspapers, and blogs.

Credibility is harder to come by for some companies than for others. When people learn they've been deceived, they tend to remember it for a long time. Third-party verification and reporting can be the beginning of a former miscreant firm's journey back into the public's good graces.

Many third-party certifications or eco-seals demonstrate rigorous standards for environmental and social performance. Others, however, don't; and consumers don't always know the difference. Says sustainability scholar Marc Epstein, "Independent verification is an important component of external reporting . . . however there is little standardization of social and environmental management systems, performance systems and reporting structures. Correspondingly, there are no generally accepted worldwide auditing or reporting standards."[26]

The value of third-party certifications for sustainability is eroded not only by the lack of generally accepted standards but also by the sheer number of eco-seals and certifications now on the market (see Photo 13-3). Ecolabelling.org reports that currently there are more than three hundred. In a *Wall Street Journal* article from April 2009, we read: "Recently, Kevin Owsley went searching for a reputable organization that could validate the eco-friendly traits of his company's carpet-cleaning fluid. But after canvassing a dozen competing groups hawking so-called 'green certification' services—including one online outfit that awarded him an instant green diploma, no questions asked—he grew disillusioned about how meaningful any endorsement would be to his customers."[27]

PHOTO 13-3 What's behind the label? Increasingly consumers want to know what terms like "eco-friendly" really mean.

Consumer Education

It's impossible to overstate the importance of consumer education to SMC. Educated consumers can be valuable partners in marketing organizations' efforts to become sustainable. But as discussed in Chapter 5, not all consumers are well informed about the need for sustainability or the benefits to be had from it. Early attempts at developing greener products and services often left consumers dissatisfied. Unfortunately, many consumers still believe that more sustainable products are also lower in quality, or they believe that consuming more sustainably requires a sacrifice in terms of quality of life. These concerns are no longer founded, and effective marketing communication is the best way to educate hesitant consumers.

Marketers can help consumers make more sustainable choices in a number of ways. Sustainable marketing consultant Jackie Ottman suggests that, "The best educational efforts make environmental benefits tangible through compelling illustrations and statistics."[28] For example, compare CO_2 reductions of product use with a certain number of cars off the road annually. Cars are much easier for consumers to visualize than CO_2 parts per million. Redesigned or recycled plastic containers can be related to gallons of oil saved.

Other consumer education tactics, recommended by authors Jill Ginsberg and Paul Bloom in *Sloan Management Review*,[29] include using packaging or in-store displays to provide environmental information, point-of-sale demonstrations to explain environmental issues, and free samples to overcome customers' initial reluctance to try something new.

Opportunities may also exist for an organization to enlist other members of its marketing channels in its educational efforts. Effective marcom managers should consider the following questions: Are our channel partners (e.g., suppliers, clients, and business customers) aware of our environmental initiatives? Are they willing to support our communication efforts?

Finally, not all customer education needs to focus on information and persuasion regarding sustainability. Emotional appeals often are more powerful than intellectual arguments in shaping consumer choices. Appealing to the right emotions is important, and leads to the following discussion of value congruence.

Value Congruence

Consumers are unlikely to get very much out of marketers' efforts to educate them about sustainability unless they see the relevance to issues they care about personally. For this reason, SMC must tap into deeply held customer values. It needs to hit them where they live. In the case of marketing communication, **value congruence** is the extent to which a marketing message is harmonious or consistent with a target customer's values. For the increasing numbers of consumers who do care about sustainability and are well informed about the differences among products, brands, and certifications, reaching them is largely a matter of providing clear and accurate information.

However, not all consumers are equally motivated to choose products based on their sustainability attributes, which is, of course an issue of market segmentation. For those customers who are unaware of the benefits of consuming more sustainably for themselves, for their families, for the Earth, and for society, the key to persuasion lies in linking sustainable consumption to values they do hold important, such as family health, economic value, attractiveness, or fashion.

THINK ABOUT IT

Lessons from Big Tobacco

Billions of dollars and a lot of brainpower have been spent over the years by the cigarette industry, governments, and activist organizations to educate and influence consumers regarding the consumption of cigarettes. By what methods have cigarette marketers attempted to influence smokers to choose their brands? What methods have governments, activists, and marketers used to reduce cigarette consumption? How might these tactics be used in efforts to promote more sustainable consumption?

One interesting case of value congruency, called **fun theory**, comes straight from the world of marketing communication. Fun theory may sound like something out of a psychology or sociology textbook, but it actually originates as the subject of a viral ad campaign by Volkswagen and the advertising agency DDB Stockholm.[30] Fun theory operates on the assumption that people are more willing to do constructive things when they provide the added benefit of enjoyment or amusement. Volkswagen and DDB have been harnessing the power of fun with a series of videos, posted on YouTube, testing that very assumption. The most popular experiment to date, with about 10 million views and 13,000 reviews on YouTube, is called Piano Stairs. It purports to demonstrate that people are 66 percent more likely to use stairs rather than an escalator if it's fun to do. Extending the concept, DDB has even hosted a contest, the Fun Theory Award, with cash prizes for people with the best new inventions to demonstrate the concept.[31] Apparently, even tackling the problem of sustainable consumption is fun if you make a game of it.

VIRTUAL FIELD TRIP

The Fun Factor

Go online to www.thefuntheory.com and explore VW's Fun Theory videos. Do they influence your feelings about Volkswagen as a brand? Are you more inclined to associate VW products with fun or enjoyment after seeing the videos? Use your Web search feature to find recent Volkswagen ads featuring different models in different media, including television and print media. What kinds of themes can you identify in the advertising? What do they communicate about VW owners? How well do you think the messages are integrated across the various media? To what extent does VW's overall communication strategy exemplify SMC? Does any aspect of the advertising seem to violate sustainability principles?

Other values related to fun—sexiness and coolness (or hipness or whatever)—also appeal deeply to consumers. One question at the current forefront of SMC is "how do we make sustainability sexy?" Advertising executive Marc Stoiber puts it this way: "Sustainability. Sexy. Two words you don't often see together. Sustainability is a serious word. It's about saving the world from ecological disaster. Getting humanity on track for survival. Heady stuff best left to academics, unions of concerned scientists, and earnest tree-huggers. Sexy . . . now that's a fun word. A word that implies pleasure. Tied to advertising, it's a hook that's been used to raise sales curves on everything from cars to cognac. A very big opportunity awaits if we—marketers, producers, and media—manage to somehow join these two words at the hip."[32] College students at University of Georgia, thinking that making sustainability sexy sounded like fun, produced a calendar featuring students covered by nothing but symbols of greener living.[33]

Back to Basics: AIDA

AIDA is a long-used and well-worn acronym for four basic stages—*attention, interest, desire, action*—in the process of persuasive communication.[34] It can also be a useful SMC guideline. Let's look at how AIDA relates to the effectiveness of SMC at Annie's Homegrown, makers of organic and all-natural foods.[35] Company founders Annie Withey and Andrew Martin initially got consumers' *attention* with communication that matched the company's natural, no fuss corporate image. In the early days of the company Withey handwrote letters in response to consumers, and in the process, she captured their hearts and minds with her openness and transparency.[36] Annie's Homegrown maintained consumers' *interest* with clever stories communicated on the packaging. Boxes for macaroni and cheese products featured images of Bernie the Rabbit and told of life on the Withey's organic farm in the Connecticut countryside. With a focus on "natural comfort food," Annie's Homegrown piqued consumers' *desire* for simple, hearty, natural foods and, by extension, lifestyles. Brand loyalty runs deep among Annie's Homegrown customers. Their collective *action* has allowed the company to celebrate its twentieth year in 2009.[37] Even the company's direct public offering was offered first to loyal customers, who learned about the offer from a flyer in boxes of macaroni and cheese.[38]

BARRIERS TO SUSTAINABLE MARKETING COMMUNICATION

Not all attempts to create SMC are equally effective. Several common mistakes create barriers to the success of SMC efforts. Ironically, perhaps, some of these missteps can be a direct result of being enthusiastic about sustainability.

Losing Sight of the Basics

It's important to keep in mind that being sustainable and promoting sustainability are only two among the many goals for SMC. One common error is concentrating on sustainability goals to the point of overlooking traditional marketing objectives. Relative sustainability is a **secondary benefit** of most products and services, meaning that if the **primary** or **core benefit** is delivered competitively, then being more sustainable may be a significant competitive advantage. However, if the product fails to deliver on its primary function, sustainability alone is an insufficient reason to purchase it. For example, if a mobile phone is the greenest phone in the world—made entirely from recycled products, with renewable energy and low water usage, by people who are paid and treated well—and yet lacks the basic features customers want in a phone, it's doomed to fail. In marketing messages, focusing on sustainability benefits while overlooking other benefits that may be more important to the target market is risky business. It's a bit like throwing a great party and forgetting to send out the invitations.

Clouding the Brand Story

The same basic rules apply to the brand message. Sustainability is only one part of the story for most brands, even from the most sustainable companies. The best brands are those that maintain clear and consistent identities while being able to evolve with changing market forces. BMW is one example of a company that is serious about becoming more environmentally and socially sustainable. It integrates sustainability throughout its operations, monitors its progress for continuous improvement, and reports the results in detailed sustainable value reports that meet the stringent requirements for transparency laid out by the Global Reporting Initiative (GRI).[39] Consider this statement from BMW board chairman, Norbert Reithofer: "The world is changing faster than ever. Environmental and climate protection, shortage of resources and demographic change are just a few of the enormous challenges society faces and which demand the involvement of all forces of society.... We believe our company is not only responsible for finding solutions—but, more importantly, for implementing them consistently."[40] Check out the BMW Group's website to explore the range and depth of its commitment to sustainability, but don't expect to see the green message overshadow the core brand message in the company's advertising. BMW is unlikely to ever let you forget who builds "The Ultimate Driving Machine."

Misreading the Target Audience

A related barrier to successful SMC stems from a failure to correctly understand the target audience. As discussed in Chapter 7, the so-called green market is anything but uniform and homogeneous. Different segments look for different benefits, even within the same product categories. They have different price sensitivities, different understandings of sustainability, different lifestyles, and that's just the beginning of the differences. To make it more complicated, markets segment differently from one industry to the next. To know how much and what to communicate about sustainability requires a company and its marketing communication providers to have a rich understanding of its target customers.

Getting the marketing communication basics right is critical, but not enough, to achieve SMC. A company can have perfect understanding of its target customers, a clear and consistent brand story, and the perfect shade of green in its external communication and still end up in trouble. This is especially true if the organization's sustainability messaging crosses the line into erroneous claims, exaggeration, or misleading information.

THE CARDINAL SINS OF SUSTAINABLE MARKETING COMMUNICATION: GREENWASHING, ASTROTURFING, AND OTHER GREEN LIES

By now it's pretty clear that consumer interest in environmental health and human well-being is growing steadily. It's also clear that more and more businesses are recognizing the importance and strategic advantages of being environmentally and socially responsible. However, the increasing enthusiasm for sustainability on all fronts also increases the danger that companies will overstate their green or humanitarian credentials. And whether they do it deliberately or not, it makes for bad press and can do serious damage to a company's image and credibility.

Greenwashing

Organizations can easily find themselves accused of **greenwashing**, that is, exaggerating sustainability claims or using marketing communication to make products and services appear more sustainable than they truly are. The term *greenwashing* brings together the concept of "green" as in environmentally friendly and "whitewash" as in covering up or concealing defects. Greenwashing tends to fall under the headings of puffery or spin. Donald Fuller notes that businesses "have been regularly accused of taking green issues out of context, putting a spin on them, and using them as a marketing ploy in an attempt to fatten short-term, bottom-line profits at the customer's expense."[41] Greenwashing may be purposeful or it may be accidental. Either way, whenever marketers actively participate in or passively allow the greenwashing of the firm, the company and brand images suffer. Many marketing managers have learned the hard way. According to Jackie Ottman, "Criticism can emanate from many sources, including regulators, environmentalists, the media, consumers, competitors, and the scientific community. Unsuspecting marketers can run afoul of inconsistent state environmental marketing laws. They can butt up against advocacy groups who question the right of former polluters to tout green credentials of any kind, and they can unintentionally create skeptical consumers among a general public short on facts."[42]

The responsibility to make true and complete sustainability claims falls squarely on the firm. As a guide for avoiding greenwashing, TerraChoice publishes "The Seven Sins of Greenwashing."[43] The seven sins are:

1. Sin of the Hidden Trade-Off: Suggesting a product is "green" based on selective attributes ignoring other important environmental issues (e.g., "energy efficient" products containing hazardous materials)
2. Sin of No Proof: Making a claim that can't be substantiated by reputable and easily accessible sources (e.g., products labeled "organic" with no verifiable certification).
3. Sin of Vagueness: Making broad, ambiguous claims that are likely to be misunderstood by consumers (e.g., "All-natural" products that contain naturally occurring substances, like heavy metals, that also happen to be toxic).
4. Sin of Worshiping False Labels: Giving the impression, through words or images, of third-party endorsement where no such endorsement exists (e.g., a label bearing a green-leaf image and mention of a standard that is made up by and unique to the firm).
5. Sin of Irrelevance: Making claims that are truthful but meaningless (e.g., claiming "CFC-free" even though CFCs have been banned for 20 years).
6. Sin of Lesser of Two Evils: Making a claim that's true but that avoids or distracts from a much more serious issue (e.g., organic cigarettes).
7. Sin of Fibbing: Making claims that are false; gaining eco-certifications under false pretenses (e.g., rigging tests to get unearned Energy Star ratings).

In a study of randomly selected U.S. consumer marketing campaigns, TerraChoice found that out of over 2,200 environmental claims, 98 percent had committed some form of greenwashing.[44]

Mini Case Study

Johnson & Johnson

The name Johnson & Johnson tends to evoke thoughts of baby shampoo and Band-Aids, not necessarily leadership in sustainability. At a 2009 Net Impact Conference,[45] Al Iannuzzi, senior director of J&J's Worldwide Environmental Health & Safety unit, recounted his experience as a corporation-hating environmentalist in the 1970s. He steered clear of corporate jobs until he read J&J's Credo,[46] established in 1943, which proclaims the company's dedication to serving customers, employees, communities, and stockholders. He joined J&J, and nearly 30 years later, he feels compelled to tell the story of its sustainability efforts. But he's also wary of greenwashing. According to Iannuzzi, J&J has tended to work quietly but steadily on its sustainability goals. His concern is, "If we're not saying anything, people assume we're not doing anything."[47] That said, J&J has been a top-performer on *Newsweek* magazine's Green Rankings List (number 3 in 2009).[48]

Dig a little deeper into J&J's sustainability-related activities. Given everything the company is doing, do you think J&J should be more vocal about its efforts? Why or why not? What effects would publicizing sustainability goals and actions have on J&J's brand messages? Can you find any cases of J&J committing one or more of the Seven Sins of Greenwashing?

Astroturfing

Greenwashing's disreputable cousin, **astroturfing**, refers to the creation of a phony grassroots movement to project a false image of widespread public support. In the United Kingdom, this common practice is called rent-a-crowd. A UK agency by the same name bills itself as ". . . a people management company made up of fun, young, respectable group of 18–25 year old men and women who will attend your celebrations in the strictest confidence. . . ."[49] In the United States, astroturfing campaigns often target government officials in efforts to influence environmental or social legislation or policy changes. Recent examples of astroturfing are cited by the NGO,

SourceWatch. Here's one of them: "In July 2009, public relations firm Bonner & Associates was caught forging letters to Representative Tom Perriello. The letters were supposedly from Virginia-based minority groups, like the Charlottesville NAACP or Creciendo Juntas—complete with their stationery—and urged him to oppose the Waxman-Markey Climate Bill. ... Perriello is one of the co-sponsors of the Clean Water Protection Act, which would slow the practice of Mountaintop removal. The American Coalition for Clean Coal Electricity (ACCCE), a coal industry front group, later admitted that Bonner was working on its behalf."[50]

As mentioned earlier, green lies such as greenwashing and astroturfing can have serious negative consequences for their perpetrators although, based on the continued prevalence of the practices, many organizations apparently still believe it's worth the risk. As a result, the U.S. government has gotten increasingly involved with the issues.

Government Actions

Environmental NGOs began taking companies to task over greenwashing and other deceptive practices, and by late 1980s they had helped to encourage government action for consumer protection. The attorneys general of 10 states joined forces and issued the *Green Report*. They included the following recommendations for guidelines:

1. Environmental claims should be as specific as possible, not general, vague, incomplete, or overly broad.
2. Environmental claims relating to disposability (e.g., degradable or recyclable) should not be made unless the advertised disposal option is currently available to consumers in the area in which the product is sold and the product complies with the requirements of the relevant waste disposal programs.
3. Environmental claims should be substantive.
4. Environmental claims should, of course, be supported by competent and reliable scientific evidence.[51]

In 1992, the Federal Trade Commission (FTC) published the *Guides for the Use of Environmental Marketing Claims* that "deals mainly with establishing norms for the use of environmental terminology and the manner in which the FTC will apply its existing deception policy and substantiation policy statements in the environmental context."[52] In brief, four areas for regulation included:

- Qualifications and disclosures: Disclosures should be sufficiently understandable to prevent deception.
- Distinction between benefits of product, package, and service: A claim should make clear whether the environmental attribute or benefit being asserted refers to the product, the product's packaging, a service, or to a portion or component of the product, package, or service.
- Overstatement of environmental attribute: A claim should not overstate the environmental attribute or benefit.
- Comparative claims: Environmental marketing claims that include a comparative statement should be presented so the basis for the comparison is sufficiently clear to avoid consumer deception.[53]

This regulatory action proved insufficient, so in 1996, the FTC announced an improved version of the guidelines. The agency included guidance "on the use of environmental seal-of-approval logos and the chasing-arrows symbol, as well as for such marketing claims as 'environmentally preferable,' 'non-toxic' and 'chlorine free.'"[54]

Federal guidelines and their enforcement still leave a lot of room for unscrupulous marketers to maneuver. Some companies continue to call for more concrete and definitive regulations and stricter enforcement. For example, Dr. Bronner's Magic Soaps, a 60-year-old product, is certified organic by the USDA's National Organic Program.[55] Company owners, descendants of the original Dr. Bronner, have accused other soap manufacturers of false advertising for using "organic" on their labels when their products are less than 100 percent organic.[56]

Some companies choose to take a proactive approach to avoiding greenwashing. When Clorox went to package its sustainable household cleaner, Green Works, it chose to list the ingredients on the label "even though there was no regulatory requirement to do so. The marketers' biggest fear was being labeled as 'greenwashers.'"[57] Concerns about greenwashing are not limited to product manufacturers. Retailers and channel members close to the customer end of the value chain need to make sure supplier claims are accurate. For example, the FTC accused Kmart of violations for advertising biodegradable American Fare private-label paper products, and the retailer was forced to remove the claims from the products.[58]

CRITICAL THINKING ACTIVITY

Developing an SMC Strategy

In developing an SMC strategy, a good place to start is with a clear understanding of customers' values and perspectives with respect to sustainability. Choose a product or service you know well. If you were the chief marketing officer for the firm, describe what you might learn about your customers' understanding with these guiding questions:

- How knowledgeable are your consumers on the environmental issues that affect your industry, company, and products?
- What types of messages do you need to get to consumers about the issues to improve your positioning in the long term?
- What do consumers need to know in order to use, recycle, and safely dispose of your products and packaging?
- What opportunities exist to develop environmental education programs or curricula?
- What types of programs can you sponsor to reach children with your message? Community projects? Environmental clubs? Children's media?
- What opportunities exist to enlist your employees' support in getting your message out?
- What are the most important environmental issues facing your key retailers in their trading areas?
- What types of education and training do buyers and sales personnel require about environmental issues for your brand/category?

Chapter Summary

The overall purpose of SMC is to help an organization achieve its marketing and sustainability objectives, which can be expressed in terms of triple-bottom-line gains or as achieving economic success while building both natural and human capital. As discussed in previous chapters, sustainable marketing requires the collaboration of a wide variety of stakeholders. SMC is the mechanism that allows them to collaborate, despite having different or even conflicting interests and ideologies.

In this chapter, we've described SMC as integrated marketing communication done with integrity, accountability,

transparency, and credibility. We've shown how SMC leverages resources by engaging and mobilizing communities.

These elements are woven into messages aimed at educating the target market, and demonstrating value congruence between consumers and sustainable brands. Marketers need to emphasize both the core product features and benefits alongside the sustainability features benefits. Above all, marketers need to guard against greenwashing, astroturfing, and other deceptive communication. Government regulations and media watchdog groups provide guidelines for SMC tactics.

Review of Chapter Objectives

In this chapter, you learned about:

- The nature of sustainable marketing communication
- The keys to success in sustainable marketing communication

- The barriers to success in sustainable marketing communication
- Cardinal sins of sustainable marketing communication: greenwashing, astroturfing, and other green lies

Key Concepts

Sustainable Marketing Communication (SMC)   185
Integrated Marketing Communication (IMC)   186

External Marketing Communication   186
Internal Marketing Communication   186
Integrity   186
Leverage   186

Community of Purpose   188
Stakeholder Dialogue   190
Puffery   190
Spin   190
Value Congruence   192

Fun Theory   193
Secondary Benefit   194
Primary (or Core) Benefits   194
Greenwashing   195
Astroturfing   196

Endnotes

1. Macalister, Terry (2007), "Big Oil Lets Sun Set on Renewables," *Guardian*, December 11, http://www.guardian.co.uk/business/2007/dec/11/oil.bp, accessed April 5, 2010.

2. Alter, Lloyd (2007), "Greenwash Watch: BP Stands for Beyond the Pale," *TreeHugger*, Dec. 28, http://www.treehugger.com/files/2007/12/greenwash_watch_12.php, accessed January 20, 2010.

3. http://webecoist.com/2009/03/22/greenwash-worlds-worst-greenwashers/, accessed January 20, 2010.

4. A.C. Nielsen (2007), *Trust in Advertising: A Global Nielsen Consumer Report*, http://asiapacific.acnielsen.com/site/documents/TrustinAdvertisingOct07.pdf, accessed January 20, 2010.

5. Sweney, Mark (2009), "Advertisers Launch Body to Restore Public Trust," *Guardian*, October 19, http://www.guardian.co.uk/media/2009/oct/19/advertisers-launch-body-public-trust, accessed April 3, 2010.

6. Fuller, Donald, A. (1999), *Sustainable Marketing: Managerial-Ecological Issues,* Thousand Oaks, CA: Sage (p. 225).

7. Armstrong, Gary and Philip Kotler (2009), *Marketing: An Introduction,* Upper Saddle River, NJ: Pearson Prentice Hall.

8. Lukovitz, Karlene (2009), "Naked Juice Launches Viral Eco Campaign," *Marketing Daily*, September 14, https://www.mediapost.com/publications/index.cfm?fa=articles.showarticle&art_aid=113460, accessed January 16, 2010.

9. McAlexander, James H., John W. Schouten, and Harold J. Koenig (2002), "Building Brand Community," *Journal of Marketing*, 66 (January): 38–54.

10. Muñiz, Albert M., Jr. and Thomas C. O'Guinn (2001), "Brand Community," *Journal of Consumer Research*, 27 (March): 412–432.

11. http://www.harley-davidson.com/wcm/Content/Pages/MDA/Muscular_Dystrophy_Association.jsp?locale=en_US&bmLocale=en_US, accessed January 6, 2010.

12. Schouten, John W. and Diane M. Martin (2010), "Communities of Purpose," A working paper for *Changing Consumer Roles—An Anthology*, ed. Karin M. Ekström and Kay Glans, Routledge, forthcoming.

13. Hawken, Paul (2007), Blessed Unrest: How the Largest Movement in the World Came into Being and Why No One Saw It Coming, New York: Viking (p. 4).

14. Thompson, Craig J. and Maura Troester (2002), "Consumer Value Systems in the Age of Postmodern Fragmentation: The Case of the Natural Health Microculture," *Journal of Consumer Research*, 28 (4, March): 550–571.

15. LOHAS (2009), http://www.lohas.com/about.html, accessed January 17, 2010.

16. Thompson, Craig J. and Gokcen Coskuner-Balli (2007), "Countervailing Market Responses to Corporate Co-optation and the Ideological Recruitment of Consumption Communities," *Journal of Consumer Research*, 34 (2, August): 135–152.

17. Local Harvest (2009), http://www.localharvest.org/csa/, accessed January 17, 2010.

18. Carrotmob, http://carrotmob.org/about/, accessed January 17, 2010.

19. McAlexander, James H., John W. Schouten, and Harold J. Koenig (2002), "Building Brand Community," *Journal of Marketing*, 66 (January), 38–54.

20. Belz, Frank-Martin and Ken Peattie (2009) *Sustainability Marketing: A Global Perspective,* Chichester, UK: Wiley (p. 84). "What Assures Consumers on Climate Change?" (2007), AccountAbility and Consumers International.

21. Werbach, Adam (2009), *Strategy for Sustainability: A Business Manifesto,* Boston, MA: Harvard Business Press (p. 103).

22. Hart, Stuart. L. (1995), "A Natural-Resource-Based View of the Firm," *Academy of Management Review,* 20 (4), 986–1015.

23. http://www.openfordiscussion.iupload-stage.com/default.asp?item=2365328, accessed January 17, 2010. Also see http://www.slate.com/id/2221246/pagenum/all/, accessed March 8, 2010.

24. McDonagh Pierre (1998), "Towards a Theory of Sustainable Communication in Risk Society: Relating issues of sustainability to marketing Communications," *Journal of Marketing Management,* 14: 591–622 (p. 23).

25. Fuller, Donald, A. (1999), *Sustainable Marketing: Managerial-Ecological Issues,* Thousand Oaks, CA: Sage (p. 242).

26. Epstein, Marc J. (2008), Making Sustainability Work: Best Practices in Managing and Measuring Corporate Social, Environmental, and Economic Impacts, San Francisco, CA: Berrett-Koehler Publishers (p. 236).

27. Bounds, Gwendolyn (2009), "As Eco-Seals Proliferate, So Do Doubts," *Wall Street Journal*, April 2, http://online.wsj.com/article/SB123862823846680371.html, accessed January 17, 2010.

28. Ottman, Jacquelyn A. (1998), *Green Marketing: Opportunity for Innovation,* New York: J. Ottman Consulting Inc. (p. 115).

29. Ginsberg, Jill Meredith and Paul N. Bloom (2004), Choosing the Right Green Marketing Strategy, *MIT Sloan Management Review*, 46 (1-Fall): 82.

30. http://www.thefuntheory.com/, accessed January 18, 2010.

31. http://www.thefuntheory.com/fun-theory-award, accessed January 18, 2010.

32. Stoiber, Marc (2005), "Making Sustainability Sexy, from an Ad Man's Point of View," *Grist*, November 30, http://www.grist.org/article/stoiber/, accessed January 18, 2010.

33. Hampton, Vince (2009), HAPPY NUDE YEAR! UGA students strip for greener goals, *Red and Black*, January 22, http://www.redandblack.com/2009/01/22/happy-nude-year-uga-students-strip-for-greener-goals/, accessed January 18, 2010.

34. Strong, E.K. (1925). Theories of Selling. *Journal of Applied Psychology* 9: 75–86.Heinz M. Goldman, *How to Win Customers*, Pan Books, London, 1958.

35. http://www.annies.com/products, accessed March 11, 2010.

36. http://www.fundinguniverse.com/company-histories/Annies-Homegrown-Inc-Company-History.html, accessed March 11, 2010.

37. http://www.annies.com/20years, accessed March 11, 2010.

38. http://www.fundinguniverse.com/company-histories/Annies-Homegrown-Inc-Company-History.html, accessed March 11, 2010.

39. http://www.globalreporting.org/AboutGRI/WhatIsGRI/, accessed January 19, 2010.

40. http://www.bmwgroup.com/publikationen/e/2009/pdf/BMW_Sustainability_Broschuere_2009_en.pdf, accessed January 18, 2010.

41. Fuller, Donald, A. (1999), *Sustainable Marketing: Managerial-Ecological Issues,* Thousand Oaks, CA: Sage (p. 226).

42. Ottman, Jacquelyn A. (1998), *Green Marketing: Opportunity for Innovation,* New York: J. Ottman Consulting Inc. (p.129).

43. http://sinsofgreenwashing.org/findings/the-seven-sins/, accessed January 20, 2010.

44. TerraChoice (2009), *Greenwashing Report 2009*, http://sinsofgreenwashing.org/findings/the-seven-sins/, accessed January 20, 2010.

45. http://www.netimpact.org/displaycommon.cfm?an=1&subarticlenbr=3006, accessed January 20, 2010.

46. http://www.jnj.com/wps/wcm/connect/c7933f004f5563df9e22be1bb31559c7/our-credo.pdf?MOD=AJPERES, accessed January 20, 2010.

47. http://www.triplepundit.com/2009/11/johnson-johnsons-sustainability-strategy-includes-avoiding-greenwashing/, accessed November 17, 2009.

48. http://greenrankings.newsweek.com/, accessed January 20, 2010.

49. http://www.adeex.co.uk/services/more-ads/rent-a-crowd, accessed January 20, 2010.

50. http://www.sourcewatch.org/index.php?title=Astroturf, accessed January 20, 2010. See also: McNeill, Brian (2009), "Forged Letters to Congressman Anger Local Groups," *Daily Progress* (Charlottesville, Virginia), July 31.

51. As reported in Fuller, Donald, A. (1999), *Sustainable Marketing: Managerial-Ecological Issues,* Thousand Oaks, CA: Sage (p. 228).

52. Fuller, Donald, A. (1999), *Sustainable Marketing: Managerial-Ecological Issues,* Thousand Oaks, CA: Sage (p. 228).

53. FTC Guidelines for use of environmental marketing claims http://www.ftc.gov/bcp/grnrule/guides980427.htm, accessed January 4, 2010

54. Ottman, Jacquelyn A. (1998), *Green Marketing: Opportunity for Innovation,* New York: J. Ottman Consulting Inc. (p. 215).

55. http://www.drbronner.com/, accessed January 10, 2010

56. Seireeni, Richard and Scott Fields (2009), *The Gort Cloud: The Invisible Force Powering Today's Most Visible Green Brands.* White River Junction, VT: Chelsea Green Publishing.

57. Werbach, Adam (2009), *Strategy for Sustainability: A Business Manifesto,* Boston, MA: Harvard Business Press (p. 50).

58. "It Isn't Easy Claiming To Be Green" Source: GoodandGreen.biz, accessed June 24, 2009.

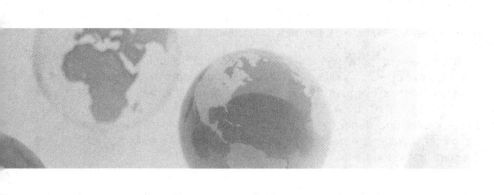

Sustainability in the Promotion Mix—Methods, Media, and Customer Relationships

INTRODUCTION: TOYOTA'S UNFORTUNATE SECRETS

In other sections of this book, Toyota has served as an example of doing things right with respect to sustainability, and Toyota's leadership in many areas of sustainable marketing is inspiring. In this chapter, however, Toyota provides a classic example of a hard lesson in sustainable marketing communication.

At the beginning of 2010, Toyota's practice of keeping secrets from its stakeholders caught up with the company and sent its reputation into a downward spiral. In February 2010, Toyota was deep into three different recalls for safety-related problems across a wide range of its vehicles.[1] Millions of cars and owners were affected. Several people had been killed and many others injured in broadly publicized accidents. Recalls aren't anything new in the auto industry, even for perceived quality leaders like Toyota and Honda, but what made this one different was the revelation that Toyota had been hiding the problems. As reported in *Business Week*: "Toyota Motor Corp. 'knowingly hid a dangerous defect' that caused its vehicles to accelerate unexpectedly, the U.S. said, for the first time accusing the world's largest automaker of breaking the law . . . . Toyota waited at least four months before telling U.S. regulators that gas pedals might stick . . . . Companies have five business days to report safety defects, the Transportation Department said."[2]

An Associated Press (AP) investigation learned that on January 16, 2010, five days before Toyota announced the recall for accelerator problems, an internal email from Irv Miller, VP for environment and public affairs, warned that, "'We are not protecting our customers by keeping this quiet. The time to hide on this one is over. We need to come clean.' . . . In a memo earlier that day, Katsuhiko Koganei, executive coordinator for corporate communications at Toyota Motor Sales USA, suggested the company should not discuss mechanical failures in accelerator pedals."[3] Other documents obtained by AP showed that the same accelerator problem had been found and reported by Toyota in Europe as early as the previous September.

Toyota's public relations disaster has had devastating consequences for the company. Relations with the U.S. government are strained, with the transportation secretary calling for an unprecedented maximum possible fine of $16.4 million.

Consumer trust in the company has eroded, with sales and stock prices falling. And matters continued to get worse for Toyota's reputation. It seems that once the public is tuned in to a company's troubles, the press finds other troubles to report. News released on April 11, 2010, by AP reveals that, "Toyota has routinely engaged in questionable, evasive and deceptive legal tactics when sued, frequently claiming it does not have information it is required to turn over and sometimes even ignoring court orders to produce key documents."[4]

THINK ABOUT IT

Preventive Public Relations

Traditionally, public relations, as a part of the promotion mix, has two main roles: first, to build positive relations with stakeholders and, second, to perform damage control when problems develop that can harm those relations. In an era of instant and widespread communication through blogs and social networks, it's getting harder for companies to keep secrets and harder to perform damage control either fast enough or well enough to head off serious reputational harm. How might Toyota have prevented some of the severe reputational harm from its safety recalls? Could Toyota have engaged stakeholders (e.g., customers and the U.S. government) differently to turn its quality and safety problems to its advantage? Might a practice of transparency in marketing communication have helped prevent the disaster in the first place?

This chapter digs deeper into the topic of sustainable marketing communication by examining its implementation in various elements of the promotion mix.

CHAPTER OBJECTIVES

In this chapter, you will learn about applications of sustainable marketing communication in:

- Advertising
- Public relations and publicity
- Sales promotions
- Personal selling and trade shows
- Customer relationship management and direct marketing

As discussed in Chapter 13, sustainable marketing communication (SMC) fosters truth and transparency in achieving both traditional marketing objectives as well as sustainability-related objectives. In SMC, messages should connect sustainable behaviors to deep, positive values, helping to educate and enrich consumers in their desire for well-being.[5] Marketing scholars emphasize that no single "green" strategy is right for every organization.[6] Marketers can draw from a variety of methods, including advertising, public relations, personal selling, direct marketing, sales promotions, and others, to communicate an organization's brand message and its marketing programs. The chosen combination of communication methods, generally referred to as the promotion mix, can use a wide variety of media such as the Internet, television, radio, movies, magazines, face-to-face meetings, newspapers, brochures, and even smart phones such as the iPhone and Blackberry. Messages and media may be targeted broadly or very narrowly, as in the case of customer relationship management.

ADVERTISING

Advertising is the paid placement of messages in a variety of media. We are an advertising culture. From television to transit, banner ads to bus stops, we find advertising everywhere. By some estimates, the average American consumer sees about 1,500 ads per day. Amid all the advertising clutter, green claims are proliferating rapidly. According to a study by TerraChoice, "Looking at 18,000 ads in recent issues of *Time*, *Fortune*, *National Geographic*, *Sports Illustrated* and *Vanity Fair*, TerraChoice found that more than 10 percent of all ads in 2008 made some sort of 'green' claim. That's up from about 3 percent in 2006."[7]

FIGURE 14-1 Eco Claim Arms Race

Advertising Appeals

The use of advertising in SMC demands careful thought about the likely response from an over-inundated and skeptical audience. One important choice involves the nature of the **advertising appeal**, or the central theme of an ad selected in order to reach a particular target audience. Advertising may use rational appeals or emotional appeals, or both, simultaneously, in its attempts to influence audiences' beliefs, attitudes, and behaviors with respect to sustainability.[8] **Rational appeals** tend to stress a product's overall value, especially in terms of functional product benefits, and this often requires a certain amount of consumer education. In the realm of sustainable marketing, rational appeals often focus on a product's lifetime costs to the customer. These include price, usage costs and, increasingly, the costs of disposition or disposal. Lifetime cost-benefit appeals have been used to overcome customer barriers to purchasing goods such as CFLs, energy saving appliances, and home energy conservation products. Other rational appeals focus on functional benefits such as convenience, durability, and reliability. Rational appeals are prevalent in business-to-business (B2B) marketing where costs and efficiencies are critical to financial, environmental, and social performance. Comparative advertising, using side-by-side product comparisons, is a common tool for emphasizing the functional benefits of more sustainable purchases. Testimonials from experts, celebrities, or customers can also help deliver rational appeals regarding overall value and sustainability.

Emotional appeals in advertising stress symbolic or experiential benefits of product use or ownership. They may attempt to link a brand's or a product's sustainability to positive feelings, such as hope, belonging, and self-esteem, or to the avoidance of negative feelings, such as guilt or fear. Self-esteem appeals associate more sustainable behaviors with positive personal attributes such as intelligence, attractiveness, hipness, goodness, or sophistication, or with positive role-performances, such as "good parent." Fear appeals tend to capitalize on social anxiety or concern for health or safety. Many environmental advertisements from NGOs play on fears about the future. Other NGOs appeal to combinations of empathy (e.g., for disadvantaged children) and guilt (perhaps stemming from a consciousness of one's own high levels of consumption). Zeitgeist appeals portray sustainability as the characteristic spirit of the times, implying that the advertised product, brand, or company is in sync with prevailing norms and values.[9]

Hybrid appeals combine both rational and emotional appeals.[10] Health and safety appeals are a case in point. For example, an ad for natural grass-fed beef may appeal to consumers' rationality by instructing them in the health benefits of the products; at the same time, depicting a happy, healthy family in the ad may appeal emotionally to the consumer's desire for self-esteem as a good parent or smart provider. Advertising appeals tend to work better when they relate directly to a consumer's personal situation and when they express environmental gains in terms that the average reader can understand. For example, rather than stating carbon emission reductions in terms such as metric tons, it's more meaningful to consumers to think in terms such as the equivalent number of passenger cars taken off the road, or the output of a coal-fired power plant.

Consider Portfolio 21, a successful investment firm that invests only in opportunities that fit its narrow criteria of sustainability. In looking for the right appeal to communicate its market position and differentiate itself from big Wall Street firms and other green firms, Portfolio 21 enlisted Seattle communication agency egg to help with branding. The firm wanted to highlight Portfolio 21's innovation and inspiration. For example, Portfolio 21's home page features a photograph of a young child and falling leaves with a green background. The headline reads: "What is your idea of a healthy return?" The rest of the page outlines the investment strategy that includes renewable energy and efficient production funding.[11] These elements together suggest that a "healthy return" is more than just financial success.

THINK ABOUT IT

Check out Portfolio 21's home page at http://www.portfolio21.com/. Which advertising appeals can you identify? Why would this investment company choose these appeals? If you were asked to choose different advertising appeals for this company, what would you choose? Why?

Storytelling

Perhaps the most powerful advertising campaigns are those that tell a compelling story that encourages retelling. People think in terms of narratives. In other words, we tend to organize our understandings of our world and ourselves, including facts, feelings, and motivations, in terms of stories. Advertising in SMC works especially well when it tells a story that consumers can appreciate and retell. **Consumer folklore**, made up of stories passed from consumer to consumer, carries a mantle of authority and authenticity that lends it credibility and staying power.[12] Within communities of purpose, such as brand communities or other groups with similar values and goals, a powerful brand story can become central to a social identity. Apple is one brand that has excelled because of a brand story that begins with Steve Jobs and ends with a message that includes reliability, user-friendliness, and visionary design. See how one blogger helps retell the Apple story for *Fast Company*: "Steve Jobs . . . in 1983, asked John Sculley of Pepsi-Cola to be his CEO by saying, 'Do you want to spend the rest of your life selling sugared water to children, or do you want a chance to change the world?' His intent was to always change the world. His brand story exemplifies powerful perseverance that connects with us because he is a true visionary, in a world where those individuals are scarce."[13]

For some consumer goods, packaging can be effective media for telling the sustainability story. For example, Ben & Jerry's proudly displays the Forest Stewardship Council logo on its pint containers, hoping to pique the interest of consumers who may then read the company's entire sustainability story on its website.[14] Similarly, Green Mountain Coffee Roasters uses its cups and bags for socially and environmentally responsible messages.[15]

Just like all promotional messages, the content of sustainability stories should vary depending on the audience. The more environmentally sophisticated the audience, the more in-depth and science-based the story can be.[16] Most consumers still have rather simplistic understandings of sustainability. Grail Research's "The Green Revolution" report shows that over 80 percent of consumers think of green products as those that are made of recyclable or reusable material, or include such packaging. Similarly, nearly 80 percent associate green products with energy efficiency or renewable power. Over 70 percent associate green products with natural or organic ingredients. However, only about 30 percent associated green products with sustainable use of water.[17]

While most consumers equate sustainability with green or environmental practices, firms can't afford to be focused too narrowly on environmental sustainability stories. The green marketing firm Conscientious Innovation (Ci) found that social issues including community engagement, fair trade, and buying local are also important to many consumers. According to its survey, "Seventy-two percent of North Americans say they want to know about the socially responsible behavior of the brands that they buy—yet the majority of the population answered 'I Don't Know' when asked to identify specific companies as socially responsible."[18] It would appear that there is a void to be filled by marketers with powerful stories to tell about social sustainability.

The Power of Pictures

We've all heard the arithmetic of the picture and a thousand words. One suggestion for telling a powerful story of sustainability is to "exploit the inherent visual power in environmentalism . . . ."[19] Pictures make problems, issues, and results come to life. They move concepts from the general and abstract to the specific and concrete. For example, ShoreBank, with operations in the Midwest, Washington, D.C., and the Northwest uses pictures of real clients on its website, accompanying specific stories of successful investments in social and environmental sustainability. Its commitment to supporting sustainable businesses is found in its motto: "Let's change the world."[20]

VIRTUAL FIELD TRIP

Explore the Visual

Go to the Web and seek out the best environmental ads (e.g., use Google Images or check out http://www.thedailygreen.com/environmental-news/latest/environmental-ads-44102408?src=nl&mag=tdg&list=dgr&kw=ist) and consider the impact of some of the pictures you find there. Which are the most powerful images in terms of emotional impact? Which ones are the most thought provoking? Which ones use humor? Which use beauty, or its opposite, or a stark contrast between the two?

Next, take a look at print ads for the laundry detergent, Method (e.g., use Google or check out http://www.flickr.com/photos/maayanpearl/4333508956/). How does the company use un-named competitors' packaging to visually make its claims of "different and therefore better"?

Finally, explore the storytelling power of video. Go to http://www.toyota.com/prius-hybrid/commercial.html and analyze the advertisement for Toyota Prius. What creative aspects of the ad make it especially entertaining? What is its underlying message about the product, people, and the planet? What lasting impression does it make regarding the Prius? Regarding Toyota?

Advertising Agencies: Partners in Sustainable Marketing Communication

Marketers looking to develop SMC don't have to go it alone. Advertising agencies and marketing communication consultancy firms specializing in sustainability are popping up around the world. These firms are committed to providing clients with promotion materials that avoid greenwashing. For instance, the global advertising holding firm Publicis Groupe, one of the largest advertising conglomerates in the world, recently released a policy "forbidding greenwashing among any of its companies (including Saatchi & Saatchi, Leo Burnett, Fallon, Starcom, MS&L, Digitas, and VivaKi)."[21] The Seattle advertising agency, egg, developed its position as an SMC provider because the employees "wanted to work only with sustainable brands."[22]

Agencies live and die by industry awards for outstanding advertising campaigns. Sustainable product and branding campaigns are starting to pick up some prestigious awards. For instant, the Martin Agency was recognized in 2008 with a prestigious Silver Jay Chiat Planning Award. Its "campaign highlighted Walmart's commitment to environmental responsibility and featured products such as organically grown coffee, compact fluorescent light bulbs, natural cleaning products and T-shirts made from recycled Coke bottles."[23]

Calling something "green" doesn't make it sustainable.

Agencies are not only producing materials that follow sustainable marketing ideals, but they are implementing sustainable processes in their organizations. "British Sky Broadcasting Group plc (BskyB), one of the leading satellite television providers in the world . . . negotiated discounts for employees to purchase hybrid [cars]" and gave employees a substantial subsidy to buy the cars. These and other initiatives made it possible for BskyB to stake its claim as the "first carbon-neutral media company" in 2006.[24] Long before YouTube, advertising agencies were using online video rather than tapes and DVD to deliver creative content. This practice allows agencies to get their creative assets delivered more quickly while reducing major amounts of toxic waste from the atmosphere and from landfills. Videotapes each take about a gallon of oil and toxic substances to manufacture. Quality control issues demanded they be discarded after only being used once.[25]

PUBLIC RELATIONS AND PUBLICITY

Public relations efforts attempt to leverage the credibility of media sources that are independent and relatively (compared to paid advertising) objective. Thus, the media play a vital role in spreading awareness about sustainability issues. Managing media exposure is the job of **public relations (PR),** referring to activities designed to generate commercially favorable **publicity,** or messages, in independent media.

Generally, with respect to sustainability, businesses use PR to build the credibility of their social and environmental activities and to try to offset any negative publicity they may have received. The use of PR has been especially visible in efforts to influence public attitudes around climate change. NGOs have been the main actors in attempting to publicize scientific reports that stress the urgency of action on greenhouse gases.[26] Companies such as ExxonMobil have supported the use of PR to cast doubt on those same scientific findings. A 2007 article in *Newsweek* reported, "A conservative think tank long funded by ExxonMobil offered scientists $10,000 to write articles undercutting the new report and the computer based climate models it is based on."[27] Meanwhile other companies support greenhouse gas reduction by announcing their own climate goals and achievements publicly. For example, when computer chip maker AMD announced that it had, "reduced greenhouse gas emissions by more than 50% between 2002 and 2007 exceeding its 40% goal," the story was picked up by Internet-based Sustainable Life Media.[28]

The objectives of public relations in SMC are similar to those for advertising and other methods. PR should contribute to the telling of a brand's sustainability story. To be perceived by stakeholders as authentic, PR and publicity should be rooted in meaningful actions by the

What's wrong with this PR picture? Hint: The globe is a tank at a California oil refinery.

company and its people. Occasionally, an organization's activities are noteworthy enough that they get reported in national or global news media. However, stories in local or industry-specific media also contribute significantly to the brand story. Activities that can stimulate good press include support for and involvement in community projects, research advances, and talks at industry conferences.

PR may be underutilized by some firms, especially if they believe that publicizing their sustainability efforts is likely to attract scrutiny and charges of greenwashing. In such cases, firms may engage in "**greenmuting**,"[29] meaning that they deliberately downplay their environmental and social initiatives.

PR professionals look for newsworthy examples of sustainability-related policies and practices to share with stakeholders, and they use press releases, feature articles, or even news conferences to attract the attention of reporting media.[30] Product innovation is one good source of sustainability news. For example, one such story in the airline industry was an innovation in airline design inspired by biomimicry. By imitating wing structures, called winglets, of bats and butterflies, Boeing made modification to the wings of its 737 airplane to reduce air resistance. "Thousands of Boeing 737s are now equipped with winglets. Every 737 with the winglets saves about 3 percent of its fuel use. Across aviation, this will save billions of gallons of fuel."[31] This innovation provided Boeing and its customers, including most major U.S. air carriers, the opportunity to describe the environmental benefits of the winglets to passengers in media such as in-flight magazines.[32] The move to paperless, or cell-phone, boarding passes also made airline news, especially for Continental, which was the first to try the technology in the United States.[33]

Another brand that makes liberal use of sustainability initiatives in PR is Silk Soymilk. For example, through its GreenCaps program, Silk donates 30 kilowatt-hours in carbon offsets for every UPC code customers enter at its website—enough to run a refrigerator for a couple of weeks. Those same customers are automatically entered in a contest to win a green home makeover. Other newsworthy Silk initiatives include offsetting its electricity use with wind power investments and tree plantings (over 20,000 acres per year); a "zero waste" program at company headquarters that includes major recycling and composting programs; and 92 percent employee participation in a local community Food Share program,[34] a food program for people living in poverty in Silk's hometown of Boulder, Colorado, that provided 6.6 million pounds of food in 2009.[35]

"CURTIS, I WANT YOU TO FIND A WAY TO BLAME ALL THIS ON EL NINO."

THINK ABOUT IT

Consider your role as a consumer. Where do you learn about news of your regular brands or products? Which of these firms seem to be in the news often? Does hearing about company news increase your brand loyalty? Which ones, in your opinion, do a good job of sharing company news with the public?

Sharing from the Top

PR professionals may be the ones who get the press interested in their firms, but often, the person most desirable to tell the story is the charismatic founder, the visionary whose innovations made the firm more sustainable. For example, Spencer Brown, founder of Earth Friendly Moving, talked about his innovative moving box rental company on MSN.com.[36] Brown tells the story of how he's created a business renting durable plastic boxes made from loads of plastic detergent jugs recovered from landfills.[37] An interesting, truthful story about detoxifying landfills while reducing the demand for cardboard boxes makes compelling news for MSN.com. Interface Carpet CEO Ray Anderson regularly makes speeches and documentaries extolling the environmental and business benefits of sustainable practices. Top managers can also be expected to make comments regarding special accolades, such as the American Marketing Association's Special Edison Award for Environmental Achievement, which has been "won by Fortune 1000 firms including 3M and Procter & Gamble as well as by a raft of up-and-coming firms with a deep-green orientation, such as Natural Cotton Colours, Patagonia, and Tom's of Maine."[38]

Mini Case Study

Positive publicity from an unlikely source

Ice cream makers Ben Cohen and Jerry Greenfield of Ben & Jerry's use the power of stories to differentiate their brand and develop relationships with consumers. The long-time friends made acting responsibly a core value of their company. In 1984, big business came after the little guys. Pillsbury, the million-dollar company behind Häagen-Dazs, felt threatened by the rapid growth of Ben & Jerry's. In an attempt to shut down the young upstarts, Pillsbury gave Ben & Jerry's distributors throughout Boston an ultimatum: "Sell Häagen-Dazs or sell Ben & Jerry's, but not both." Cohen and Greenfield resolved to fight back. Finding little hope in their legal options, the two decided to use PR. They launched the now famous "What's the doughboy afraid of?" campaign and began taking it as public as they could. From placing advertisements on the sides of buses to renting banner planes for flying around major sporting events, Cohen and Greenfield did whatever they could think of to gain support for their little business. They took out a classified ad in *Rolling Stone* magazine asking readers to "help two Vermont hippies fight the giant Pillsbury Corporation." Greenfield even took to being a one-man picket outside the headquarters of Pillsbury in Minneapolis, handing out pamphlets that read, "What's the doughboy afraid of?" Later that year, Cohen and Greenfield came up with the idea of putting a 1-800 number on every pint of Ben & Jerry's ice cream. "We started getting like a hundred calls a night," recalls Greenfield, "most of them between the hours of midnight and 3 a.m." Many callers even offered to form gangs of Doughboy busters. Public interest and media attention surrounding the issue began to grow, most of which portrayed Pillsbury in a negative light—an evil corporate giant trying to put two young guys out of business. Eventually, all the bad press led Pillsbury to renege on its ultimatum.[39]

Pillsbury eventually settled with Ben & Jerry's out of court.[40] That same year, Ben & Jerry's sales more than doubled from the year before.[41]

What aspects of the public fight with Pillsbury made it successful for Ben & Jerry's? What impact do you think the affair had on Ben & Jerry's brand? What impact did it have on the Häagen-Dazs brand? Prior to the media showdown, was Häagen-Dazs openly linked to its parent company Pillsbury? Why might Pillsbury have preferred to keep that connection out of the press?

PR may seek to publicize organizations' success stories or, as in the case of Ben & Jerry's, their difficulties. When tiny TerraCycle was sued by Scotts Miracle-Gro in 2007, the company created a special website, SuedByScotts.com. TerraCycle used its position as the upstart David to the Goliath of Scott's Miracle-Gro to garner more press.[42] The parties settled the suit when TerraCycle agreed to change its packaging and stop claiming its product's superiority to Miracle-Gro, but analysts agreed that all the media attention from the lawsuit was a real advantage for TerraCycle.[43]

Tapping into Celebrity

Sometimes it seems that, short of natural disasters, nothing interests the media like celebrity. Ben & Jerry's once again provides an excellent example. In 2007, the company announced a new ice cream flavor in honor of the famous comedian (and famously self-promoting patriot) Stephen Colbert. Stephen Colbert's Americone Dream, which Ben & Jerry's called "the sweet taste of liberty in your mouth," made news, not only on Comedy Central's *The Colbert Report* but also on legitimate news reports. Colbert is donating his share of profits to charity through the newly established Stephen Colbert Americone Dream Fund.[44] In another example, the popularity of the Toyota Prius hybrid got a major boost when news reported that large numbers of Hollywood celebrities, such as Leonardo DiCaprio, Cameron Diaz, and Will Farrell, had become vocal Prius drivers.[45]

Linking a well-known person to a brand works best when the values of both parties align. When Te Casan shoes wanted to develop a line of luxury vegan shoes, it tapped actress and vegan activist Natalie Portman.[46] In some cases, the celebrity is also truly the designer. Stella McCartney was already famous for being the daughter of former Beatles member Sir Paul McCartney. Her clothing line contains no fur or leather and she favors organic materials. Along with her ready-to-wear line, she also designs for athletic-wear powerhouse, adidas.[47]

Sustainability, Risk, and Investor Relations

B Corporation creates brand value for member companies by auditing and certifying their sustainability efforts. Investors take a deep interest in the vulnerabilities of companies in their stock portfolios. Traditional threats to stock gains have included business issues such as competitor innovation, international tariff changes, and government regulatory changes. Now investors are also paying attention to firms' relative sustainability. According to Richard Liroff of the Investor Environmental Health Network (IEHN), "A wave of shareholder activism has been growing in recent years, with investors increasingly filing resolutions proposing specific operating policies or requesting information about the financial risks companies face from environmental and social issues, such as climate change."[48]

As investors sense the shift in consumer preferences for more sustainable products and services, they want to protect their wealth from consumer backlash over social and environmental problems. For example, a 2008 report by IEHN "examined disclosures on supply chain

weaknesses before and after the 2007 toy recalls due to lead paint . . . [and] concluded that major industrial and other sectors affected by product toxicity risks are doing a poor job of informing shareholders of market risks they face due to toxic chemicals in their products."[49]

Professional financial planners and individual investors are also finding investing opportunities among sustainable firms. For example, Portfolio 21 carefully screens all companies in its investment portfolio for "companies designing ecologically superior products, using renewable energy, and developing efficient production methods."[50] Associations, such as the Advocacy & Policy Program, provide information on advocacy and policy issues affecting the socially and environmentally responsible investing industry.[51]

Investors aren't the only ones concerned about the risks associated with undisclosed use of toxic chemicals and supply chain weaknesses. Insurance companies are beginning to see social and environmental problems as risks that affect a firm's value. A 2009 U.S. Securities and Exchange Commission (SEC) decision made it easier for shareholders and insurance companies to "request climate change risk disclosure from public companies."[52]

Voluntary Reporting

Responding to the needs of investors, insurers, and the public, many companies now add voluntary sustainability reporting to their PR efforts. In 2009, the Social Investment Forum reported that, "66 S&P 100 companies produced a formal sustainability report with performance data in 2008, compared to 49 reports produced only one year earlier. And 55 companies made reference to the GRI (Global Reporting Initiative) in their sustainability reports, more than double the 24 that did so in 2004."[53]

The increase in voluntary reporting means a lot of corporations have to learn how and what to include in their annual reports. Many firms rely on the GRI (see Chapter 6) as a useful structure for reporting sustainability progress. For example, Bristol-Myers Squibb adopted GRI guidelines as the basis for its environmental reporting, which covers environmental policies and systems, relevant stakeholder relationships, reviews of product performance, and an overview of the company's sustainability encompassing everything from packaging guidelines to water use.[54]

Rules for avoiding greenwashing in advertising and packaging also apply to environmental policy statements. While it is helpful to include commitment to specific environmental policies, firms need to walk their talk. Researchers found that although firms across industry sectors commit to environmental policies, there is variation in the degree to which they actually implement those policies.[55]

SALES PROMOTIONS

A common barrier to the sales of more sustainable products is consumer doubt about product performance. The most effective way to remove such doubt is to get the customer to try the product. For this purpose, marketing managers regularly turn to **sales promotions**, defined as activities designed to stimulate sales in the short term. Sales promotions such as cents-off coupons, rebate offers, contests, and "buy-one, get-one" free deals regularly appear in newspapers, email inboxes, Internet banner ads, and product packaging. Any of these tactics, alone or in combination with other forms of promotion or advertising, may be useful to motivate consumers to try a more sustainable product or service. When IKEA first began marketing compact fluorescent light bulbs (CFLs) in its native Scandinavia, the company offered one free CFL to every household in Sweden.

Other in-store merchandising techniques can boost the effectiveness of sales promotions. For example, when Wal-Mart made it a company-wide goal to push CFLs, they used end-cap displays, favorable shelf space, sale prices, and customer information displays to persuade customers to try the new "squiggly" bulbs.

Many sustainability-related sales promotions occur only online, and are designed to drive customer traffic to company websites, where additional information about a firm's sustainability initiatives may be available. For example, Sony offers limited time offers through its "weekly deals" link on the company website,[56] and Seventh Generation offers coupons via its website.[57]

Anyone who has wandered the aisles of a Costco or similar warehouse store on a weekend understands the promotional value of providing free samples. **Sampling** is a particularly

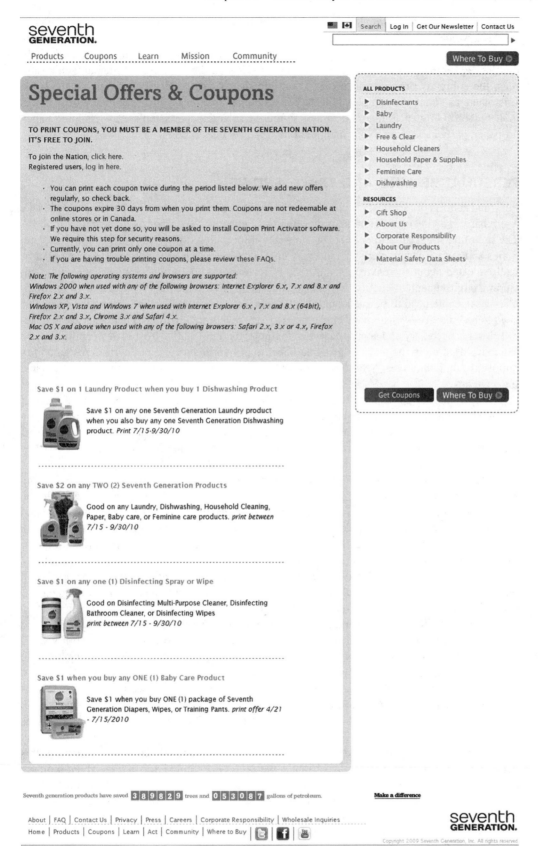

Home cleaning company Seventh Generation offers $1 and $2 coupons via its website: http://www.seventhgeneration.com/coupons.

effective way to encourage customers to try a new or unfamiliar product, such as many "green" products typically are. A good sample is one that provokes an immediate purchase or provides an experience that sticks in the customer's mind. For example, YOLO sells house paint made without the environmental toxins present in most paints. Rather then supplying little paint chip samples, the company provides poster-sized sample sheets with repositioning tape on the back. Customers can hang the sample up in the room and get a better idea of how the color works in their home. YOLO encourages customers to reuse the large paper samples "as wrapping paper, art paper, party hats . . . use your imagination."[58]

PERSONAL SELLING AND TRADE SHOWS

Personal selling, or face-to-face communication with the goal of persuading a customer to make a purchase, is a vital element of the promotion mix, and as such, it also has roles to play in SMC. The use of personal sales to deliver sustainability information differs according to product categories and industry characteristics. In every case, however, "it is crucial that sales personnel be well educated about the environmental factors surrounding the products they represent,"[59] including environmental benefits, regulatory issues, and environmental certification. To be credible, sales people need to be sufficiently well trained to answer customers' questions. They also need to be sensitive to customers' current knowledge levels, and willing to help educate at whatever level is necessary and appropriate. For example, the sales staff at Toyota dealerships receive extensive training in the technologies and benefits of hybrid cars and in Toyota's sustainability philosophy and initiatives.[60] Sustainable selling, like all aspects of SMC, is founded on truth and transparency.

Personal selling is especially important in B2B marketing, and this holds true in the area of sustainability as well. Many manufacturers use B2B sales to push sustainability information down the channels to customers at the retail interface. For example, Seventh Generation trains its brokers to share good stories about the product, which often come from customers, when they are working with retailers that carry the products.[61]

Travel industry professionals are finding that sustainability drives purchases among many of their most loyal users: older adults traveling in groups. Tour operators provide the bulk of these opportunities and have developed personal selling tactics to reach the estimated 55 million Americans who seek socially and environmentally responsible tourism. Robin Tauck of Tauck Tours promotes low-impact travel (combining bicycling, walking, and motor coach travel), voluntourism (which combines travel with volunteer service), authentic cultural experiences (which emphasize experiences with local people, locally grown foods, and local products), ecotourism, and suppliers that partner with significant conservation organizations and nonprofits. As for the personal selling of such tourism products, Tauck recommends a combination of salesperson awareness, education, personal familiarization with locations and providers, and involvement with conferences and other efforts to promote sustainability within the travel industry.[62] In other words, in selling high-end sustainability products, the key is to develop expertise and relationships.

Trade shows are an important setting for personal sales and PR, especially in industries that rely heavily on B2B sales and marketing, such as consumer electronics, information technologies, gift items, and building supplies. Trade shows also serve particular consumer interests such as motor sports, collectibles, or model trains. Environmentally focused businesses have found that trade shows serving business and consumer interest in sustainability can provide access to this demographically diverse market. For example, the 2009 Greenbuild Expo, a large green-building conference, included nearly 1,100 exhibitors. According to GreenBiz, "The expo floor at Greenbuild has become populated with billion-dollar companies . . . [including] large construction companies (DPR, Turner), building automation and controls manufacturers (Honeywell, Johnson Controls), office furniture makers (Herman Miller, Steelcase), architecture firms (Gensler, HOK), flooring manufacturers (Interface, Shaw), and others."[63] Similarly, the Go Green Expo in New York City allowed corporate buyers and trade professionals to visit the show on Friday (before it opened to the general public) in an effort to "encourage organizations to embrace the large-scale use of earth-friendly products, services and ideas."[64] 3,000 exhibitors and 52,000 visitors participated in the 2010 Natural Products Expo in Anaheim, California. Show promoters promised to save 487 full-grown trees by producing a Show Directory Map in place of a Buyers'

The Go Green Expo trade show features eco-friendly products.

Guide and encouraging show goers to "use the Online Buyers' Guide and Show Directory to create your own personal Expo Plan." Show badges were distributed onsite, rather than mailed ahead of time "saving 4 metric tons of CO_2 emissions" and mailing costs.[65] Sustainability-oriented trade shows have expanded from B2B to include B2C (business-to-consumer). Weekend attendance at the New York City Go Green Expo was geared for consumers. Co-op America also runs Green Festivals in San Francisco, Chicago, Seattle, and Washington, D.C.[66]

CUSTOMER RELATIONSHIP MANAGEMENT AND DIRECT MARKETING

Marketers know that the era of "telling customers what to buy" is well in the past. The marketplace has moved from transaction-based marketing to relationship marketing. The firm and, more importantly, the brand must be an authentic point of contact for a sustainable relationship with customers. A strong relationship with consumers is built on transparency and trust. For example, Seventh Generation, the household cleaning manufacturer, notes that including all the ingredients on its packaging provides transparency that gives its customers a sense of comfort. Marketers at the ad agency imc2 note that, "[loyal] consumers are more likely to forgive mistakes and stick with a brand even in tough times . . . . Brands committed to sustainable relationships tend to nurture these connections and focus on continually strengthening them."[67]

Customer Relationship Management

Customer relationship management (CRM) is generally defined as a strategy that integrates information technology with other marketing efforts in order to identify, target, attract, and retain the best mix of customers. Common elements of CRM systems include customer databases, which profile customers in great detail, and **loyalty programs** designed to reward customer support and motivate continued patronage. One example of CRM occurs at retail checkout counters. Stores can use scanner data to record and analyze customer purchases, including purchases associated with social or environmental sustainability. Based on the analysis, a store can provide customers with highly targeted coupons (e.g., for other green products) printed right at the register. Someone who routinely purchases organic produce may then receive coupons for earth-friendly cleaning supplies or nontoxic personal hygiene items.

Despite CRM's emphasis on technology, the main contributions of attention to customer relationships lie in open and regular communication. In the words of author Adam Werbach, without open channels of communication, "How do you know when your product is making people sick? How do you know if your packaging is ruined when the customer takes it home? How do you know when your customer has an idea for you to improve?"[68] Customer research can provide certain kinds of information, but it's limited to the topics of research and the times when research is fielded.

Loyalty programs, or rewards programs, conventionally provide economic rewards to the consumer, such as frequent flyer miles, cash back, or opportunities for premium services. In efforts to achieve SMC, they can also link customer loyalty to noneconomic rewards, particularly to social or environmental initiatives. The EcoUnit concept is one example of a program that rewards more sustainable consumption.[69] It's the result of collaboration between Organic Valley, which is America's largest cooperative of organic farmers, and Ray's Food Place, a family-owned supermarket chain in Southern Oregon and Northern California. When customers buy Organic Valley products, they get EcoUnit credits at the checkout register. They can later use the credits on the EcoUnit website to support their choice of local environmental initiatives such as the restoration of salmon habitat and watersheds on local rivers.[70]

Direct Marketing

The emphasis of CRM on direct and individual communication with customers favors **direct marketing**, in which the marketing message is delivered straight to customers through individually accessed media such as phone, mail, or the Internet. Telemarketing and direct mail are perceived as annoyances to most consumers, and between advancing technology and legislation, these forms of direct marketing seem headed for extinction in the consumer market. Nevertheless, the telephone still serves as an important tool, particularly in B2B marketing where efficiency is valued and telephone messages tend to be highly targeted and even welcomed. For purposes of increasing sustainability, the phone is especially green in terms of materials use and transportation costs for salespersons. For example, the company Eco1 employs telemarketers "with a passion for eco marketing" who were "born with recycled spoons in their mouths" to achieve three strategic objectives: (1) appointment making, or prearranging face-to-face or online sales meetings; (2) telesales, including persuasive selling or order-taking directly over the telephone; and (3) market research, which helps clients focus their direct marketing efforts.[71]

Direct mail marketing has been praised within the direct mail industry for its focus on precision[72] and reviled outside the industry as a junk mail generator. As authors Frank-Martin Belz and Ken Peattie point out, "The concept of 'junk mail' has made direct mail a target for environmental activist campaigns and also for grumbling by many householders. Ironically, it is also one of the major communication tools employed by environmental organizations in their efforts to raise funds for their campaigns."[73] Three keys to increasing the sustainability (or minimizing the environmental damage and consumer annoyance) of direct mail are to: (1) make sure that customer targeting is dead on and that nonresponsive customers are dropped from the program, (2) use eco-friendly printing techniques and paper products, and (3) offset carbon emissions from printing and transportation through investments in renewable power and reforestation.

The growing reality in direct marketing is its migration to electronic media, which is the focus of Chapter 15.

CRITICAL THINKING ACTIVITY

TNSF and the Nuts and Bolts of SMC

Compare and contrast the different methods and media of the promotion mix in terms of the four conditions of a sustainable society as outlined in The Natural Step Framework. Which methods and media are the most sustainable? Are any of them inherently unsustainable (meaning that they can't exist without violating system conditions)? If the most sustainable method of communication is storytelling, then what promotion techniques can be most effective in telling and encouraging the retelling of the sustainability story?

Chapter Summary

Making the most of SMC means applying sustainability principles to each part of the marketing mix. The single-most sustainable kind of communication is storytelling. An authentic, memorable, and relevant brand story is likely to be told and retold among consumers, even to the point of creating enduring consumer folklore. Any of the various elements of the promotion mix can enhance the telling of the brand story. The most familiar element, advertising, requires marketers to consider the central theme or appeal that will best reach a particular target audience. Both rational and emotional appeals can be effective, depending on the needs of the target audience and the nature of the product being advertised. Rational appeals can educate consumers about sustainability advantages of a brand; whereas emotional appeals provide a hook that connects the brand to basic psychological needs. Advertising can also bring powerful visual images to the story. Many advertising agencies are developing sustainability into their creative output and organizational practices. A challenge for advertising based on sustainability claims is that, in an environment tainted by greenwashing, consumers often don't trust it.

PR can also provide important support for the brand story. Marketers use it to generate positive publicity in media that consumers tend to trust, and they use it to counter negative publicity that may result from poor product performance or bad business behavior. PR can be used proactively to prevent consumer backlash; the key is to encourage transparency and integrity in all of an organization's decisions and communication, knowing that in the Internet age it is becoming impossible to keep secrets. By voluntarily reporting successes, challenges, and ongoing sustainability efforts, firms increase the level of trust with their stakeholders. Sales promotions are particularly valuable in SMC, especially when customers need an extra incentive to try products, such as more sustainable alternatives, that are unfamiliar to them. Personal selling and trade shows have always been vital to marketing in certain industries, and "green" business is no exception. The success of personal selling relies on salespeople who are well informed and able to communicate both expertise and authenticity. CRM uses very narrow targeting to reach, interact with, reward, and retain an organization's best customers. CRM relies largely on databases to identify specific customer segments, and on direct marketing to communicate with them. One of the promising aspects of CRM is the ability to identify "green" consumers of various shades by their purchase behaviors and to introduce them to new "green" alternatives that are likely to appeal to them.

Review of Chapter Objectives

In this chapter you learned about applications of SMC in various elements of the promotion mix, including:

- Advertising
- Public relations and publicity
- Sales promotions
- Personal selling and trade shows
- Customer relationship management and direct marketing

Key Concepts

Advertising 202	Hybrid Appeals 204	Greenmuting 207	Customer Relationship
Advertising	Consumer	Sampling 210	Management (CRM) 213
Appeal 203	Folklore 204	Sales Promotions 210	Loyalty Programs 213
Rational Appeals 203	Public Relations 206	Personal Selling 212	Direct Marketing 214
Emotional Appeals 203	Publicity 206	Trade Shows 212	

Endnotes

1. Woodyard, Chris (2010), "Toyota PR Blitz Plays Catch-Up After Storm of Problems," *USA Today*, February 10, http://www.usatoday.com/money/autos/2010-02-10-toyotaad10_ST_N.htm, accessed April 11, 2010.
2. Greiling, Angela Keane and Alan Ohnsman (2010), "Toyota Hid Pedal Defect, Violating Law, U.S. Says," *Business Week*, April 6, http://www.businessweek.com/news/2010-04-06/toyota-hid-pedal-defect-in-violation-of-u-s-law-lahood-says.html, accessed April 11, 2010.
3. Margasak, Larry and Ken Thomas (2010), "Irving Miller: Toyota Exec's Email Told Colleagues 'We Need To Come Clean' About Recall," Associated Press, April 7, http://www.huffingtonpost.com/2010/04/08/irving-miller-toyota-exec_n_529825.html, accessed April 11, 2010.
4. Anderson, Curt and Danny Robbins (2010), "AP IMPACT: In Toyota Cases, Evasion Becomes Tactic," Associated Press, April 11, http://www.google.com/hostednews/ap/article/ALeqM5i-N2d0exucAO44cR2JAz_bjytnjAD9F11E900, accessed April 11, 2010.
5. Crane, Andrew (2000), *Marketing, Morality and the Natural Environment,* London, UK: Routledge. And Grant, John (2007), *The Green Marketing Manifesto,* West Sussex, UK: John Wiley & Sons Ltd.

6. Ginsberg, Jill Meredith and Bloom, Paul N. (2004), "Choosing the Right Green Marketing Strategy," *MIT Sloan Management Review*, 46 (1-Fall): 79.

7. Environmental Leader (2009), Green Ads on the Rise, May 1, http://www.environmentalleader.com/2009/05/01/green-ads-on-the-rise/, accessed January 22, 2010.

8. Schuhwerk, Melody E. and Roxanne Lefkokk-Hagius (1995), "Green or Non-Green? Does Type of Appeal Matter When Advertising a Green Product?" *Journal of Advertising,* 24 (2, Summer): 45–54.

9. Banerjee, Subhabrata, Charles S. Gulas and Easwar Iyer (1995), "Shades of Green: A Multidimensional Analysis of Environmental Advertising," *Journal of Advertising*, 24 (2, Summer): 21–31.

10. Belz, Frank-Martin and Ken Peattie (2009), *Sustainability Marketing: A Global Perspective,* Chichester, UK: Wiley (p. 187). And Rose, C., Dade, P. and Scott, J. (2007), "Research into Motivating Prospectors, Settlers, and Pioneers to Change Behaviours that Affect Climate Emissions," London, UK: Campaign Strategy.

11. Portfolio 21, http://www.portfolio21.com/, accessed January 15, 2010.

12. Schouten, John W. and James H. McAlexander (1995), "Subcultures of Consumption: An Ethnography of the New Bikers," *Journal of Consumer Research* (June): 43–61. And Holt, Douglas B. (2004), *How Brands Become Icons: The Principles of Cultural Branding*, Cambridge, MA: Harvard University Press.

13. Eustacia K. (2008), "The Best Brand Stories Win," *Fast Company*, September 28, http://www.fastcompany.com/blog/eustacia-k/story-behind-brand-powerful, accessed April 12, 2010.

14. Seireeni, Richard with Scott Fields (2009), *The Gort Cloud: The Invisible Force Powering Today's Most Visible Green Brands*, White River Junction, VT: Chelsea Green Publishing.

15. Seireeni, Richard with Scott Fields (2009), *The Gort Cloud: The Invisible Force Powering Today's Most Visible Green Brands*, White River Junction, VT: Chelsea Green Publishing.

16. Seireeni, Richard and Scott Fields (2009), *The Gort Cloud: The Invisible Force Powering Today's Most Visible Green Brands*, White River Junction, VT: Chelsea Green Publishing.

17. Environmental Leader (2009), "'Natural,' 'Recyclable,' 'Renewable' Terms Resonate Most with Consumers," October 1, http://grailresearch.com/About_Us/FeaturedResearch.aspx?aid=90, reported in http://www.environmentalleader.com/2009/10/01/natural-recyclable-renewable-terms-resonate-most-with-consumers/, accessed January 6, 2010

18. Sustainable Life Media (2008), "Why Your Green-Marketing Message May Be Missing the Mark," May 1, http://www.sustainablelifemedia.com/content/story/brands/why_your_green_marketing_message_may_be_missing_the_mark, accessed May 9, 2008

19. Ottman, Jacquelyn A. (1998), *Green Marketing: Opportunity for Innovation,* New York: J. Ottman Consulting Inc. (p. 119).

20. Shore Bank, http://www.shorebankcorp.com/bins/site/templates/splash.asp, accessed January 15, 2010.

21. Strategy for Sustainability, http://www.strategyforsustainability.com/blog/, accessed December 12, 2009.

22. egg, http://www.eggusa.net/

23. The Martin Agency, http://martinagency.com/index.php?/site/single_entry_news/walmart_sustainability_campaign_earns_silver_in_jay_chiat_planning_awards/, accessed March 12, 2010.

24. Werbach, Adam (2009), *Strategy for Sustainability: A Business Manifesto,* Boston, MA: Harvard Business Press (p. 137).

25. Stewart, Brad (2010), "Green: Video," *MediaPost*, January 27, http://www.mediapost.com/publications/?fa=Articles.showArticle&art_aid=121388, accessed January 29, 2010.

26. "ENN: Environmental News Network—Know Your Environment" From: R. K. Pachauri, Science and Development Network, More from this Affiliate. Published June 24, 2009, 10:40 AM, accessed January 15, 2010.

27. Begley, Sharon (2007), "The Truth about Denial," *Newsweek*, August 13, http://msl1.mit.edu/furdlog/docs/2007-08-13_newsweek_global_warming_denyers.pdf, accessed January 21, 2010.

28. Sustainable Life Media (2007), "AMD Sets Ambitious Climate Change Goals," August 2, http://www.sustainablelifemedia.com/content/story/climate/08022007_2, accessed April 11, 2010.

29. Makower, Joel, and Cara Pike (2009), Strategies for the Green Economy: Opportunities and Challenges in the New World of Business, Hightstown, NJ: McGraw-Hill.

30. PR-Insider.com, http://www.pr-inside.com/, accessed November 28, 2009.

31. Werbach, Adam (2009), *Strategy for Sustainability: A Business Manifesto,* Boston, MA: Harvard Business Press (p. 19).

32. United Hemispheres, http://www.hemispheresmagazine.com/2010/04/01/fuel-intentions/, accessed April 12, 2010.

33. Hensel, Jr., Bill (2007), *Houston Chronicle,* "Cell Phone Boarding Passes Going Into Use Here First," December 12, http://www.chron.com/disp/story.mpl/front/5349969.html, accessed January 24, 2010.

34. "The Great Lakes Zephyr – Wind Energy & Hydrogen Journal," http://gl-zephyr.blogspot.com/2008_05_01_archive.html, accessed January 15, 2010.

35. Boulder and Broomfield Counties Food Bank, http://www.communityfoodshare.org/, accessed March 12, 2010

36. Seireeni, Richard with Scott Fields (2009), *The Gort Cloud: The Invisible Force Powering Today's Most Visible Green Brands.* White River Junction, VT: Chelsea Green Publishing.

37. Seireeni, Richard and Scott Fields (2009), *The Gort Cloud: The Invisible Force Powering Today's Most Visible Green Brands.* White River Junction, VT: Chelsea Green Publishing.

38. Ottman, Jacquelyn A. (1998), *Green Marketing: Opportunity for Innovation,* New York: J. Ottman Consulting Inc. (p. 13).

39. Carmichael, Evan, "Lesson #5: Don't Be Afraid to Go After the Big Guys," http://www.evancarmichael.com/Famous-Entrepreneurs/945/Lesson-5-Dont-Be-Afraid-to-Go-After-the-Big-Guys.html, accessed January 15, 2010

40. Alexander, Charles P. (2005), "A Stock Scoop for Ice Cream," April 18, http://www.time.com/time/magazine/article/0,9171,1050535,00.html, accessed January 15, 2010

41. Carmichael, Evan, "Lesson #5: Don't Be Afraid to Go After the Big Guys," http://www.evancarmichael.com/Famous-Entrepreneurs/945/Lesson-5-Dont-Be-Afraid-to-Go-After-the-Big-Guys.html, accessed January 15, 2010

42. Seireeni, Richard with Scott Fields (2009), *The Gort Cloud: The Invisible Force Powering Today's Most Visible Green Brands*, White River Junction, VT: Chelsea Green Publishing.

43. Loten, Angus (2007), *Inc.*, "After a Good Fight, David Forced to Settle with Goliath," September 24, http://www.inc.com/news/articles/200709/terracycle.html, accessed January 15, 2010.

44. MSNBC, http://www.msnbc.msn.com/id/17152896/, accessed January 15, 2010

45. Hybrid Cars (2006), "Celebrity Hybrid Drivers," March 24, http://www.hybridcars.com/hybrid-drivers/celebrities.html, accessed January 24, 2010.

46. Doan, Abigail (2008), "Inhabitat Natalie Portman Te Casan Vegan Shoes for Spring," April 13, http://www.inhabitat.com/2008/04/13/natalie-portman-vegan-shoes/, accessed March 13, 2010.

47. Stella McCartney, http://www.stellamccartney.com/us/en/stellasworld/green/, accessed March 13, 2010.

48. Liroff, Richard (2009), *GreenBiz.com,* "The Benefits of Coming Clean on Your Company's Toxic Footprint," December 4, http://www.greenerdesign.com/blog/2009/12/04/benefits-coming-clean-your-companys-toxic-footprint, accessed December 4, 2009.

49. Liroff, Richard (2009), *GreenBiz.com,* "The Benefits of Coming Clean on Your Company's Toxic Footprint," December 4, http://www.greenerdesign.com/blog/2009/12/04/benefits-coming-clean-your-companys-toxic-footprint, accessed December 4, 2009.

50. Portfolio 21, http://www.portfolio21.com, accessed on January 16, 2010.

51. Social Investment Forum, www.sriadvocacy.org, accessed on November 21, 2009.

52. Climate Biz (2009), "New Ruling Opens Door for Increased Shareholder Activism on Climate," October 28, http://www.greenbiz.com/news/2009/10/28/shareholders-could-vote-more-climate-resolutions-under-new-sec-rule, accessed November 1, 2009.

53. Kropp, Robert (2009), "CSR Reporting Improves in 2009 – Though Not for All," *GreenBiz.com*, December 30, http://www.greenbiz.com/news/2009/12/29/csr-reporting-improves-2009-thought-not-everyone, accessed March 13, 2010.

54. Kolk, Ans (2000), "Green Reporting," *Harvard Business Review*, 78 (1, Jan/Feb): 15–16.

55. Ramus, Catherine A. and Ivan Montiel (2005), "When Are Corporate Environmental Policies a Form of Greenwashing?" *Business & Society,* 44 (4, December): 377–414.

56. Sony, http://www.sonystyle.com/webapp/wcs/stores/servlet/ContentDisplayView?cmsId=STATICS_Outlet_Special_Offers&hideHeaderFooter=false&storeId=10151&catalogId=10551&langId=-1, accessed January 17, 2010.

57. Seventh Generation, http://www.seventhgeneration.com/coupons accessed January 17, 2010.

58. Seireeni, Richard and Scott Fields (2009), *The Gort Cloud: The Invisible Force Powering Today's Most Visible Green Brands,* White River Junction, VT: Chelsea Green Publishing (p. 248).

59. Fuller, Donald, A. (1999), *Sustainable Marketing: Managerial-Ecological Issues,* Thousand Oaks, CA: Sage (p. 257).

60. Belz, Frank-Martin and Ken Peattie (2009), *Sustainability Marketing: A Global Perspective,* Chichester, UK: Wiley (p.182).

61. Seireeni, Richard and Scott Fields (2009), *The Gort Cloud: The Invisible Force Powering Today's Most Visible Green Brands.* White River Junction, VT: Chelsea Green Publishing.

62. Tauck, Robin (2008), "Selling Sustainable Travel Performance, Media Group Virtual Home-Based Key Note," May, http://www.robintauck.com/selling-sus-travel/selling-sus-travel.html, accessed on March 6, 2010.

63. Makower, Joel (2009), *GreenBiz.com*, "Searching for Greenwash at Greenbuild," November 16, http://www.GreenBiz.com/blog/2009/11/16/searching-greenwash-greenbuild, accessed November 17, 2009.

64. Beuschel, Vanessa (2009), "Environmental Network News: ENN Interviews President/CEO of New York's Go Green Expo," April 17, http://www.enn.com/top_stories/article/39716/print, accessed April 21, 2009.

65. Natural Products Expo West, http://www.expowest.com/ew10/public/enter.aspx, accessed March 13, 2010.

66. Greenfestival, http://www.greenfestivals.org/, accessed March 13, 2010.

67. http://relationshipera.files.wordpress.com/2009/11/winningintherelationshipera_v2-2.pdf, accessed January 16, 2010.

68. Werbach, Adam (2009), *Strategy for Sustainability: A Business Manifesto,* Boston, MA: Harvard Business Press (p. 31).

69. Ecounit, http://www.ecounit.com/, accessed January 24, 2010.

70. Triplepundit, http://www.triplepundit.com/2009/12/ecounits-green-affinity-marketing/eco_logo_final/, accessed January 16, 2010.

71. Eco, "The Green Sales Generator," http://www.eco1.biz/2.html, accessed on January 17, 2010.

72. Direct Marketing Association, http://www.the-dma.org/index.php, accessed on January 17, 2010.

73. Belz, Frank-Martin and Ken Peattie (2009), *Sustainability Marketing: A Global Perspective,* Chichester, UK: Wiley (p. 182).

Digital Media and Sustainable Marketing

INTRODUCTION: HIGH STAKES SKIRMISH IN SOCIAL MEDIA

It began as an attack by Greenpeace on Nestlé and grew into what blogger Bernhard Warner of Social Media Influence called "the most successful social-media-influence campaign yet."[1] A provocative, one-minute protest video posted on the Greenpeace Facebook page and linked to a Nestlé Facebook page challenged viewers to protest Nestlé's purchases of palm oil from an Indonesian company responsible for destroying vast tracts of virgin rainforest and Orangutan habitat.[2] Public reactions to the ad were tweeted and re-tweeted around the world on Twitter. On its own Facebook page,[3] Nestlé fought back with censorship of posts and a ban on the use of its logo. Nestlé fans were upset, insulted, and alienated by the heavy-handed response. Nestlé shortly apologized to its Facebook fans, and, soon after, company chairman Peter Brabeck-Letmathe announced in a letter to Greenpeace that Nestlé would stop procuring palm oil from unsustainable sources.[4]

The letter evoked praise from some fans and condemnation from others, who dismissed it as greenwashing. Referring to a similar situation in his March 23, 2010, blog, Warner also reports: "Two years ago . . . Rainforest Action Network members flooded onto the open comments area of General Motors' site GMNext questioning its commitment to the environment. GM responded at first by deleting the critical comments, but then agreed to meet with its accusers in a series of one-on-one interviews, winning some grudging praise from its biggest accusers. 'This is a great chance to speak directly to a major corporate executive,' RAN later told its members."[5]

THINK ABOUT IT

Social Media Hijacking

In the above examples, two huge multinational corporations found that their own interactive media vehicles had been turned against them by targeted attacks from activists. In each case, who were the winners? In the end, who were the losers? Or *were* there any losers? Expand your analysis to include stakeholders beyond just the companies and the activists. Does that affect your conclusions?

SOCIAL MEDIA MARKETING MADNESS

This chapter explores some of the special characteristics of electronic and social media and their relationship to sustainable marketing.

CHAPTER OBJECTIVES

In this chapter, you will learn how digital media fit into the world of sustainable marketing. We will cover:

- Digital communication and sustainable marketing
  - Rapid innovation and change
  - Consumer preference for digital media
  - Enhanced product sustainability through dematerialization
  - Increased process sustainability
  - Digital communities driving sustainability
- Current uses of digital media in sustainable marketing communication
- Digital danger zones and antisocial media

Storytelling is perhaps the most sustainable form of communication. Good stories get told and re-told, often outliving their storytellers. As individuals, we use stories to piece together our understandings of our lives and ourselves. As groups, we use stories to define who we are and what we stand for. The best, most compelling stories rise to the level of mythology and create the very foundations of cultural understanding. This chapter stands apart from the other chapters on sustainable marketing communication because it deals with technologies that are unique in their ability to transmit stories. It begins with a general discussion of digital communication technologies as they relate to sustainability in marketing, and it ends with a glimpse into the dark side of social media.

DIGITAL COMMUNICATION AND SUSTAINABLE MARKETING

Recall from Chapter 14 how ad agencies' use of online video to deliver creative content reduces emissions and toxic materials in the biosphere. The rapid growth of digital communication continues to result in opportunities for increased sustainability. Emails, tweets, and social networking sites are replacing personal letters, notes, and form letters. Digital streaming and downloads are replacing videotapes and DVDs. By the time you read this chapter, some of the technologies mentioned here may already be obsolete. They certainly will have advanced. The principles behind them, however, are still relevant. Here are five principles governing the roles of communication technology in sustainable marketing:

- Digital information and communication technologies advance rapidly, driving innovation and change.

- Digital media sources are becoming consumers' first recourse for market information.
- Digital products help dematerialize consumption.
- Digital communication makes marketing processes more sustainable.
- Digital communication links people to communities.

Principle #1—Rapid Innovation and Change Are the Norm

Information and communication technologies advance rapidly, driving innovation and change. **Moore's Law** states that the computing capacity of a given sized transistor or chip doubles roughly every two years. The combination of increasing power and decreasing size of computer chips fuels innovation in all kinds of industries, including **digital communication**, defined as the electronic transmission of digitally encoded information. In his second law, Moore also recognizes that this continuously doubling capacity is extremely expensive, with every new gain in performance costing more than the previous one. Finally, Moore cautions that such gains are not infinitely sustainable. At the present time, however, high-tech performance curves continue to arc upward.

Moore's Law has at least two direct consequences for the sustainability of digital communication. First, the increasing capacity and miniaturization of electronics means that less and less material is required to manufacture each device. Second, each device is capable of more and more functions. The net impact is that, in practically every avenue of life and business, communication processes are becoming more energy-efficient and materials-efficient. For example, cellular phones in 1990 were veritable bricks in terms of size and weight, and they had one function only: the telephone call (see Photo 15-1). Contrast those with smart phones circa 2010 that weigh a few ounces and contain functions, such as global positioning, navigation, and video cameras, which would have been considered science fiction in 1990. The flip side of rapid change in hardware capabilities is rapid obsolescence. Cell phones, which contain hazardous materials, are a major source of electronic waste. According to the U.S. Environmental Protection Agency, "The average cell phone life span is about 18 months. They are discarded at an alarming rate of more than 125 million phones per year, resulting in more than 65,000 tons of waste."[6]

It's not only hardware technology that's advancing at a breakneck pace. The same is true of the systems that connect the devices and the software that allows them to operate and communicate with each other. Remaining competitive in such an environment of rapid change requires an organization to be learning constantly. The term *Web 2.0* may have been replaced with another term by the time you read this sentence, and 3G networks may seem cumbersome and limiting.

PHOTO 15-1 A mobile phone from the 1990s—In communication technology, rapid innovation and obsolescence are the norm.

The way you communicate in business 10 years from now may consign current communication technologies to the same scrap heap as typewriters and floppy discs.

A company's communication capabilities need to be continually evaluated and updated as new technologies emerge. For the sake of long-term competitive advantage, each new opportunity also needs to enhance a firm's sustainability. An effective process for evaluating new technologies can be created following the principles of backcasting developed in The Natural Step Framework. Backcasting helps to uncover violations of the conditions for sustainability, and it helps planners avoid unwanted trade-offs to the triple bottom line.

Rapid change also affects our overall understanding of sustainability. As sustainable marketing consultant Jackie Ottman put it, "No matter how well companies do their homework, what is accepted as 'green,' today may wind up being viewed as 'brown,' tomorrow."[7] Savvy companies keep abreast of trends in a variety of ways. Some work with independent research firms, called trend spotters, which monitor youth culture.[8] Others take the pulse of new trends by staying in close contact with their best customers. Engaging your best customers in authentic, open dialog keeps them interested and gives you more eyes and ears to track what's being said about your brand, your products, and possible unmet needs.

Principle #2—Consumers Increasingly Prefer Digital Media

More and more people turn first to **digital media**, which include platforms like the Internet, Web, and mobile phone networks, for all kinds of information. Phone books are relics of the past in many neighborhoods. They get dropped off on doorsteps and go straight to recycling bins. Websites like Google, Bing, and Wikipedia are the first contact for many information searches. Company websites are becoming the norm for all businesses and nonprofits. Consumers expect them, and they expect them to be artfully designed, informative, and easy to navigate. As the organization's virtual "front door," the homepage is a critical point of interaction with consumers. Brand elements found in traditional media should be found on the company's homepage, driving consumer interest and continuing the established brand story. Content is an integral part of the homepage. Content should be organized for different users and to facilitate different patterns of shopping and information search. Web content can influence the buying process by hooking people and pacing them through a transaction to finish a purchase online, request more information, or go to a retail store (see Figure 15-1).

The Internet has influenced every aspect of marketing communication. Online advertising, for example, may be more popular and more effective with some consumers than television advertising. Author David Meerman Scott reports that, unlike television, the online context

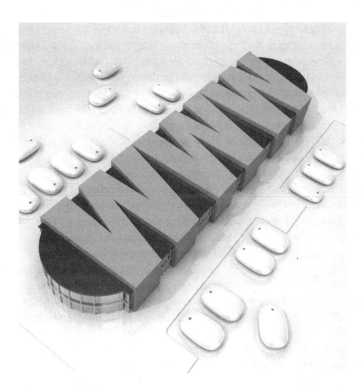

FIGURE 15-1 The worldwide web is an electronic supermall.

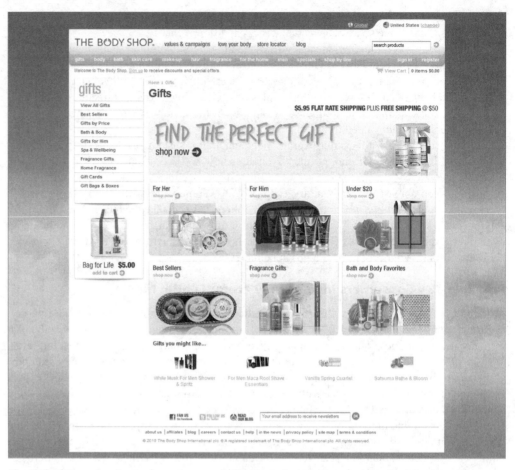

The Body Shop makes it easy for consumers to find just what they are looking for. http://www.thebodyshop-usa.com/index.jsp.

allows marketers to deliver useful content to consumers at the precise moment it is needed. Scott also comments on the Internet's influence on public relations: "The Internet has made public relations public again, after years of almost exclusive focus on media. Blogs, online news releases and other forms of Web content let organizations communicate directly with buyers."[9] In fact, one hallmark of the Internet as a communication medium is that it offers organizations and stakeholders the opportunity to speak more directly and interactively.

The Internet has changed the face of direct mail as well. Email marketing programs offer marketers the convenience of regular communication with customers without the costs and waste, such as paper, printing, transportation, and delivery, attributed to physical mail. The most effective and least objectionable form of email marketing is called **permission marketing**, which is conducted only with the explicit consent of recipients. Permission marketing is highly and accurately targeted. Because recipients have already indicated their desire to receive an organization's information, they are more likely to consider and act upon it. Unsolicited email, or spam, naturally has the opposite effect and has been the target of both legislative action and tactical defenses (e.g., spam filters) within the online industry.

Broadcast media (i.e., radio and television) have also migrated to the Internet and taken on different forms there. Streaming audio most closely approximates a traditional radio experience. Some online stations, like Radio Paradise or National Public Radio, control their content but have large target audiences who tune in for it. Other services, such as Pandora, allow consumers to customize their listening experiences according to their own preferences and even their moods. Podcasts more closely resemble audio essays or magazine articles. Users can subscribe to feeds from specific sources representing a wide variety of information and entertainment. Videocasting adds a visual dimension to a podcast, making it suitable for television or TV-style content. Through YouTube, for example, users can download or upload original videos, commercials, TV and movie clips, mini-films, educational webinars, or other kinds of video content.

Marketers have followed consumers out of their homes and businesses and now seek to communicate with them through **mobile marketing**, which directs marketing messages to

The Green Guide Network is an online resource for information about local businesses striving for sustainability.

mobile phones.[10] Customers increasingly rely on smart phones, which use specialized software applications, to simplify tasks like shopping, navigation, or checking stock prices or weather reports. For example, applications have been created to help shoppers choose safe, healthy, and more sustainable products. The GoodGuide mobile app includes over 50,000 products and ratings that can be accessed by scanning the bar code of the product with the phone's camera to see detailed ratings for health, environment, and social responsibility.[11]

Consumers don't seem to mind commercial content on their phones, as long as they can control when it appears. Apps such as Urban Spoon carry links to restaurants and bars. AroundMe directs smart-phone users to a wide variety of businesses based on their proximity. In a brilliant example of specialization, *The Portland Mercury* app, Cocktail Compass, displays information on the closest happy hours along with distances, addresses, phone numbers, and readouts of how much time is remaining before the happy hour ends. When the eating and drinking is done, Cocktail Compass also provides a one-button taxi call.

From an environmental standpoint, digital media appear to be more sustainable than print forms. However, the differences may not be as great as they seem. Print media are rapidly becoming more sustainable through use of recycled papers and vegetable-based inks available for many applications. Digital media come with hidden environmental costs, especially those associated with the production of hardware and the energy requirements of computing. Online radio,

Increasing numbers of consumers around the world prefer to receive information electronically.

podcasts, and videocasts may not be noticeably more sustainable than conventional broadcasting media from an ecological perspective. However, digital media may provide gains in terms of economical and social sustainability. Placing content on Internet sites is still cheaper than purchasing airtime on television or radio, especially during time slots when ratings are high. When people do come in contact with marketing messages via the Internet, it is often because they have either sought out the information or received it from a friend. Either way, it is well targeted and contributes to an overall brand story.

Principle #3—Digital Products Dematerialize Consumption

Digital products are potentially more sustainable than conventional ones in that they dematerialize consumption. As discussed in Chapters 2 and 9, dematerialization results in consumers receiving the product benefit without having to deal with its material aspects. Digital content and delivery systems require less energy and less material than conventional goods and services, components of which are manufactured, packaged and transported. For example, teleconferencing is replacing travel technology in many business applications. Likewise, digital entertainment is replacing solid media such as DVDs. Email is preferred in most cases over the humble snail mail, and university libraries are adding research databases and electronic journals at a much faster rate than hard copies. Electronic readers, such as the Kindle, and devices such as smart phones and the iPad have become popular for accessing content such as magazines, books, and newspapers that previously were available only in print. For example, the *New York Times* has an online version and versions or applications for smart phones, the iPad, and various e-readers.

The travel industry has digitized its services to a great degree. For many years, travel agency services have been migrating to Internet-based platforms, largely for cost savings and to accommodate an increasingly tech-savvy customer base. Sustainability has more recently become a differentiator for more materially focused travel businesses, and for the online services that promote them. Travelocity, for example, as a member of the Tourism Sustainability Council (TSC), has developed a Green Hotel Directory as part of a program called Travel for Good,[12] which promotes social responsibility through volunteerism and green travel through carbon offsets and eco-friendly hotels. According to the Travelocity website: "Each of the hotels in our directory has been endorsed by a leading green hotel certification provider, appears in the Rainforest Alliance's Eco-Index of Sustainable Tourism, or is making significant strides in at least three of the four areas the TSC's criteria."[13]

Despite the dematerialization that digital technology facilitates, computing technology still leaves a broad and deep environmental footprint. The manufacturing of hardware is a dirty, water-intensive business, and computing both requires and wastes enormous amounts of energy. A semiconductor plant can easily use more than 240,000 kilowatt hours of electricity and from two to five million gallons of water every day, and the manufacturing processes use a host of toxic chemicals, including arsenic, benzene, cadmium, lead, and toluene.[14]

As for computing, data centers of the sort operated by Google are enormously energy intensive, producing large amounts of greenhouse gases. Even simple online operations contribute significantly. For example, researchers have determined that conducting two relatively complex Google searches from a desktop computer generates about the same amount of carbon dioxide as boiling a tea kettle; and over the course of a year, maintaining an avatar on Second Life uses about as much electricity as the average Brazilian uses just to live.[15]

One of the main tasks for the future of digital technology is to increase its sustainability. Companies such as Google and Microsoft are constantly exploring ways to make computing more energy efficient,[16] and scientists at MIT are working to design thermal diodes that can capture waste heat and convert significant amounts of it back to electrical energy.[17]

Principle #4—Digital Communication Aids Process Sustainability

Digital communication systems can make marketing processes such as sales, logistics, and order fulfillment more sustainable. For example, the company TNT has invested in digital telepresence or videoconferencing systems to substitute for travel services, replacing many international business flights and reducing costs and carbon footprints. Of course, efficiency without effectiveness is wasted. If an organization's virtual meetings fail to accomplish their intended purposes, you can bet that airline reservations aren't far behind.

Certain innovations radically improve both efficiency and effectiveness. For example, because of online communication systems Amazon doesn't need to warehouse huge inventories. It merely has to facilitate direct shipping from buyer to seller; and that shipping tends to be handled by specialists like UPS that continue to innovate and drive their own technological improvements. But the Amazon story doesn't end with a more efficient business model. Author Chris Anderson describes how the combination of message reach, product variety, and site searchability has made Amazon a game changer in the world of retail marketing. Even low-demand products with hard-to-identify markets can thrive.[18]

Multinational corporations aren't the only ones benefiting from technological advances. Small businesses also reap advantages. For example, the digital infrastructure provided by eBay allows small businesses with limited resources to survive, or even to compete, in global markets. And in remote areas of rural Africa and India, cell phone service has improved market opportunities and negotiation power for farmers. In areas with no telephone landlines, villagers used to have to walk miles to learn the value of their coffee or other crops on the world market. Now they can use cell phones to access the information quickly and reliably, allowing them to protect themselves from unscrupulous middlemen.[19]

Principle #5— Digital Communities Drive Sustainability

Digital communication links people who have never been linked before. It allows companies to communicate with stakeholders and stakeholders to communicate with companies. It allows communities of purpose to organize, collaborate, create, and accomplish goals that might be nearly unreachable otherwise. Those communities range in scope from local, as in flash mobs, to global, as in mobilizations of humanitarian aid to disaster-stricken areas like Haiti after the 2010 earthquake.

Social media have, of course, accelerated the formation of online communities. Platforms like Facebook and Twitter may become important tools for consumer relationship management. Consider the words of PR professional Jen Maxwell-Muir, "Twenty-five years ago, companies were asking if they really needed to invest in building websites, and we all know the answer to that question today. A similar debate about resource allocation rages in 2010, but now it's over social media. It's OK to start slowly, but companies need to engage. At minimum, they should protect their brand online by registering Twitter and Facebook accounts, and start listening to what their consumers have to say."[20]

The principles for success in social media are the same as many of the principles for success in sustainability: transparency, authenticity, stakeholder involvement, and innovation. Like all consumer contact, communication through social media works best if managers treat it as two-way communication between individuals. The following hints can help with the task of managing an organization's use of social media.

1. *Treat customers as a community, not as a target.* Community members help to build and maintain the neighborhood; target customers just come looking for deals.
2. *Be completely honest in what you communicate.* Stakeholders are more forgiving of honest mistakes than of dishonest claims.
3. *Appeal to both logic and emotion.* Customers want to feel good, and they want to understand why they feel good.
4. *Be consistent in your social media presence.* If you're fortunate enough to get regular riders on your social-media bus, don't leave them standing at the curb wondering where you are.
5. *Communicate something of value.* Each post should be meaningful, so planning an editorial calendar can be helpful. Take your topics from stakeholder concerns.

Within existing online communities, digital communication can spread rapidly, turning customers and other stakeholders into co-marketers, critics, or even adversaries.[21] They actively communicate with other consumers, influencing them both through word of mouth and through word of mouse. The latter, called **viral marketing**, results when Internet-mediated marketing communication receives wide distribution in online communities, forums, customer review sites, and social media.[22]

Brand stories conveyed from person to person carry a weight of approval and authenticity not found in company-sponsored communication. Word of mouth has always been considered the most effective and cost-effective form of marketing communication, and digital communication

technologies expand its reach. A story that hits the Web can go global in a matter of minutes. Of course, this is a double-edged sword for companies. Digital media don't discriminate between good press and bad. They don't even discriminate very well between fact and fantasy, or between truth, lies, and everything that lies in between. Bad news about a brand or product can reverberate around the world before companies have time to plan and carry out damage control. The Nestlé-Greenpeace interaction from the chapter introduction is a good example of social media getting out of control.

Within existing brand communities and fan communities, word can travel especially fast and far. For example, when Cindy Gordon, vice president of new media and marketing partnerships at Universal Orlando Resort, launched the theme park attraction, The Wizarding World of Harry Potter, she initially told only seven people about it. Those seven, who were active at Harry Potter fan sites, spread the word to thousands more. Eventually the mainstream media picked up the story and reached an estimated 350,000 people about the new attraction. Using traditional advertising and public relations would have cost millions of dollars to accomplish what passionate fans did for free.[23]

CURRENT USES OF DIGITAL MEDIA IN SUSTAINABLE MARKETING COMMUNICATION

With some of the basic "whys" out of the way, let's focus more on the "who, what, where, and how" of digital media and its applications in sustainable marketing communication. Given the fast pace of innovation in the area, the lists are bound to be incomplete and changing.

Who Communicates to Whom?

The easy answer is, it could be just about anybody (see Photo 15-2). Digital media is so abundant and readily accessed that people almost anywhere in the world can join in discussions about sustainable living and business. From the standpoint of a marketing organization, however, two key questions are: (1) Who should speak for us? and (2) To whom should we pay special attention?

Transparency, credibility, and trust between an organization and its stakeholders are best served by external communication from knowledgeable employees who are passionate about the

PHOTO 15-2 Online social networks have emerged as important tools for sustainable marketing communication.

brand. Those employees, acting as brand advocates, may be executive officers, sustainability officers, product designers, or anyone else who is engaged with bringing sustainability to the organization's products or operations.

Whoever an organization's online advocates are, it is vital that they identify themselves openly and honestly. To do otherwise invites justifiable backlash. For example, in 2007, the CEO of Whole Foods, John Mackey, authored online attacks against its competitor, Wild Oats Markets, Inc. Hiding behind a false name, Mackey bashed Wild Oats, predicting plummeting stock prices, when in fact, his company was planning to acquire the smaller competitor.[24]

In 2009, Mackey once again unwittingly demonstrated the dangers of global digital communication. Writing an opinion piece for the *Wall Street Journal*, he came out strongly against health-care reform. The repercussions in the electronic media among customers and stockholders who disagreed with his opinions were immediate and severe. Blogs calling for boycotts were picked up and passed along through social media. Some loyal customers announced they were defecting, and others that they were selling their Whole Foods stock.[25]

Mackey's problem is that he has repeatedly aired his own opinions and values, even when they have been offensive to the values of large segments of the Whole Foods customer base. In direct contrast, Matt Flannery, co-founder of the online lending platform, Kiva, publishes his opinions regularly in "The Kiva Chronicles,"[26] a blog hosted on the website Social Edge. Flannery is a successful spokesperson for his company because he sticks to the business and the core values of Kiva, including success stories of customers who have benefited from Kiva's microlending programs.

THINK ABOUT IT

Shared Values

Corporate leaders may not always have value systems that match those of their customers. Think about a cause or issue that is personally important to you. Now think of one of your favorite brands. Imagine that the executive in charge of that brand has come out publicly against your interests. How would you feel? If that brand's closest competitor openly supported your cause, would you be tempted to switch?

Digital media allow companies to have ongoing conversations with suppliers, customers, sustainability advocates, and experts, or any other interested stakeholders. There are many important reasons to pay attention to customer and stakeholder concerns. As illustrated above, one reason is to stay tuned to customers' values and concerns.

Another reason for close communication with customers is that they may become co-marketers for the organization. Green home-cleaning products company Seventh Generation exemplified this principle with its Million Baby Crawl, a grassroots effort designed to urge Congress to pass stronger regulations on chemicals used in household products. The company website uses the catch phrase: "We cannot stand, but we stand for something. Babies of all ages are crawling to Washington D.C.[27] Seventh Generation argues that since the passage of the Toxic Substances Control Act in 1976, the government has required testing on only about 200 of more than 80,000 chemicals now found in household products. The online initiative hopes to engage parents in the creation of crawling-baby avatars to participate in a virtual march, or crawl, on Washington, D.C. to advocate for legislative action on toxics."[28]

Another example of recruiting customers as co-marketers comes from the fair trade and organic chocolate company, Green & Black's, which invites customers to add their own stories to the company website. It calls the promotion "Live in the &." The & is where Green meets Black and represents a life in balance between ethics and indulgence. The company's position is that, "We can be consciously respectful of our earth while also indulging in the best things life has to offer." Reader-customers are invited to contribute their stories about living in balance in exchange for special discounts and the chance to be featured on the website.[29]

Another reason to engage stakeholders is a phenomenon called **crowdsourcing**. The basic concept is to get outsiders, preferably customers, to swarm together or collaborate online in the completion of a project, such as designing a product or an ad campaign.[30] Pepsi made news in February 2010 with a campaign to use crowdsourcing to guide millions of dollars of philanthropic donations. The grant money came from funds that would normally have been spent on Super Bowl advertising. As reported by Ariel Schwartz in a 2010 *Fast Company* article, "Starting February 1, readers can vote to give grants to a number of health, environment, culture, and education-related organizations. Pepsi plans to give away multiple grants each month, including two $250,000 grants, 10 $50,000 grants, and 10 $25,000 grants. Visitors are also encouraged to submit their own organizations and grant ideas."[31]

MIT studies crowdsourcing through its Center for Collective Intelligence. According to its website, "New communication technologies—especially the Internet—now allow huge numbers of people all over the planet to work together in new ways."[32] Author Adam Werbach cites three advantages of crowdsourcing. First, it allows an organization to create a bigger team for a project by enlisting talents and ideas from outside. Second, the organization saves money, because it only pays for those ideas that yield results. And third, the organization can explore various kinds of solutions and ideas simultaneously through the efforts of independent teams.[33]

One company, Innocentive, uses crowdsourcing contests to help companies and other organizations develop solutions to a variety of problems, including human health, social, and environmental problems. Innocentive matches "seekers" looking for solutions to specific problems with "solvers" who propose solutions. One example of an Innocentive problem is the search for a design for a "robust and easy to assemble river turbine . . . for platform-mounted use on the rivers of the Peruvian jungle. The power produced will be used to electrify Peruvian villages, schools and medical centers."[34]

VIRTUAL FIELD TRIP

Starbucks Crowdsourcing

Visit the crowdsourcing site, My Starbucks Idea, and explore some of the ideas that customers have contributed (http://mystarbucksidea.force.com/ideaHome). One user-generated idea, to offer Starbucks card holders a small credit for refilling their cards, generated over 200 comments (see the posting at http://mystarbucksidea.force.com/ideaView?id=087500000004DACAA2#comments-top).

How and Why Do They Communicate?

Communicating with stakeholders can be done through various vehicles for various reasons. Probably the most prevalent media vehicles are web logs, or **blogs**, with which you undoubtedly are familiar. A blog is basically just a website created and maintained for the purpose of personal reporting. The blogger posts entries, usually at regular intervals, and often related to a single theme about which the blogger has special interest or expertise. The blog site also offers readers the opportunity to post comments, which may agree or disagree with the blogger's position, or which may extend or expand upon the blogger's argument. In many cases, a debate emerges, revealing multiple sides of a story or issue and adding credibility to the blog itself.

Marketing organizations can use blogging either passively or actively. They may choose to simply follow blogs that tend to relate to their industries, brands, customers, or other relevant topics. Such passive use may reveal information such as what customers are saying about the organization's brands. In a somewhat more active mode, organizations may attempt to shape the discussions initiated by bloggers. For example, in a blog that is critical of a company's sustainability claims, someone from the company may wish to clarify or defend its position with comments in response. An even more active use would be for a company to create its own blog, such as the case of the Kiva Chronicles mentioned earlier. A company blog may be maintained by a single employee, or it may feature multiple contributors. Starbucks stays engaged at every level. Several employees blog actively about what's going on in their parts of the organization. What's more, the blogosphere regularly carries messages about Starbucks from fans and detractors alike, making it important that the company remain tuned in.

Blogs offer numerous advantages to their creators, if they are done well. One advantage is that blogs help to build credibility for their authors and institutions. Blogs help writers to sell books, consultants to attract clients, and companies to build goodwill among stakeholders. In areas related to sustainable business, numerous blogs serve to disseminate information and to solidify connections and community. Another advantage of blogs is that they often are treated as newsworthy, getting picked up and reproduced by other media, thus reaching many people beyond the normal community of followers.

Mini Case Study

HP Blog Central

Hewlett-Packard backs blogging. HP employees are encouraged to blog in a wide variety of arenas, and their posts are hosted on the HP Community website.[35] Categories of regular business-related postings include innovation and creativity, inside HP, networking, international news and business, digital photography, IT management, printing and imaging, security software, servers, services, enterprise software, storage, and technology trends. HP also hosts a wide variety of employees' personal blogs, covering everything from motherhood to outdoor sports, cooking to gaming, and anything else that piques the interests of HP people. HP bloggers adhere to a nine-point code of conduct.

HP thinks strategically about blogging. For example, Eric Kintz, HP's vice president of Global Marketing Strategy & Excellence, initiated collaboration with other non-HP senior marketing executive bloggers to create the following model depicting the importance and impact of blogging. They call it "Why Blogging Matters: 6 Degrees of Perspective."[36] A few of the benefits they cite include:

- Expanding and humanizing *public relations*
- Reaching and *influencing* customers in micro-segments
- Amplifying and extending traditional *advertising*
- Strengthening an organization's web *strategy* by engaging customers
- Building customer relationships through *conversation*
- Driving *creativity* through interaction and feedback.

Outside of HP's own blogosphere, the company also leverages the blogging of others to help create social benefits. For example, in February 2010, it launched "Create Change in 2010: Blogger contests with HP" on which it offered HP laptop-and-printer bundles as prizes for "stories about how individuals and technology are creating change in the world."[37] The catch is that HP doesn't choose winners or award prizes directly. All of that is done by a group of six independent bloggers focused on nonprofits and social change.

How would you evaluate HP's overall blogging strategy? In what ways does it exemplify sustainable marketing communication? How does it make the most of renewable resources? How does it affect corporate transparency and perceptions of authenticity? What are the strategic marketing benefits?

Many, if not most, blogs offer connectivity options called **RSS (really simple syndication) feeds** to "push" posts to their regular followers. An RSS feed allows a reader to subscribe to a blog and automatically receive new content every time it's generated. A blogger's subscribers constitute a market niche or community of people with common or overlapping interests. Desktop alerts are similar to RSS feeds from a user perspective, in that they provide instant notification of messages from user-selected companies.

The relative ease of shooting, editing, and embedding digital video into Web content has made video blogging, or Vlogging an increasingly popular vehicle for online communication. Vlogs may be instructional, journalistic, or entertaining, depending on their intended audience and purpose.

Among the most promising forms of digital communication for marketing are **social media**, Internet-based platforms that facilitate and encourage social interaction among users. Social media stress user-generated content (UGC) rather than strictly corporate or institutional messages. Author David Meerman Scott discusses some of the marketing implications of social media such as Facebook: "People join Facebook groups because they want to stay informed about subjects they're interested in, and they want to do it on their own time. Just like blogs, the best way to maintain a Facebook group is simply to make valuable information available. Unlike intrusive e-mail updates, which arrive only when the sender chooses, Facebook groups can be visited at the member's convenience."[38]

Although general-interest platforms such as Facebook and MySpace are the most well-known social media, other platforms, such as Ning, allow users to create their own online networks or social spaces that focus narrowly on special interests. For example, in the area of sustainability, The Natural Step Network maintains a site on Ning called "Transform Agents: A Community of Strategic Sustainability Leaders for Transformation."

Another social networking technology with some promise of usefulness to marketers is Twitter, which is based on "the exchange of quick frequent answers to one simple question: What are you doing?"[39] It's a collection of networks that follow each other's brief status updates. Content is limited to 140 characters per tweet, or message, which may also limit its usefulness for many kinds of communication. Particularly interesting messages often are forwarded or "re-tweeted" from users to their own networks of followers, giving them the ability to spread very broadly and rapidly.

Among the most popular sites for UGC is the video-sharing site, YouTube. On this site and others like it, users can upload content and make it public. UGC also includes formats like comments, ratings, and reviews, and other use comment mechanisms. TV ads and other videos may "go viral" when users load them on YouTube.

What Are They Communicating?

According to research by J.D. Power and Associates, the content and tone of sustainability-related blogs has been changing. They report that, "More than half—62%—of online posts discuss various solutions to environmental issues. This is a shift from 18 months ago when people were still spending much of their time discussing sustainability by debating whether or not the environmental crisis was real. Consumers in the blogosphere group discuss sustainability solutions into two categories: broad social, organizational, and political change; and incremental personal change."[40]

Many blogs or **electronic newsletters** carry news items about gains or challenges in the world of sustainable business. For example, the World Business Council for Sustainable Development (WBCSD), "a CEO-led, global association of some 200 companies dealing exclusively with business and sustainable development,"[41] produces several newsletters, from quarterly to biweekly, for subscribers regarding WBCSD projects relating to a wide range of industry sectors and sustainability concerns. The electronic publisher, Sustainable Life Media (SLM),[42] produces free newsletters including the marketing-oriented *Sustainable Brands Weekly*. The e-publications contain both news and editorial content, and they serve to promote SLM membership, conferences, and virtual events such as online seminars. Member companies receive the added benefit of the frequent association of their brands with sustainability issues and initiatives.

News and other informational content can be linked with varying degrees of brand promotion. Primarily, news-related messaging, like that in the WBCSD newsletters, does little to directly promote brands, especially in the realm of consumer marketing. However, in the spheres where member organizations operate, which often are business-to-business, the reported activities build much recognition and goodwill. Messaging such as that from SLM has a more openly promotional appeal, often featuring consumer brands as the subjects of stories, displaying logos, and recognizing members of the SLM organization in event promotions and announcements. Editors of the SLM newsletters, mainly authors and consultants, also benefit from the credibility and publicity they receive. Finally, programs like Travelocity's Green Hotel Directory, mentioned earlier, openly promote specific brands and services, using their sustainability programs as a means of differentiation.

There are certain assumptions that many marketers tend to make around digital media and its audiences, and these assumptions affect the marketers' choices of tone and content. One assumption is that these media are basically youth oriented. Not necessarily so. Peter Corbett, the CEO of iStrategyLabs, has been following Facebook and blogging and tweeting about it. He reports that, as of January 2009, the fastest growing demographic is the 35–54 year-old age group. The second fastest growing demographic: 55 and older. Corbett concludes, "Parents and professionals are rapidly adopting Facebook. Should a marketer be concerned about this shift if they're focused on youth marketing? No. Facebook's ad targeting enables zero waste from an age targeting perspective."[43]

Another common assumption is that young users of digital media are actively seeking information about sustainability. Also not necessarily so. Researching promotion for a new green product launch, one firm reported that significant numbers in the 18- to 24-year-old group turned first to ads, product labels, and news coverage for green product information. An equally large segment claimed to get green product info first from friends and family. For both segments, Internet searches were lower on the list of important information sources.[44]

The lessons here are that (1) users of social media are segmented just like any other markets, (2) they don't necessarily go out of their way to hunt down sustainability information, and (3) online media don't magically create buzz for organizations' sustainability initiatives. Even in the fast-paced world of digital media, marketing sustainably and marketing sustainability require attention to fundamental principles of good marketing.

DIGITAL DANGER ZONES AND ANTISOCIAL MEDIA

For all the opportunity inherent in social media and the Internet, cyberspace is not an entirely safe place for its users. For many organizations, including businesses, public services, and even governments, cyberattacks are a serious potential danger. **Cyberattacks** are malicious acts targeting computer systems, networks, and/or databases through the Internet. The intent of such acts may be to disrupt operations or to destroy or steal information. Identity theft is a particular concern. Perpetrators of cyberattacks may be independent hackers, criminal organizations, hostile governments, or corporate spies. *Computer World* recently reported one particularly notorious and massive cyberattack: "Security researchers at Herndon, Va.-based NetWitness Corp. have unearthed a massive botnet affecting at least 75,000 computers at 2,500 companies and government agencies worldwide. The Kneber botnet . . . has been used to gather login credentials to online financial systems, social networking sites and e-mail systems for the past 18 months . . . ."[45]

Another Internet danger zone is **cyberstalking**, defined as the use of electronic media for purposes of harassing, threatening, menacing, or otherwise bringing harm to another individual. Some of the more insidious forms of cyberstalking include sexual predation, cyberbullying, and character assassination.

CRITICAL THINKING ACTIVITY

Dell and the Blogs

Bloggers can have significant impact on corporate sustainability practices. On Earth Day in 2008, Dell was hit with an onslaught of complaints from blogs including Consumerist and Gizmodo. Writers took Dell to task for using excessive and wasteful packaging in its delivery of parts and accessories. Dell immediately responded to the complaints with a pledge to engage its suppliers in designing more eco-efficient packaging. Dell had invited intense scrutiny from environmentalists by announcing its intention to become the "greenest technology company in the world."[46]

What does the Dell case imply for an organization's need to be aware of bloggers? How might Dell use blogs to succeed in becoming "the greenest technology company in the world?" Log onto Dell's official blog sites (en.community.dell.com/blogs/direct2dell). Do you see evidence of two-way communication with stakeholders? What does Dell's blogging strategy seem to be? What, if anything, would you recommend that Dell do differently?

Chapter Summary

This chapter has explored some of the special characteristics of electronic and social media and their relationship to sustainable marketing. It began with a discussion of five principles of digital communication and its role in sustainable marketing. It examined the nature of digital media, including who communicates to whom, why, by what methods, and with what kinds of content related to sustainable marketing. Finally, it presented a glimpse of the darker underside of electronic media.

Review of Chapter Objectives

In this chapter, you learned how new media fit into the world of sustainable marketing. We covered:

- Digital communication and sustainable marketing
  - Rapid innovation and change
  - Consumer preference for digital media

- Enhanced product sustainability through dematerialization
- Increased process sustainability
- Digital communities driving sustainability
- Current uses of digital media in sustainable marketing communication
- Digital danger zones and antisocial media

Key Concepts

Moore's Law   220
Digital Communication   220
Digital Media   221
Permission Marketing   222

Mobile Marketing   223
Viral Marketing   225
Crowdsourcing   227
Blog   228

RSS (Really Simple
    Syndication) Feed   230
Social Media   230

Electronic Newsletters   230
Cyberattacks   231
Cyberstalking   232

Endnotes

1. Warner, Bernard, editorial director of Social Media Influence, in *The Big Money*, March 19 and 23, 2010, see: http://scribe.thebigmoney.com/blogs/c-tweet/2010/03/19/nestl-s-no-logo-policy-triggers-facebook-revolt?page=full, and http://www.thebigmoney.com/blogs/c-tweet/2010/03/23/ will-nestl-ever-reclaim-its-facebook-page-protesters-0, accessed April 17, 2010.

2. Greenpeace (2010), "Need a Break? So Does the Rainforest." http://www.greenpeace.org/international/campaigns/climate-change/kitkat, accessed April 17, 2010.

3. Nestlé (2010), http://www.facebook.com/Nestle, accessed April 17, 2010.

4. Nestlé (2010), Statement on deforestation and palm oil, http://www.nestle.com/MediaCenter/SpeechesAndStatements/AllSpeechesAndStatements/statement_Palm_oil.htm, accessed April 17, 2010.

5. Warner, Bernhard (2010), "Will Nestlé Ever Reclaim Its Facebook Page from Protesters?" *The Big Money*, March 23, http://www.thebigmoney.com/blogs/c-tweet/2010/03/23/will-nestl-ever-reclaim-its-facebook-page-protesters-0, accessed April 17, 2010.

6. http://www.rethinkrecycling.com/residents/throw-buy/materials-name/cell-phones, accessed February 7, 2010.

7. Ottman, Jacquelyn A. (1998), *Green Marketing: Opportunity for Innovation,* New York: J. Ottman Consulting Inc. (p. 91).

8. Trendwatching "Eco-Iconic" products (June 2008) http://trendwatching.com/trends/ecoiconic.htm, accessed August 12, 2009.

9. Scott, David Meerman (2009), The New Rules of Marketing & PR: How to Use News Releases, Blogs, Podcasting, Viral Marketing & Online Media to Reach Buyers Directly. Hoboken, NJ: John Wiley & Sons, Inc.

10. Mobile Marketing Association, 2009.

11. http://www.goodguide.com/about/mobile, accessed February 7, 2010.

12. http://www.travelocity.com/TravelForGood/index.html, accessed February 12, 2010.

13. http://leisure.travelocity.com/Promotions/0,,TRAVELOCITY%7C5019%7Cgreen_hotel_popup,00.html, accessed February 12, 2010.

14. Holden, Jason and Christopher Kelty (2009), "The Environmental Impact of the Manufacturing of Semiconductors," http://cnx.org/content/m14503/latest/, accessed February 8, 2010.

15. Leake, Jonathan and Richard Woods (2009), "Revealed: The Environmental Impact of Google Searches," *The Sunday Times*, London, January 11, http://technology.timesonline.co.uk/tol/news/tech_and_web/article5489134.ece, accessed February 8, 2010.

16. Oiaga, Marius (2008), "Microsoft Explores Next-Generation Computing," *Softpedia*, April 29, http://news.softpedia.com/news/Microsoft-Explores-Next-Generation-Computing-84468.shtml, accessed February 8, 2010.

17. http://www.alternative-energy-news.info/waste-heat-battery-life-laptops-cell-phones/, accessed February 8, 2010.

18. Anderson, Chris (2006), The Long Tail: Why The Future of Business Is Selling Less of More, New York: Hyperion.

19. Werbach, Adam (2009), *Strategy for Sustainability: A Business Manifesto,* Boston, MA: Harvard Business Press (p. 55).

20. http://naturalfoodsmerchandiser.com/tabId/107/itemId/4360/Fads-that-last-Experts-reveal-continuing-trends-f.aspx, accessed February 10, 2010.

21. Gummesson, Evert (2005, July), "From One-to-One to Many-to-Many Marketing in the Network Society," Academy of Marketing and AMA Conference, DIT, Dublin.

22. Scott, David Meerman (2008), The New Rules of Viral Marketing: How Word-of-Mouse Spreads Your Ideas for Free, free e-book available at: http://www.davidmeermanscott.com/documents/Viral_Marketing.pdf, accessed July 16, 2009.

23. http://www.davidmeermanscott.com/documents/Viral_Marketing.pdf, pp. 5–7, accessed July 16, 2009.

24. Associated Press (2007), "Whole Foods CEO's Anonymous Online Life: Postings on Financial Forums Attacked a Rival Company Trying to Buy," MSNBC, July 12, http://www.msnbc.msn.com/id/19718742/,

25. Goldstein, Katherine (2009), "Whole Foods Backlash: Bloggers Outraged over CEO's Anti-'ObamaCare' Column," *Huffington Post*, August 18, http://www.huffingtonpost.com/2009/08/18/the-whole-foods-health-ca_n_262471.html, accessed February 10, 2010.

26. http://www.socialedge.org/blogs/kiva-chronicles, accessed February 10, 2010.

27. http://www.seventhgeneration.com/million-baby-crawl/ accessed January 25, 2010.

28. "Seventh Generation Launches the Million Baby Crawl for Toxic Chemical Reform," Kathryn Siranosian, November 19, 2009.

29. http://greenandblacks.com/us/live-in-the-and.html, accessed January 25, 2010.

30. http://www.techcrunch.com/2008/02/18/first-look-klusters-market-approach-to-crowdsourcing/, accessed January 24, 2010.

31. Schwartz, Ariel (2010), "Pepsi Ditches the Super Bowl, Embraces Crowdsourced Philanthropy Instead," *Fast Company*, January 24.

32. http://cci.mit.edu/, accessed February 10, 2010.

33. Werbach, Adam (2009), *Strategy for Sustainability: A Business Manifesto,* Boston, MA: Harvard Business Press (p. 97).

34. https://gw.innocentive.com/ar/challengePavilion/index?pavilionName=Clean+Tech, accessed February 10, 2010.

35. http://www.hp.com/hpinfo/blogs/index.html, accessed March 15, 2010.

36. http://darmano.typepad.com/logic_emotion/2006/10/open_post_to_al.html, accessed March 15, 2010.

37. http://www.communities.hp.com/online/blogs/thechangingfaceofmedia/archive/2010/02/05/lt-strong-gt-create-change-in-2010-blogger-contests-with-hp-lt-strong-gt.aspx, accessed March 15, 2010.

38. Scott, David Meerman (2009), The New Rules of Marketing & PR: How to Use News Releases, Blogs, Podcasting, Viral Marketing & Online Media to Reach Buyers Directly. Hoboken, New Jersey: John Wiley & Sons, Inc. (pp. 230, 233).

39. Scott, David Meerman (2009), The New Rules of Marketing & PR: How to Use News Releases, Blogs, Podcasting, Viral Marketing & Online Media to Reach Buyers Directly. Hoboken, New Jersey: John Wiley & Sons, Inc. (p. 243).

40. JD Power & Associates, September 2008. http://www.sustainablelifemedia.com/content/column/brands/sustainable_business_trends_2010, accessed February 11, 2010.

41. http://www.wbcsd.org/, accessed February 12, 2010.

42. http://www.sustainablelifemedia.com/, accessed February 12, 2010.

43. http://www.istrategylabs.com/2009/01/2009-facebook-demographics-and-statistics-report-276-growth-in-35–54-year-old-users/, accessed March 14, 2010.

44. Kustin, Adam (2010), *How to Market Green to the Wired Generation,* Green Biz, January 12, http://www.greenbiz.com/blog/2010/01/12/how-market-green-wired-generation, accessed January 16, 2010.

45. Vijayan, Jaikumar (2010), "Over 75,000 Systems Compromised in Cyberattack," *Computer World*, February 18, http://www.computerworld.com/s/article/9158578/Over_75_000_systems_compromised_in_cyberattack, accessed March 14, 2010.

46. http://www.sustainablelifemedia.com/content/story/strategy/dell_bows_to_bloggers_on_green_packaging_demands, accessed May 12, 2008.

GLOSSARY

Accountability Taking responsibility for actions and consequences and acting in a manner that is both trustworthy and transparent.

Advertising Paid placement of commercial messages in a variety of media.

Advertising appeal The central theme of an ad selected in order to reach a particular target audience.

Alternative consumption Rejection of consumerism and of the notion that happiness and well-being are derived from the accumulation of material goods.

Anti-consumption A socio-political movement against consumerism, including resistance to commodity culture and corporate brands; it is fueled by a desire to feel more authentic and to demonstrate love for the natural world.

Appropriate technology Technology that is designed to be ideally suited to the environmental, economic, and social situations in the community in which it is employed.

Astroturfing The creation of a phony grassroots movement to project a false image of widespread public support.

Backcasting Evaluating an organization's current position with respect to its vision of a sustainable future and then working from this desired end state to identify possible steps to create the future.

Balance A business's ability to accommodate conflicting stakeholder interests or moral standards.

Bartering The direct trading of goods and services without using money as an exchange medium.

Baseline performance Starting point from which to measure and track improvements.

Benchmarks Standards against which to compare performance.

Benefit segmentation Segments based on the combinations of benefits or solutions that consumers desire from a product.

Benefits profile The unique combination of functional, symbolic, and hedonic benefits that a product offers to consumers.

Biomimicry The redesign of industrial processes according to biological models.

Biosphere The part of the Earth and its atmosphere that is capable of supporting life.

Biotechnology Biological processes, living organisms, or systems used to develop or modify products or processes.

Blog Web log; a website created and maintained for the purpose of personal reporting.

Brand Identifying trademarks of a product or company and all the meanings invested in those trademarks by their stakeholders.

Brand communities Socially constructed networks of people based on their devotion to a brand and what it represents.

Business-to-business (B2B) sustainable segments Businesses that sell sustainable products and services to other businesses.

Buycotts Active campaigns to buy the products or services of a particular company or country in order to achieve a specific social or environmental goal; generally considered to be the opposite of boycotts.

Cap and trade A policy that sets legal limits on emissions and then allows organizations that pollute less than the limit to sell allowances to those that pollute more.

Carbon footprint calculators Calculators that help individuals, households, and organizations estimate how many tons of carbon dioxide and other greenhouse gases they create each year.

Chain of custody The documented ability to trace the movement and possession of materials from their current places back to their origins.

Channel power The relative influence of one member of the marketing channel over the actions or circumstances of other members.

Citizen groups Community-based and Internet-based groups of people who seek to influence public policy and business practices; also called watchdog groups.

Co-branding When two organizations combine their brands to benefit both brands.

Co-marketers Partners in the marketing process; in the case for consumers, those who willingly attempt to persuade other consumers to try or adopt a product or a brand.

Communitarian A philosophy that emphasizes individual sacrifice for the common good.

Community of purpose A group of people united by common or overlapping goals, working collaboratively to achieve specific outcomes.

Competitive advantage Advantage over one's competitors, often due to continual innovation, anticipating regulatory changes, reducing costs, stabilizing supplies of limited resources, driving product and process innovation, attracting and retaining talented workers, and establishing a strong and authentic market position.

Competitor collaboration Situations that create a mutual advantage for competitors including agreements on standards in areas where they prefer not to compete, such as labor conditions in foreign plants or environmental practices throughout the supply chain.

Competitor environment The actions of firms vying for the same consumer.

Complementary currencies Nonmonetary means of paying for goods and services.

Conflicting ideologies Belief systems that contradict each other or arrive at irreconcilable conclusions when considering an issue.

Consumer Behavior The activities and experiences of people engaged in buying, using, and disposing of goods and services.

Consumer decision process The string of mental processes involved in purchasing, using, and disposing of a product.

Consumerism Creating and fostering a desire to purchase commodity goods in ever greater amounts.

Consumer folklore Stories passed from consumer to consumer with high levels of perceived authority and authenticity.

Co-producers Partners in the production process; in the case of consumers, those who undertake value-creation tasks traditionally performed by members of the marketing channel.

Cost The sum of money, time, and resources associated with a purchase or an activity.

Cost advantages The ability to operate at lower costs than one's competitors.

Cost-based pricing Determining a product's price by adding a fixed amount or a percentage to the product's cost.

Cradle-to-cradle certification Third-party assurances that products are designed to be reabsorbed by nature or the technosphere at end of life and that they are produced with renewable energy, efficient use of water, and fair treatment of people.

Cradle-to-cradle design Design of products and processes such that all waste is returned to productive uses.

Cross-functional teams Teams comprising three or more people from different functional areas of an organization.

Crowdsourcing Encouraging outsiders, preferably customers, to collaborate in the completion of a project.

Corporate social responsibility (CSR) Corporate policies for self-regulation, intended to integrate triple-bottom-line concerns into the business plan.

Culture The learned system of behaviors and beliefs that guide and structure life in society.

Cultural Creatives Consumers who make conscientious purchasing and investing decisions based on social and cultural values.

Customer relationship management (CRM) A strategy that integrates information technology with other marketing efforts in order to identify, target, attract, and retain the best mix of customers.

Cyberattacks Malicious acts targeting computer systems, networks, and/or databases through the Internet.

Cyberstalking The use of electronic media for purposes of harassing, threatening, menacing, or otherwise bringing harm to another individual.

Dematerialization The process that allows fewer resources to be used to create the same or equivalent benefits.

Demographics Individuals' characteristics, such as age, sex, and ethnicity.

Deontology A philosophy that prioritizes moral duty and adherence to rules.

Design for disassembly Design that allows products to be more easily and safely reduced to their component materials at end of life.

Developed nations Countries with the highest levels of production, consumption, and overall standard of living.

Developing nations Nations that have large populations of people that are deeply poor, ruled by a minority that is very rich, and with a small middle class.

Digital communication The electronic transmission of digitally encoded information.

Digital media Various platforms for digital communication such as the Internet, World Wide Web, and mobile phone networks.

Direct marketing Marketing communication in which the marketing message is delivered straight to customers through individually accessed media such as phone, mail, or the Internet.

Disintermediation Reducing the number or roles of intermediaries in a marketing channel.

Disposition behaviors (also known as disposal behaviors) All the behaviors associated with a product once a consumer no longer uses it.

Disposition costs (also known as postuse costs) Any cost incurred for the disposal of a product, including fees for trash hauling, recycling, or other postuse collection.

Downstream channel members A company's customers and their customers, on down to final consumers of the company's product.

Eco-efficient services Services that are either closely related to products or substitute for products, thereby reducing the use of material and energy.

Ecological footprint The amount of Earth's resources required to support a particular lifestyle.

Ecologically sustainable development (ESD) A perspective that combines sustainable economies, ecosystem management, worldwide food security, and population impacts on ecosystems.

Economic development The overall standard of living of people in a nation, usually attributed to industrialization, the adoption of new technologies, and levels of production and consumption.

Economic environment The prevailing economic factors, including employment, income, inflation and interest rates, which influence consumer and business behavior.

Economic sustainability The ongoing ability of an economic system to provide for all human needs.

Ecosystem services Collective activities of natural systems that renew resources and sustain life.

Electronic newsletters Periodic, subscription-based electronic publications containing news and editorial content.

Embedded water (also called virtual water)All the water used in the production of a particular product.

Emerging nations Those countries with medium (and usually growing) levels of production, consumption, and overall standard of living.

Emotional appeals Stress the symbolic or experiential benefits of product use or ownership.

Environmental regulation The laws designed to protect the natural environment against undue harm by individuals or organizations.

Environmental sustainability The ongoing preservation of essential ecosystems and their functions.

European Union emissions trading scheme The world's largest international cap-and-trade system for atmospheric carbon.

Evaluation of alternatives The mental weighing of potential costs and benefits associated with one or more products being considered for purchase.

Extensive problem solving An extended or intensified information search and evaluation of purchase alternatives, generally to reduce the perceived risk associated with a purchase.

External audits Audits wherein third-party certifiers observe and document business practices for compliance with standards that are typically voluntary.

External marketing communication Communication that helps to maintain connections or relationships with customers and other external stakeholders.

External reporting Providing information for use by individuals outside of an organization.

Externalized costs (also known as externalities) Negative impacts of economic activity that are borne by people not directly involved in or benefiting from the activity.

Financial capital The monetary resources available to a firm.

Functional benefits (also known as utilitarian benefits) Product usage outcomes that primarily solve problems or ease burdens.

Fun theory The proposition that people are more willing to do something constructive when it provides the added benefit of enjoyment or amusement.

Genetically modified (GM) foods Foods derived from organisms created by genetic engineering.

Green Market Sustainability-oriented consumers and the businesses that serve them.

Greenmuting An organization's deliberate downplaying of its sustainability efforts or successes.

Green Products Generally meaning products that are less damaging to the environment or human health than traditional equivalents.

Greenwashing Making false or exaggerated claims to project a more sustainable image than is warranted by actual practice.

Hedonic benefits (also known as experiential benefits) Product usage outcomes that are valued for the qualities of the experiences they provide.

Higher-order scales Individual metrics that contain more rather than less information about the differences in a phenomenon.

Human capital Consists of all the resources that people provide, including labor, talent, and creativity.

Human sustainability The opportunity for all people to maintain fulfilling, productive lives while preserving or replenishing the natural and economic systems that make their well-being possible.

Hybrid appeals Combine both rational and emotional appeals.

Information search The active pursuit of information regarding any aspect of a potential purchase.

Innovation The development of new products, services, and processes that can keep a business running ahead of its competitors.

Intangible services Substitute systems, often technology-based, for products.

Integrated marketing communication (IMC) A condition such that all the messages from an organization, in all media, work together holistically to convey the organization's desired image or market position.

Integrity Honesty; consistency of words and actions.

Internal branding The development of a culture among employees that values and supports the brand story.

Internal marketing communication Communication that maintains connections or relationships with employees and serves to motivate employees to be effective ambassadors for the organization.

Internal reporting Providing information for use within an organization.

LEED (Leadership in Energy and Environmental Design) Rating program, which evaluates a building's environmental sustainability, has provided guidance leading to huge strides in energy and water conservation, the reduction of building waste, and the use of renewable and nontoxic materials.

Leverage Achieving the greatest possible impact using the least necessary resources.

Libertarian A philosophy that prioritizes individual rights.

Life-cycle assessment Evaluation of a product's impact across its entire life, including raw material acquisition; materials manufacture; production; use, reuse, and maintenance; and waste management and disposal.

Life-cycle costing The attempt to account for all costs associated with a product throughout all stages of its life.

Lifestyle segmentation A form of psychographic segmentation that focuses on overall patterns of consumer choices and behavior.

Lifestyles of health and sustainability (LOHAS) An organization of businesses that monitors the changing U.S. marketplace for goods and services that focuses on health, the environment, social justice, personal development, and sustainable living.

Limited problem solving Selective or minimal external information search and evaluation, generally associated with low-risk purchases.

Lithosphere The outer part of the Earth, consisting of the crust and upper mantle, approximately 100 km (62 mi) thick.

Local Exchange Trading Scheme (LETS) Community-based networks of people that trade goods and services, often by listing "wants" and "offers" in local directories.

Locavores A segment of consumers who stress the environmental, social, and economic value of eating products grown close to home.

Loyalty programs Marketing programs designed to reward customer support and motivate continued patronage.

Macroculture The overarching value systems and way of life of a society.

Manufactured capital The technological resources available to a firm.

Market-penetration pricing Setting initial prices artificially low in order to speed up sales of a new product.

Market position A clear, unique, and advantageous perception in the marketplace of a product or a brand with respect to its competitors.

Market-skimming pricing Setting high initial prices for new products in order to recover maximum revenues before substitutes appear in the market.

Marketing channels The means whereby goods, services, and value move between producers and consumers.

Marketing mix Product, price, place, and promotion and people (understanding and honoring human needs), planet (maintaining healthy systems), and progress (research, strategy, and innovation).

Marketing opportunities Possible actions for creating or increasing value for customers, the firm, and stakeholders.

Marketing sustainably Conducting marketing operations in a manner that is environmentally and socially sustainable; the first of two main objectives of sustainable marketing.

Marketing sustainability Using marketing functions and influence to help bring about a culture in which striving for sustainability is the norm; the second of two main objectives of sustainable marketing.

Maslow's hierarchy of needs A framework that organizes human needs in order of their importance or urgency from the most basic physical needs, such as survival and safety, up through psychological needs, such as belonging, esteem, and self-actualization.

Material culture Refers to human-made objects and natural objects that have been given special purpose for human use.

Measurement The process of determining the essential qualities or quantities of a phenomenon, such as its number, strength, or duration.

Merchandising The processes and techniques used by retailers to communicate with customers, including product displays, signage, sampling, and décor.

Methodological Information A form of secondary research that includes strategic frameworks, measurement processes, and individual metrics.

Metrics Measurements or scales.

Microculture The defining characteristics of a distinct subgroup of society.

Mobile marketing Marketing messages directed to mobile phones or other mobile devices.

Moore's Law The expectation that computing capacity of transistors or chips will double roughly every two years.

Motivation A desired end state, or the activation of consumer behavior for the purpose of achieving some desired end state.

NAFTA North American Free Trade Agreement. An international trade agreement between the United States, Canada, and Mexico.

Natural capital Consists of all the resources nature provides, including both materials and ecosystem services.

Natural capitalism An approach to capitalism that fully values all forms of capital, with an emphasis on restoring nature and increasing human well-being.

Natural environment All living and non-living things occurring naturally on Earth, including plants, animals, climate, water, air, metals, and soil.

Natural resources Resources occurring naturally in the environment such as wood, water, soil, minerals, coal, and petroleum.

Need recognition The onset of awareness of a need or a goal.

Nongovernmental organizations (NGOs) Organizations created without participation or representation of any government.

Performance indicators Summary measurements meant to give a quick and general assessment of a situation and, in some cases, to trigger an immediate response.

Permission marketing Marketing communication via email, which is sent with the explicit permission of recipients.

Personal selling Face-to-face communication with the goal of persuading a customer to make a purchase.

Political-legal environment Laws, agencies, and regulations that influence businesses and individuals.

Positioning The use of marketing communication to create a distinctive identity for it in the minds of consumers.

Post-purchase behaviors Both product usage behaviors and disposition or disposal behaviors.

Prestige pricing Setting and maintaining a high price on a product in order to convey an image of higher quality or desirability.

Price The monetary value of a product as agreed upon by a buyer and a seller.

Primary benefits (also called core benefits) The main functional benefits a product or service is designed to deliver.

Primary conservationists Individuals who make major changes in their lives in an effort to reduce consumption.

Product mix All of the goods and services a company offers to its customers, along with the packaging that accompanies them.

Product stewardship Understanding, controlling, and communicating a product's environmental, health, and safety related effects throughout its life cycle, from production (or extraction) to final disposal or reuse.

Product services Extending the life of a product through maintenance, upgrading, repair, guarantees, and product take-backs.

Product strategy A firm's decisions concerning the best combination of goods and services to deliver value to its target market.

Product-use costs All the costs incurred for using of a product, including maintenance, wear and tear, energy, and supplies.

Product usage behaviors All the behaviors associated with a consumer's use of a product after it is purchased but before it is used up or discarded.

Psychographics Individuals' characteristics such as needs, values, attitudes, lifestyles, and aesthetic preferences.

Publicity News about individuals or organizations in independent media.

Public relations Activities designed to generate commercially favorable messages in independent media.

Puffery Marketing messages that rely on exaggeration or ungrounded opinion; empty claims of superiority.

Purchase costs All the costs to a customer, including money and time, of searching for and acquiring a product.

Purchase decision process All the decisions necessary to complete a transaction.

Quick wins Actions that move a company closer to sustainability while creating short-term cost savings and efficiencies.

Radical resource productivity Making the most of limited and irreplaceable resources.

Radical transparency An organization's complete and public openness about its practices.

Rational appeals Stress a product's overall value, especially in terms of functional product benefits.

REACH (registration, evaluation, authorization, and restriction of chemical substances) A European Union regulation governing the manufacture and use of chemicals aimed at the protection of human health and the environment through the better and earlier identification of the intrinsic properties of chemical substances.

Redesign of industrial processes A means of closing the production loop and allowing zero waste by following biological models.

Reductionism The tendency to focus on individual components of a system rather than on the system as a whole.

Reinvestment Using the dividends, interest, or profits from an investment to buy more of that investment.

Research Investigation of a phenomenon involving the gathering and analysis of information.

Result services Work toward satisfying customer needs while reducing the need for material products altogether.

Reverse logistics The systematic movement of waste backward through marketing channels, in order to convert it back into usable raw materials.

RoHS (Restriction of Hazardous Substances Directive) A European Union policy that restricts the use of specific hazardous materials found in electrical and electronic products.

Routine purchasing Habitual purchasing made with little or no external search.

RSS (really simple syndication) feed A device that automatically delivers new blog posts to subscribers.

Sampling Offering a free sample to encourage customers to try a new or unfamiliar product.

Sales promotions Activities designed to stimulate sales in the short term.

Science-based decision framework A methodology for decision making that grounds each decision in basic scientific facts.

Scorecard A measurement tool comprising multiple indicators to compare sustainability performance in a given category.

Secondary benefit A product benefit that is ancillary or considered only in addition to a primary benefit.

Secondary conservationists Individuals who seek to offset their impact through reusing, recycling, and the use of developing technologies.

Secondary markets Markets that provide used or surplus goods at prices that are usually well below initial retail prices.

Service-dominant logic Focusing strategy on what needs people are trying to meet rather than on what products they will buy.

Service economies Economies that emphasize meeting consumer with services and viewing goods as means of service delivery.

Social-cultural environment Forces and trends external to an organization that relate to a society's values and belief systems.

Social media Internet-based platforms that facilitate and encourage social interaction among users.

Social sustainability The ongoing ability of communities to provide for the well-being of all their members.

Spin A highly biased or distorted portrayal of a situation or set of facts, often considered deceptive or manipulative.

Stakeholder dialogue An ongoing and meaningful exchange between a firm and its stakeholders.

Stakeholders People and groups that influence the business but are not necessarily shareholders.

Strategic alliances Relationships with people and organizations from outside the company including industry experts, such as suppliers and distributors, and nonindustry experts, such as thought leaders from government and nongovernmental organizations.

Strategic flexibility Having the resources required to take advantage of future strategic opportunities.

Storage costs Any costs incurred for the storage of product not in use, including fees for rent and transportation.

Substantive information A form of secondary research that includes the size, structure, and segmentation of markets.

Sustainable brand The economically enduring trademarks and meanings of a product or company; its associations in the minds of customers and other stakeholders rightfully include social justice and ecological sustainability.

Sustainable consumption The use of goods and services that meets people's current needs without compromising the ability of other people to meet their needs, either now or in the future.

Sustainable development Development that meets the needs of the present without compromising the ability of future generations to meet their own needs.

Sustainable distribution Emphasizes efficiency and carbon neutrality, prioritizes local production, incorporates material backflows from consumers to manufacturers, and helps convert refuse to resources, allowing manufacturers to replace virgin materials with recyclables more easily.

Sustainable marketing The process of creating, communicating, and delivering value to customers in such a way that both natural and human capital are preserved or enhanced throughout. Marketing must be done in a sustainable manner so that all the marketing processes are environmentally and socially benign while helping to bring about a society in which striving for sustainability is the norm.

Sustainable marketing communication (SMC) Messages and media directed to any stakeholder of an organization for the purpose of achieving the organization's marketing and sustainability objectives.

Sustainable marketing strategies Statement of an organization's marketing goals and a plan for achieving them while preserving or enhancing both natural and human capital.

Sustainable packaging Manufactured, transported, and recycled using renewable energy and clean production technologies and maximizes the use of renewable or recycled source materials, providing for optimal end-of-life disposition.

Sustainable price A price that accounts fully for the economic, environmental, and social costs of a product's manufacture and marketing while providing value for customers and a fair profit for business.

Sustainability The ability of a system to maintain or renew itself perpetually.

Sustainability audits Certified, independent, third-party assessment of materiality, completeness, and responsiveness of a firm's sustainability performance.

Sustainability labeling Communicating information such as carbon footprints and chemical contents, thereby enabling consumers to make more informed purchase decisions.

Symbolic benefits (also known as self-expressive benefits) Product usage outcomes that are valued for what they communicate about the user.

System conditions Four essential characteristics of a sustainable society.

Target market A market segment a firms chooses to serve, usually one with which the company has some competitive advantage or special expertise.

Technology environment New and existing technologies that influence products and marketing systems.

Technosphere Human-made technological systems.

Teleology A philosophy that prioritizes the consequences of an action.

The Natural Step Framework A science-based set of guidelines for increasing sustainability.

Third-party certifications Seals that indicate a product meets certain standards for social or environmental performance.

Throughput system A linear view of a system, in which materials come in and go out, with no accounting for the materials' ultimate origination or destination.

Time banks Also called service exchanges; barter systems that allow participants to provide and receive services using time spent as expertise.

Tiered pricing Charging different prices in different countries or markets according to consumers' ability to pay.

Total product costs Costs that include all direct (e.g., materials and labor) and indirect costs (e.g., company overhead) of a product for purposes such as inventory valuation, profitability analysis, and pricing.

Trade shows Shows that serve particular customer interests.

Transparency The extent to which an organization's operations and practices are open and visible to outside observers; a key element in sustainable marketing.

Transparent Open and visible to outside observers.

Triple Bottom Line (TBL) A framework that addresses the areas of economic, environmental, and social sustainability where managers find opportunities to build competitive advantage.

Usage segmentation Market segments based on the amount or quantity purchased within a given product category.

Use services Allow the benefit of use without the need to buy the product.

Upstream channel members A company's supply chain.

Value The creation of long-term value for both the business and society.

Value-based pricing Pricing set according to the value customers perceive a product to have.

Value chain The chain of activities and institutions that add value to a product on its way from manufacture to its end consumer.

Value circles Closed-loop value chains that include end users as suppliers of raw materials and component parts for manufacturers.

Value congruence The extent to which a marketing message is harmonious or consistent with a target customer's values.

Viral marketing Marketing activities that result from Internet-mediated communication such as forums, blogs, customer review sites, and social media.

Voluntary simplicity Simple living or the option to live with less, reducing one's material consumption by choice.

Water crisis Planetary depletion of freshwater flows.

Waste from electrical and electronic equipment (WEEE) A European Union directive that mandates the treatment, recovery, and recycling of electric and electronic equipment for all applicable products in the EU market after August 13, 2006.

Whole-system approach (also called systems thinking) Examining every action for its consequences to global eco-systems and society.

World Bank An organization that provides low-interest loans, interest-free credits, and grants to developing countries for a wide array of purposes.

WTO (World Trade Organization) An organization that intends to supervise and liberalize international trade.

INDEX

Numbers

3M, 208
The 11th Hour, 44

A

Acadamic Search Premier, 76
AccountAbility, 80
accountability
    in business, 32–33, 109–110, 189–190
    individual, 35, 37–38
    transparent, 32, 142, 148, 161, 185, 189–190
ACUPCC (American College & University Presidents' Climate Commitment), 43
Adidas, 161, 209
advertising. *See also* promotion mix sustainability; public relations (PR) and
        publicity
    agencies and consulting firms, 205–206
    appeals, 203–204, 205, 215, 225, 231
    lack of trust in, 184
    sales promotions, 210–212, 211p
    storytelling, 204, 207, 215, 219
Advertising Association, 184
Advocacy & Policy Program, 210
AES, 42
AFM, 100
agriculture
    beef industry, 57, 58fig, 159–160, 173–175
    CSA (community-supported agriculture), 165–166, 188
    genetically modified foods, 116
    organic growing, 61, 129–130, 162–163, 175, 193–194, 228
Air Quality Act, 15
Alcoa, 42, 72
The Alliance for Sustainability in Minneapolis, 45
all®Small and Mighty, 125, 147
Alstom, 42
alternative consumption segments, 97
alternatives, evaluation of, 65, 67
Amazon, 30, 63, 90, 146, 225
American Coalition for Clean Coal Electricity (ACCCE), 197
American College & University Presidents' Climate Commitment
        (ACUPCC), 43
American Electric Power (AEP), 29
American Marketing Association, 7, 10
American Recovery and Reinvestment Plan, 46
Anderson, Chris, 89, 225
Anderson, Ray, 24, 63, 131, 208
Annie's Homegrown, 193–194
anti-consumption, 97
Apple, 204
appropriate technology, 112
AroundMe, 223
Ashby, Jeff, 101, 101p
Association for Consumer Research, 62
Association for the Advancement of Sustainability in Higher Education, 43
astroturfing, 196–197
Attenborough, David, 8
Aveda, 141, 156
Avelle's Bag Borrow or Steal, 124

B

B Corporation, 209
backcasting, 23, 75, 221
backhauling, 112–113
Backpacker Magazine, 99
balance, 32, 35–37
Baranowski, Mitch, 141
barriers to sustainability, 33–34, 39, 59, 117, 174–176, 194–195, 210
bartering, 180
baseline performance, 72–73, 75

BASF, 114
Batcha, Laura, 61
BBMG, principles of branding, 141–143
Beckerman Public Relations, 44
beef industry, 57, 58fig, 159–160, 173–175
Belz, Frank-Martin, 214
Bemporad, Raphael, 141
Ben & Jerry's, 90, 204, 208–209
benchmarks, 76
benefit segmentation, 92–94
benefits profile, 93, 123, 142, 194
Best Buy, 158
Bing, 221
Biofuels, 33
biomass, 48fig, 134, 179
biomimicry, 20, 156–157, 207
biosphere, 2, 22, 22figs, 34, 38–39t, 75, 78, 156–157, 170, 172fig
bio-swales, 21, 21p, 164
biotechnology, 47
Blackberry, 202
blogs, 229–231
Bloom, Paul, 192
BMW, 60, 194
Boeing, 207
Bon Appétit Management Company, 162, 162fig
Bonner & Associates, 197
Boston Scientific, 42
BotP (bottom of the pyramid), 177
BP (British Petroleum), 32–33, 114, 184
BP America, 42
Brabeck-Letmathe, Peter, 218
brand, 140–141, 208–209. *See also* sustainable branding
brand communities, 60, 124, 187–188, 204, 208–209, 225–226
branding, 124
Braungart, Michael, 156
Brent Spar, 30
Brilliant Earth, 99
Brin, Sergey, 179
Bristol-Myers Squibb, 210
British Sky Broadcasting Group plc (BskyB), 206
broadcast media, 222–224
Brown, Spencer, 208
Browne, John, 32
The Brundtland Commission, 18–19. *See also* World Commission on
        Environment and Development
Burley bicycles, 125
Burr, Andrew C., 46
business customers, 131–132
Business for Social Responsibility, 129
business-to business (B2B) practices, 100–102, 117, 124, 133–134, 203, 212
buycotts, 59, 188–189

C

C.A.F.E. (Coffee and Farmer Equity), 179–180
cap and trade, 109–110
capital, 11, 19–20, 72. *See also* human capital; natural capital
Capri Sun, 153
carbon dioxide concentration levels, 53fig, 58fig
carbon emissions. *See* greenhouse gases (GHGs)
carbon footprint, 57, 82–84, 84fig, 85, 156fig, 176fig
carbon offsets, 178, 207
Cargo Cosmetics, 147
Carrotmob, 59, 188–189
car-sharing, 68, 124. *See also* Zipcar
Carson, Rachel, 8
Cascio, Jamais, 57
Caterpillar, 42, 158
cell phones, 220, 220p, 222–223, 225
CERES (Coalition for Environmentally Responsible Economies), 77–79

certifications, third party, 135, 148–150, 161, 191
CFCs (chlorofluorocarbons), 106, 195
CFLs (compact fluorescent light bulbs), 33, 99, 167, 179, 210
  labeling, 204
chain of custody, 161
Chang, Jack, 113
channel power, 160
Cheerios, 20
cheeseburger footprint, 57, 58fig
Chevron, 30
Chicago Climate Exchange, 49
Chrysler, 42, 98
Chrysler Aspen, 98
citizen groups, 45–46, 108
Clark, Helen, 8
Clean Water Act, 15
cleaning products industry, 129, 228
Clif Bar, 153
climate change, 1–2, 15, 42, 51, 106–107, 110, 116–119, 206. *See also* global
  warming
Clooney, George, 179
Clorox, 11, 93, 129, 142, 197, 197–198
Clorox Green Works, 65
Cloud Institute for Sustainability Education, 44
CNAD (Center for a New American Dream), 94–95, 94–95figs
CNW, 64
co-branding, 148–149
Coca-Cola, 11, 110, 141
Cocktail Compass, 223
codes of conduct, 73, 77–78, 161
Cohen, Ben, 208
Coke, 139
Colbert, Stephen, 209
Colgate-Palmvolive, 10
collaboration, 11, 47, 141, 143, 160–161, 188–189
Collins Companies (Collins Pine), 4–5
Colorado's Best Beef, 173
Columbia Sportswear, 111
co-marketers, 59, 228
Commoner, Barry, 4
communication. *See* sustainable marketing communication
communication technology, 219–226, 228. *See also* digital media and
  sustainable marketing
communitarian perspective, 33
communities of purpose, 188–189, 204, 225
community and sustainability, 5
competitive advantage, 15–18, 19, 72, 188–189, 190, 221
competitive pricing barriers, 174
competitor environment, 47
Conflict-Free Diamonds, 61
conflicting ideologies, 33–34
ConocoPhillips, 42
Conscientious Innovation (Ci), 205
Conservation International, 11, 179
consumer behavior. *See also* digital media and sustainable marketing;
  sustainable branding; sustainable consumption; sustainable products and
  services
  alternative consumption segments, 97
  brand communities, 60, 124, 187–188, 204, 208–209, 225–226
  consumer motivation (needs), 60–63, 128–129
  education, 192
  as focus of primary research, 77
  folklore within, 204
  global consumers and sustainable marketing, 116–119, 175
  government as consumer, 131–132
  involvement and sustainability, 59–60, 67
  merchandising methods influencing, 166–167
  post-purchase, 66–67
  preference for digital media, 221–224
  pricing and, 177, 178fig, 179–180
  responsibility within, 35–39, 38–39t
  reverse logistics, 157–158
  role of culture in sustainable consumption, 67–68
  shift toward sustainability, 90–92, 92fig, 141
consumerism, 97, 171
Continental Airlines, 207

Co-op America, 63, 213
co-producers, 60
Corbett, Peter, 231
corporate social responsibility (CSR), 30–31, 79, 139, 143, 161, 165, 177
cost
  advantages, 16
    gasoline, 173, 175
    pricing related, 171–174, 177
CoStar Group, 46
Costco, 210
cradle-to-cradle design, 20, 22, 60, 125–126, 156–157, 157p
credibility, 185–186, 190–191, 204, 206, 212, 229
cross-functional teams, 23–24, 75, 130
crowdsourcing, 228
CSA (community-supported agriculture), 165–166, 188
Cuba, Jorge, 108
cultural creatives, 95–97
cultural diversity in sustainable marketing, 19, 67–68
cultural pricing barriers, 175
customer relationship management (CRM), 213–215
cyberattacks, 231–232
cyberstalking, 232
cycles of sustainability, 22, 22fig

D

Dana Undies, 166
DDB Stockholm, 193
Dell, 160, 161, 232
dematerialization, 123–124, 136, 224
demographics, 91–92
deontology, 33
design for disassembly (DfD), 125–126, 157
DesJardins, Joseph R., 31
developed/developing nations, 112–114, 180
Diamond, Jared, 141
Diaz, Cameron, 209
DiCaprio, Leonardo, 8, 44, 209
digital communities, 225–226
digital media and sustainable marketing. *See also* advertising; promotion mix
  sustainability
  antisocial media and danger zones, 231–232
  blogs, 229–231
  communication technology, 219–226, 228
  consumer preference for, 221–224
  crowdsourcing, 228
  dematerialization, 123–124, 136, 224
  digital communities, 225–226
  environmental impact of, 220, 224
  how and why of communication, 229–230
  mobile marketing, 222–223
  permission marketing, 222
  processes sustainability, 225
  rapid innovation and change, 220–221
  what is being communicated, 231
  who is communicating, 225–226
Digitas, 205
direct marketing, 214
disintermediation, 166fig
Disney, 139
Disposition Decision Taxonomy, 92, 93fig
Dodge Durango, 98
Dow Chemical, 42, 47
downstream channel members, 161
Dr. Bronner's Magic Soaps, 197
Drano, 129
Duke Energy, 42
DuPont, 42, 47

E

Earth Day, 9
Earth Friendly Moving, 208
Earthbound Farm, 61
Earthkeeper, 146
eBay, 166, 225
Ecol, 214

ecological issues
  ecolabeling, 191
  ecological laws, 4
  ecologically sustainable development (ESD), 18
  ecosystems, 22–23, 32, 34, 39t, 51, 53fig, 128, 131–132, 135, 170, 172fig
  ecotourism, 135, 212, 224
  footprint, 4, 6fig, 57, 58fig, 82–85, 84fig, 117, 126, 156fig, 175–176, 176fig, 224
Ecomat-Cleaners, 134–135
economic factors
  developed and developing nations, 112–114
  ethical consequences, 29
  global challenges, 110–114
  sustainability, 4, 6fig, 9–10
The *Economist*, 46
educational influences on sustainability, 43–44
egg, 204, 205
Ehrlich, Anne, 8
EICC (Electronic Industry Citizenship Coalition), 47
Electrolux, 24
electronic newsletters, 231
Elkington, John, 19, 155
EMAS (Eco-Management and Audit Scheme), 79–80
embedded water, 107, 107t
emerging nations, 112–114
emotional appeals, 203
Energy Policy Act, 15
Energy Star, 149
ENGO, 46
Enron, 141
Environmental Defense Fund, 16, 42
environmental matters. *See also* global environmental issues
  activism, 116
  awakening, 7–11, 9t
  conduct code, 77–78
  crises, 1–4, 22, 30, 118, 131–132, 132p
  digital media, 220, 224
  environmental standards, 77–80
  environmental sustainability, 4, 10, 22, 90
  regulation, 15, 42–43, 50–51, 109–110, 114–116, 197, 228
EPA (Environmental Protection Agency), 51, 105, 109, 145, 220
Epstein, Marc J., 161, 178, 191
e-readers, 224
ESI (environmental services industry), 100
ethical dimensions
  conflicting ideologies, 33–34
  consumer responsibility, 35–39
  economic consequences, 29
  international marketing regulations, 115
  responsible business, 28–35
European Union Emissions Trading Scheme, 110
e-waste, 111, 116, 159–160, 220
experiential (hedonic) benefits, 93–94, 125, 203
extensive problem solving, 67
external marketing communication, 186
externalized costs, 172–173, 177
Exxon Valdez, 30
ExxonMobil, 206

F

Facebook, 187–188, 218, 230–231. *See also* social networking
Fairtrade, 149
Fairtrade products, 61, 61fig
fair-trade products, 163
Fairtrade products, 177, 228
Fallon, 205
Farrell, Will, 209
Federal Resource Conservation and Recovery Act, 8
Federal Trade Commission (FTC), 44, 197
FedEx, 128
FedEx Kinko's, 32
financial capital, 19
fishing industry, 1, 47, 48, 49fig, 115, 149, 161
Flannery, Matt, 227
FLO International, 61
Food Alliance, 149

food-service companies, 134, 161–162
Ford, 37, 42
Ford Motor Company, 100
Forest Stewardship Council (FSC), 5, 32, 61, 128, 146, 161, 204
ForestEthics, 128
frameworks for marketing strategies, 18–23
Frayne, Shawn, 17
Freegans, 97
Friedman, Milton, 29
Friends of the Earth, 8
FTC (Federal Trade Commission), 50–51, 197
Fuller, Donald A., 23, 123, 172, 181, 185, 195
fun theory, 193
functional benefits (utilitarian), 93
Future Energy Research Corporation, 177

G

gasoline costs, 173–175
GATT (General Agreement on Tariffs and Trade), 115
G-Diapers, 126p
GDP (gross domestic product), 71, 112
General Electric, 42, 47, 74, 139
General Mills, 20, 147
General Motors (GM), 11, 14–15, 42, 140, 218
genetically modified foods, 116
GfK Roper, 90, 92, 116
Gips, Terry, 38
Glade, 129
global environmental issues. *See also* greenhouse gases (GHGs)
  climate change, 1–2, 15, 42, 51, 106–107, 110, 116–119, 206
  consumers and sustainability, 175
  economic challenges, 110–114
  the global greenhouse, 109–110
  global marketplace, 110–112
  global warming, 52, 52fig, 53figs, 106–107, 118, 162fig
  government and regulation, 114–116
  trends, 29
  water issues, 105, 106–109, 122, 128
Global Footprint Network, 5
The Global Impact of SmartWood Certification, 32
global warming, 52, 52fig, 53figs, 106–107, 118, 162fig
Globe Aware, 62
GlobeScan, 116
GNH (gross national happiness), 71–72
GNP (gross national product), 71, 131
Goleman, Daniel, 142
Gonen, Ron, 181
GoodGuide, 84–85, 86p, 223
Google, 63, 76, 140, 221, 224
Google Scholar, 76
Gordon, Cindy, 226
Gore, Al, 8, 44, 63
government as consumer, 131–132
governmental initiatives
  environmental efforts, 8
  federal legislation, 9, 15, 42–43, 50–51, 109–110, 114, 197, 228
  intergovernmental marketing regulations, 115–116
  state-level, 50–51, 197
  subsidies, 115, 173, 175–177, 179
GPI (genuine progress indicator), 72
Grail Research, 204
Grand Central Baking, 149
Green & Black's, 228
green building, 46, 133–134, 159, 163–164, 212. *See also* LEED (Leadership in Energy and Environmental Design)
Green Confidence Index, the, 82
Green Gauge Report, 90–91, 92
Green Guide Network, 223p
Green Hotel Directory, 224, 231
green market, the, 90–98, 96t, 101–102
Green MicroGym, 95
Green Mountain Coffee Roasters, 204
Green Power Market Development Group, 47
green products, 10, 64p, 65, 93, 96t, 141, 204–205, 231. *See also* sustainable products and services
Green Report, the, 197

Green Seal, 134, 148–149, 148fig
Green Source, 134
Green Star®, 149
Green Works, 129, 197
GreenBiz directory, 44
Greenbuild Expo, 212
Greendex, 116–117
Greenfield, Jerry, 208
greenhouse gases. *See also* carbon footprint
greenhouse gases (GHGs)
    producers of, 112–113, 224
    reduction efforts, 32–33, 73, 76, 159, 165, 206
    regulation of, 15, 42–43, 109–110
greenmuting, 207
Greenpeace, 30, 111, 218
greenwashing, 64, 195, 205, 207, 218
Greenwashing Index, 64
GRI (Global Reporting Initiative), 79, 194, 210

H

H&M (Hennes & Mauritz), 161
Häagen-Dazs, 208
Hamburger Helper, 147
Hansen, James, 8
Harley-Davidson, 187
Hart, Stuart L., 190
Hartman Group, the, 77, 90, 91–92, 92fig
Hawken, Paul, 2, 10, 63, 115, 116, 188
Heinz, 150
Henkel, 148
Herman Miller, 60, 97, 157p
Hewlett-Packard, 229
higher-order scales, 76
Hill, Julia Butterfly, 8
Hindustan Unilever, 177
Home Depot, 32
Honda Motors, 15, 46, 98, 142
honest representation, 227
Hot Lips Pizza, 166
HP Blog Central, 229–230
human capital, 11, 20, 21, 72, 89, 111–113, 112p, 128–129, 136, 163
human needs, 61–63
human rights issues, 111, 112p
human survival, 3–4, 22, 61
human well-being, 34, 71–72, 128–129, 176
humanitarian marketing, 99, 100p
Humdinger Wind Energy, LLC, 17
Hummer, 64
hybrid cars. *See under* Toyota, 62, 64, 98, 142

I

Iannuzzi, Al, 196
IBM, 139
IBM's Real Estate and Site Operations (RESO) Group, 73
IDC Architects, 49
IDEO, 129
IKEA, 17, 32, 60, 146, 210
An Inconvenient Truth, 44, 62
individual consumer responsibility, 35–39
information search, 63–65, 67, 76–77, 221
Innocentive, 228
innovation, 16, 47, 113, 130, 133–134, 143, 220–221
Institute of Food Technologists, 148
integrity, 141–143, 186, 225
Intel, 139
Interbrand, 139
Interface Carpet, 63, 131, 208
Interface Inc., 24
intergovernmental marketing regulations, 115–116
internal branding, 144
internal marketing communication, 186
International Center for Technology Assessment, 173
International Organization for Standardization (ISO), 79
Internet, 63–64, 76, 89–90, 221–222. *See also* digital media and sustainable marketing; Internet; social networking
investment sustainability issues, 204, 209–210

Investor Environmental Health Network (IEHN), 209–210
iPad, 224
iPhone, 202
Irv, Miller, 201
ISO (International Organization for Standardization), 79
iStrategyLabs, 231
Ithaca Hours, 180

J

Jackson, Andrew, 8
Jaffe, Dan, 105
J.D. Power and Associates, 231
Jill Ginsberg, 192
Jobs, Steve, 204
Johnson & Johnson, 42, 47, 196
Jones, Van, 8
JTS (Journey to Sustainability), 5

K

K2 Eco inline skates, 130p
Keen Footwear, 98
Kelloggs' Cocoa Krispies, 150
Kellogg's Froot Loops, 150
Kennedy, Robert F., 71
Kintz, Eric, 229
Kiva, 227
Kleanthous, Anthony, 143
Kmart, 198
Kodak, 123, 140
Kohlberg, Kravis & Roberts (KKR), 16
Kroger's Fred Meyer, 65
Kyoto Protocol, 49, 110

L

labeling. *See* sustainable labeling
labor. *See* human capital; workforce
Langert, Bob, 190
Larson, Jonathan, 125
laser tattoos, 148
Lazarus, Shelley, 142
LED lighting, 113, 176
LEED (Leadership in Energy and Environmental Design), 49–50, 61, 61fig, 93, 133–134, 164
LEGO, 89, 129, 140, 141–142
Leo Burnett, 205
leverage, 186–187
Levitz Furniture, 17
libertarian viewpoint, 33
life-cycle assessment (LCA), 82, 83fig, 84fig, 123, 136, 149, 173
life-cycle costing, 173–174
lifestyle segmentation, 91
Lincoln, Abraham, 8
Linens 'N Things, 17
Liroff, Richard, 209
lithosphere, 2, 22, 22figs, 34, 38t
LIVE (Low Input Viticulture & Enology), 149
LocalHarvest, 188
locavores, 97
Lockwood, Charles, 134
LOHAS (Lifestyles of Health and Sustainability), 95, 96t, 117, 188
loyalty programs, 213–214
Lynas, Mark, 107

M

Mackey, John, 227
macroculture, 43
Macy's, 112
Malden Mills, 100
manufactured capital, 19
manufacturing processes, 126, 128
marcom (marketing communication), 184
Marine Stewardship Council, 64, 142, 161
Marine Stewardship Council (MSC), 161
market position, 16, 97–99

market segmentation
   benefit segment, 92–95, 92fig
   business-to business (B2B), 100–102, 117, 124, 133–134, 203, 212
   communication issues within, 194–195
   cultural creatives, 95–97
   digital media in, 231
   green market, 90–92
   LOHAS (Lifestyles of Health and Sustainability), 95–96
   positioning for sustainability, 97–99
marketing. *See* market segmentation
   direct, 214
   humanitarian, 99, 100p
   media influences on, 44–45
   metrics (measurement) in, 71–85
   mobile, 222–223
   opportunities, 24, 159–160
   permission, 222
   strategy frameworks for, 18–23
   word-of-mouth/mouse, 59–60, 225
marketing channels
   building sustainable channel capacity, 162–163
   communication and collaboration, 160, 163, 192
   cradle-to-cradle, 20, 22, 60, 125–126, 156–157, 157p
   developing sustainable channel operations, 163–166
   linear flows and waste, 155–156
   marketing opportunities, 159–160
   retailing, 166–167
   reverse logistics, 157–158
   secondary markets, 158–159
   shorter channels, 165–166, 166fig
   transparency and chain of custody, 161
   value chains, 154–155, 158fig
marketing environments
   competitor environment, 47
   economic environment, 46
   natural environment, 51–53
   political-legal environment, 49–50
   social-cultural environment, 43–46
   technology environment, 47–48
market-penetration pricing, 178–179
market-skimming pricing, 177
Marrone Bio Innovations, 132
Martin, Andrew, 193
Martin Agency, 205
Maslow's Hierarchy of needs, 61–63
material culture, 67–68
Max-Neef, Manfred A., 34, 35–36
Maxwell-Muir, Jen, 225
McCartney, Sir Paul, 209
McCartney, Stella, 209
McDonald's, 128, 139, 190
McDonough, William, 156
McKinsey & Company, 177
measurement. *See also* metrics
   in branding sustainability, 144
   company metrics and scorecards, 80–82
   environmental code of conduct, 77–78
   importance of, 72–74
   life-cycle assessment (LCA), 82, 83fig, 84fig, 123, 136, 149, 173
   principles, 74–76
   standards, 79–80
   sustainability audits, 80
   of wellbeing, 71–72
media. *See* digital media and sustainable marketing
Menken, Greg, 44–45
merchandising methods, 166–167
methodological information, 76
metrics, 72–85. *See also* measurement
Metro Paint, 158
microculture, 43, 44. *See also* nongovernmental organizations
Microsoft, 139, 224
Miller Zell, 46
mobile marketing, 222–223
Mobility Car Sharing, 37
Monsanto, 116
Moore's Law, 220

mother's milk contamination, 28
motivation, 60–63
Mr. Muscle, 129
MS&L, 205
MSC (Marine Stewardship Council), 149
Muir, John, 8
Mythic Paint, 99

N

NAFTA (North American Free Trade Agreement), 115
Naked Juice, 186–187, 187p
Nash, Steve, 130
National Geographic, 116
National Green Pages, 63, 64p
National Public Radio, 222
The National Wildlife Federation, 8
natural capital, 11, 19, 21, 72, 128
Natural Capitalism, 19–21, 124
Natural Cotton Colours, 208
Natural Products Expo, 212
natural resources, 2, 4, 9–10, 16, 20, 78
The Natural Resources Defense Council, 8, 11, 42, 108
The Natural Step Framework (TNSF)
   backcasting, 23, 75, 221
   ethics and responsible business within, 34–35
   individual accountability, 38–39t
   pricing, 171–172
   principles for measurement, 74–76
   product marketing and goals of, 25
   product sustainability, 124–129
   strategic flexibility, 23
   sustainability goals, 21
   sustainable consumption, 59
   system conditions, 21–23
The Nature Conservancy, 8, 11, 42
Nau, 66, 66p, 142
need recognition, 63, 128–129
negative PR, 201–202, 206, 207p, 208–209, 227
Nelson, Gaylord, 9
Nestlé, 110, 218
Nestlé Waters North America, 107–108
NetWitness Corp., 231
New Seasons Market, 65–66
New York State's Citizens' Environmental Coalition, 45
Nike, 11, 24, 25, 49, 99, 111, 127, 130, 142, 157, 161
Nike, Considered Design Index (CDI), 80, 81fig, 130
Nike Trash Talk, 130
Nilsson, Roland, 35
Nokia, 139
nongovernmental organizations (NGO), 9, 9t, 11, 45, 76–78, 141–142, 179, 190, 197, 203, 206
Northwest Natural Gas, 176
NRG Energy, 42
Nvey Eco, 65

O

Oakland Public Library's "Tool Lending Library," 124
OFF! 129
Office Depot, 98, 98p
Ogilvy & Mather, 142
Ogoni, 30, 31
organic agriculture, 61, 129–130, 162–163, 175, 193–194, 228
Organic Agriculture and Products Education Institute, 61
Organic Trade Association, 61
Organic Valley, 61, 214
Origins cosmetics, 147
Ottman, Jacquelyn A., 146, 179, 192, 195, 221
OurPower.org, 62
outsourcing, 111, 175
ozone layer, 106, 118

P

PACE (Property Assessed Clean Energy), 174
Pacific Building Care (PBC) Janitorial Services, 134
Package Flow Technology, 165

packaging, 145–147, 145f, 160, 204
Page, Larry, 179
pallets, shipping, 16, 155–156
Panasonic, 157
paper vs. plastic, 82, 83fig, 84fig
Patagonia, 65, 74, 100, 126–127, 144, 208
Patagonia's Footprint Chronicles, 74
Peattie, Ken, 214
Peck, Jules, 143
Pepsi, 228
PepsiCo, 42
performance indicators, 76
permission marketing, 222
Pew Center on Global Climate Change, 42
Pew Charitable Trusts, 173
PG&E, 42
pharmaceuticals in drinking water, 122
Philadelphia Eagles, 44
Phillips, 157
philosophy of marketing, 6
photovoltaic (PV) power. See solar power
Pillsbury, 208–209
plastic vs. paper, 82, 83fig, 84fig
Pledge, 129
political pricing barriers, 174–175
political-legal environment
    federal legislation, 50–51
    states sustainability initiatives, 50, 197
    sustainable municipalities, 49, 51, 114
pollution and pollutants. See global environmental issues, 9, 15, 105, 109, 125, 165
Pollution Prevention Act, 8
population growth, 5, 14
Porritt, Jonathon, 8
Portfolio 21, 204, 210
Portland General Electric, 134
Portman, Natalie, 8, 209
positioning for sustainability, 97–98
post-purchase behaviors, 66–67
prestige pricing, 179–180
primary (core) benefit, 194
primary conservationists, 91, 97
primary research, 76–77
Procter & Gamble, 77
product design, 125
product innovation, 207
product mix, 122, 129–130
product stewardship, 123, 127
profitability, 14, 16, 23, 32–35, 155, 173
promotion mix sustainability
    advertising, 202–206
    customer relationship management (CRM), 213–215
    direct marketing, 214
    personal selling and trade shows, 212, 215
    public relations (PR) and publicity, 206–210
    risk and investor relations, 209–210
    sales promotions, 210–212, 211p
ProQuest, 76
psychographics, 91–92
public relations (PR) and publicity
    celebrity power, 8, 44, 50, 63, 179, 206–210
    negative PR, 201–202, 206, 207p, 208–209, 227
    proactive use of, 215
    voluntary reporting, 210
Publicis Groupe, 205
puffery, 190, 195
Pur Minerals, 65
Pura, 117
purchase decision process, 65–66

Q

QUEST (Quality Utilizing Employee Suggestions and Teamwork), 24, 131
quick wins, 23

R

radical resource productivity, 20, 186
radical transparency, 142

Radio Paradise, 222
RadioShack, 140
Raid, 129
Rainforest Action Network, 218
Rainforest Alliance, 149
Rainforest Alliance's Eco-Index of Sustainable Tourism, 224
rational appeals, 203
Ray's Food Place, 214
REACH (Registration, Evaluation, Authorization and Restriction of Chemical substances), 116
ReBuilding Center, the, 159
RecycleBank, 181
recycling, 8, 38–39t, 49, 60, 66, 101, 111, 153, 156–157, 167, 186–187
reinvestment, 21
Reithofer, Norbert, 194
renewable energy, 17, 113, 126, 134, 179, 207. See also solar power
reporting systems, 74, 79
research, 76–77, 90–92
responsibility of individual consumers, 35–39
responsible business, 28–35, 39, 77–78
result services, 133
retailing influences, 166–167
reverse logistics, 157–158
Rio Tinto, 42
RiskMetrics Group, 77
Robèrt, Karl-Hendrik, 21
Rocky Mountain Recycling, 101, 159
Roosevelt, Theodore, 8
Rosen, Christine Meisner, 148
routine purchasing (limited problem solving), 67
Royal Dutch Shell plc, 31
RSS (really simple syndication) feeds, 230

S

Saatchi & Saatchi, 44, 205
Safe Lube, 126
Safechoice, 100
Safecoat, 100
Safeway, 65, 107
Sainsbury's, 176
Salmon Safe, 149
sampling, 210–212
Sam's Club, 147
Saran, 129
SC Johnson, 80, 129–130
S.C. Johnson, 142
SC Johnson, 160, 161
Scandic Hotels, 35
Schneider, 112
Schor, Juliet, 94
Schultz, Howard, 144
Schumacher, E. F., 8
Schwartz, Ariel, 228
Schwarzenegger, Arnold, 8, 50, 179
science-based decision framework, 33–35. See also The Natural Step Framework (TNSF)
scorecard, 80–82
Scott, David Meerman, 221, 230
Scott, Lee, 45, 47, 147
Scott's Miracle-Gro, 209
Scrubbing Bubbles, 129
Sculley, John, 204
secondary benefit, 194
secondary conservationists, 91
secondary research, 76–77
self-storage, 36, 173
SERA Architects, 49–50
service economies, 20
Service Employees International Union, 45
service-dominant logic (SDL), 123–124
services. See sustainable products and services
Seventh Generation, 65, 125, 125p, 129, 210, 212, 213, 228
sexy sustainability, 193
Seyfang, Gill, 180
SFI (Sustainable Forests Initiative), 150
Shadman, Farhang, 107

Shapiro, Robert B., 116
Shell, 30–31, 42, 117, 184
Shepherd's Grain, 149
ShoreBank, 205
Shrivastava, Paul, 160, 172
Siemens, 42
Sierra Club, 8, 11
Silk Soymilk (PR initiatives), 207
Singer, Peter, 32, 115, 116
Smart Choices, 150
Smithsonian Bird Friendly, 149
social media, 230–232
social networking, 186, 188, 218–219, 225, 230–232
social sustainability, 10–11, 34
social-cultural environment, 43–46
Sodexo, 134
Sokol Blosser Winery, 127–128
solar power, 67, 113, 114, 174
Solid Waste Disposal Act, 8
Sommestad, Lena, 8
Sony, 210
Sony Ericsson, 73
The South Pole Challenge, 118
spin, 190, 195
Sports Business Journal, 44
sports industry and marketing, 44–45
Sprint, 146
Sprint Nextel, 99
stakeholders, 19, 32, 34–35, 76, 80, 141–142, 184, 186–187, 189–190, 214, 227–228
standard of living increase, 113–114, 163
standards. *See* measurement
Stanton, William J., 157–158
Starbucks, 144, 179–180, 228, 229
Starcom, 205
Starr, Amory, 94
Steelcase, 157
Steffen, Alex, 157
Stoiber, Marc, 193
Stonyfield Farms, 143
storytelling, 219
Stranahan, Susan, 122
strategic alliances, 24
strategic flexibility, 23
substantive information, 76
Suez, 108–109
Super Sandwich Bale™, 101, 101p
sustainability. *See also* barriers to sustainability; life-cycle assessment (LCA)
    defining, 2–5, 10–11, 21–22, 22fig
    educational influences on, 43–44
    U.S. Army move towards, 79, 79fig
sustainability metrics. *See* measurement
sustainable branding, 204
    brand communities, 124
    brand definitions, 140–144, 140p, 208–209
    clarifying, 194
    in digital media, 221
    labeling, 145f, 148–150
    packaging, 145–147
sustainable cities, 49, 49fig, 51, 114
sustainable consumption, 36, 38–39t, 58–59, 60–63, 67–68, 84–85, 94, 94–95figs, 192–193
sustainable distribution, 163–164
Sustainable Forests Initiative (SFI), 150
Sustainable Harvest Coffee, 163
Sustainable Harvest Coffee (SHC), 163, 177
sustainable labeling, 148–150, 191
Sustainable Life Media (SLM), 231
Sustainable Logistics LLC, 165
sustainable marketing communication. *See also* advertising; digital media and sustainable marketing; greenwashing; public relations (PR) and publicity; sustainable branding
    accountability and transparency, 189–190
    AIDA (attention, interest, desire,action), 193
    astroturfing, 196–197
    barriers to, 194–195

communities of purpose, 188–189
    consumer education, 192
    credibility, 190–191
    government actions, 197–198
    greenwashing, 64, 195, 205, 207, 218
    integration, 186
    leverage, 186–187
    nature of, 184–185
    stakeholder dialogue, 190, 214
    value congruence, 192–193
sustainable marketing strategies. *See also* market segmentation; measurement; sustainable pricing; The Natural Step Framework (TNSF)
    backcasting, 23, 75, 221
    and competitive advantage, 15–18
    creating and implementing, 23–25
    cross-functional teams in, 23–24
    frameworks for, 18–23
    importance of training in implementing, 24
    marketing mix, 24, 213–214
    marketing opportunities, 24
    strategic alliances, 24
    Sustainable Value Networks (SVNs), 24
    target market, 24, 117, 203–204
    unsustainable marketing, 6–7, 19–20
sustainable packaging, 145–147, 145fig, 204
Sustainable Packaging Coalition (SPC), 146
sustainable pricing
    barriers to, 174–176
    beyond cost strategies for, 177–180
    complementary currencies, 180
    costs, 171–175
    keys to, 176
    local exchange trading scheme (LETS), 180
    market-penetration pricing, 178–179
    market-skimming pricing, 177
    sustainable price, 171, 172fig
    time banks, 180–181
sustainable products and services
    for business and government, 131–132
    business-to business (B2B), 133–134
    consumer, 134–135
    dematerialization, 123–124
    design of, 125
    development of new consumer, 129–131
    eco-efficient, 132–133
    Green Guide Network, 223, 223p
    The Natural Step Framework (TNSF), 124–129
    product mix, 122, 129–130
    product stewardship, 123, 127
    service-dominant logic (SDL), 123–124
Sustainable Value Networks (SVNs), 24
Swan, Robert, 118, 118p
Swiss Re, 117
symbolic benefits (self-expressive), 93
system conditions, 21–23
Szaky, Tom, 153

T
Target, 153, 166
target market, 24, 117, 203–204
Tauck, Robin, 212
Tauck Tours, 212
Te Casan shoes, 209
technology. *See also* digital media and sustainable marketing; Internet innovation, 207
    marketing environment, 47–48
    promotion mix, 213–214
    sustainability and, 2–3
technosphere, 156
Teledyne, 15
telemarketing, 214
teleology, 33
Ten Thousand Villages, 177
TerraChoice, 195, 202
TerraCycle, 153, 154p, 159, 209

Tesla Roadster, 179, 179p
Texaco, 30
The 11th Hour, 44
third-party certifications, 135, 148–150, 161, 191
throughput system, 155
Tide Coldwater, 77
tiered pricing, 177
Timberland, 146
time banks, 180–181
TNSF. *See* The Natural Step Framework (TNSF)
TNT, 224
Tom's of Maine, 10, 147, 208
Tonkon Torp LLP, 134
Tourism Sustainability Council, 224
Toyota, 212
  Camry, 46
  and hybrid car development, 15
  on Interbrand list, 139
  Logistics Services, 21, 126, 164
  negative PR, 201–202
  as one of largest car manufacturers, 14
  Prius, 46, 62, 62fig, 64, 73, 74p, 93, 178–179, 209
trade shows, 212–213
trademark, 140
transoceanic toxins, 105
transportation industry, 165
transportation options, 37, 68, 133. *See also* car-sharing; hybrid cars
Travel for Good, 224
travel industry
  airline innovation, 207
  ecotourism, 135, 212, 224
  sustainable tourism, 224
Travelocity, 224
Traverse City Light & Power, 179
Treehugger.com, 46
Triple Bottom Line (TBL), 10, 19, 19fig, 23, 34, 134, 140, 146, 185
Tully, Shawn, 108

U

UCG (user-generated content), 230
UGB (Urban Growth Boundaries), 51
U-Haul, 37, 133
U.N. Food and Agriculture Organization, 47
Unarco Industries, 16
UNEP (United Nations Environmental Programme), 79
UNESCO (United Nations Educational, Scientific and Cultural Organization), 19, 43, 108
Unilever, 142, 147
United Bottle, 108
United Nations Framework Convention on Climate Change, 116
United Nations Global Compact, 89
United Nations Intergovernmental Panel on Climate Change, 52
United States Climate Action Partnership (USCAP), 42
Universal Orlando Resort, 226
unsustainable economic activity, 4, 9–10
unsustainable growth, 2, 6fig
unsustainable marketing, 6–7, 19–20
UPS (United Parcel Service), 133, 133fig, 165, 225
upstream channel members, 160
Urban Spoon, 223
U.S. Army, 79, 79fig
U.S. Consumer Confidence Index, 82
U.S. Consumer Product Safety Commission, 51
U.S. Environmental Protection Agency, 76
U.S. Green Building Council, 61
U.S. Securities and Exchange Commission (SEC), 210
usage segmentation, 95
USCAP (United States Climate Action Partnership), 42–43

V

value, in responsible business, 31–32
value, individual, 35–36
value chains, 153–167, 158fig
value circles, 158, 158fig, 160, 163
value congruence, 192–193
value of a healthy planet, 170

value of quality of life, 71
value of sustainable living, 167
value-based pricing, 177–178, 178fig
viral marketing, 59, 186–187, 193, 206, 208, 210, 225
VivaKi, 205
Vodka360, 148
Volkswagen (fun theory), 193
voluntary reporting, 210
voluntary simplicity, 97
V-Power, 117

W

Wagoner, Rick (GM CEO), 14
Wal-Mart, 11, 16, 24, 25, 45, 47, 65, 80–83, 101, 116, 128, 144, 146–147, 153, 160, 163, 166–167, 176, 191, 205, 210
Wal-Mart Watch, 45
Warner, Bernhard, 218
waste handling, 126, 130, 131, 155–157, 164. *See also* e-waste
watchdog groups, 45–46, 64, 189
water issues
  bottled water, 107–108
  embedded water, 107, 107t
  fresh water endangerment, 128
  global challenges, 106–107
  pharmaceuticals in drinking water, 122
  privatization, 108
  transoceanic toxins, 105
  water-for-profit, 108
websites, 221–222, 225
WEEE (Waste from Electrical and Electronic Equipment), 116
Werbach, Adam, 19, 80, 190, 214, 228
Whole Foods, 127p, 227
whole-system approach, 33–34, 75, 155, 185–186
Wikipedia, 221
Wild Oats Markets, Inc., 227
Willard, Bob, 123
Willis, Margaret, 94
WinCo, 65
wind power. *See* renewable energy
Windbelt™, 17
Windex, 129
Withey, Annie, 193
The Wizarding World of Harry Potter, 226
word-of-mouth/mouse marketing, 59–60, 225
workforce, 16, 20, 111–113, 112p. *See also* human capital
workplace safety, 78, 100
World Bank, 115
World Business Council for Sustainable Development (WBCSD), 77, 90, 231
World Commission on Environment and Development, 3, 18
World Resources Institute, 42
The World Wildlife Fund, 8, 11
World Wildlife Fund, 142, 143
Wrangler, 91
WRAP (Worldwide Responsible Accredited Production), 161
WTO (World Trade Organization), 115
Wyeth, Nathaniel, 8

X

Xerox, 124
XStrata, 159–160

Y

YOLO, 212
YOLO Colourhouse, 99
youth attitudes toward sustainability, 46
YouTube, 222, 230

Z

zebra mussels, 132, 132p
Zen Home, 124
Zequanox, 132
Zikmund, William G., 157–158
Zipcar, 37, 37p, 68, 124
Ziploc, 129